BELGIAN NATIONAL INCOME DURING THE INTERWAR PERIOD
RECONSTRUCTION OF THE DATABASE

STUDIES IN SOCIAL AND ECONOMIC HISTORY
edited by Herman Van der Wee
Leuven University Press

Volume 27

Stef Peeters
Martine Goossens
Erik Buyst

Belgian National Income during the Interwar Period
Reconstruction of the Database

Leuven University Press
2005

Published with the support of K.U.Leuven Commissie voor Publicaties

© 2005 Leuven University Press / Universitaire Pers Leuven / Presses Universitaires de Louvain
Blijde-Inkomststraat 5, B-3000 Leuven (Belgium)

All rights reserved. Except in those cases expressly determined by law, no part of this publication may be multiplied, saved in an automated data file or made public in any way whatsoever without the express prior written consent of the publishers.

ISBN 90 5867 349 9
D/2005/1869/44
NUR: 696

PREFACE

Historical national accounting is nowadays recognized as an important field of research in economic history. Nevertheless the sub discipline also receives a lot of criticism. Several estimates would be based on shaky data material so that the outcome would in part reflect the personal opinion of those who produced the series. Moreover in some publications the estimation methods are explained in very vague terms thereby making a duplication of the results almost impossible. This book tries to remedy these critiques. The estimation procedures of the various components of Belgian national income between 1920 and 1939 are thoroughly discussed and explained.

The book also falsifies the proposition that "Belgium is a country without statistics". There are many series available but they are scattered over many publications and therefore often difficult to find. One merit of this book is that it brings together quantitative material from very diverse sources and origins. Not only economic historians will benefit from the wealth of statistics presented here, but also e.g. social historians.

Erik Buyst
Center for Economic Studies

INTRODUCTION

Post-war economic historiography of Belgium is remarkable for the fact that, in contrast to other Western countries, little or no interest was displayed in Belgium in the first few decades after 1945 in a research undertaking which, at that time, was engaging the attention of numerous economists and historians elsewhere : the reconstruction of the National Accounts for the nineteenth and early twentieth centuries. In response to the work of the American economist and later Nobel Prize winner Simon Kuznets, research centres were set up both in the United States and in Europe with a view to reconstructing the National Accounts, but this subject was not for the time being taken up in Belgium itself [1].

The unfortunate consequence was that, in contrast to other Western countries, no fundamental pioneering studies were carried out in Belgium between 1950 and 1980 on the structural development of the Belgian economy over the previous 200 years[2]. The lack of a historical databank on the essential parameters of the country's economic past also explains - at least in part - why the early nineteenth century Belgian Industrial Revolution has still not yielded its secrets[3].

The subject of the National Accounts did not engage the attention of Belgian economic historians until the mid-1970s, when the Liège *Groupe d'étude d'histoire quantitative et de développement,* headed by Professor Pierre Lebrun, presented a concrete and ambitious plan of work aimed at the reconstruction of Belgium's National Accounts from 1830 to 1913. Although the Liège initiative resulted in the publication in subsequent years of a series of highly commendable specialist studies on the basic components of the nineteenth century Belgian economic structure[4], the publication of quantitative time-series for Gross National Product during the period 1830-1948 still failed to materialize.

---

[1] For a survey of the activities in this field in other countries, see VAN DER WEE, H. DANCET G., *De Belgische Nationale Boekhouding, 1920-1982: Geschiedenis van haar reconstructiemethodologie,* in: "Actuele economische problemen. Theorie en politiek", VAN ROMPUY, V. (ed.), Leuven 1986, pp. 146-150 and pp. 155-158; BUYST, E., SMITS, J.P. and VAN ZANDEN, J.L., *National Accounts for the Low Countries, 1800-1990,* in: "Scandinavian Economic History Review", vol. 43, 1995, pp. 53-76.

[2] The studies by MATTHEWS R.C.O. et al., *British Economic Growth, 1856-1973,* Oxford 1973 and MADDISON A., *Dynamic Forces in Capitalist Development. A Long-Run Comparative View,* Oxford, New York, 1991, may be regarded as prototypes of the kinds of pioneering studies that had become possible into the National Accounts in historical perspective. Of earlier date, and the main source of inspiration for later research in this field, is KUZNETS S., *Economic Growth of Nations. Total Output and Production Structure,* Cambridge, 1971.

[3] In contrast to the UK or the US, there is for example no "industrialization debate" in Belgium.

[4] GADISSEUR J., *Le produit physique de l'économie belge, 1831-1913. Présentation critique des données statistiques* (Ph.D. Dissertation Economics Department State University of Liège, 1979-

It is against this background that the *Leuven Workshop on Quantitative Economic History*, until 1993 directed by Herman Van der Wee and since 1993 by Erik Buyst, decided in 1984 to embark on a large-scale research project entitled the "Reconstruction of the National Accounts of Belgium". In contrast to the Liège project, the Leuven project consisted from the outset of two specific elements : (i) a statistical research phase with the aim of reconstructing Gross National Product in accordance with the methodology currently employed by the National Institute of Statistics, and (ii) a research phase, not forming the exclusive preserve of the working group, concerned with the economic interpretation of the databank.

Six specialist studies have in so far been published as part of the overall research project : one by Erik Buyst on investment in residential building between 1890 and 1961, one by Martine Goossens on the economic development of Belgian agriculture in the period 1812-1846, one by Jan Blomme on the economic development of Belgian agriculture in the period 1880-1980, one by Chris Schroeven on private consumption between 1920 and 1939, one by Piet Clement on public spending and one by Michelangelo van Meerten on capital formation. Other publications are forthcoming and a number of less extensive working documents have also been published[5].

The present publication is concerned with the reconstruction of National Income during the period 1920-1940. In terms of approach, the present study is at once narrower and broader than the six previously published works: in contrast to

---

1980, 9 vol.) ; DEGREVE D., *Le commerce extérieur de la Belgique, 1830-1913. Présentation critique des données statistiques*, Brussels, 1982 ; PIRARD J., *Le pouvoir central belge et ses comptes économiques, 1830-1913*, Brussels, 1980-1985 ; LEBRUN P. et al., *Essai sur la révolution industrielle en Belgique, 1770-1847*, Brussels, 1979.

[5] BUYST E., *An Economic History of Residential Building in Belgium between 1890 and 1961*, in: "Studies in Belgian Economic History", vol. 1, Brussels, 1992 ; GOOSSENS M., *Economic Development of Belgian Agriculture : A Regional Perspective, 1800-1846*, in :"Studies in Belgian Economic History", vol. 2, Brussels, 1992 ; BLOMME J., *The Economic Development of Belgian Agriculture, 1880-1980. A Quantitative and Qualitative Analysis*, in: Studies in Belgian Economic History, vol. 3, Brussels, 1992. SCHROEVEN C., *Consumer Expenditure in Interwar Belgium, 1920-1939*, in: "Studies in Belgian Economic History", vol. IV, Brussels, 1994; VAN MEERTEN M., *Capital Formation in Belgium (1900-1995)*, Leuven, 2003; CLEMENT P., *The Growth of a Welfare State in Belgium: A History of Belgian Public Finances, 1830-1940*, Leuven, 2000. The most important working documents include : GOOSSENS M., *Reconstructie van werkgelegenheidscijfers voor het Interbellum. Methodologie en resultaten*, in: "Workshop on Quantitative Economic History", vol. 87.01. Leuven, 1987 ; BUYST, E., NACKAERTS, P., and PEPERMANS, G., *Some Aspects of Gross Domestic Fixed Capital Formation in Manufacturing and in Dwellings: Belgium, 1920-1939*, in: "Workshop on Quantitative Economic History", vol. 87.03. Leuven, 1987; GOOSSENS M., *Het looninkomen van arbeiders in privé-dienst tijdens het Interbellum, 1920-1939: berekeningsmethode en resultaten*, in: "Workshop on Quantitative Economic History", vol. 87.06, Leuven, 1987 ; HENAU A., *De Belgische huishuren gedurende het Interbellum*, in: "Workshop on Quantitative Economic History", vol. 91.01, Leuven, 1991; BUYST, E., *Het inkomen uit onroerend vermogen toevloeiend aan particulieren: België, 1920-1939*, in : "Workshop in Quantitative Economic History. Research Paper 94.01", Leuven, 1994.

the latter, the present study is confined to the *reconstruction of a databank*, whereas the previously published studies also contain a good deal of interpretation. The present work covers the *entire economic system* of inter-war Belgium, whereas the three previously published studies are confined to the construction of a databank for one particular sector of economic activity.

In terms of the conceptual framework used for the National Accounts, the classical methods for calculating the central concept in the system of National Accounts, namely gross National Product (GNP), are the *income method*, the *expenditure method* and the *output method*. The term GNP refers to the *total market value of the final goods and services produced in a country in a given year*. As such, GNP serves as a measure for the growth of the national economy. Under the income approach towards GNP, it is assumed that goods and services can only be produced given the input of factors of production - land, labour and capital - for which a reimbursement is paid; the sum of these factor costs - rent, wages and interest respectively - accordingly corresponds with the GNP of the national economy[6].

In other words, this study concentrates on the incomes earned in Belgium in the inter-war period. The methodology is based on the method of calculation devised by the *National Institute for Statistics* (Nationaal Instituut voor de Statistiek, NIS) in the 1950s, and which was used until the early 1990s for calculating National Income. This methodology fully complies with the relevant OECD international standards, meaning that the research results should be usable for both national and international comparative research purposes[7].

The NIS methodology has been followed as faithfully as possible for the period 1920-1939, and thus determines the structure of this study. More specifically, this means that each chapter is concerned with one of the sub-headings in the present NIS national accounts; each chapter is introduced by a practical commentary on the heading in question and a theoretical explanation of its place in the system of National Accounts, after which an attempt has been made to calculate the relevant category for the inter-war period in as much detail and as accurately as possible.

The major obstacle to the application of the NIS methodology in the inter-war period consisted of the deficiencies in the source material. Only rarely are the same statistical sources available for the inter-war and post-war period, so that for most headings different source material had to be used. The basic statistical material on

---

[6] This equation is only approximately correct : in a strict sense National Income and Gross National Product are only equal if National Income is increased by depreciation and net indirect taxes and reduced by subsidies. This will also be shown in the general concluding chapter. Under the *output approach* the final production of the services and agricultural and industrial products effectively realized by the national economy is calculated, while the *expenditure approach* examines how the income is spent. The advantage of these three independent methods of calculation is that they can each be used to verify the others, thereby ensuring that the ultimate figure for GNP approximates reality more closely. For a more detailed analysis of the various methods for measuring GNP and the technical variants on this concept, see VAN ROMPUY P. et al., *Inleiding tot de economie*, Leuven, 1988, p. 281 ff.

[7] See in this respect VAN DER WEE H., DANCET G., *o.c.*, p. 155.

wages and salaries and the social security contributions paid by employers and employees, for example, comes in the 1990s from the various agencies of the Department of Social Security, an institute that did not exist in the inter-war period. Similarly the tax and accounting systems of the central and regional governments have undergone major changes since 1945, so that here too a special approach had to be adopted. The major challenge, therefore, consisted of finding the most comparable source in the inter-war period, so that the present NIS system of national accounts could still be followed as closely as possible.

This quest for alternative source material was highly laborious and not always rewarding. Much official statistical material has been lost due to the poor administration of government archives; and manpower shortages at the General State Archives mean that important archives such as the tax records of the Ministry of Finance remain inaccessible to the public. In many cases, therefore, it was necessary to do with fragmentary published data, such as the fiscal statistics published for a number of years in the Parliamentary Papers.

Nevertheless the search for alternative source material also yielded positive results. It turned out, for example, that the social security system - although not known as such at that time - grew rapidly, especially from the 1930 depression onwards, resulting in a series of new sources that harmonized unusually well with those of the post-war period. The most notable example of these are the Reports on the Implementation of the Industrial Accidents Act.

As noted above, this study is confined to the *reconstruction* of National Income in the period 1920-1939 ; the *interpretative* part will be dealt with in a following study[8]. This implies that the general conclusion of this study is confined to the presentation of a database representing the Belgian national income during the inter-war period.

The authors wish to thank the participants in the Leuven "Workshop on Quantitative Economic History" and more especially Jan Blomme, Guido Pepermans, Antoon Soete and Michelangelo van Meerten for their valuable advice. They also owe a considerable debt of gratitude to the directorates-general and officials of the Ministries of Economic Affairs and Finance, and to the statisticians of the NIS for the facilities and information they gave us during our research.

Scientific research requires substantial financial means. These were provided by the Fonds voor Kollektief Fundamenteel Onderzoek (Fund for Collective Fundamental Research), the Nationale Bank van België (National Bank of Belgium), the Ministry of Science, and the Algemene Spaar- en Lijfrentekas (General Savings and Annuity Fund).

---

[8] For a preview, see BUYST, E., *Economic Growth in an Era of Severe Macroeconomic Imbalances: Belgium, 1910-1934*, in: "Exploring Economic Growth", HEIKKINEN, S., VAN ZANDEN, J.L. (eds.), Amsterdam, 2004, pp. 167-181. Interpreting the database on national income is only relevant if the database is expressed in *real terms*, which implies the construction of a *GNP-deflator* for the inter-war period. See BUYST, E., *New GNP Estimates for the Belgian Economy During the Interwar Period*, in "Review of Income and Wealth", vol. 43, 1997, pp. 357-375.

CONTENTS

PREFACE	5
INTRODUCTION	7
TABLE OF CONTENTS	13
LIST OF ABBREVIATIONS	19
LIST OF TABLES AND GRAPHS	21

CHAPTER 1. PAY OF MANUAL WORKERS IN THE PRIVATE SECTOR IN BELGIUM . 27

Section 1. Definitions and summary of contents of the six chapters concerning income from paid employment 27
    Paragraph 1. Definition of the concept of income from paid employment 27
    Paragraph 2. Summary of the six chapters concerning income from paid employment 30
        1. NIS Classification 30
        2. Classification for the inter-war period 32

Section 2. Pay of manual workers employed in enterprises in industry, trade and other service sectors 34
    Paragraph 1. Evolution of the industrial accident insurance 35
        1. Scope 36
        2. Possibilities for complying with the Act 38
    Paragraph 2. The insured wagebill in the official publications concerning the industrial accident legislation 39
    Paragraph 3. Adjustments to the insured wagebill 41
        1. Deduction of incorrectly included occupational categories 43
            a) The insured wagebill of a proportion of the government employees and a proportion of the agricultural workers 43
                - Civil servants 43
                - Agricultural workers 44
            b) The insured wagebill of white-collar workers up to and including 1932 45
            c) Insured wagebill of non-residents employed in Belgium 51
        2. Addition of the wagebill of workers not included in the Reports 52
            a) Wagebill of non-insured manual workers 52
            b) Wagebill of non-insured manual workers whose employers contributed to the Guarantee Fund 54

        c) Wagebill of non-insured manual workers whose employers were exempted from contributing to the Guarantee Fund 55
    3. Conversion of insured wagebill into actually earned wagebill .. 55
        a) Adjustment for minimum- and maximum wage 55
        b) Adjustment for non-declared earnings 58
Section 3. Pay of homeworkers, agricultural workers, fishermen and seamen 59
    Paragraph 1. Pay of homeworkers 60
    Paragraph 2. Pay of agricultural workers 62
    Paragraph 3. Pay of fishermen and seamen.................... 62

CHAPTER 2. PAY OF WHITE-COLLAR WORKERS IN THE PRIVATE SECTOR 65

Section 1. Definition of the heading 65
Section 2. Employment of white-collar workers in industry and commerce 68
    Paragraph 1. The censuses of 1920, 1926, 1930 and 1937 as a source of employment data 68
    Paragraph 2. Employment, unemployement and total workforce of white-collar workers in industry and commerce in 1920, 1926, 1930 and 1937 71
        1. Employment, unemployement and total workforce in industry and commerce on 31 december 1930 71
        2. Employment, unemployement and total workforce in industry and commerce on 27 februari 1937 72
        3. Employment in industry and commerce on 31 december 1920 .. 72
        4. Employment in industry on 31 october 1926 72
        5. Deduction of manual workers in positions of authority 72
    Paragraph 3. Employment, unemployement and total labour force of white-collar workers in industry and commerce in 1920-193 73
Section 3. Pay of white-collar workers in industry and trade 74
Section 4. Employment and pay of other white-collar workers 74

CHAPTER 3. PAY OF DOMESTIC STAFF, BORDER-WORKERS AND SEASONAL WORKERS EMPLOYED ABROAD 75

Section 1. Definition of the heading 75
Section 2. Pay of domestic staff 78
    Paragraph 1. Number of individuals 78
        1. Domestic staff in the censuses of 1920 and 1930 78
        2. The problem of part-time charwomen 79
        3. Inter- en extrapolations for the non-census years 80
    Paragraph 2. Pay 81

    1. Brussels wages of domestic staff and construction of an overall loan index for all domestic staff 82
        a) The payroll records of the Brussels Labour Exchange 82
        b) Wages of domestic staff in the wage lists of the Brussels Labour Exchange and of comparable personnel in Brussels 83
        c) Overall wage index for all domestic staff 83
    2. Unit pay of the various categories of domestic staff van het huis- en dienstpersoneel 85
    3. Wagebill of domestic staff 87

Section 3. Pay of border-workers 87
    Paragraph 1. Number of Belgian border-workers in France 87
    Paragraph 2. Unit remuneration and wagebill 90

Section 4. Pay of seasonal workers employed abroad 92
    Paragraph 1. Number of Belgian seasonal workers in France 93
    Paragraph 2. Average working hours 95
        1. Average number of months of employment per year 95
        2. Average number of working days per month 96
        3. Average number of working hours per working day 96
        4. Average number of workin days per year 97
    Paragraph 3. Average hourly wage and total wagebill 97

CHAPTER 4. EMPLOYERS' SOCIAL SECURITY CONTRIBUTIONS 99

Section 1. Definition of the heading 99
Section 2. Employers' contributions to mineworkers' pensions 102
Section 3. Employers' contributions to manual workers' pensions 103
Section 4. Employers' contributions to white-collar workers' pensions ... 104
Section 5. Employers' contributions to family allowances 106
Section 6. Employers' contributions to job-related sickness benefit 108
Section 7. Employers' contributions to industrial accident insurance 108

CHAPTER 5. PAY AND PENSIONS OF GOVERNMENT STAFF 109

Section 1. Definition of the heading 109
Section 2. Central government : civil service, state education and military establishment : total pay and pensions 109
Section 3 . Provinces and municipalities : civil service 111
    Paragraph 1. The provinces 111
    Paragraph 2. The municipalities 111
Section 4. Provincial and municipal education (including pay subsidies) . 112
Section 5. Free education 112
Section 6. State railways/NMBS 113

Section 7. RTT, the postal service and the Belgian aviation authority 113
Section 8. Public companies controlled by the provinces and municipalities 113

CHAPTER 6. INCOME FROM PAID EMPLOYMENT : ADDITIONS AND ADJUSTMENTS 115

Section 1. Content of the heading 115
Section 2. The additions and corrections made 117
    1. Free coal and coke 117
    2. Voluntary employers' contributions not fitting into the compulsory social security system 118
    3. Undeclared manual workers' income 119
    4. Occupational costs borne by employees 119

CHAPTER 7. INCOME FROM ENTREPRENEURSHIP IN AGRICULTURE, HORTICULTURE AND FORESTRY 121

Section 1. Content of the chapter and principal sources 121
    Paragraph 1. Definition of the concept of incime from entrepreneurship in the agricultural sector 121
    Paragraph 2. Summary of the principal sources 122
Section 2. Gross value of agricultural and horticultural production 123
    Paragraph 1. Livestock production 124
        1. Meat production 124
        2. Dairy production 124
        3. Egg production 125
        4. Wool production 125
        5. Changes in the numbers of livestock 125
        6. Livestock prices 126
    Paragraph 2. Arable crop production 126
    Paragraph 3. Horticultural production 127
Section 3. Inputs and income from entrepreneurship in agriculture and horticulture 128
    1. Rents 128
    2. Wages of agricultural labourers 129
    3. Fertilizers 130
    4. Animal feedstuffs 130
    5. Planting stock and seed 131
    6. Interest on borrowed operating capital 131
    7. Depreciations 132
    8. General overheads 132
    9. Indirect taxation 133
    10. Subsidies 133

Section 4. Self-employed income from woods not controlled by the forestry commission 133

CHAPTER 8. ENTREPRENEURIAL INCOME OF THE PROFESSIONS, INDEPENDENT TRADERS, CRAFTSMEN AND PARTNERSHIPS 135

Section 1. Definition of the heading 135
Section 2. The system of income tax and the fiscal statistics relating to trade tax 137
    Paragraph 1. Income taxes in Belgium during the interwar period 137
    Paragraph 2. The fiscal statistics relating to trade tax on natural persons 140
    Paragraph 3. Numbers of independent traders and industrial entrepreneurs: comparison of the fiscal statistics with the censuses 144
Section 3. Entrepreneurial income of independent traders and craftsmen . 148
    Paragraph 1. Homogenisation of taxable income 149
    Paragraph 2. Conversion of taxable income into actual income 150
        1. Arguments in favour of increasing taxable income 151
            a) Tax fraud 151
            b) Tax avoidance : fictitious remuneration of family members helping in business 153
            c) Fixed assessment of taxpayers with no business accounts ... 153
        2. The incremental coefficients of the NIS and Baudhuin 153
        3. Incremental coefficients for the interwar period 154
    Paragraph 3. Inter- en extrapolations of the missing years 154
    Paragraph 4. Entrepreneurial income of independent traders and craftsmen (secondary occupation) 154
Section 4. The entrepreneurial income of the professions 154
Section 5. The entrepreneurial income of partnerships 155

CHAPTER 9. INTEREST PAYMENTS TO THE PERSONAL SECTOR 157

Section 1. Definitions and survey of contents of the three chapters dealing with income from property accruing to the personal sector 157
Section 2. Interest from saving deposits 160
    Paragraph 1. Interest on savings deposits held with the ASLK 162
        1. Capitalised interest accruing tot the personal sector 162
        2. Interest paid in the course of the working year accruing to the personal sector 162
        3. Interest on the endowment passbooks of returned services 163
        4. Interest on deposit passbooks of partnerships 164
    Paragraph 2. Interest on savings deposits held with private savings banks 164

  Paragraph 3. Interest on savings deposits held with municipal savings banks 166
  Paragraph 4. Interest on savings deposits held with public credit institutions (excluding ASLK) 166
Section 3. Interest on bank deposits accruing to the personal sector 167
Section 4. Imputed interest on the actuarial reserves of life insurance companies 169
Section 5. Interest on government securities accruing to the personal sector 172
Section 6. Interest from bond loans transacted by companies 174
Section 7. Interest on mortgage loans accruing to private persons 174
Section 8. Imputed interest relating to services provided free of charge by banks and other financial intermediaries 175

CHAPTER 10. RENTS (RECEIVED OR IMPUTED) PAYABLE TO PRIVATE INDIVIDUALS 177

Section 1. Definition of the heading 177
Section 2. Gross rent from improved properties 179
  Paragraph 1. The average rent per household in 1935 179
  Paragraph 2. A rent-index for inter-war Belgium 180
Section 3. Gross rent from unimproved properties 181
Section 4. Charges and net rent 181
  Paragraph 1. Depreciation and maintenance costs 182
  Paragraph 2. Mortgage interest 182

CHAPTER 11. DIVIDENDS, RETURNS ON INVESTMENT ABROAD, BONUSES AND GRANTS ACRRUING TO PRIVATE INDIVIDUALS 185

Section 1. Definition of the heading and discussion of the sources 185
  Paragraph 1. Definition of the heading 185
  Paragraph 2. Discussion of the sources 186
    1. The return-on-capital statistics of the National Bank of Belgium 186
    2. Fiscal data ralating to the financial assets tax 189
     a) Characteristics of the financial assets tax 189
     b) The fiscal statistics relating to income subject to financial assests tax 190
Section 2. Dividends distributed by Belgian companies principally trading in Belgium 191
Section 3. Dividends paid out by Belgian companies principally trading in the colonies or abroad 194
Section 4. Earnings from investments abroad 194
Section 5. Directors bonuses 195
Section 6. Corporate grants 197

CHAPTER 12. RESERVED PROFITS OF CORPORATIONS 199

Section 1. Definition of the heading 199
Section 2. Non-distributed profits of joint-stock companies 200
   Paragraph 1. Estimate according to the NIS method 200
      1. Net profits 201
      2. Reserved profits 205
   Paragraph 2. Comparison with alternative figures 206
Section 3. Undistributed profits of autonomous public institutions 207

CHAPTER 13. DIRECT TAXATION OF COMPANIES OF ALL LEGAL FORMS 209

Section 1. Definition of the heading 209
Section 2. Trade tax 210
   Paragraph 1. Estimate for the 1930 tax year 210
   Paragraph 2. Estimate for the tax years for which the fiscally reserved
      profits are known 211
Paragraph 3. Estimate for the financial years for which the fiscally reserved
      profits are unknown 212
Section 3. Financial securities tax 213
Section 4. Land tax 213
Section 5. National crisis tax 214

CHAPTER 14. INCOME FROM PROPERTY AND ENTREPRENEURIAL INCOME
ACCRUING TO THE GOVERNMENT 215

Section 1. Imputed net rent 215
Section 2. Interest, dividends, rent income, profits and losses 216
   Paragraph 1. Central government 216
   Paragraph 2. Statutory pension funds : interest on actuarial reserves .. 218
      1. Interest on actuarial reserves of statutory pension funds 218
      2. Interest on the actuarial reserves of industrial accident insurance
         funds 219
   Paragraph 3. Other government 220
      1. Municipalities 220
      2. Public Welfare Committees 222
      3. Provinces 222

CHAPTER 15. INTEREST ON THE PUBLIC DEBT 223

Section 1. Definitions and summary of contents 223
    Paragraph 1. Why is the interest on the public debt deducted form national income ? 223
    Paragraph 2. Definition of public debt 225
    Paragraph 3. Definition of local government debt 227
Section 2. Interest on the state debt 228
Section 3. Interest on local government debt 233

CHAPTER 16. DEPRECIATION 235

Section 1. Definition and reconstruction problems 235
Section 2. The post-war estimates by DULBEA and the NIS 237
Section 3. Estimate of depreciation during the inter-war period 238
    Paragraph 1. Depreciation of dwellings 239
    Paragraph 2. Depreciation of other buildings in the private sector 240
    Paragraph 3. Depreciation of plant and equipment in the private sector 242
    Paragraph 4. Depreciation in the government sector 243
    Paragraph 5. Total depreciation 244

CHAPTER 17. INDIRECT TAXES AND SUBSIDIES 245

Section 1. Indirect taxes 245
    Paragraph 1. Definitions 245
        1. General distinction between direct and indirect taxes 245
        2. Indirect taxes according to the standardized system of the OECD 245
        3. Indirect taxes in the national accounts of the NIS 246
    Paragraph 2. Indirect taxes during the inter-war period 246
Section 2. Subsidies 248
    Paragraph 1. Definition 248
    Paragraph 2. Subsidies during the inter-war period 248

GENERAL CONCLUSION 249

ANNEX 257

BIBLIOGRAPHY 409

ABBREVIATIONS

1) CENSUSES[1]

- CC : Commercial census (1910, 1930, 1937)
- ESC 1937 : Economic and Social Census of February 1937
- IC : Industrial census (1910, 1926, 1930, 1937)
- ICC : Industrial and commercial census (1910, 1930)
- OC : Occupational census in the framework of the industrial and commercial census (1910, 1930)
- PC : Occupational survey in the framework of the population census (1910, 1920, 1930)

2) OTHER SOURCES[2]

- Report : Report on the implementation of the Act for the Reimbursement of Injury arising from Industrial Accidents (Verslag over de uitvoering der wet op de vergoeding der schade voortspruitende uit arbeidsongevallen)
- Statistics : Industrial Accident Statistics (Statistiek van de arbeidsongevallen)

3) INSTITUTIONS

- ASLK : General Savings and Annuity Fund (Algemene Spaar- en Lijfrentekas)
- NBB : National Bank of Belgium (Nationale Bank van België)
- NIS : National Institute for Statistics (Nationaal Instituut voor de Statistiek)
- RMZ : National Social Security Agency (Rijksdienst voor Maatschappelijke Zekerheid)

---

[1] See Bibliography for the exact references of these censuses.
[2] Idem.

LIST OF TABLES AND GRAPHS

TABLES

Table 1 : Wagebill of manual workers employed in enterprises in industry, trade and other service sectors (in BF millions)

Table 2 : Comparison between total insured wagebill - manual workers plus white-collar workers) in the Reports and the Statistics (in BF millions)

Table 3 : Wagebill of insured persons employed in vocational training schools, municipal services and certain branches of special agriculture (in BF millions)

Table 4 : Wagebill of insured manual workers : adjustment for the insured domestic staff (1920-1932) (in BF millions)

Table 5 : Problem of the insured white-collar workers : attempt at solution by alternative estimate of the insured manual workers' and white collar workers' pay

Table 6 : Wagebill of workers not protected against industrial accidents (1910-1931) (in BF millions)

Table 7 : Wagebill of non-insured manual workers for whom payments made to the Guarantee Fund (in BF millions)

Table 8 : Wagebill of non-insured manual workers whose employers were exempted from contributing to the Guarantee Fund (in BF millions)

Table 9 : Adjustment of insured wagebill for wagebill above maximum wage and wagebill below minimum wage (in BF millions)

Table 10 : Wagebill of homeworkers (in BF millions)

Table 11 : Wagebill of fishermen and seamen (in BF millions)

Table 12 : Pay of manual workers employed in the private sector in Belgium (in BF millions)

Table 13 : Pay of white-collar workers in the private sector : simplified table (in BF millions)

Table 14 : Employment, unemployment and total workforce of white-collar workers and manual workers in positions of authority according to the industrial and commercial census of 31 December 1930

Table 15 : Employment, unemployment and total workforce of white-collar workers and manual workers in positions of authority according to the Economic and social census of 27 February 1937

Table 16 : Estimate of white-collar workers and manual workers in positions of authority in industry and commerce on 31 December 1920 : men

Table 17 :	Estimate of white-collar workers and manual workers in positions of authority in industry and commerce on 31 December 1920 : women
Table 18 :	Estimated employment level for white-collar workers and manual workers in positions of authority in industry on 31 October 1926
Table 19 :	Percentage of manual workers in authority in combined total of white-collar workers and manual workers in authority on 27 February 1937
Table 20 :	Estimated level of unemployment of white-collar workers in industry and commerce
Table 21 :	Employment, level of unemployment and total workforce of white-collar workers (excluding manual workers in positions of authority) in census years
Table 22 :	Employment of white-collar workers (excluding manual workers in positions of authority) in industry and commerce : 1920-1939
Table 23 :	Estimate of average pay of white-collar workers in 1937
Table 24 :	Combined index of average pay of railway staff and average hourly wage of skilled manual workers in industry
Table 25 :	Total pay of white-collar workers (excluding manual workers in postions of authority) in industry and commerce : 1920-1939 (in BF millions)
Table 26 :	Estimate of pay of white-collar workers not listed in the industrial and commercial censuses
Table 27 :	Total wagebill of domestic staff, border-workers and seasonal workers employed abroad. Summary table (in BF millions)
Table 28 :	Domestic staff in the censuses of 1920 and 1930
Table 29 :	Domestic staff in the censuses of 1910, 1920, 1930 en 1947
Table 30 :	Wages of domestic staff in Brussels (in BF)
Table 31 :	Total wagebill of domestic staff (in BF millions)
Table 32 :	Number of Belgian or West Flanders border-workers employed in the Department du Nord or in the rest of France according to various sources
Table 33 :	Possible indicators for the evolution of the number of border-workers employed in France
Table 34 :	Average annual pay of border-workers employed in France (including employers' social security contributions)
Table 35 :	Total wagebill of Belgian border-workers employed in France (including employers' social security contributions) (in BF millions)
Table 36 :	Average annual pay of seasonal workers employed in France (including employers' social security contributions)
Table 37 :	Total wagebill of seasonal workers employed in France (including employers' social security contributions) (in BF millions)
Table 38 :	Statutory employers' social security contribution (in BF millions)
Table 39 :	Employers' contributions to white-collar workers pensions (in BF millions)

Table 40 : Employers' contributions to family allowances (in BF millions)
Table 41 : Employers' contributions to industrial accident insurance (in BF millions)
Table 42 : Pay and pensions of government staff (in BF millions)
Table 43 : Income from employment : additions and adjustments (in BF millions)
Table 44 : Estimate of voluntary employers' contributions (in BF millions)
Table 45 : Estimate of undeclared income of manual workers (in BF millions)
Table 46 : Self-employed income from agriculture, horticulure and forestry (in BF millions)
Table 47 : Operational inputs in agriculture and horticulture (in BF millions)
Table 48 : Self-employed income from woods managed by the forestry commission (in BF millions)
Table 49 : Entrepreneurial income of the professions, independent traders, craftsmen an partnerships. Summary table (in BF millions)
Table 50 : Direct taxes received by the central government (annual figures - in BF millions)
Table 51 : Number of tax payers, tax receipts and taxable income of industrial proprietors, independant traders, craftsmen and the professions (tax receipts and taxable income in the year in which income was earned - in BF millions)
Table 52 : Comparison of the numbers of independent traders and industrial entrepreneurs according to the censuses and the fiscal statistics
Table 53 : Number of industrial entrepreneurs and independent traders according to the adapted fiscal statistics
Table 54 : Taxable income of industrial proprietors, independent traders and craftsmen : homogenization of the fiscal statistics (in BF millions)
Table 55 : Estimated taxable income from invested capital of industrial proprietors, independent traders and craftsmen : 1920-1928 (in BF millions)
Table 56 : Entrepreneurial income of independent traders and craftsmen : incremental coefficients of the NIS
Table 57 : Conversion of taxable into actually earned entrepreneurial income of independent traders and craftsmen (in BF millions)
Table 58 : Estimated entrepreneurial income of independent traders and craftsmen in years without fiscal statistics (in BF millions)
Table 59 : Number of independent traders and craftsmen as secondary occupation on 31 december 1930
Table 60 : Entrepreneurial income of independent traders and craftsmen (secondary occupation) (in BF millions)
Table 61 : Capitalized interest on savings deposits held by private individuals with the ASLK (in BF millions)
Table 62 : Interest on ex-servicemen's endowment passbooks with the ASLK (in BF millions)

Table 63 :	Interest on savings deposits with private savings banks (in BF millions)
Table 64 :	Interest on savings deposits : summary overview (in BF millions)
Table 65 :	Interest on bank deposits (in BF millions)
Table 66 :	Imputed interest on the actuarial reserves of life insurance companies (in BF millions)
Table 67 :	Interest from mortgage loans accruing to private individuals (in BF millions)
Table 68 :	Interest for private individuals. Various categories (in BF millions)
Table 69 :	Rent (received or imputed) credited to private individuals (in BF millions)
Table 70 :	Rent index for all dwellings in Belgium (1935=100)
Table 71 :	Gross income from improved properties credited to private individuals
Table 72 :	Gross income from unimproved properties credited to private individuals (in BF millions)
Table 73 :	Total charges (in BF millions)
Table 74 :	Dividends, proceeds from investment abroad, directors' bonuses, donations to private individuals resident in Belgium : summary table (in BF millions)
Table 75 :	Dividends paid by Belgian companies principally trading in Belgium (in BF millions)
Table 76 :	Dividends paid by Belgian companies principally trading in the colonies or abroad (in BF millions)
Table 77 :	Income from investments abroad (including dividends from Belgian companies) (in BF millions)
Table 78 :	Directors' bonuses and corporate grants to households or non-profit making organizations serving households (in BF millions)
Table 79 :	Saving of corporations : summary table (in BF millions)
Table 80 :	Net profit of Belgian joint-stock companies principally trading in Belgium (in BF millions)
Table 81 :	Profits reserved by Belgian joint-stock companies principally trading in Belgium (in BF millions)
Table 82 :	Reserved profits : comparison with results from other sources (in BF millions)
Table 83 :	Non-distributed profits of autonomous public companies (in BF millions)
Table 84 :	Direct taxes of companies : summary table (in BF millions)
Table 85 :	Estimate of trade tax paid by companies (annual figures - in BF millions)
Table 86 :	Estimate of financial securities tax and land tax paid by companies (annual figures - in BF millions)
Table 87 :	Imputed net rent accruing to the government (in BF millions)

Table 88 :	Income from property and entrepreneurial income accruing to the central government : total excluding income derived from the railways, post office, telegraph and telephone (in BF millions)
Table 89 :	Income from property and entrepreneurial income accruing to the central government : income derived from the railways (in BF millions)
Table 90 :	Income from property and entrepreneurial income accruing to the central government : income derived from the post office and the telegraph and telephone company (in BF millions)
Table 91 :	Income from property and entrepreneurial income accruing to the central government : total (in BF millions)
Table 92 :	Statutory pension funds : interest on actuarial reserves (in BF millions)
Table 93 :	Interest on actuarial reserves of statutory pension funds (in BF millions)
Table 94 :	Interest on actuarial reserves of industrial accident insurance funds (in BF millions)
Table 95 :	Income from property and entrepreneurial income (excluding imputed rent) accruing to other government (in BF millions)
Table 96 :	Income from property and entrepreneurial income (excluding imputed rent) accruing to the municipalities and public welfare committees (in BF millions)
Table 97 :	Income from property and entrepreneurial income (excluding imputed rent) accruing to the provinces (in BF millions)
Table 98 :	Interest on the government debt (in BF millions)
Table 99 :	Interest on the public debt (in BF millions)
Table 100 :	Interest on government funds (1933-1939) according to the return on capital statistics (in BF millions)
Table 101 :	Interest on the intergovernmental debt : 1929-1940 (in BF millions)
Table 102 :	Interest on local government debt (provinces and municipalities (in BF millions)
Table 103A :	Depreciation of dwellings (in BF millions)
Table 103B :	Depreciation of other buildings and plant and equipment, public sector (in BF millions)
Table 104 :	Depreciation of other buildings and plant and equipment, private sector, and totals (in BF millions)
Table 105 :	Indirect taxes (in BF millions)
Table 106 :	Subsidies (in BF millions)
Table 107 :	Belgian GNP, 1920-1939 (nominal terms, in BF millions)
Table 108 :	Share of the various income categories, 1920-1939 (nominal terms)

GRAPHS

Graph 1 :   Belgian GNP, 1920-1939 (nominal terms)
Graph 2 :   Share of total income from employment in GNP, 1920-1939
Graph 3 :   Share of income from employment of employees in the private sector in GNP, 1920-1939
Graph 4 :   Share of employers' social security contributions in GNP, 1920-1939
Graph 5 :   Share of income from capital accruing to the personal sector in GNP, 1920-1939
Graph 6 :   Share of companies in the formation of GNP, 1920-1939
Graph 7 :   Share of government revenues in GNP, 1920-1939

CHAPTER 1

PAY OF MANUAL WORKERS IN THE PRIVATE SECTOR IN BELGIUM

The reconstruction of income from employment is subdivided into six chapters. Before examining the actual method of reconstruction, the first section of this chapter discusses the meaning of income from paid employment in terms of the OECD's standardized system of national accounts. The following text therefore relates not just to the first chapter but also to the five succeeding chapters. A brief survey is also provided of the content of the six first chapters, which follow the present classification of the *National Institute for Statistics* (Nationaal Instituut voor de Statistiek, NIS) with reference to income from paid employment. The second section of the first chapter relates to the wages of manual workers in enterprises in industry, trade and other service sectors, while the third section examines the pay of homeworkers, agricultural workers and wage-earning fishermen and seamen.

SECTION 1. DEFINTIONS AND SUMMARY OF CONTENTS OF THE SIX CHAPTERS CONCERNING INCOME FROM PAID EMPLOYMENT

Paragraph 1. Definition of the concept of income from paid employment[1]

By income from paid employment is understood every form of remuneration in cash or in kind payable by an employer of whatever description (i.e. companies, private individuals, non-profit organisations, government agencies or foreign employers) to wage and salary earners normally resident in Belgium.

This definition implies that neither nationality nor the location of employment determines whether or not remuneration is included as part of national income. The residence criterion, for example, means that the remuneration paid to an Italian living in Belgium employed in the Liège steel industry is counted as part of Belgian national income. By contrast the pay of a Dutch national who crosses the border to work in Belgium but resides in the

---

[1] *A standardized system of national accounts,* Paris, OECD, 1958, pp. 79-81; NIS, *Commissie van het Nationaal Inkomen, Het Belgisch nationaal inkomen van 1948 tot 1954* (unpublished file, December 1955, pp. 1-3); *Het Belgisch nationaal inkomen van 1948 tot 1954*, in: "Statistisch Bulletin", vol. 42, 1956, pp. 587-588; *De nationale rekeningen van België 1953-1962*, in: "Statistisch Tijdschrift", vol. 49, 1963, p. 1143.

Netherlands forms part of Dutch national income. Belgians who earn their livelihood abroad but reside in Belgium contribute towards Belgian national income. This applies during the inter-war period to a large group of Flemish workers employed in the Northern France industrial basin or the surrounding rich agricultural areas of Artois and Picardy[2]. The remuneration paid to Belgian colonials in the former Belgian Congo, however, does not form part of Belgian national income since these individuals did not live in Belgium. The non-repatriated element of foreign remuneration of Belgian residents (i.e. that proportion of their earnings spent in other countries) is counted as part of Belgian national income[3].

An exception to the residence criterion is formed by the members of the armed forces stationed abroad and diplomatic staff posted abroad[4]. The pay of Belgian soldiers quartered in Germany therefore forms part of Belgian national income. Similarly the pay of ambassadors or other official Belgian representatives abroad is treated as part of Belgian national income. The pay of locally engaged staff, on the other hand, forms part of the national income of the host country.

Income from paid employment may be regarded as consisting of wages and salaries on the one hand and the employer's social security contributions on the other. Wages and salaries are included in national income before deduction of taxes and before deduction of employees' social security contributions. This means *gross pay*. On the other hand transfer payments such as unemployment benefits or pensions are not regarded as income from paid employment and do not therefore form part of national income. The reason for this is that the income approach towards national income deals solely with the primary distribution of income, i.e. with the factor payments corresponding to a contribution towards national product. An exception is formed by the pensions and other social security benefits of permanently appointed government employees. These payments are regarded not as a transfer but as a (deferred) wage and are therefore included as part of national income.

Social security benefits comprise the entitlements under social security legislation. Employers' social security contributions therefore only comprise the contributions required under law and not the extra-legal benefits paid on a voluntary basis, such as contributions to a supplementary pension.

When pensions or other social benefits are directly assigned by the employer to the beneficiary, i.e. without prior employers' contributions being made to specially established funds or insurance companies, such pensions and social benefits must be added to the wages and salaries item and not be entered as

---

[2] The fact that these agricultural workers sometimes left their country for several months to work in France does not detract from the fact that Belgium was their normal place of residence.
[3] *Het Belgisch nationaal inkomen van 1948 tot 1954*, p. 592.
[4] *A standardized system*, p. 33.

employers' social security contributions[5]. The latter is the case with pensions and the social security benefits paid to permanent government employees[6].

Apart from the normal cash payments, the wages and salaries item includes extra remuneration for special services, gratuities and the cash equivalent of benefits in kind (provided free or at reduced cost), in so far as these represent a net benefit for the beneficiary. By net benefit is meant the fact that certain consumer goods or a part thereof no longer need to be purchased by the parties concerned[7]. This applies for example if the wage or salary earner enjoys free board and lodging. In some cases this also applies to the clothing issued by the employer. Benefits in kind must be valued at the cost price to the employer.

Premiums (e.g. for dangerous work), bonuses (e.g. end of year bonuses), profit-sharing schemes and other benefits assigned to employees (e.g. a thirteenth-month pay) are counted as part of wages and salaries. Such additional sources of income were particularly important for white-collar workers in the inter-war period.

Travel and other business expenses reimbursed by the employer are not counted as part of pay. The reimbursement for travel costs which a commercial traveller receives from his employer is not therefore treated as extra remuneration. If such expenses are not reimbursed they are deducted from pay. This applies for example if a miner has been required to buy his own lamp and equipment without financial assistance from the mine proprietor.

It may be asked whether or not the travelling expenses paid by the employer for an employee to travel between home and work should be deducted from pay. According to the standardized system such expenses should not be regarded as occupational expenses and are consequently not deducted from pay[8] as these expenses are not inherently bound up with the exercise of the profession[9]. Although not explicitly spelt out anywhere in the standardized system, this line of argument implies that if the employer reimburses the costs of travelling to and from work such reimbursement should be regarded as a form of pay.

---

[5] Despite the fact that holiday bonuses are not paid directly by employers but via specially established funds maintained by the employers, the NIS treats employers' annual leave contributions as part of wages and salaries and not as part of employers' social security contributions. *De nationale rekeningen van België 1953-1962*, p. 1143.

[6] Central government and local authorities do not pay employers' social security contributions for their permanent staff. Pensions, sickness benefits, industrial accident payments and the like are paid directly to the permanent staff and may be regarded as (deferred) pay. The situation for temporary government employees is the same as that for employees in the private sector: the employer (in this case the government) pays employers' contributions to the social security funds and these employers' contributions are included as such in the national accounts.

[7] OLISLAEGERS O., *Naar een uitbreiding van de nationale rekeningen. Tweede deel. Het Europese stelsel van geïntegreerde economische rekeningen*, in: "Statistisch Tijdschrift", vol. 55, 1969, p. 992.

[8] *Het Belgisch nationaal inkomen van 1948 tot 1954*, p. 596.

[9] Save in exceptional cases (e.g. lack of housing near the place of employment) such costs can be avoided by moving closer to the place of employment.

Such methodological considerations concerning travel and other expenses are of particular interest in a theoretical sense. They are, however, of less importance for the concrete reconstruction of pay since little data is generally available on the subject.

Finally it should be noted that if a self-employed person is assisted by members of his family, the latter are not regarded as wage or salary-earners, unless they effectively receive a wage or salary.

Paragraph 2. Summary of the six chapters concerning income from paid employment

Following a discussion of the present classification of the NIS, the classification used for the inter-war period is examined, with special reference to points of correspondence with or discrepancy from the NIS classification.

1. NIS Classification

In the national accounts of the NIS, income from employment is subdivided into four main categories (see Annex 1). The classification is based not on functional distinctions, e.g. by economic sector (companies, households or government) or by occupational category, but on an institutional criterion, namely whether or not the pay was subject to the general social security regulations. Since the introduction of the compulsory system of social security on 1 January 1945 (Act of 28 December 1944) three bodies in Belgium have been responsible for administering these arrangements: the *National Social Security Agency* (Rijksdienst voor Maatschappelijke Zekerheid, RMZ[10]), the *National Miners' Pension Fund* (Nationaal Pensioenfonds voor Mijnwerkers, NPM) and the *Merchant Seamen's Social Security Agency* (Dienst voor Maatschappelijke Veiligheid der Zeelieden ter Koopvaardij, DMVZK[11]).

The first and also major category consists of the *Wages and salaries received by employees subject to the general social security regulations*. In the first place, this category consists of the pay of the manual and white-collar workers employed in the private sector in Belgium, namely in the primary, secondary (including homework) or tertiary sectors (with the exception of domestic staff). This NIS heading also includes the pay of the personnel of public utilities and semi-government agencies (if not on the state payroll) and the temporary workers and white-collar workers employed by the state and provincial and municipal authorities.

---

[10] Currently "Rijksdienst voor Sociale Zekerheid" (RSZ).
[11] Currently "Hulp- en Voorzorgkas voor Zeevarenden" (HVKZ).

In contrast to permanent officials, trainees and manual workers, temporary government staff (employed by the State, provinces, municipalities and in some cases public corporations) are subject to the general social security regulations. The arrangements for temporary government staff are comparable to those for employees in the private sector: both the employee and the employer (in this case the government) pay contributions for all forms of social security (i.e. pensions, health insurance and unemployment and disability insurance, etc.). Temporary government staff are consequently subject to the general social security regulations. The situation for permanent civil servants and trainees is totally different. The employer (the State, provinces, municipalities and certain public corporations, such as the National Belgian Railways) do not pay employers' contributions and the employee's contribution is confined to just a few aspects of social security (e.g. a contribution for widows' and orphans' pensions). As employer, the government does not pay a contribution as it simply continues to pay out all or the majority of pay in the event of sickness, invalidity or the attainment of retirement age on the part of permanent staff. A contribution for unemployment insurance would also be superfluous since permanent staff cannot by definition be dismissed except for serious personal misdemeanors.

The heading "Wages and salaries received by employees subject to the general social security regulations" is further subdivided into three subheadings: the *wages of manual workers* (figures drawn from the RMZ and NPM), the *wages of white-collar workers* (figures drawn from the RMZ and NPM) and finally a small category covering the *pay of merchant seamen* (figure drawn from the DMVZK).

The second category consists of *Employees subject to certain but not all of the social security provisions*. This concerns the pay of domestic and personal servants, border workers and seasonal workers working abroad.

Employers' social security contributions form the subject of the third category.

The fourth category consists of the *Pay of employees who are not subject to the general social security regulations*. This group comprises the permanent and trainee staff of the State, provinces, municipalities, certain semi-government agencies (if on the State payroll), private education[12], a number of government corporations (National Belgian Railway Company, Telegraph and Telephone Corporation and the Airwaves, Post, Radio and Television Agency) and the public utilities controlled by the provinces or municipalities (e.g. gas, water and electricity utilities). The employees coming under the fourth heading are not affiliated to the RMZ because their pensions, family allowances and other social benefits are paid directly by the employer without payment of prior contributions.

---

12   Free education in Belgium is primarily provided by the Catholic Church or affiliated organizations.

For this reason these social benefits have been included not under "Employers' social security contributions" but under "Wages and salaries"[13].

Finally a fifth NIS-category - which is not explicitly taken up in Annex 1 - contains a number of supplements and adjustments to the remuneration as shown in the previous items. The most important of these adjustments relate to earnings not notified to the RMZ (e.g. pay for moonlighting).

2. Classification for the inter-war period

In order to ensure continuity with the post-war figures, every effort was made to draw up a classification for the inter-war period that corresponded with the classification currently employed by the NIS. This was not, however, always possible, since the institutional framework on which the NIS classification is based, differed radically during the inter-war period from that after the Second World War. During the 1920s and 1930s there was no generally compulsory system of social security and the RMZ - the annual statistics of which provide the most important source for the pay recorded by the NIS - was not established until 1945. It would therefore be an anachronism to refer in relation to the period 1920-1939 to "Employees subject to social security", "Employees subject to certain social security provisions", "Employees not subject to the general social security regulations", etc. For this reason the nomenclature of the various headings has been adapted where necessary, without however losing sight of the substantive correspondence with the post-war figures.

Income from employment is subdivided in this publication into six chapters. Chapters 1 and 2 correspond approximately with the first principal NIS category. The next four chapters each correspond with one category in the post-war national accounts.

The first chapter comprises the remuneration of manual workers employed in the private sector in Belgium (with the exception of the domestic staff[14]). All Belgian merchant seamen are also included under this chapter, irrespective as to whether they had manual worker or white-collar status. Chapter 2 deals with the remuneration of white collar workers employed in the private sector in Belgium. These two chapters largely correspond with the "Wages and salaries of employees subject to social security" in the present national accounts. The most important

---

[13] The pensions and other social benefits of these employees are regarded not as a transfer but as (deferred) wages (cf. above).

[14] The description "private sector" is not entirely correct, in the sense that in principle the wages and salaries of the staff of public corporations and semi-government agencies (where such employees are not on the State payroll) have been included in the pay in chapters 1 and 2. On the other hand it would also be incorrect to speak of the enterprises sector, since the most important public enterprises (Railways, Telegraph and Telephone, Post Office) have been included under Chapter 5, in line with the NIS.

difference is that temporary government staff have not been recorded in the inter-war period.

The third chapter deals with the pay of domestic and personal servants, border workers and seasonal workers employed abroad, corresponding with the NIS heading "Wages and salaries of employees subject to certain social security provisions".

The fourth chapter relates to the employers' social security contributions. The content of this heading corresponds with that of the NIS.

The fifth chapter deals with the pay and pensions of government employees. This chapter corresponds with the NIS heading "Remuneration of employees not subject to the general social security regulations", with the difference that temporary staff were also included in the inter-war period. The reason is twofold: in the first place the sources for the inter-war period contain insufficient information to enable a distinction to be drawn between permanent and temporary staff and secondly it is more logical from a substantive viewpoint to group together the remuneration of all government personnel[15]. Finally, Chapter 6 brings together a number of additions and corrections which correspond as far as possible with the content of the eponymous NIS heading.

A detailed survey of the contents is provided in the introductory section to each chapter. The first chapter, in which the remuneration of manual workers employed in the private sector in Belgium is reconstructed, is subdivided into two sections. Section 2 deals with the total wages and salaries of manual workers employed in enterprises in industry, commerce and other service sectors. This is one of the largest headings in the income approach. The wages of the manual workers in question are largely reconstructed on the basis of figures relating to industrial accident insurance. Section 3 handles a number of more minor occupational categories: homeworkers, agricultural workers, fishermen and seamen.

---

[15] The pay of all public servants (i.e. including temporary employees) can also be established from the national accounts of the NIS. Heading 4 ("Other employees not subject to the general social security regulations") shows the income of all public servants (including temporary staff), on the basis of the government's accounts. The pay of temporary staff is then deducted in order to avoid duplication with heading 1 ("Employees subject to the general social security regulations"). The pay figures in question are drawn from the annual accounts of the State Social Security Agency.

SECTION 2. PAY OF MANUAL WORKERS EMPLOYED IN ENTERPRISES IN INDUSTRY, TRADE AND OTHER SERVICE SECTORS[16]

The total wages and salaries for the group of workers concerned can be reconstructed for the inter-war period in two ways[17]. The first possibility consists of estimating annual employment figures which are then multiplied by an average hourly wage and an average number of man-hours per year[18]. The first two of these three variables can be approximated on the basis of industrial and commercial censuses, unemployment statistics and hourly-wage indices. No macro-economic statistics are, however, available on the average number of man-hours per year in the inter-war period.

An alternative approach is provided by the published figures on the wagebill insured against industrial accidents[19]. Under the Act of 24 December 1903, Belgium had a compulsory system of industrial accident insurance that applied to nearly all workers in contractual employment. Total insured wages and salaries were published each year by the Ministry of Industry and Labour and for certain years by the *Central Bureau of Statistics* (Centraal Bureau voor de Statistiek, CBS), the precursor of the NIS.

Since the actually earned pay provided the basis for determining the wagebill to be insured, these statistics provide a suitable basis for these calculations. The insured wagebill implicitly covers all variables that determine total wages and salaries: the number of employees, the hourly wage and working hours. On account of the sharp fluctuations in the level of economic activity, the working hours varied considerably during the inter-war period; there were both periods with a substantial amount of overtime (in the late 1920s) and periods with partial

---

[16] This section is largely based on GOOSSENS M., *Het looninkomen van arbeiders in privé-dienst tijdens het Interbellum (1920-1939): berekeningsmethode en resultaten*, in: "Workshop on Quantitative Economic History", Discussion paper 87.06, Louvain, 1987.

[17] Among other things, the "other" service sectors include the banking and insurance system, personal care (especially hairdressers), organizations concerned with sport, cultural affairs and leisure/relaxation and maintenance and security firms. These sectors are included in the Statistics under the heading "Miscellaneous enterprises".

[18] This method was for example applied to manual workers in industry by SCHOLLIERS P., *Loon-indexering en sociale vrede*. Among other things, the "other" service sectors include the banking and insurance system, personal care (especially hairdressers), organizations concerned with sport, cultural affairs and leisure/relaxation and maintenance and security firms. These sectors are included in the Statistics under the heading "Miscellaneous enterprises". *Koopkracht en klassenstrijd in België tijdens het Interbellum*, in: "Centrum voor Hedendaagse Sociale Geschiedenis", Brussels, VUB, 1985, pp. 340-341.

[19] This source has been previously used: COPPIETERS B., *De statistieken over de arbeidsongevallenverzekering als bron voor de berekening van de totale loonsom der arbeidersklasse in België*, in: "Tijdschrift voor Sociale Geschiedenis", vol. 13, 1987, pp. 94-111. Coppieters takes the published statistics as they stand without any correction, which involves a substantial distortion of the actually earned total wagebill.

unemployment (the larger part of the 1930s). In addition working hours were, to a somewhat lesser extent, affected during the period in question by statutory provisions and strike action.

Since, in contrast to the first approach, the available source material for the second approach does implicitly take account of the number of hours worked at macro-economic level, it was decided to opt for the latter method. This also fits in well with the present working method of the NIS, which mainly draws its information on paid employment from the annual reports of the RMZ and NPM, which also include total wages and salaries.

As the scope of the industrial accident legislation was subject to change in the period under review, a survey is first provided of the changes over time in the legislation (Paragraph 1). The publications in which the insured wagebill is included are then discussed Paragraph 2. In order to arrive at the actually earned wagebill of workers employed by enterprises in industry, commerce and other service industries, a number of adjustments need to be made to the figures on the insured wages. These adjustments are discussed in Paragraph 3.

Before discussing the statutory framework, the final result of the calculations is shown in Table 1. Column 1 indicates the insured wagebill as shown in the statistics on industrial accident insurance. Columns 2-7 show the corrections carried out in order to arrive at the actually earned wages and salaries in column 8. The adjustments that most affected the size and especially the movements in total wages and salaries are the correction for insured domestic staff (column 3) and the correction for that element of the wagebill above the maximum wage and below the minimum wage (column 7). The need for these adjustments should become clearer after the statutory framework has been discussed.

Paragraph 1. Evolution of the industrial accident insurance legislation[20]

The following paragraph examines which categories of employees were covered by the Act, and on what element of their pay the benefits were calculated. The way in which employers were able to discharge their obligations is examined in the second paragraph.

---

[20] For a survey of the legislation relating to industrial accident insurance see: COPPIETERS B., *o.c.*, pp. 94-103; HAIDANT P. *Précis de législation industrielle et sociale*, Brussels; Liège; Paris, 1939^2, pp. 129-145; VELGE H., *Les lois belges d'assurance et de prévoyance sociales,* Brussels, 1993, pp. 10-116. The statistical publications on industrial accident insurance also contain a considerable amount of useful information on the statutory framework.

1. Scope

The Industrial Accidents Indemnification Act of 24 December 1903 is a milepost in Belgian social history. Before that date, the victim of an industrial accident claiming indemnity had to demonstrate culpability on the part of the employer[21]. Under the Act of 24 December 1903, the victim in principle became entitled to indemnification irrespective as to whether the employee, employer or a third party was responsible for the accident.

The payment was calculated as a percentage of the employee's pay during the year preceding the accident, subject however to an upper and a lower limit. If for example the accident resulted in a temporary and complete incapacity for work, the employee was entitled to a daily reimbursement of 50% of his average daily pay during the period of employment invalidity[22]. The pay used for calculating the daily payment was, however, subject to an upper limit of an equivalent annual wage of BF 2,400 and a lower limit of BF 365. If a worker earned more than BF 2,400, this daily reimbursement was limited to an equivalent annual sum of BF 1,200 (i.e. 50% of the upper limit). If the manual worker earned less than BF 365 he or she was entitled, in the event of total inactivity, to a daily reimbursement corresponding to an annual sum of BF 182.5 (50% of the lower limit).

Initially not all manual workers were protected by the Act of 24 December 1903. The obligation to pay a reimbursement was confined to the following private and public cooperations:
- industrial companies in industries with a high accident risk, such as mines, steel mills, the chemical industry and transport companies[23], as well as companies from other industries where these rely on mechanical power;
- industrial companies with a low accident risk, provided that they employed at least five manual workers;
- trading and other service companies with an average of at least three manual workers;
- agricultural enterprises with an average of at least three manual workers.

Manual workers were regarded as all staff attached to the company under a contract of employment as laid down in the Act of 10 March 1900[24]. Apprentices, even if they received no pay, were equated with manual workers, as were white-collar workers earning less than BF 2,400 who were exposed to the same dangers as manual workers in exercising their profession. In contrast to the manual workers, white-collar workers who earned more than BF 2,400 did not qualify for

---

[21] COPPIETERS B., *o.c.*, p. 96.
[22] Under the Act of 15 May 1929, which came into operation from 1 January 1930, this percentage was increased to 66.7% and in certain cases to as much as 80% (*Report 1927-1928-1929*, p. 9).
[23] Section 2 of the Act of 24 December 1903 provides a summary of the industries with a high accident risk.
[24] The Act of 10 March 1900 laid down the reciprocal rights and obligations of employers and

any form of statutory reimbursement, even if they performed hazardous work.

The comparatively small number of manual workers not falling into any of the above categories remained covered by the former system. Where they considered they qualified for compensation, they had to demonstrate that the accident was due to liability on the part of the employer.

The Act of 24 December 1903 was repeatedly amended. These amendments are of relevance in reconstructing total wages and salaries only in so far as the scope was extended to other categories of workers or if the minimum or maximum wage was increased. Until 1930 the changes remained confined to increases in the lower and upper wage limits on which the compensation was calculated[25], and to increases in the pay which white-collar workers subject to the same accident risk as manual workers could earn in order to qualify for statutory protection.

No radical modification to the scope of the legislation occurred until the Act of 18 June 1930 and the Royal Decree of 28 December 1930, both of which came into force on 1 January 1932. From that date onwards all manual workers, irrespective of the size or degree of risk of the enterprise by which they were employed, were protected against the financial consequences of an industrial accident. Similarly all white collar workers whose contracts of employment were determined under the Acts of 7 August 1922 and 2 May 1929 now benefited from the statutory protection[26].

No further changes were made to the scope of the Act for the remainder of the 1930s, meaning that from 1 January 1932 onwards only the following categories of employees fell outside the statutory framework[27]:
- domestic and personal servants
- homeworkers
- manual workers employed by an employer who did not employ at least one person for at least two months a year
- white-collar workers earning more than BF 24,000 (category that was not mentioned in the Acts of 7 August 1922 and 2 May 1929 concerning the contracts of employment for white-collar workers)
- fishermen and seamen

---

manual workers. The Act does not, however, provide any clear definition of the concept of manual worker. Section 1 of the Act does, however, explicitly state that foremen and chargehands should be classed as manual workers (and not, therefore, as white-collar workers).

25 For a survey of these amendments between 1920 and 1939 see Table 9 columns 4 and 5.
26 The Act of 7 August 1922 concerning contracts of employment for white-collar workers was modified in various respects by the Act of 2 May 1929. Among other things it was laid down that the contract of employment for white-collar workers earning more than BF 24,000 were not subject to the Act (in 1922 the limit was BF 12,000 a year). As in the case of the Act of 10 March 1900 concerning contracts of employment for manual workers, the acts on the contracts of employment for white-collar workers did not provide any clear definition of a white-collar or a manual worker.
27 HAIDANT P., *o.c.*, p.130; *Statistics 1937*, p. IX.

- government employees, including the employees of the *National Belgian Railway Company* (Nationale Maatschappij van de Belgische Spoorwegen, NMBS), the *Telegraph and Telephone Corporation* (Regie van Telegrafie en Telefonie, RTT) and the Post Office.

The first four of these categories had no statutory protection against industrial accidents, while the latter two were covered by separate arrangements. Fishermen and seamen enjoyed separate insurance arrangements under the Act of 20 December 1929, while the government continued to pay its staff in the event of an industrial accident.

Needless to say the statutory protection extended only to employees working in Belgium. Belgian residents employed abroad were not covered, while foreigners in salaried employment in Belgium enjoyed the same benefits as their Belgian colleagues.

2. Possibilities for complying with the Act

Under the Act of 24 December 1903 an employer was discharged from his responsibility to pay compensation if he had taken out an insurance contract with an insurance agency recognized by the State. This could be either a private insurance company or an employer's cooperative insurance fund. Employers who had not taken out any insurance remained personally liable for the financial consequences of an industrial accident, meaning that they had to pay the victim the compensation provided for under law out of their own pocket. To guard against the possibility of non-payment (e.g. if an employer went bankrupt), the legislator decided to set up a *Guarantee Fund* (Waarborgfonds). This fund, which was administered by the government, was supported by the compulsory contributions made by employers who had not taken out separate insurance arrangements. Payment was made from the Guarantee Fund only if it had been legally established that the company in question or, if an insurance scheme had been taken out, the insurance company, had failed to meet its obligations. In essence this meant that the Guarantee Fund intervened in the event of the insolvency of the employer or insurance agency. The contribution to the Guarantee Fund therefore in no way absolved the non-insured employer of his financial responsibility towards the victim of an accident[28].

The Act also laid down that, following a favourable report by the Industrial Accident Commission, an uninsured employer could be absolved by ministerial order of his obligation to make payments towards the Guarantee Fund provided that he could provide sufficient guarantees that he was capable of paying the compensation determined under law in the event of an accident. The requirements were however so strict (a company needed for example to have a workforce of at

---

[28] COPPIETERS B., *o.c.*, p. 100.

least 500)[29] that only extremely large companies qualified for exemption. These companies are sometimes referred to in the sources as "personal liability insurers"[30].

To sum up, employers coming under the scope of the Act could choose from the following possibilities:
1) The employer could conclude an insurance scheme with a private insurance company or employers' insurance fund, thereby eliminating liability for the financial consequences of an industrial accident.
2) The employer did not conclude an insurance contract and remained personally liable. In this case one of the two following situations arose:
   a) The employer paid a contribution to the Guarantee Fund, which then reimbursed the victim in the event of insolvency on the part of the employer.
   b) The employer did not contribute towards the Guarantee Fund if he was able to provide sufficient guarantees of his ability to pay compensation to victims, which applied only in the case of very large enterprises.

The figures reveal that the vast majority of manual workers worked for employers who had taken out insurance arrangements[31]. Clearly, also employers not coming under the Act could take out an insurance. As they remained liable for the financial consequences of an industrial accident if it could be shown that they had been at fault, it was advisable to insure against such risks.

Paragraph 2. The insured wagebill in the official publications concerning the industrial accident legislation

The legislation on industrial accidents resulted in two series of statistical publications, which form the basic material for the reconstruction of the earnings from paid employment of manual workers employed in the private sector. These publications are the *Report on the implementation of the Act for the*

---

[29] Royal Decree of 22 December 1904. This provision was amended to some extent by the Royal Decree of 26 April 1932 in that the requirement was changed to 250 white-collar workers or 500 manual workers plus white-collar workers.

[30] In fact the term "personal liability insurers" to describe the companies that retained financial liability and were exempted from contributing to the Guarantee Fund is somewhat misleading since the other employers who had not concluded an insurance contract but had made contributions to the Guarantee Fund also remained liable. They could therefore equally as well be regarded as personal liability insurers. To avoid any misunderstanding, the terminology used in the sources has been retained in the remainder of this discussion, meaning that the term "personal liability insurers" refers solely to those employers who had not taken out separate insurance arrangements and who had been exempted from making payments to the Guarantee Fund.

[31] See Table 1, which provides a survey of the insured (column 1) and the non-insured (columns 4, 5 and 6) wagebill.

Reimbursement of Injury arising from Industrial Accidents and the *Industrial Accident Statistics*[32]. The "Reports" were published by the Ministry of Manufacturing Industry, Labour and Social Security. The "Statistics" were published by the same Ministry up to the end of 1922, and from 1931 onwards by the CBS.

The Reports were published every three years, but contained annual figures. Their essential purpose was as a check on the financial solidity of the insurance companies and employers' insurance funds in the industrial accident sector[33]. The insurance agencies were obliged by law to advise the government of their financial structure. One of the elements of that structure was the insured wagebill. In this respect, the Reports provide annual figures on the coal mines on the one hand and on the all the other sectors combined on the other[34]. Up to and including 1932 no distinction was drawn between the insured of manual workers and white-collar workers respectively. From 1933 onwards separate series were published for manual workers and white-collar workers.

In contrast to the Reports, the Statistics were not drawn up with the aim of facilitating an evaluation of the financial position of the insurance institutions. They primarily contain information on industrial accidents themselves. Thus the Statistics note the number of accidents per sector, with details on the causes, the resultant payments, relationship between the insured wagebill and the amounts paid out, etc.

Another difference is the fact that the Statistics were drawn up for a few years only (during the inter-war period: 1921, 1922, 1931, 1937, 1938 and 1939), whereas the Reports contain annual figures.

The Reports and the Statistics were drawn up independently of one another, but the basic material for both publications was provided by the insurance

---

[32] *Rapports relatifs à l'exécution des lois coördonnées sur la réparation des dommages resultant des accidents du travail*, Brussels, Ministère de l'Industrie et du Travail - Ministère du Prévoyance Sociale, 1905-1940 ; *Statistiques des accidents du travail élaborées d'après les documents fournis en exécution de la loi du 24 décembre 1903 sur la réparation des dommages résultant des accidents du travail*, Brussels, Ministère de l'Industrie et du Travail - Ministère des Affaires Economiques, 906-1913, 1921, 1922, 1931, 1937-1940. In the remaining discussion "Reports" refers to the first series of publications while the term "Statistics" refers to the second series.
[33] COPPIETERS B., *o.c.*, p. 97; GOOSSENS M., *o.c.*, p. 2.
[34] The "other enterprises" comprise enterprises in industry (with the exception of coalmines), commerce, other service industries and what was known as "special agriculture". The latter covers a wide range of activities, including market gardening, maintenance of parks and properties, floristry and forestry. The "Reports" and "Statistics" do not contain any wage data on agriculture in the narrow sense (i.e. arable and pastoral farming) as the insurance premiums for the agricultural industry were calculated on a fixed basis (per hectare) rather than on the basis of wages paid out (*Statistics 1938-1939-1940*, p. 9).
[35] COPPIETERS B., *Schatting van de koopkracht en de loonevolutie van arbeiders en bedienden in de privé-sector 1906-1945 op basis van de statistieken betreffende de arbeidsongevallenverzekering*, in: "Centrum voor Politicologie", vol. 4, Brussels, VUB, 1985, pp. 6-7.

institutions[35], for which reason the insured wagebills in both publications correspond reasonably well (see Table 2). The major deviation in 1938 is undoubtedly attributable to the excessively high figure in the Statistics[36]. The cause of the unduly high figure could not, however, be determined. Nor could any explanation be found for the comparatively small discrepancies in the remaining years.

With respect to the reconstruction of income from paid employment, the Statistics have the advantage that they provide information on 20 sectors (17 industrial sectors[37], special agriculture[38], commerce, and miscellaneous enterprises[39]), subdivided for certain years (1922, 1931, 1937) into subsectors. By contrast, the Reports only provide sectoral figures for the coalmines. The major disadvantage of the Statistics, however, is the irregular and much lower frequency of publication. For this reason, the insured wagebill as shown in the Reports has been taken below as the basic material for the reconstruction of wages. A number of significant adjustments do, however, need to be made in order to arrive at the actually earned pay of all manual workers from the insured pay of the insured manual workers. These corrections are outlined in the next paragraph.

Paragraph 3. Adjustments to the insured wagebill

The adjustments to the total insured wagebill in the Reports have a twofold objective: in the first place, adjusting the figures in such a way that they relate to a homogeneous category, namely all manual workers (excluding white-collar workers) employed in enterprises (including those who were not insured), and, secondly, to convert the insured wagebill into the actually earned wagebill. Three kinds of adjustments may be distinguished:
1) Insured remuneration that does not relate to manual labour in enterprises engaged in industry, commerce and other service sectors must be deducted. Three corrections were made:
   a) The total insured wagebill includes the remuneration paid to certain agricultural workers (namely those employed in "special agriculture").

---

36   This could be determined on the basis of the figures relating to the coalmines - an industry for which alternative figures are available - drawn from the General Directorate of Mines and published in the Yearbook of the Central Bureau of Statistics (CBS). According to this alternative source, the total wagebill for mineworkers in 1938 amounted to BF 1,947 million (*Yearbook CBS*, vol. 64, 1942, p. 200). The Reports provide a figure of BF 1,927 million for the insured wagebill for mineworkers in 1938, while the Statistics provide an insured sum of BF 2,644 million.

37   One of these 17 sectors is transport (excluding the State Railways and the National Belgian Railway Company.

38   See footnote 34.

39   Among other things the "miscellaneous enterprises" include the banking and insurance system, personal care (especially hairdressers), sporting, cultural and leisure facilities and maintenance and security firms.

These must be deducted, as the wagebill for all agricultural workers is calculated elsewhere[40]; without this deduction there would be a double-count. The same applies to the pay of teachers in the vocational training schools of the private education system and manual workers employed by the municipalies, since these workers form part of the public sector[41].

b) Up to and including 1932 the insured pay of white-collar workers was included in the same series as the insured wages of manual workers. An estimate consequently needs to be made for the period 1920-1932 of the insured pay of white-collar workers, which then needs to be deducted from the total wagebills.

c) The pay of the non-residents employed by a Belgian employer needs to be deducted as these individuals do not form part of Belgian national income.

2) The pay of manual workers whose employers had not taken out insurance are not included in the Reports and need to be added to the insured wagebill. Four estimates are required for this purpose:

a) An estimate of the wagebill of the manual workers lacking statutory protection against industrial accidents up to and including 1931 (manufacturing enterprises with a low accident-risk employing fewer than five manual workers and trading and other service enterprises with fewer than three manual workers), and for whom the employer had not taken out insurance on a voluntary basis.

b) An estimate of the wagebill of the non-insured manual workers whose employers had made payments to the Guarantee Fund.

c) An estimate of the wagebill of the non-insured manual workers whose employers were exempted from making payments to the Guarantee Fund (the so-called personal liability insurers).

d) An estimate of the wagebill of the manual workers employed by an employer who did not employ at least one worker for at least two months. This provision covered manual workers who sporadically performed odd jobs, often after their normal daily task[42].

3) The insured wagebill needs to be converted into the actually earned wagebill. The insured wagebill of the insured manual workers differs from their actually earned pay in four respects:

a) The manual workers who earned more than the maximum wage were only insured up to that maximum amount. The difference between the

---

[40] Cf. below.

[41] The pay of teachers in the free education system comes under the public sector in the Belgian National Accounts. Teachers are included in Chapter 5. No correction need be made for teachers in official education as their pay does not form part of the insured wagebill.

[42] The pay in question - the scale of which is of course totally unknown - is included under an all-inclusive correction heading, "Non-reported income of manual workers", in Chapter 6, "Additions and adjustments".

actual wage and maximum wage is not included in the insured wagebill, so that the latter is less than the actually earned pay.

b) Manual workers who earned less than the minimum wage were nevertheless insured up to that minimum amount. The difference between the minimum wage and actual pay is included in the insured wagebill, so that the latter exceeds the actually earned pay[43]. The same applies to apprentices who, even if they earned nothing at all, were nevertheless insured for this minimum amount.

c) Pay not reported by the employer to the insurance institutions has of course not been included in the insured wagebill, so that the latter underestimates the actually earned pay.

1. Deduction of incorrectly included occupational categories

a) The insured wagebill of a proportion of the government employees and a proportion of the agricultural workers

* *Civil servants*

With a view to continuity with the post-war figures of the NIS, an attempt has been made to harmonize the contents of Chapters 1 and 2 (Pay of the manual workers and white-collar workers employed in the private sector in Belgium) as far as feasible with the NIS heading "Income from paid employment of the employees subject to the general social security provisions"[44]. In the first place, this heading covers the pay of employees employed in the private sector in Belgium. It also covers the personnel of public enterprises and semi-government agencies (if not paid under the state budget) and the temporary manual workers and white-collar workers employed by the State and the provincial and municipal authorities.

The employees coming under the budget of the State, provinces or the municipalities (with the exception of temporary employees), as well as the personnel of the NMBS, the RTT, the Post Office and the public corporations controlled by local government are not subject to the general social security regulations and are included by the NIS under a different heading ("Other employees not subject to the general social security provisions"). This heading largely corresponds with Chapter 5 of this study for the inter-war period ("Pay and pensions of civil servants"). The only difference is that the pay of temporary civil servants was not included under Chapters 1 and 2, but was amalgamated with the wagebill of permanent civil servants in Chapter 5[45]. On this point, therefore, there is a discrepancy from the post-war classification. For the remainder, efforts have

---

43 The discrepancies arising from the maximum and minimum insured pay have been estimated according to the same method. For this reason they have been treated together below.
44 Cf. above.
45 Cf. above.

been made to arrive at comparable categories. It was therefore established whether the wagebill insured against industrial accidents also included the pay of employees that were defined as civil servants, as these would need to be deducted from the insured wagebill in order to avoid double-counts with Chapter 5.

The accompanying text to the 1938-1939-1940 Statistics reports that the manual workers in the majority of the public sector (State, provinces, municipalies, semi-government agencies and NMBS) were not insured and consequently were not included in the statistics[46]. An examination of the Statistics for 1922, 1931 and 1937, which contained a detailed classification of all insured manual workers, revealed that only the staff of certain vocational training schools and municipal services were insured. By contrast the manual workers employed by public corporations in the transport and communications sector NMBS, Telegraph, Telephone and Post Office) were clearly not insured, which is in accord with the post-war classification based on the applicability/non-applicability of the social security regulations. The only adjustment required in this case therefore concerned the personnel of certain vocational training schools and municipal agencies. As noted earlier, these are deducted from the total insured wagebill.

Table 3 (columns 2 and 4) shows the remuneration referred to in the Statistics of 1922, 1931 and 1937. For the remaining years the wagebill was estimated on the basis of these figures, together with the evolution of the total insured wagebill in the Reports.

Agricultural workers
Up to and including 1931 for an agricultural enterprise with at least three paid employees and from 1932 onwards irrespective of the size of the enterprise, agricultural workers came under the industrial accident legislation. In contrast to manual workers in the secondary and tertiary sector, agricultural workers were not insured in accordance with their actual pay but on a fixed basis[47]. For this reason, neither the Reports nor the Statistics provide agricultural workers' wages. An exception relates to "special agriculture", a heterogeneous category in the Statistics, the most important subcategories in which were market gardening, floristry, forestry and the maintenance of parks and properties. Workers employed in special agriculture were not insured on a lump-sum basis, but in proportion to their actual pay. Their remuneration does consequently form part of the insured wagebill in the Reports and the Industrial Accident Statistics.

The wagebill of a proportion of the subcategories in special agriculture, such as the remuneration of manual workers employed in market gardening and floristry, is included under the income of agricultural workers, which has been estimated in its totality in the remainder of this study[48]. In order to avoid double-

---

[46] *Statistics 1938-1939-1940*, p. 9.
[47] The insurance premium was calculated on the basis of farm acreage.
[48] The remuneration of agricultural workers is examined later.

counts, this pay must be deducted from the total insured wagebill (see Table 3 columns 6 and 7). The same method was followed as that for vocational training schools and the municipal agencies. The remuneration of other special agriculture subcategories (for example forestry and the maintenance of parks and properties) do not relate to agriculture. Since these categories do not overlap with the income of agricultural workers, their remuneration need not be deducted from the insured wagebill.

b)   The insured wagebill of white-collar workers up to and including 1932

A clear distinction between the pay of manual workers and white-collar workers was not made in the Reports and the Statistics until 1933 (see Table 4 columns 2 and 3)[49]. Prior to 1933 only one pay series was printed (column 1), but from the accompanying commentary in the Statistics and the Reports it is not clear whether this relates to the wagebill of manual workers only or whether the total figure also includes the remuneration of the insured white-collar workers. If the latter is the case, the insured pay of white-collar workers needs to be estimated for the period 1920-1932 and deducted from the total wagebill as this chapter is solely concerned with the reconstruction of the wages of manual workers.

It will be shown below that the insured wagebill for 1920-1932 also includes the pay of white-collar workers. This may be deduced by comparing the figures for industrial accident insurance on the one hand and an alternative reconstruction of the insured wagebill on the other. This alternative reconstruction also enables an approximation to be made of the share of the insured white-collar workers' pay in the total insured wagebill. Before examining this problem in more detail, it may be desirable to recall the industrial accident legislation with respect to white-collar workers.

With respect to the statutory arrangements for white-collar workers two different periods may be distinguished. From 1 January 1932 all white-collar workers in the private sector earning less than BF 24,000 a year were protected under law against the financial consequences of an industrial accident. Before 1932 such statutory protection applied only to white-collar workers exposed to the same dangers as manual workers in the exercise of their profession and not earning more than BF 12,000[50]. Employers were of course also at liberty to insure white-collar workers who did not come under the statutory provisions.

The insured wagebill of manual workers was reconstructed as follows. On the basis of the known insured wagebill of manual workers in 1933, the unknown

---

[49]   The criterion for distinguishing white-collar workers from manual workers is not made clear. What is clear is that manual workers in positions of authority (i.e. foremen and chargehands) were classed as manual workers and not as white-collar workers. *Statistics 1931*, p. V; *Statistics 1937*, p. X.
[50]   In 1903 the maximum sum amounted to only BF 2,400 and was repeatedly increased after the First World War to, ultimately, BF 12,000 in 1926 (Act of 3 August 1926).

insured manual workers' pay in 1932 was estimated on the basis of employment and wage figures. This estimate was then compared with the known total insured pay in 1932, with a view to establishing whether the latter variable also included the pay of white-collar workers. This working method was then repeated for the year 1931, so that it can be established whether the changed legislation for white-collar workers from 1932 onwards is reflected in the figures for the insured pay in that year. Finally the estimation method was also applied for the period 1933-1939, for which the insured manual workers' pay is known. A comparison between the observed rate of growth of the insured manual workers' pay and the estimated growth rates provides an indication of the reliability of the estimates.

On the basis of these estimates it will be sought to demonstrate that:
1) the wagebill in 1920-1932 (Table 4 column 1) also includes the insured white-collar workers' pay;
2) the three-yearly Reports did not take account of the amendments to the legislation for white-collar workers, which came into force on 1 January 1932, until 1933 (= Report 1933-1934-1935). This implies that in relation to 1932 - as also for 1920-1931 - column 1 includes in addition to the insured manual workers' pay only the remuneration of white-collar workers with the same accident-risk as manual workers, provided always that they did not earn more than a legally determined amount.

Table 5 provides an alternative estimate of the insured manual workers' pay in detail. This was based on the following formula[51]:

$$\overset{\circ}{y} = \overset{\circ}{w} + \overset{\circ}{h} + \overset{\circ}{p} + \overset{\circ}{r} \qquad [1]$$

where

    y = manual workers' wagebill
    w = hourly wage
    h = annual number of man-hours per manual workers
    p = active population (population aged 15-65)
    r = participation rate (% of the active population employed as a manual worker in the private sector)
    $\circ$ = growth rate

No direct information is available for any of these variables, meaning that approximations must be used instead. As an alternative to the rate of growth in the hourly wages of all manual workers (w) the rate of growth of the hourly wage of industrial workers may be used (Table 5 column 1). In the absence of data the

---

[51] This formula is only approximate: the higher the growth rates (in absolute terms) the greater the discrepancy between the left-hand and right-hand sides of the equation.

growth in the active population (p) is replaced by the growth in the total population (column 2). As an approximation of the changes in the rate of participation (r) the rate of employment of workers in industry has been used, in which the rate of employment (in %) equals 100 - the rate of unemployment (column 4). No macro-economic figures are available on the evolution of the annual number of hours worked per worker (h). For the time being it has been assumed that this variable remained constant (i.e., h = 0). Finally, it has been assumed that the insured wagebill corresponds with the actually earned wagebill (y). The latter assumption is defensible because nearly all manual workers were insured in the 1930s and the minimum and maximum wage levels to be insured were respectively so low and high that the remuneration of the vast majority of manual workers fell within these limits[52].

On the basis of formula [1], column 5 shows the *estimated growth* in the wagebill of manual workers, while column 6 shows the *observed* growth in the insured wagebill of manual workers. The observed insured wagebill of manual workers from 1933 onwards is shown in column 8. Manual workers' pay in 1932 has been estimated (columns 9) on the basis of the observed wage-sum of the workers in 1933 (BF 9,710 million) and the estimated growth in 1933 (-0.8%). The wagebill of the manual workers in 1931 has been estimated in an analogous way. Finally column 11 estimates the insured pay of white-collar workers in 1931 and 1932 by deducting the estimated manual workers' pay (column 9) from the observed total insured pay (column 10).

How may the results be interpreted? Before answering this question it should be emphasized that the method employed necessarily rests on various assumptions. In particular, as will be seen below, the assumption of a constant number of annual man-hours is at variance with reality.

Before analysing the results for 1931 and 1932, the reconstructed growth rates for the period 1934-1939 (column 5) are compared with the observed growth rates (column 6). The discrepancies between the two figures are sometimes positive and sometimes negative (column 7). A comparison of these discrepancies with the economic cycle, as expressed for example by industrial production (column 13) and exports (column 14), indicates that in years of recovery (1935, 1936, 1937) the observed growth in total manual workers' pay exceeded the estimated growth rate. In years of economic downturn the reverse applies: the observed growth is less than the estimated rate. These results clearly indicate the weak point in this method of reconstruction, namely the average number of hours worked per year per worker, which, in the absence of macro-economic figures, has been taken as constant. It is logical that in the comparatively favourable years, the average number of man-hours was higher, and that it was lower in poorer years. For this reason, the reconstructed wagebill has been underestimated for the favourable years and overestimated for the unfavourable ones[53].

---

52 Cf. below.
53 This exercise clearly reveals that if account is not explicitly or implicitly taken of the average

Columns 9, 10 and 11 clearly reveal that the total insured wagebill in 1931 and 1932 also covers white-collar workers' pay. At first sight, a comparison of the estimated insured white-collar workers' pay in 1932 of BF 1,152 million with the known insured white-collar workers' pay in 1933 (BF 1,883 million, see column 12) suggests an extraordinary situation. Since the statutory provisions in 1932 and 1933 remain unchanged, such a sharp increase in the insured pay of white-collar workers between 1932 and 1933 is, a priori, highly implausible.

To what may this enormous increase be attributed? An initial possible explanation derives from the fact that the annual number of hours worked per manual worker has been kept constant. From the test relating to 1934-1939 it was evident that the predictions of manual workers' pay were underestimated in years of economic upswing and overestimated in years of economic decline. The importance of this explanatory factor in this case is, however, presumably minimal since the state of the economy in 1933 was only marginally better than that in 1932, so that it may be assumed that the number of hours worked per manual worker was much the same in both years[54].

A second possible explanation for the marked difference between the estimated insured pay of white-collar workers in 1932 and the known insured wages in 1933 derives from the inadequate application of the Act in 1932. On 1 January 1932 the Act of 18 June 1930 and the Royal Decree of 28 December 1931, which determined that henceforth all white-collar workers earning less than BF 24,000 per annum were protected against the financial consequences of an industrial accident, came into force. It is not inconceivable that the amended legislation was not observed on a large scale until 1933.

A final possible explanation resides in the fact that the insured wagebill in 1932 was published in the three-yearly Reports relating to 1930-1932 while the wagebill for 1933 was included in the 1933-1935 series. It is quite possible that the compilers of the Report for 1930-1932 wished to provide figures on a homogeneous category of insured persons, and consequently included only those servants who were already insured before 1932.

The estimate of the insured pay of white-collar workers for 1931 is even more problematical. A fall from BF 1,610 in 1931 to BF 1,152 million in 1932 is impossible. This anomaly is undoubtedly due to the assumption of a constant number of man-hours per manual worker. There can be no doubt that the average number of hours worked per worker in 1932 was lower than in 1931 on account of the marked economic decline in the latter year (see columns 13 and 14). This

---

number of man-hours an estimate of the total wages and salaries of manual workers in the inter-war period will always lead to distorted results. The fact that the wagebill insured against industrial accidents implicitly includes the labour-duration variable indicates the exceptional importance of this source for the reconstruction of national income.

[54] If the economy in 1932 was less favourable than in 1933, the wagebill of manual workers has been overestimated in 1932 and the insured pay of white-collar workers consequently underestimated.

means that the estimated insured wagebill of manual workers in 1931 is underestimated and that of white-collar workers consequently overestimated.

What can be concluded from all this? In the first place it is clear that the total insured wagebill in the Reports included white-collar workers' pay up to and including 1932. It is also probable that this pay did not just relate to those who were compulsorily insured (i.e. white-collar workers with the same accident-risk as manual workers) but that many employers also voluntarily insured their non-legally protected white-collar workers. The latter is not illogical since the employer of non-insured staff was personally liable in the event of an accident due to an error on his part. Many employers are unlikely to have been willing to incur this risk and, when insuring their manual workers and white-collar workers with the same accident-risk, will have taken out a policy at the same time for their remaining white-collar staff. The number of white-collar workers in most companies was in fact very low, so that the additional cost of insuring them was of little consequence.

Secondly it appears that the Reports do not take account until 1933 of the amended legislation for white-collar workers that came into force on 1 January 1932. This implies that up to and including 1932 the Reports included in addition to insured manual workers' wages only the pay of white-collar workers subject to the same accident-risk as manual workers (providing they did not earn more than BF 12,000) and of the voluntarily insured white-collar workers (see Table 4 column 1). By contrast the insured pay of white-collar workers from 1933 onwards (see column 3) refer presumably to a larger group than those covered by column 1, namely all white-collar workers, with the exception of those earning more than BF 24,000 per annum.

What adjustment should now be made to the total insured wagebill between 1920 and 1932 with a view to isolating out the insured pay of white-collar workers? The underlying assumption is that the 1920-1932 series (total insured wagebill, see Table 4 column 1) and the 1933-1939 series (insured wagebill of manual workers, see column 2) are each homogeneous. To begin with, the insured pay of white-collar workers is estimated for 1920 and 1932, followed by an interpolation for the intervening years. Finally the estimated wagebill of white-collar workers is deducted from the total insured wagebill for the period 1920-1932. The outcome of this procedure is the insured wagebill of workers in 1920-1932 - a series that corresponds with the insured wagebill of manual workers in the Reports in 1933-1939 (see column 8).

According to the reconstruction carried out in Table 5, the insured wagebill of manual workers in 1932 amounted to BF 9,785 million and that of white-collar workers BF 1,152 million (see Table 5 columns 9 and 11). The latter sum represents 10.53% of the total insured pay. It is assumed that this share - which has been rounded up to 11% - roughly corresponds with reality[55]. In this way, the

---

55 By rounding off the share of the pay of white-collar workers in 1932 upwards, allowance is made for the fact that the economy in 1933 had improved slightly on the year before. The average

insured manual workers' wagebill in 1932 is estimated at BF 1,203 million (see Table 4 columns 6 and 7).

For 1920, the insured white-collar workers' pay was estimated on the basis of the results of a survey conducted by the Ministry of Industry and Labour on 15 April 1920[56]. This survey covered 23,173 white-collar workers in the private sector - both men and women - employed in seven sectors[57]. Among other things, the respondents were asked whether of not they were insured against industrial accidents. 21,083 respondents replied to this question, of whom 9,308 (44.1%) proved to be insured. Of these 9,308 persons 4,955 (53.2%) had taken out insurance themselves while for the remaining 4,353 white-collar workers (46.8%) the employer had done so[58].

On the basis of these figures and the total earnings of all white-collar workers in 1920, it is possible to estimate the insured white-collar workers' pay in 1920. The total pay of all white-collar workers in 1920 has been estimated in Chapter 2 at BF 885 million[59]. If it is assumed that the full pay was insured and that the average pay of the non-insured persons was the same as that of insured persons, the insured pay amounts to BF 390 million (44.1% of BF 885 million). The problem does however arise that 53.2% of the policies were taken out by the white-collar workers themselves and it is not known whether these insurance contracts were included in the Reports on Industrial Accidents. If the latter is assumed not to have been the case, the total insured wagebill in the Reports includes white-collar workers' pay in 1920 amounting to BF 183 million (45.8% of BF 390 million). This sum corresponds to 20.6% of the total white-collar workers' pay (183÷885) and with 4.9% of the total insured wagebill in the Reports.

A comparison of these figures with the results for 1932 provides an indication of the reliability of these assumptions. In 1932, the insured white-collar workers' pay was estimated at BF 1,203 billion, or 34.4% of the total white-collar workers'

---

number of man-hours per annum in 1933 is consequently likely to have been a little higher than in 1932. No allowance was, however, made for this in the estimates in Table 5, meaning that the estimated insured manual workers' pay in 1932 is likely to have been overestimated to some extent and that of white-collar workers to have been slightly underestimated.

[56] *Enquête sur la situation des employés privés (15 April 1920)* Brussels, Ministry of Industry and Labour, 1923.

[57] The seven sectors are industry, wholesaling, retailing, banks and credit institutions, insurance institutions, stockbrokers and exchange brokers and the staff of members of the liberal professions. The survey was also conducted among commercial travellers and among white-collar workers of various enterprises (education, newspapers, religious institutions, hotels, etc.), but the results of the survey for the latter two groups were not published. In total 97,004 white-collar workers were sent a questionnaire, of which 30,381 returned a reasonably completed form. If commercial travelers, the white-collar workers employed by various enterprises, those not specified and the unemployed are deducted from the latter figure, one arrives at a total of 23,173 white-collar workers (*Enquête sur la situation des employés*, pp. 3-7).

[58] Own calculations on basis of *Enquête sur la situation des employés*, passim.

[59] See Chapter 2 Table 13 column 3.

pay and 11.0% of the total insured wagebill in the Reports[60]. The increase in the insurance cover of white-collar workers' pay[61] from 20.6% in 1920 to 34.4% in 1932 appears plausible as it is likely that more and more employers will have voluntarily ensured their white-collar workers in the course of the 1920s[62]. The increase in the share of insured white-collar workers' pay in the total insured pay (from 4.9% in 1920 to 11.0% in 1932) is a manifestation of the same phenomenon. It must also be taken into consideration that the ratio between the total number of white-collar workers and the total number of manual workers increased considerably between 1920 and 1932.

For the intervening years (1921-1931) it has been assumed that the share of the insured white-collar workers' pay in the total insured wagebill increased on a linear basis (see Table 4 column 6). By multiplying this share by the total insured wagebill the insured white-collar workers' pay was arrived at (column 7). Finally that pay was deducted from the total insured wagebill in order to arrive at the insured wagebill of the manual workers (column 8).

c) *Insured wagebill of non-residents employed in Belgium*

As noted in the introductory section to this chapter, the pay of non-residents employed in Belgium has, in accordance with the standardized system of the OECD, been added not to Belgian national income but to the national income of the country where they are normally resident. No indication is provided in the Reports and the Statistics whether such pay has been included in the insured wagebill. There is however no reason whatever to assume that this will not have been the case as the legislation does not draw any distinction between the treatment of residents and non-residents. This means that for the reconstruction of national income, the pay of the non-residents has to be deducted from the insured wagebill. The problem is that no reference whatever is made to this wagebill. The fact that no reference is made in the literature to the non-residents employed in Belgium indicates that this phenomenon may have been unimportant in the inter-war period. The opposite applies to Belgian residents who earned their living abroad, especially in Northern France. According to the occupational census in 1930, no fewer than 79,626 Belgian residents were employed as border-workers in the North France industrial basin[63]. According to the same occupational census,

---

[60] In 1932 the income from paid employment of white-collar workers amounted to BF 3,501 million (see Chapter 2 Table 13 column 3).

[61] This relates solely to insurance taken out by employers.

[62] The same phenomenon of growing voluntary insurance also applied to employers who fell outside the scope of the Act until 1932 (i.e. enterprises with fewer than three workers in the tertiary sector or fewer than five workers in industry, which were not mechanically powered and which belonged to an industry with a low accident risk, cf. below).

[63] *Le recensement de l'industrie et du commerce au 31 décembre 1930. Analyse sommaire des résultats. Première partie: recensement professionnel*, in: "Revue du Travail", vol. 43, 1934, pp. 748-749.

the number of Belgian border-workers in other countries was limited: 4,887 in the Netherlands, 1,427 in the Grand Duchy of Luxembourg, 312 in Germany and 57 in Britain.

If it is assumed that no French residents were employed in Belgium and that the number and pay of the Dutch, Luxembourg, German and British residents earning their livelihood in Belgium was equal to the number and pay of the Belgian residents employed abroad, the problem outlined above can then be resolved more or less satisfactorily. No adjustment is made to the insured wagebill, while Chapter 3 makes allowance only for the Belgian border-workers in France.[64] This means that the figures in this chapter have been overestimated and those in Chapter 3 underestimated. These are however small amounts which, if the assumptions are correct, cancel one another out and consequently do not affect the size of national income.

2. Addition of the wagebill of workers not included in the Reports

a) Wagebill of non-insured workers

Up to and including 1931 manufacturing companies in industries with a low accident-risk fell outside the scope of the Industrial Accidents Act, at least if they employed fewer than five workers and were not mechanically powered. The same applied to enterprises in the tertiary sector with fewer than three workers. The bosses of these companies were of course at liberty to ensure their workers on a voluntary basis.

No direct information is available on the wagebill of workers falling outside the scope of the Act for whom no insurance was taken out. This wagebill has been reconstructed as follows. To begin with, an estimate has been made of the number of non-insured companies falling outside the Act. It has been assumed that on average these companies employed two workers. The number of workers is then multiplied by an average hourly wage and an average working hours.

The average hourly wage of the non-protected workers is based on the *Economic and Social Census of February 1937* (Economische en Sociale Telling van 1937, ESC 1937), the trimesterial hourly-wage index of the *National Bank of Belgium* (Nationale Bank van België, NBB) and the annual hourly-wage index for industrial workers published by Cassiers. The ESC 1937 provides the average hourly wage per industry, by size of company and by sex. It has been assumed that the hourly wage of the non-protected workers in February 1937 was equal to the weighted average hourly wage of workers in industrial enterprises employing fewer than five workers. The hourly wage determined in this way for February 1937 has then been increased into an hourly wage for 1937 as a whole by means

---

[64] See Chapter 3.

of the trimesterial hourly-wage index of the NBB[65]. The hourly wage for 1927 was then linked to Cassiers' annual hourly-wage index[66].

The estimate of the annual wage was based on a constant number of working hours per year (2,400 hours = 300 paid days x 8 hours). 300 working days may be regarded as the normal working year of a manual worker who was not unemployed or ill for any part of the year, as this figure corresponds with one unit of labour in the Statistics[67].

A comparison of the number of enterprises that had taken out insurance or contributed to the Guarantee Fund in 1910 with the total number of enterprises according to the industrial and commercial census of 1910, indicates that some 40,000 employers had not taken out insurance in that year or made a contribution to the Guarantee Fund[68]. The number of companies that fell outside the scope of the Act was of much the same order, implying that no more than a few entrepreneurs had taken out voluntary insurance in 1910. This is not illogical in view of the fact that the Industrial Accidents Act had been in force for only a few years and managers saw little advantage in insuring their workers if that was not required by law.

A similar comparison with the total number of enterprises according to the industrial and commercial census of 1930 reveals that on the eve of the legislative amendment of 1930-1931 nearly all enterprises - including therefore small businesses with a low accident-risk that fell outside the Act - were insured or had contributed towards the Guarantee Fund[69]. The number of companies that fell outside the scope of the Act and had not taken out insurance may be put at no more than 1,000. The managers of small businesses with a low accident-risk had therefore taken out insurance in the course of the 1920s with a view to avoiding the risk of being held personally liable in the event of an accident - a risk that continued to apply with respect to accidents for which they were to blame.

Table 6 provides an estimate of the number of companies with non-protected manual workers based on the assumption that 40,000 companies were in this situation in 1910 and 1,000 in 1931. Interpolation in between these two years was conducted on the basis of the growth in the number of insured companies. By multiplying the number of companies employing non-insured workers with the

---

[65] According to the NBB's quarterly index of wages (1936-1938 = 100) the index in March 1937 stood at 98, in June 1937 at 101, in September 1937 at 104 and in December 1937 at 106, providing an average figure for 1937 of 102.25. The latter figure is 4.3% more than the figure for the first trimester (*Belgische economische statistieken 1929-1940*, in: "Tijdschrift voor Documentatie en Voorlichting van de Nationale Bank van België", special number, 1940, p. 199.

[66] CASSIERS I., *Une statistique des salaires horaires dans l'industrie belge, 1919-1939*, in: "Recherches Economiques de Louvain", vol. 46, 1980, pp. 73. Cassiers' hourly-wage index is based on the hourly-wage index of the National Bank of Belgium (*Belgische economische statistieken 1929-1940*, p. 199), which does not however commence until 1929. For the period 1919-1928 her data have also been derived from the NBB. The data consist of the results of a retrospective survey conducted on behalf of the NBB in 1943 (known as the Davin survey - the results of which, however, were never published by the NBB.

assumed average number of workers per company (namely two) and the average yearly wage, the total wagebill of the relevant group of manual workers was obtained.

The main weakness in this method of reconstruction is of course the assumption - in the absence of macro-economic data on the average number of hours worked per year per worker - that this latter variable remained constant. However, given the comparatively small size of this category of manual workers, it may safely be assumed that this erroneous assumption has resulted in no more than a minor distortion in the total wagebill of all workers.

b) Wagebill of non-insured manual workers whose employers contributed to the Guarantee Fund

The manual workers in this category came under the scope of the Industrial Accidents Act and were employed by an employer who had not taken out any insurance and therefore remained personally liable in the event of an accident. These employers had not applied for or obtained any exemption from contributing to the Guarantee Fund. The wagebill for this group of manual workers has been estimated along the same lines as the method employed in the previous section: to begin with an estimate has been made of the number of employees in question, which has then been multiplied by an average yearly wage.

Up to and including 1931, it was possible to calculate the number of manual workers precisely. The legislator had laid down that each non-insured employer coming under the Act was required to pay a fixed annual premium to the Guarantee Fund. In addition a sum of BF 12 had to be paid per manual worker. This proportional premium remained unchanged between 1920 and 1931. Since the Reports specify the total sum of proportional premiums to the end of 1931, the number of manual workers could be straightforwardly calculated. Table 7 clearly reveals that the group in question was extremely small and moreover that it fell substantially in the course of the 1920s. From 1932 onwards, it was no longer possible to calculate the number of manual workers in question and the declining trend was roughly extrapolated. Since most of the companies contributing to the Guarantee Fund had only a few employees[70], it has been assumed that the manual

---

[67] The Statistics show the number of insured labour-units per industry. A labour-unit corresponds with the employment of one individual for 300 days. In view of the fact that many workers worked less than 300 days per year on account of partial unemployment or part-time employment, the number of labour units is lower than the number of workers. Example: 3 workers working 200 days per year = 2 labour units.

[68] For the specific calculations see GOOSSENS M., *Het looninkomen*, pp. 12 and 20-21.

[69] Idem.

[70] JULIN A., *Enquête sur les charges sociales de l'industrie*, Brussels, Editions du Comité Central Industriel de Belgique, 1933, pp. 13-14. The small scale of most of the companies contributing to the Guarantee Fund is also evident from Table 7 (compare column 1 with column 3): in 1920 these enterprises employed an average of just eight workers, a number that was to fall in the succeeding years to four in 1931. .

workers in question received the same annual pay as the non-insured manual workers of the very small enterprises who were discussed in point b above.

c) Wagebill of non-insured workers whose employers were exempted from contributing to the Guarantee Fund

Large companies that were not insured and which could guarantee that they were able to absorb the financial consequences of possible accidents were exempted from contributing to the Guarantee Fund. The wagebill for such enterprises - sometimes referred to as personal liability insurers - paid to their employees is known for only three years. Julin provides figures for 1926 and 1929[71], and the Industrial Accident Statistics contain the sum relating to 1939 (see Table 8 column 1)[72]. The wagebill reported in the Statistics relates just to manual workers, while the sums quoted by Julin possibly also include white-collar workers' pay. If this is indeed so the sum in question will have been comparatively small: in 1939 the pay of white-collar workers employed by exempt employers amounted to just BF 14 million, compared with a wagebill for manual workers of BF 481 million[73]. For this reason no adjustment has been made to the wagebill for 1926 and 1929. The wagebill for the missing years has been calculated on the basis of the three known years on the one hand and the evaluation of the adjusted wagebill of the insured manual workers on the other (see column 3).

3. Conversion of insured wagebill into actually earned wagebill

a) Adjustment for minimum and maximum wage

The main drawback of using the wagebill insured against industrial accidents to measure the income from paid employment arises from the fact that paid earnings were insured only up to a certain level - the maximum wage - meaning that the wagebill in the Reports on Industrial Accidents is underestimated in respect of manual workers earning more than the maximum wage. A corresponding problem - although in this case resulting in an overestimation of the actually earned wagebill - is the fact that wages had to be insured up to at least the minimum wage, even if actual earnings were lower.

Clearly, the size of the distortion of the insured wagebill as a measure for the actually earned wagebill is heavily determined by the level of the maximum and minimum wage. In the extreme case, in which the maximum wage is so high and the minimum wage so low that every worker's pay lies within these limits, there

---

[71] JULIN A., *o.c.*, pp. 12 and 14. The author provides no indication of the source from which his data were obtained.
[72] *Statistics 1938-1939-1940*, p. 259.
[73] Idem.

would of course be no distortion. In order to obtain an idea of the distortion it is therefore necessary to compare the minimum and maximum wages with average pay[74].

Table 9 columns 4 and 5 show the evolution of the minimum and maximum wage which, on account of inflation, were repeatedly raised in the 1920s. Columns 1, 2 and 3 provide an estimate of the weighted average annual pay of all male and female manual workers in industry and commerce[75], assuming average working hours of 2,400 hours a year[76]. The method is completely analagous with that developed for estimating the average annual pay of the unprotected and non-insured manual workers whose employers made a contribution towards the Guarantee Fund[77].

A comparison of the evolution of the average wage (column 3) with that of the minimum wage (column 4) indicates that the latter was so low throughout the inter-war period that any distortion of the insured wagebill in an upward sense must be presumed minimal. By contrast, the maximum wage does cause serious problems, more especially in the 1920s. Particularly in 1920-1921 and, to a lesser extent, during the remainder of the decade, the average wage was close to the maximum wage, revealing that many manual workers earned more than the maximum wage and that the insured wagebill consequently underestimates the actual level of pay. In the 1930s the underestimation may be negligeable as the maximum wage was sharply increased from 1 July 1929. On the basis of these considerations it may be concluded that the insured wagebill falls short of the actually earned wagebill in the 1920s but that any distortion in the 1930s is of little to no account.

Having outlined the problem, the question is how a satisfactory solution can be found. Clearly, an alternative source needs to be found with the same positive characteristics as the Reports (e.g. the implicit inclusion of the annual number of working hours per manual worker) but that is not distorted by a maximum or a minimum wage. A comparison of the wagebill as determined by the alternative source with those in the Reports can then help establish the distortion in the latter more precisely.

There is only one source that complies with these requirements, namely the wagebill of the miners included annually in the *Statistical Yearbook*[78], in turn based on information supplied by the Mining Industry General Council (column

---

[74] The spread of wages also needs to be taken into account, in that the greater the variation of individual wages around the average wage the greater the distortion.

[75] No breakdown by sex is provided anywhere in either the Reports or the Statistics.

[76] Needless to say the assumption of a constant number of hours per employed worker is liable to a good deal of justified criticism; the sole object of the exercise in question, however, is to obtain an impresion of the impact of the maximum and the minimum wage on the size of the insured wagebill.

[77] Cf. above.

[78] *Statistisch Jaarboek voor België en Belgisch Congo,* Brussels, NIS, 1920-

7). A comparison of the wagebill in this source with the insured wages in the coalmines according to the Reports[79] (column 6) confirms the conclusions reached earlier of a marked downward distortion of the insured wagebill in 1920-1921, a less pronounced but nevertheless substantial distortion during the remainder of the 1920s and a negligible distortion in the 1930s.

It may next be asked whether the percentage deviations between the miners' wages in the Statistical Yearbook on the one hand and those in the Reports on the other (column 8) can be used as an overall adjustment factor for the insured wagebill in all sectors. Before taking this step it needs to be established (i) whether all miners' wages were in fact insured, and (ii) whether the volume and evolution of miners' wages were representative for those in the other sectors.

As a hazardous industry, the mines were subject to the industrial accident legislation through the inter-war period. This does not, however, mean that the miners were necessarily insured, since insurance was not compulsory and mineowners could if they so chose make a contribution instead to the Guarantee Fund or could act as a personal liability insurer. Since the employers who made payments to the Guarantee Fund generally employed no more than a few people and a mine is necessarily a medium-sized to large commercial undertaking, the former alternative may be ruled out. The second alternative was also considered improbable, for the following reasons: (i) the high correlation in the 1930s between the insured wages and the wages in the Statistical Yearbook and (ii) the fact that the mines were a well organized industry with highly developed employers' insurance funds[80].

This leaves the problem of the representativeness of miners' wages. The latter exceeded the level of pay in most other industries[81], thereby implying a priori that the overall adjustment factor must be lower than that in column 8. Despite this assumption it was decided not to scale down the adjustment factor for the mine industry. This was because an attempt was made to obtain an impression of the overall adjustment factor by an alternative method. This approach was based on the estimated average annual wage shown in column 3 (with the most important distortion being the assumption of a constant number of annual hours of work per employee) and the distribution of wages around the mean in February 1937[82]. It was assumed that the distribution of wages around the mean remained unchanged during the inter-war period. On the basis of these figures and assumptions a frequency distribution of the wages was drawn up for each year and

---

[79] The Reports contained the insured wages for the coalmines on the one hand and those for all the other industries on the other.
[80] This is evident from the fact that nearly all miners' wages were insured with the "communal funds" and only a negligible proportion with the private insurance companies (or what were known as the "fixed-premium insurance companies"). In 1930 the wagebill of miners insured with the employers' funds amounted to BF 2,417 and that with private insurance companies to only BF 0.6 million (*Report 1930-1931-1932*, pp. 230).
[81] See for example the ESC 1937, vol. IV, p. 48.

it was established what percentage of the wagebill was above the maximum wage and what percentage below the minimum wage. From this an adjustment factor could be derived and compared with the adjustment factor for the mines in column 8.

The results of this test were as follows. The minimum wage does not exert any influence, nor does the maximum wage in the 1930s. In the 1920s, however, the insured wagebill needs to be augmented. The order of magnitude of this adjustment factor is the same as that for the mines[83], but the annual fluctuations are considerably greater. The cause of the less pronounced fluctuations in the adjustment factor for the mines may be attributable to the delayed application of the changes in the legislation with respect to the maximum wage. As a result possible sudden fluctuations resulting from an increase in the maximum wage were spread out over several years. In the alternative estimate of the adjustment factor for all industrial and commercial sectors it was (perhaps incorrectly) assumed that a change in the legislation was immediately observed, thereby leading to greater annual variations in the adjustment factor.

As the order of magnitude of the adjustment factor for the mines is the same as that produced by the alternative estimate for industry and commerce in general and since it appears plausible that an amendment to the legislation would not have been always or universally applied promptly, it was decided to apply the adjustment factor for the mines to the total insured wagebill. The overall adjustment arrived at in this manner is shown in column 10.

b)   Adjustment for non-declared earnings

Leaving aside the minimum and maximum wages, companies were required to insure the total wagebill of their manual workers with the insurance institutions. In determining the level of the insurance premiums and any pay-outs, account was also taken of the benefits in kind[84]. Contractually, the insurance companies were authorized to check whether the insured wages corresponded with those actually paid out as shown in the books of the company in question[85]. An examination of the payroll records for the Van der Wee shoe factory in Lier revealed that such checks were effectively conducted[86]. In addition the tax authorities were entitled

---

[82]   The ESC 1937 provides a detailed frequency distribution for the hourly wages of workers in each industry (ESC 1937, vols. IV and V).

[83]   It is unclear while why the order of magnitude of the overall adjustment factor (for all manual workers in industry and trade) on the basis of the alternative method should be the same as the adjustment factor for the miners on the basis of the miners' wages according to the Mining Industry General Council as shown in column 8, as it would be expected that the former would be lower since the miners' wages were on average higher than those in other industries.

[84]   COPPIETERS B. *o.c.*, pp. 102-103.

[85]   COPPIETERS B., Idem.

[86]   The payroll records cover the period 1924-1943. The wage records were audited by the insurance company inspector in December 1924, December 1927 and December 1932. The Van der

to check the observance of the statutory provisions with respect to industrial accident insurance[87]. Despite this system of verification allowance needs to be made for possible evasion. As far as the level of undeclared wages is concerned one is of course groping in the dark. Nor is it clear to what extent some wages were consciously not declared and to what extent the non-declaration was the result of ignorance or carelessness. Since the fiscal/para-fiscal burden was much lower in the 1920s than it is now, it may be that fewer conscious efforts were made during the inter-war period to avoid or evade social security contributions and income tax. On the other hand it may be assumed that the audits conducted by the authorities in the 1920s and 1930s were less effective than those after the Second World War because the tax department was less effectively equipped.

There are therefore many elements of uncertainty, as a result of which any adjustment to correct for the underestimation of the actually earned wagebill is necessarily arbitrary. A rough estimate has been made in Chapter 6, "Income from paid employement : Additions and adjustments"[88].

SECTION 3. PAY OF HOMEWORKERS, AGRICULTURAL WORKERS, FISHERMAN AND SEAMEN

This section provides an estimate of the income of private sector manual workers who were not subject to the general legislation on industrial accidents (i.e. homeworkers, fishermen and seamen)[89]. Belgian residents who went abroad to work (i.e. border and seasonal workers) were not included in the Reports and the Industrial Accidents Statistics. By way of analogy with the NIS classification, their income was shown in separate headings (Chapter 3). The same applies to domestic staff, who were however insured by law. The income of agricultural workers, who did come under the statutory regime but were insured on a lump-sum basis rather than on the basis of actual pay, does not form part of the insured wagebill in the Reports and the Industrial Accident Statistics. For these reasons the wages of agricultural workers have been estimated separately[90].

Wee shoe factory at Lier near Antwerp was a medium-sized family business employing 50-100 men and women. The company's payroll records form part of the family archives. The authors thank the Van der Wee family for their willingness to allow these documents to be inspected.

87 COPPIETERS B., *o.c.*, p. 103.
88 See Chapter 6.
89 Homeworkers had no legal protection against industrial accidents (HAIDANT P., *o.c.*, p. 130). Fishermen and seamen had a separate insurance system and were consequently not included in the Reports and the Statistics.
90 Under the present NIS classification the wages of homeworkers, agricultural workers and fishermen form part of the major heading "Remuneration of employees subject to the general social security regulations", subheading "Figures derived from RSZ and NPM: employees". This subheading also includes the wages of the large group of manual workers as calculated in section 2 of this Chapter. The remuneration of seamen comes under the same main heading, but within that heading comes under their own subheading.

Paragraph 1. Pay of homeworkers

In the ESC 1937 the concept of homeworker was defined as follows: "A homeworker is someone who performs labour for one or more employers in his home or in a workshop belonging to him or which he rents for that purpose, without any contractual relationship with the consumer"[91]. According to this definition, a homeworker is therefore a wage-earner rather than an independent craftsmen. In practice, however, it is sometimes difficult to draw this distinction. In fact the statute of the homeworker lies somewhere in between that of the independent craftsmen and the dependent wage-earner[92]. In this study homeworkers are regarded as wage-earners and their income consequently forms part of income from paid employment.

Homework was concentrated in the textiles, clothing and hides and leather (footwear) industry and was primarily performed by women[93]. Between 1910 and 1937, the phenomenon of homework declined sharply as the industries in question became more and more mechanized after the First World War, with a consequent shift from outwork to factory employment[94].

Since the total wagebill of homeworkers is unknown for any one year, it has been estimated by multiplying the number of workers by an average yearly wage. The most important sources for calculating the wagebill of homeworkers are the industrial censuses and the annual reports of the *General Savings and Annuity Fund* (Algemene Spaar- en Lijfrentekas, ASLK) which included statistics on the pension insurance required by law from 1926 onwards.

The total number of homeworkers is known only for the years in which an industrial census was organized, namely 1910, 1930 and 1937 (see Table 10 column 1). From 1927 onwards the annual reports of the ASLK also reported the level of pension contributions for homeworkers (column 2). The combination of both sources results in the total number of homeworkers paying pension contributions, namely 44.9% in 1930 and 63.6% in 1937. From these percentages

---

[91] *ESC 1937*, vol. I, p. 88.
[92] It could even happen that a homeworker employed other homeworkers: in that case he was both an employer and an employee (see in this connection *Recensement de l'industrie et du commerce (31 décembre 1910)*, Brussels, Ministry of Industry and Labour, vol. IV, pp. 156-157; *Le recensement de l'industre et du commerce au 31 décembre 1930. Analyse sommaire des résultats. Deuxième partie: recensement industriel, (IC 1930)* in: "Revue du Travail", vol. 44, 1935, p. 1420).
[93] Of the 45,497 homeworkers in 1930, 17,411 (11,887 women and 5,524 men) or 38.3% worked in the clothing industry, 13,809 (12,806 women and 1,003 men) or 30.4% in the textile industry and 4,926 (2,684 women and 2,242 men) or 10% in the hides and leather industry (own calculations based on *Le recensement de l'industrie et du commere au 31 décembre 1930*, pp. 1422-1429).
[94] In 1910 the total number of homeworkers was 141,456, consisting of 108,553 women and 32,903 men (*Recensement de l'industrie et du commerce 1910*, vol. IV, pp. 156-157). In 1930 the numbers had fallen to 45,497, of which 29,678 women and 15,808 men (*Recensement de l'industrie et du commerce 1930*, p. 1420). The total number of outworkers fell further in the course of the 1930s to 25,569 in 1937 (*ESC 1937,* vol. 1, p. 88; no breakdown by sex).

it is evident that the Pensions Act of 10 December 1924 (which came into force on 1 January 1926), under which all employers and manual workers, including homeworkers, were required to make pension contributions, was poorly observed, at least by homeworkers and their employers[95]. The Act was, however, gradually applied more effectively in the course of the 1930s. For the remaining years of the period 1927-1939 the proportion of pension-contributing homeworkers in relation to the total number of homeworkers was estimated on the basis of the ratios in 1930 and 1937 (column 3). The number of pension-contributors (column 2) divided by this share results in the total number of homeworkers (column 4). Finally the total number of homeworkers needs to be estimated for 1920-1926, a period for which no pension data are available. It has been assumed that the sharp reduction in the number of homeworkers between 1910 (industrial census figure) and 1927 (estimated according to the method described above) took place at a steady annual rate.

In estimating average annual pay, a distinction has been drawn between the periods 1920-1932 and 1933-1939. On account of the Act of 14 July 1930, which came into force on 1 July 1931, a proportional link was to some extent introduced between pension contributions and wage earnings[96]. It has been assumed that the relationship between the average pension contribution for an homeworker and that for an ordinary manual worker (column 8) reflects the ratio between the average wage of an homeworker and that of an ordinary manual worker. This ratio has been multiplied by a rough estimate of the average annual wage for an ordinary manual worker (column 9) to provide the average annual wage of an homeworker (column 10).

This method has only been applied from 1933 onwards since it is assumed that the average pension contribution in 1931-1932 has been distorted by contributions made in accordance with the provisions of the previous system. The latter system, which was in force from 1 January 1926 to 30 June 1931, provided for a fixed contribution irrespective of actual pay. In the case of male workers aged over 18 both the employer and the employee were required to contribute BF 3 per month. In the case of female workers and male workers aged under 18 the monthly contribution required by law was BF 1. In view of the lump-sum nature of the contributions, the method of pension contributions cannot be applied to the pre-1932 period. It has been assumed that an homeworker between 1920 and 1932 earned 55% of the average annual wage of an ordinary manual worker. This 55% is the average ratio between the pension contributions for homeworkers and those for ordinary manual workers in the period 1933-1939[97].

---

95   The pension legislation for workers is discussed in detail in Chapter 4.
96   See Chapter 4.
97   55% appears a plausible figure because outwork paid less well than factory employment and because women formed a far higher proportion of outworkers than of factory workers. The wage differentials between men and women were very substantial during the inter-war period: a male factory worker earned an average of BF 4.90 an hour in February 1937, while a female factory worker earned only BF 2.72, i.e. 55% of the male wage (*ESC 1937*, vol. IV, p.49).

By multiplying the number of homeworkers (column 4) by their average yearly wage (column 10) the total wagebill is obtained (column 11).

Paragraph 2. Pay of agricultural workers

The wagebill of agricultural workers forms part of the operating expenses of self-employed farmers. The method of reconstruction is discussed in Chapter 7, "Income from entrepreneurship in agriculture, horticulture and forestry"[98]. The resultant figures are shown in Table 12 column 3.

Paragraph 3. Pay of fishermen and seamen[99]

The wage-earnings of the fishermen and seamen were roughly calculated by multiplying an estimated number of workers by an average hourly wage and an average number of hours worked. As far as pay and working hours are concerned, the method is the same as that applied in estimating the wagebill of non-insured manual workers and of non-insured manual workers whose employer contributed to the Guarantee Fund[100]. This means that it was assumed that fishermen and seamen worked a constant annual number of hours (2,400) while testimated hourly wage is based on the ESC 1937, increased by an adjustment factor in order to allow for the wage increases in the course of 1937. The hourly wage in 1937 was subsequently linked to the hourly-wage index for industrial workers published by Cassiers (see Table 11 column 3).

The number of wage-earning fishermen was established only in the census years of 1910, 1930 and 1937 (see column 1). The remaining years were filled in by linear interpolation (column 2). The ESC 1937 reports an average hourly wage for fishermen of BF 6.14 - a high sum in view of the fact that the average hourly wage for male industrial workers according to the same count was just BF 4.90[101]. The estimated average yearly wages and the annual wagebill are shown in columns 4 and 5.

Only one figure, for 1930, has been found for the number of seamen (column 6)[102]. In the absence of data, it was assumed that this figure remained effectively unchanged throughout the inter-war period. Since the ESC 1937 does not provide any information on the hourly wage of seamen, it was assumed that this corresponded with the hourly wage for fishermen. On account of the assumptions

---

[98] See Chapter 7.
[99] This section relates solely to the earnings of wage-earning fishermen, i.e. self-employed fishermen are excluded.
[100] Cf. above.
[101] ESC 1937, vol. IV. pp. 48-49.
[102] This was for seamen living in Belgium.

in question, the estimated wagebill (column 7) may be regarded as no more than a very rough estimate of the true situation. The wage earnings of seamen, however, form such a small subcategory that any errors to which the method gives rise have little real impact on the size of national income.

CHAPTER 2

PAY OF WHITE-COLLAR WORKERS IN THE PRIVATE SECTOR

SECTION 1. DEFINITION OF THE HEADING

This chapter contains an estimate of the pay of white-collar workers in the private sector in Belgium. All white-collar workers, with the exception of government staff (Chapter 5) and domestic and personal servants (Chapter 3), belong in this category. Following the example of the NIS, the employees of the principal state-owned companies (State Railways, from 1926 onwards the *National Belgian Railway Company* (Nationale Maatschappij der Belgische Spoorwegen, NMBS), the *Telegraph and Telephone Corporation* (Regie van Telegrafie en Telefonie, RTT), the Post Office and the Airwaves, Radio and Television Agency), and employees of state-owned companies under the control of the provinces or municipalities are regarded as government staff and hence not included here. The pay of hospital staff on the other hand does form part of this chapter, even if the hospital in which they are employed is managed by the government.

In contrast to the wages of manual workers, there is little point in estimating the pay of white-collar workers on the basis of the industrial accident insurance reports[1]. This is because until 1931 employers were obliged to insure only those white-collar workers who in the execution of their duties were exposed to the same risk of an industrial accident as manual workers. Consequently, until 1931 most white-collar workers fell outside the scope of statutory industrial accident insurance.

Under the terms of the Act of 18 June 1930 and the Royal Decree of 28 December 1930, both of which came into effect on 1 January 1932, all white-collar workers whose contract of employment was subject to the Act of 2 May 1929 had to be insured. White-collar workers who earned more than BF 24,000 p.a. were not covered by the provisions of the Act of 2 May 1929 governing contracts of employment for white-collar workers, and in consequence under the terms of the Act and Royal Decree of 1930 on industrial accident insurance were not required to be insured[2]. Moreover, the maximum insurable salary was BF 20,000, so that for a white-collar worker who earned, for example, BF 22,000 p.a., insured pay was BF 2,000 less than actual earnings. Since large numbers of white-collar workers earned more than BF 20,000 p.a., insured pay remains a

---

[1] For a summary of the provisions and scope of statutory industrial accident insurance, see Chapter 1, "Pay of Manual Workers in the Private Sector in Belgium".
[2] The employer could of course insure these white-collar staff voluntarily.

downwardly distorted criterion for the actual earnings of white-collar workers during the 1930s[3]. For this reason it was necessary to look for other sources for the reconstruction of the pay of white-collar workers.

Because there are no reliable data on the total amount of white-collar workers' pay, these were estimated indirectly, namely by the annual multiplication of employment data on white-collar workers by their average pay. As in the case of manual workers there are no annual figures available regarding hours worked. However, not taking account of the hours worked has no serious negative consequences for the reliability of the estimates in view of the fact that most white-collar workers were paid monthly, regardless of the number of hours worked. As explained in the previous chapter, this was not the case for manual workers, who were mostly paid hourly, so that their total pay was greatly affected by the hours worked and in consequence also by the economic climate[4].

The employment figures were mainly estimated on the basis of the industrial, commercial, and population censuses of 1910, 1920, 1926, 1930 and 1937. Between these reference years the figures were interpolated, taking account of the level of unemployment. As far as pay in industry and commerce are concerned there are very good figures available in the ESC 1937. For the other years, however, there are no macro-economic data available[5]. Therefore the pay of white-collar workers in 1937 was linked to an index of the hourly wage of skilled manual workers in industry and an index of the annual pay of railway employees. The absence of annual macro-economic figures on white-collar workers' pay is undoubtedly the weak point in the reconstruction method.

A problem which arises here in relation to Chapter 1 is the question as to which jobs should be counted as manual labour and which should be regarded as white-collar employment. For most jobs this poses few problems: a miner or someone working in the blast furnaces and not in a position of authority is undoubtedly a manual worker, and a person performing administrative work belongs unambiguously to the group of white-collar workers. But what, for example, is one to make of warehousemen, shop staff or foremen in factories? In some statistics these employees are mainly classified with manual workers (for example, in the statistics and reports of industrial accidents), in other statistics one finds them among white-collar workers (for example, in the censuses).

---

[3] According to the calculations of this chapter, the annual average wage of a white-collar worker in industry in 1937 was approximately BF 26,000 (see Table 23, column 11). In the three-yearly industrial accident insurance reports one finds a total sum of insured pay amounting to BF 2,462 million for all white-collar workers in 1937 (see Chapter 1, Table 5, column 12). Estimates of this chapter give a total for white-collar workers' wages for that year of BF 3,932 million (see Table 13, column 3), which is 60% more than insured pay.

[4] See Chapter 1.

[5] It is true that a survey was carried out in 1920 which included white-collar workers' wages, but the results of this research are of very limited use for the reconstruction of the total wage-bill.

With the aim on the one hand of not overlooking any form of pay, and on the other hand of avoiding duplications, the definition of the group of white-collar workers should be viewed in connection with the content of Chapter 1. Manual workers' pay was estimated principally on the basis of the reports and statistics of industrial accidents. As a result the following are regarded here as white-collar workers: all employees who in the reports and statistics relating to industrial accident insurance are not included in the group of manual workers. Since the censuses are based on a broader definition of white-collar workers than in the industrial accident data, a portion of the white-collar workers in the censuses must be isolated and not included. How precisely this was done is explained below in the text.

In this chapter white-collar workers are divided into two groups: on the one hand those white-collar workers included in the censuses under the heading industry and commerce, and on the other hand the remaining white-collar workers in the private sector. The terms industry and commerce in the censuses are somewhat misleading, because they cover a broader field than simply manufacturing and purchasing and selling. In the industrial censuses the transport and fishing industries are also included, and the commercial censuses extend to the financial sector (banks, insurance companies, stockbrokers[6]), hotels and cafés and the entertainment sector. When industry and commerce are mentioned below, this refers to the definition in the censuses. The white-collar workers who are not included in the industrial and commercial censuses are principally employed in the cultural/artistic field[7], in journalism, in the medical professions[8], in the employment of other professionals, or in scientific, political associations or associations representing special interests[9]. It must, however, be emphasized that only employees are included in this chapter: the earnings of a solicitor's clerk therefore count as part of the pay of white-collar workers, the income of the solicitor himself does not[10].

White-collar workers in industry and commerce are discussed in Sections 2 and 3. In Section 2 annual employment data are reconstructed and in Section 3 an estimate of pay is given. The employment figures and the pay of the remaining white-collar workers are discussed in Section 4.

The results of the estimates are presented in Table 13.

---

6   In the censuses stockbrokers are included among commercial intermediaries.
7   For example, the artistic and administrative staff of theatres, opera houses, concert halls and ballet venues, private librarians and archivists and the staff of craftsmen.
8   For example, the staff of hospitals, sanatoriums and mental asylums.
9   For example the University Foundation, trade unions and chambers of commerce.
10 Solicitors' incomes are dealt with in Chapter 8, "Entrepreneurial income of the Professions, Independent Traders, Craftsmen and Partnerships".

SECTION 2. EMPLOYMENT OF WHITE-COLLAR WORKERS IN INDUSTRY AND COMMERCE

The employment figures for white-collar workers in industry and commerce are based mainly on the information available for four reference dates: 31 December 1920, 31 October 1926, 31 December 1930, and 27 February 1937. On these dates industrial, commercial, occupational or population censuses were organized by the government. Before presenting the employment figures for these sample dates, it is desirable to discuss briefly the scope and the principle points of difference between the various censuses (Paragraph 1). Because the censuses used differ in content they have as far as possible been adjusted in Paragraph 2 in order to arrive at homogenous figures. Finally, an explanation is given in Paragraph 3 of how the figures for the intervening years were arrived at.

Paragraph 1. The censuses of 1920, 1926, 1930 and 1937 as a source of employment data

During the inter-war period three kinds of censuses were conducted in Belgium by the government in order to obtain a detailed overview of the occupational and employment structure in the country. Since in estimating employment use was also made of the censuses of 1910 these are included in the following discussion.
1) *Occupational surveys* in the context of the *population censuses* of 31 December 1910, 31 December 1920 and 31 December 1930 (hereafter referred to as *population census/PC*). Each resident had to indicate his/her occupation, so that the population censuses embrace not only industrial or commercial occupations but every kind of work. In the population censuses the working population is subdivided into eight large categories which are in turn divided into various subcategories. The eight main categories are: agriculture and forestry, fishing, industry, commerce, the professions, government employees, domestic and personal servants and those providing personal care[11], and those without an occupation[12]. In the first four categories a distinction is also made between employers, white-collar workers, manual workers and helpers (i.e. unpaid family members giving assistance).
2) *Industrial and commercial censuses* on 31 December 1910, 31 December 1930 and 27 February 1937 (hereafter referred to as *IC, CC,* or *ICC*). Every employer in industry or commerce had to give the census agents a summary of the employment situation in his/her company. Besides the censuses of 1910, 1930 and 1937, a census was also conducted on 31 October 1926.

---

[11] The sub-heading personal care is made up largely of hairdressers and their staff.
[12] For example, housewives, school pupils, students, persons with private means, retired persons, prisoners, persons entirely dependent on public support.

However, this relates only to industrial companies employing at least ten manual workers. In the censuses a distinction was made between the number of establishments and the number of employers, white-collar workers, manual workers and helpers. The census of 1937 is an exception, giving no information on the number of employers. Another difference between the census of 1937 and the other censuses is that in 1937 a distinction is made between the economic census and the social census. The object of the economic census is comparable with that of the censuses of 1926 and 1930. The social census contains data which were not mentioned in the previous censuses, namely information on pay, hours worked, and unemployment.

3) *Occupational censuses* in the context of the industrial and commercial censuses on 31 December 1910 and 31 December 1930 (hereafter referred to as *OC*) Every employee in industry or commerce had to give his/her occupation. A distinction was made between employers, white-collar workers, manual workers and helpers. The occupational census also contained information on the number of unemployed in each job category, as well as data on cross-border employment (i.e. Belgian residents working abroad).

In all censuses a broad definition of a white-collar worker is used: besides administrative personnel, manual workers in positions of authority and management staff are regarded as white-collar workers.

There is little point in discussing at length the points of difference between the various kinds of censuses. The principle differences relating to the employment of white-collar workers in industry and commerce can be summarized as follows:

1) In the PC and OC the number of white-collar workers is higher than in the industrial and commercial censuses. The reason for this is that in the PC and the OC the employees themselves completed their own census forms and decided for themselves what job category they belonged to. In the ICC on the other hand the census forms were completed by the employer. Since the social status of a white-collar worker was still markedly higher than that of a manual worker in the first half of the twentieth century, a number of manual workers incorrectly described themselves as white-collar workers. The number of white-collar workers in the PC and OC is therefore an overestimate[13].

2) In the PC and OC the employees are classified according to the job they perform. In the ICC they are included under the sector in which they are

---

[13] The bottom line of Tables 16 and 17 shows that in 1910, according to the PC, the number of white-collar workers in industry and commerce totalled (in round figures) 114,000 (94,000 men and 20,000 women). According to the ICC the figure was 100,000 (85,000 men and 15,000 women). In 1930 the PC yielded a total of 246,000 white-collar workers in industry and commerce (182,000 men and 64,000 women), the ICC only 201,000 (148,000 men and 53,000 women).

employed. Thus, in the PC and OC, a carpenter employed in a shipyard is included in the timber industry (being a carpenter). In the ICC, however, he is classified in the metal industry (since he works in a shipyard). As regards white-collar workers this difference in approach has particularly affected commercial travellers. In the PC and OC almost all commercial travellers are included under the heading *commercial intermediaries*, forming part of commerce. In the ICC they are mostly included in the sector in which they earn their living. A commercial traveller selling on behalf of a shoe factory is therefore included in the *"hide and leather" industry*. This explains why there are more male white-collar workers in commerce and fewer in industry in the PC compared with the ICC (see Table 16).

3) In the PC no distinction is made between employees and unemployed persons who have previously been employed. As a result the figures of the PC are an overestimate as an employment indicator. In the ICC only those employed are included[14]. The figures of the OC, like those of the PC, include employees and unemployed in the same job categories, but in contrast to the PC the OCs also contain a number of separate tables in which only the unemployed are listed. It is therefore possible to calculate the number in employment on the basis of the data in the OC, namely by deducting the number of unemployed from the overall total.

Because the estimates of white-collar workers' pay are based on the pay given in the 1937 ESC, and because the various ICCs contain reliable sectoral employment data, the reconstruction of the series of employment figures is based on the ICC and not on the OC or the PC. In 1920, however, no ICC took place, and only PC data are available. In order to make these data comparable with the ICCs of 1930 and 1937, a number of adjustments must be made to the available figures. The same applies to the IC of 1926, since the latter was carried out only in industrial companies employing at least 10 manual workers. This requires an adjustment taking account of employment in companies with less than 10 manual workers. As regards commerce, no data at all are available for 1926, so that only three reference years can be used for the commercial sector. The employment figures in the ICCs of 1930 and 1937 can be included almost in their entirety without many adjustments. In the following paragraph employment in 1930 and 1937 will therefore be presented first, followed by the employment situation in 1920 and 1926.

---

[14] In 1937 a census of the unemployed was conducted, but appeared in a separate volume.

Paragraph 2. Employment, unemployment and total workforce of white-collar workers in industry and commerce in 1920, 1926, 1930 and 1937

For the four reference years employment, unemployment and total workforce (i.e. employed + unemployed) have first been calculated or estimated[15]. Subsequently, in order to avoid duplication with Chapter 1, an adjustment is made for the four reference years in order to isolate manual workers in positions of authority from white-collar workers in the strict sense. In the censuses manual workers in positions of authority are mainly regarded as white-collar workers, but in the reports and statistics of industrial accidents, on which Chapter 1 is based, they are counted as manual workers.

Before presenting the data attention must be drawn to the transport sector. In the censuses not only private transport is included under this heading, but also the public companies in the transport and communications sector (for example the Belgian State Railways/NMBS, the RTT and the Post Office). Since the pay of staff in the state-owned companies in the transport and communications sector is included in the pay of government employees in Belgian national income, the white-collar workers concerned must be deducted from the total figure for the transport sector. In some cases this separation was made possible by studying the subheadings of the census, in other cases the annual reports of the state companies concerned, which usually contained employment data, were used.

1. Employment, unemployment and total workforce in industry and commerce on 31 December 1930

In Table 14 the results of the ICC (employment) and OC (unemployment) have been added together, thus permitting the total workforce and the level of unemployment to be calculated for each industry.

As explained at the foot of the table, the employment figure for the mines was increased in order to give it the same content as in the other ICs. From a comparison of the various censuses it emerges that in 1930 a portion of the employees in the mines who in other census years were included among white-collar workers were included among manual workers. These may be manual workers in positions of authority.

---

[15] Figures for the total workforce are required so that in the next paragraph employment levels in the intervening years can be estimated on the basis of annual unemployment rates.

2. Employment, unemployment and total workforce in industry and commerce on 27 February 1937

Table 15 gives the results for the census year 1937. As noted above, the employment data derive from the economic section of the census. The unemployment figures come from the unemployment census.

3. Employment in industry and commerce on 31 December 1920

In 1920 no ICC was organized, though there was a PC. The data of the PC cannot be included as they stand, because they differ in content from the ICC, as explained above. This is clear from a comparison of the PC and the ICC in 1910 and 1930 (see Table 16 for male white-collar workers and Table 17 for female white-collar workers). However, by adjusting the data of the PC, taking account of the relative differences between the PC and ICC in 1910 and 1930, one arrives at employment figures for 1920 which are more or less comparable with the figures for the other reference years. This adjustment is also represented in Tables 16 and 17.

4. Employment in industry on 31 October 1926

Since the 1926 census included only those companies which employed more than ten manual workers, an estimate must be made of the number of employees in companies with fewer than ten manual workers. The 1937 census, for example, classifies employment according to size of company (measured by the number of manual workers employed). In 1937 it was therefore possible to calculate the ratio in each industrial sector of white-collar workers in companies with fewer than ten manual workers to white-collar workers in companies with more than ten manual workers. It was assumed that these sectoral ratios were the same in 1926 (see Table 18).

5. Deduction of manual workers in positions of authority

In order to avoid duplication, manual workers in positions of authority, who were already included in Chapter 1, had to be deducted from the white-collar workers in the censuses. Only the census of 1937 gives information on the number of manual workers in positions of authority. In all other censuses manual workers in positions of authority are included in the same category as white-collar workers in the strict sense, without any indication of the relative importance of the two groups. In the absence of data it was assumed that the proportion of manual workers in positions of authority, which can be calculated for each sector in 1937, was the same for the other census years (see Table 19).

Paragraph 3. Employment, unemployment and total labour force of white-collar workers in industry and commerce in 1920-1939

The employment of white-collar workers in industry and commerce was estimated as follows. The starting point is the number of white-collar workers employed in the census years. The number of white-collar workers employed in the census years was subsequently increased for each sector and for both sexes by the number of unemployed white-collar workers, so that the total workforce of white-collar workers in the census years was obtained. For the intervening years this total workforce was interpolated linearly by sector and sex. Subsequently annual unemployment levels were estimated for each sector. Finally employment data can be obtained by multiplying the labour force by one minus the level of unemployment.

The average level of unemployment of all white-collar workers in industry and commerce is estimated in Table 20. This is based on the level of unemployment on 31 December 1930 and 27 February 1937 (column 1). It was also possible to estimate the percentage of unemployment in April 1920, i.e. on the basis of a survey conducted among approximately one third of the total population of white-collar workers. The annual percentage unemployment of white-collar workers was estimated on the basis of trends in the level of unemployment of manual workers, which is known for all years (columns 2-6). Moreover, it was possible from 1936 onwards to make use of trends in the level of unemployment of white-collar workers insured against unemployment (columns 7-8)[16]. It should be observed that in the series of figures finally obtained (column 9) the level of unemployment in 1930 and 1937 differs from that at the time of the census (column 1). This is due to the fact that column 1 represents a single moment in time and column 9 a yearly average.

In Table 21 the total workforce of white-collar workers by sector and by sex is estimated at the point of the censuses (31 December 1920, 31 October 1926, 31 December 1930 and 27 February 1937). Subsequently the total workforce for each sector is estimated by sex by a linear interpolation of the workforce during the census years. Finally employment by sector and sex is estimated by deducting the unemployed from the total labour force. The unemployment figures were obtained on the basis of the unemployment rates by sector and sex in the census years (Table 21, column 2) and the annual level of unemployment for all white-collar workers in industry and commerce (Table 20, column 9). The results of the employment estimates are presented by sector and sex in Table 22.

---

[16] Before 1936 no separate data were published on unemployment among insured white-collar workers.

SECTION 3. PAY OF WHITE-COLLAR WORKERS IN INDUSTRY AND TRADE

The social section of the 1937 census contains a detailed overview of the monthly pay of white-collar workers (see Table 23, column 7). However, no account is taken in the figures of the pay of white-collar workers earning more than BF 50,000 per annum or of the earnings of commercial travellers. It is assumed that the former earned an average of BF 65,000 and commercial travellers BF 30,000. It was possible to determine approximately the number of white-collar workers earning more than BF 50,000 and the number of commercial travellers after a detailed comparison of the economic and social sections of the 1937 census. The economic section contains all white-collar workers, including those earning more than BF 50,000, while in the social section of the census only those white-collar workers are included who earned less than BF 50,000 (excluding commercial travellers). Annual pay calculated on the basis of the 1937 monthly salary was subsequently raised by 4% in order to take account of the pay rise in the course of that year. This percentage was arrived at through the hourly wage index for manual workers, which was published quarterly. The figure was also increased because some white-collar workers received a 13 month's pay or a share in profits. The latter percentage increases (column 10) were obtained through the 1920 survey of white-collar workers[17].

For the other years the pay of white-collar workers in 1937 was linked to the mathematical average of the index of hourly rates for skilled workers on the one hand and the index of average pay of railway personnel on the other (Table 24). The multiplication of the annual employment figures by the annual data on pay gives the total annual pay figure (Table 25).

SECTION 4. EMPLOYMENT AND PAY OF OTHER WHITE-COLLAR WORKERS

The estimate of the total pay of white-collar workers not included in the ICC is presented in Table 26. The employment figures are based mainly on the PCs of 1920 and 1930. As far as average annual pay is concerned it was assumed that for male white-collar workers this was 75% of the average wage of a male white-collar worker in industry. For female white-collar workers the proportion was assumed to be 85%. Both percentages were derived from the 1920 survey of white-collar workers.

---

17 *Enquête sur la situation des employés privés, 15 avril 1920.*

CHAPTER 3

PAY OF DOMESTIC STAFF, BORDER-WORKERS AND SEASONAL WORKERS EMPLOYED ABROAD

SECTION 1. DEFINITION OF THE HEADING

At first glance the two categories of domestic staff and Belgian residents abroad (i.e. border and seasonal workers) have little in common, but their pay is grouped together under the same heading in the post-war national accounts of the NIS as they were the sole group of workers who were subject only in part to the Belgian system of social security[1]. Although there was no generally compulsory system of social insurance in the inter-war period, the remuneration of these groups of workers have, in the interests of continuity, also been included under a separate heading for the inter-war period.

The pay estimated in this chapter has been broken down into three subheadings:
- the pay of domestic staff (Section 2)
- the pay of border-workers employed in France (Section 3)
- the pay of seasonal workers employed in France (Section 4)

Domestic staff refers to the personnel employed by private individuals. It comprises a wide range of professions, such as cooks, kitchen maids, charwomen, governesses, private chauffeurs and gardeners. Persons who carried out a similar profession for a company or a government agency (such as a cook in a restaurant or a gardener employed by the municipality) are not regarded as domestic staff.

The difference between border and seasonal work is largely based on the duration of the employment abroad. As the word itself indicates, border-workers generally live in the vicinity of the border[2]. In particular, this category consists of West Flanders industrial workers who commuted every day or every week from their place of residence in Belgium to their place of work in the textiles or metal factories in the Northern France industrial basin, mainly in the *Département du Nord*. The seasonal workers were primarily employed in agriculture. They worked for only some six months of the year abroad, although the employment was

---

[1] The pay of government employees, which (with the exception of temporary staff), falls totally outside the scope of the General Social Security Regulations, is also dealt with under a separate heading in the national accounts of the NIS; cf. Chapter 1.
[2] Some border-workers, however, lived further inland - for example in the region around Bruges - and were transported each day to France by coach.

particularly intensive (according to one survey conducted in the early 1920s they averaged 13 hours a day)[3]. Since the seasonal work was in general located in more southerly areas - especially the fertile cereals and sugar-beet areas of Artois and Picardy (in between the industrial basin of the Département du Nord and Paris) the seasonal workers generally remained in France for several months at a stretch. For this reason the Belgian seasonal workers were not recruited in border areas alone but also in more inland regions, such as the arrondissements of Aalst and Oudenaarde in East Flanders.

The income of Belgians permanently resident abroad need not be taken into account as these earnings formed part not of Belgian national income but of the national income in which the individuals concerned were established.

During the second half of the nineteenth century there was a substantial level of emigration from Belgium to France. At that time the North of France was undergoing spectacular economic development, especially in the textiles and metal industries, apart from which the low birth rate meant that it was grappling with a shortage of labour. The Belgian provinces of East and West Flanders were confronted at that time with the loss of the traditional home-industry in the textile sector and had a high birth rate. Numerous Belgians moved to France on account of the higher wages and superior employment prospects, both in industry and in agriculture[4]. At the end of the nineteenth century immigration tapered off and border and seasonal work for Belgians in France became more important. With the improvements in transport (the advent of the bicycle and the tram and the introduction of cheap rail season tickets) it became easier to live in Belgium and work in France - something that was particularly attractive on account of the higher wages in France and the lower cost of living in Belgium[5].

As discussed in Chapter 1, this chapter does no more than to provide an estimate of the income from border and seasonal employment in France[6]. In contrast to France, where a considerable number of Belgian residents were employed, only a small number of Belgian residents found employment in other neighbouring countries. According to the occupational census of 31 December

---

3   Cf. below.
4   Between 1951 and 1972 the number of Belgians who had settled in France rose from 128,000 to 348,000 (*La main-d'oeuvre frontalière dans le Nord de la France*, in : "Etudes et conjoncture. Economie francaise", 1949, p. 37).
5   For a historical survey of Belgian emigration to France and of border and seasonal work see *La main-d'oeuvre frontalière dans le Nord de la France*; LENTACKER F., *La frontière franco-belge. Etude géographique des effets d'une frontière sur la vie de relations,* Lille, 1974; MAUCO.G., *Les étrangers en France. Leur rôle dans l'activité économique*, Paris, 1932; SCHEPENS L., *Van vlaskutser tot franschman. Bijdrage tot de geschiedenis van de Westvlaamse plattelandsbevolking in de negentiende eeuw*, Bruges, 1973; THEYS J., *Een analyse van de Westvlaamse grensarbeid in Noord-Frankrijk,* Bruges, 1969.
6   On account of the lower cost of living in Belgium many French citizens had also moved to the Belgian border regions (*La main-d'oeuvre frontalière dans le nord de la France,* pp.47-48). Because these French workers were Belgian residents, their earnings form part of Belgian national income.

1930, 79,626 Belgian residents earned their living as border-workers in the North of France[7]. According to the same census, border employment in other countries came to just 6,683 units, of which 4,887 in the Netherlands, 1,427 in the Grand Duchy of Luxembourg, 312 in Germany and 57 in Great Britain. According to the estimates the number of Belgian seasonal workers in France fluctuated during the inter-war period between 11,000 and 34,000[8]. No figures could be traced for seasonal employment in other countries in the inter-war period. A rough estimate is, however, known for before the First World War, namely 400 in the Netherlands, 100 in the Grand Duchy of Luxembourg and 500 in Germany - negligible figures[9].

In the absence of data, no adjustment was made for the foreign border and seasonal workers employed in Belgium in estimating the earnings of workers and servants employed in the private sector in Belgium (Chapters 1 and 2). For the sake of simplicity it was assumed that the income they earned in Belgium (but which forms part of the national income of the country where they lived) was equal to the income of Belgian border and seasonal workers abroad, excluding France[10]. This means that the pay in Chapters 1 and 2 is slightly overestimated (as it incorrectly contains the pay of foreign residents employed in Belgium) and that the pay of border and seasonal workers is slightly underestimated (on account of the non-inclusion of border and seasonal work in the Netherlands, Luxembourg, Germany and Great Britain). Since comparatively few foreign border and seasonal workers were employed in Belgium, and in view of the fact that the border and seasonal work of Belgian residents abroad, with the exception of France, was limited, the non-inclusion of these categories has little impact on the size of Belgian national income. The ultimate distortion is in fact even smaller since the two phenomena exert a contrary effect on the size of national income and therefore to some extent cancel one another out.

The wages of the border and seasonal workers under consideration in this chapter comprise not just the repatriated incomes but also total pay, of which a portion generally was spent abroad[11]. Benefits in kind such as food and shelter, which were frequently assigned to seasonal workers, also need to be included.

Finally it should be noted that the employers' social security contributions paid by the French employers for their employees resident in Belgium should be added to the wagebill[12], since the employers' contributions in Chapter 4 only comprise the payments made by Belgian employers.

The final results of the calculations discussed below are presented in Table 27.

---

7   *OC 1930,* pp. 748-749.
8   Cf. below and Table 37.
9   RONSE E., *L'émigration saisonnière belge,* Ghent, 1913, pp. 70-71.
10 Cf. Chapter 1.
11 *Het Belgisch nationaal inkomen van 1948 to 1954,* p. 592.
12 *De nationale rekeningen van België 1953-1962,* p. 1144.

SECTION 2. PAY OF DOMESTIC STAFF

No macro-economic data are available on the pay of domestic staff. Their aggregate wages could consequently only be reconstructed by annually estimating the number of individuals concerned and multiplying that number by the estimated average pay. The number of persons has been estimated in Paragraph 1 on the basis of the censuses of 1920 and 1930. In these censuses domestic staff were divided by sex into eight categories. Wage series have been put together in Paragraph 2 by sex and by category. These are largely based on the Brussels wages for domestic staff. Because the pay in Brussels was on average higher than that elsewhere in the country, the Brussels figures have been adjusted downwards. For the categories for which no wage figures were available for domestic staff the level of pay has been taken for equivalent professions in enterprises (e.g. restaurant and café staff) or in the public sector (e.g. nightwatchmen in Brussels).

Paragraph 1. Number of individuals

Point one below compares the number of individuals in the censuses of 1920 and 1930. A rough estimate is then provided of the number of part-time working women who were not included in the censuses. Finally point three examines the numbers shown for the non-census years.

1. Domestic staff in the censuses of 1920 and 1930

The results of the censuses of 1920 and 1930 are compared in Table 28. The number of male domestic staff fell by around 6,000 or 18% from 33,000 to 27,000. By contrast the number of female personnel rose by around 19,000 or 16% (from 120,000 to 139,000). Particularly notable is the fact that some subcategories recorded a distinct fall while other groups clearly increased. For most professions the numerical evolution is plausible. This applied for example to the fall in the number of servants responsible for the care and management of animals. This reduction is logical in view of the increase in motorized transport in the 1920s[13]. The fall in kitchen staff ("Servants responsible for the preparation and handling of foodstuffs") may probably be ascribed to the introduction of labour-saving domestic appliances such as gas stoves. A possible explanation for the increase in the number of "personal servants" (e.g. nannies) and the increase in the number of housekeepers and cleaners is the increase in participation in the labour market of middle-class women, who found employment as non-manual workers or helped

---

[13] The increase in motorized transport in the 1920s may also be responsible for the increase in the number of male "personal servants", which category, among other things, included private chauffeurs.

their husband run a business. The extra earnings generated as a result enabled the family to take on extra staff to manage the household.

It is of course also possible that the shifts in the number of domestic staff are to some extent attributable to the fact that various individuals in the 1930 census were allocated to a different category from that in 1920. This is readily understandable since the domestic staff performed varying tasks and it was often difficult to decide which category they fitted into.

2. The problem of part-time charwomen

It is fairly sure that one group was not included in Table 28, namely that of charwomen in part-time employment. Where they combine these earnings on the side with another occupation they were included in the census under their main profession, since the censuses are broken down into principal occupations only. Working women who spent only a few hours a week outside the home in gainful employment were probably largely included in the category of individuals not living from the earnings of a particular occupation.

It is of course exceptionally difficult to approximate the number of part-time charwomen. The NIS estimated the total number of charwomen in 1947 at 193,000[14]. This figure differs radically from the 34,259 "Charwomen and housekeepers" recorded in the General Population, Industrial and Commercial Census of 31 December 1947[15]. This total figure consists of 26,594 charwomen and 7,914 housekeepers[16]. If it is assumed that the numbers in the census relate to full-time employment one arrives at a figure of around 166,500 cases of part-time employment as charwomen in 1947 (193,000 - 26,500). It does however need to

---

14   NIS, *Commissie van het Nationaal Inkomen*, pp. 22-24. The NIS estimates the number of persons in employment in a highly indirect way. To begin with it is assumed that there is a link between taxable income and the employment of domestic staff. For each income category in the financial statistics for the 1948 fiscal year (i.e. 1947 earnings) a coefficient was assigned in a comparatively arbitrary fashion to establish the link between taxable income and the employment of domestic staff. For example, traders, industrialists and the liberal professions falling into the income bracket of BF 25,000-50,000 were assigned a coefficient of 1/10. This category comprises 231,849 taxpayers, so that it was assumed that they employed a total of 23,185 domestic staff. To take another example, the coefficient of 2/3 was assigned to wage-owners and agricultural workers with a taxable income of between BF 100,000 and 150,000. Multiplication of the number of taxpayers in this category (29,493) by 2/3 results in 19,662 cases of employment. On the basis of a comparison between the total number of cases of employment established in this manner with the figures from the census, the NIS decided that in 1947 193,000 families employed a charwoman.
15   *General Population, Industrial and Commercial Census of 31 December 1947*, vol. VIII, p. 283.
16   NIS, *Commissie van het Nationaal Inkomen*, p. 21. It is not clear why the figures quoted by the NIS from the 1947 census without precise attribution (26,594 + 7,914 = 34,508) differ from the figure shown in the census (34,259).

be borne in mind that the number of instances of part-time employment exceeded the number of persons in part-time employment since some charwomen worked in various places.

What sort of figure should be put on the number of charwomen in the inter-war period? No concrete indications are available. It may however be assumed that the number was lower than after the Second World War, since a shift from full-time to part-time domestic staff is likely to have taken place after the war. Table 29 compares the number of domestic staff in the censuses of 1910, 1920, 1930 and 1947. The classification of the censuses of 1910, 1920 and 1930 is the same so that the figures for these years are fully comparable. In 1947 a different occupational classification was employed, for which reason the 1947 figures were adjusted to bring them into line with the results of the earlier censuses. It was assumed that the domestic staff included in the censuses were employed full-time. Between 1930 and 1947 the number of (full-time) domestic staff fell by around 51,000 units or 31%. It has been assumed that this marked decline was largely offset by an increase in the volume of part-time employment, in that it is highly plausible that the social revolution associated with the Second World War meant that it was more difficult to find people who were willing to work full-time (and generally to live in) as domestic staff, so that increasing resort was made to the services of people prepared to work for a number of half-days per week. It was estimated that there were some 166,500 cases of part-time employment as charwomen in 1947. It is assumed that this figure amounted to 120,000 in 1920 and 1930.

3. Interpolations and extrapolations for the non-census years

For both males and females, a linear interpolation has been made for the number of persons per occupational category between 1920 and 1930 on the basis of the censuses.

It is unclear how the numbers evolved in the 1930s as no figures are available for the end of the inter-war period. As shown in Table 29, the total number of male staff consistently fell according to the 1910, 1920, 1930 and 1947 censuses, for which reason it may be assumed that the number also continued to fall between 1930 and 1939. The estimates were based on the assumption that for each male occupational category the annual decline (or in some cases rise) in the numbers between 1920 and 1930 also applied between 1930 and 1939.

In the case of women in full-time employment, the problem arises that the total number rose between 1920 and 1930 but then fell appreciably between 1930 and 1947. This is not, therefore, a case of a long-term downward trend, for the number of female domestic staff rose between 1920 and 1930. Was the rising trend in that period continued in the 1930s and was the sharp decline after 1947 simply a post-war phenomenon? Or, on the contrary, did the downward trend already set in in the course of the 1930s? No indications have been found to provide an answer to these questions. It may be argued that during the depression years of the 1930s some of the factory workers who had lost their jobs sought employment as maids, cooks, chambermaids and so on, thus swelling the ranks of domestic staff (i.e. an increase in supply). On the other hand it may be assumed that as a result of the depression certain families were obliged for financial reasons to dismiss some or all of their domestic staff (i.e. a fall in demand). It is unclear whether the demand or the supply factor dominated, for which reason it has been assumed that the numbers in the 1930s per occupational category remained constant.

Finally there remain the part-time charwomen. In the absence of figures it has been assumed that these number remain constant throughout the inter-war period (120,000 cases of employment, see 2.). In line with the NIS it has been assumed that each case of employment amounted on average to three half working days[17].

Paragraph 2. Pay

As far as could be established the wages for domestic staff were published only for Brussels. The pay-levels were found by Scholliers in the payroll records of the Brussels Labour Exchange[18]. Also in relation to Brussels Van Den Eeckhout has found published pay rates for two categories of municipal personnel in positions comparable to domestic staff, namely charwomen and nightwatchmen[19]. These wages series are presented and compared in point 1 below. A single wage index has also been compiled on the basis of these figures for all categories of domestic staff.

A unit pay-rate for a base year is established in point 2 for each category of domestic staff by sex. The base year depends on the availability of data. As far as possible the Brussels figures of Scholliers and Van Den Eeckhout were used. Because Brussels wages were generally higher than the pay for equivalent occupations elsewhere in Belgium, the former figures were adjusted downwards. With respect to the categories for which no Brussels wage figures were available, the pay rates for more or less equivalent occupations in industry and commerce were sought in the ESC 1937.

Finally in point three the unit pay-rates for the base year for each category of domestic staff (these pay rates differ from one occupational category to another = point 2) have been multiplied by the wage-index for domestic staff (which is the

---

[17] Idem, p. 27.
[18] SCHOLLIERS P., *Loonlijsten van de Brusselse Arbeidsbeurs 1922-1939*, in: "Centrum voor Hedendaagse Sociale Geschiedenis. Lonen en prijzen in België in de negentiende en twintigste eeuw", Loonreeks 3, Brussels, VUB, 1979.
[19] VAN DEN EECKHOUT P., *Lonen van Brusselse arbeiders in openbare instellingen (1809-1934): bouwvakarbeiders, ziekenhuis en stadspersoneel*, in: "Centrum voor Hedendaagse Sociale Geschiedenis. Lonen en prijzen in België in de negentiende en twintigste eeuw", Loonreeks 1, Brussels, VUB, 1979.

same for all occupational categories = point 1). In this way one arrives at a complete wage series for the 1920s and 1930s for each occupational category. These wage series were then multiplied by the numbers as estimated in the previous paragraph.

1. Brussels wages of domestic staff and construction of an overall loan index for all domestic staff

a) The payroll records of the Brussels Labour Exchange[20]

As noted earlier the Brussels wage figures are largely based on the figures derived from the Brussels Labour Exchange. The latter was an official employment exchange established in 1919 at the initiative of the Ministry of Labour. From 1922 onwards a limited number of wage-lists were drawn up and sent each month to employers' associations and trade unions as well as to entrepreneurs who requested them. These lists contained the hourly or monthly wage for some 130 different occupational categories covering virtually every sector of the Brussels economy. The wage-lists of the Brussels Labour Exchange also served as the basis for the Belgian wages published by the International Labour Organization (ILO) from 1923 onwards in its comparative wage surveys for the entire world in the Revue International du Travail.

How were the Brussels Labour Exchange wage figures arrived at? Where a *Collective Labour Agreement* (Collectieve Arbeidsovereenkomst, CAO) applied in a particular industry, the agreed wage was included in the lists[21]. In those industries in which the pay was not laid down in a CAO - which undoubtedly applied in the case of domestic staff - the wages published by the Labour Exchange were determined by supply and demand, although allowance was also made for the evolution of the cost of living by linking wages to the retail price index.

Are the wages published by the Labour Exchange a faithful reflection of the situation in the Brussels Labour Market? Scholliers considers they are, on the basis of the high correlation coefficient (0.98) between the hourly wage of a Brussels bricklayer in the National Bank's wage survey and the bricklayer's wage in the Labour Exchange's wage-series[22].

---

[20] The general description of the Brussels Labour Exchange payroll records is based on SCHOLLIERS P., *o.c.*, pp. 1-6.
[21] The Brussels Labour Exchange refused offers of employment at a wage below that agreed in the CAO (Idem, p. 5).
[22] Idem, pp. 5-6. The National Bank's wage survey is published in SCHOLLIERS P., *Lonen in de Belgische nijverheid, 1913-1940: de enquête Davin,* in: "Centrum voor Hedendaagse Sociale Geschiedenis. Lonen en prijzen in België in de negentiende en twintigste eeuw". Loonreeks 2, Brussels, VUB, 1979.

b) Wages of domestic staff in the wage-lists of the Brussels Labour Exchange and of comparable personnel in Brussels

The lists of the Brussels Labour Exchange includes eight wage-series for occupations that may be counted as domestic staff. These are: cooks/maid, cook, maid, chambermaid, nanny, servant, charwoman and gardener (see Table 30 columns 1-14 and 21-22). This series was supplemented by various wages for Brussels municipal personnel: charwomen in the urban slaughterhouse and in the Stock Exchange and nightwatchmen (columns 15-20).

In order to make the wage-series comparable with one another, they were converted into indices, with 1928 as the base-year. 1928 was chosen as the base-year as it was the last year for which figures were available for all series. These indices clearly reveal that some series evolved very differently, in some instances for reasonably similar occupations. For example, the wages for a maid fell in the index between 1931 and 1934 from 150 to 117 (column 6), while the wages for a servant remained constant at 138 (column 12). The wages for a chambermaid rose between 1928 and 1931 from index 100 to 160 (column 8), while those for a nanny only rose from 100 to 122 during the same period (column 10) - even though these relate to wages in the same geographical area and in occupational categories in which wages might have been expected to evolve at the same pace. The wages for Brussels municipal personnel could also evolve very differently: between 1928 and 1930 the wages for a charwoman at the Stock Exchange rose from index 100 to 186 (column 18), while the pay of a charwoman working in the slaughterhouse rose from index 100 to just 110 (column 16).

Since the disparate evolution of the various Brussels wages may well have been distorted by a number of accidental factors there is little justification for adopting them as they stand for each occupational category and multiplying them by the numbers estimated in the previous paragraph. There is also the further, practical problem that the occupational categories in the censuses are not fully comparable with the occupational categories for which wage figures are available. Another practical difficulty consists of the fact that wage series covering the entire 1920-1930 period are not available. In the case of certain occupational categories in the censuses, such as the lady-companion and the servants responsible for tending and leading animals, no wage figures at all were available. On the assumption that the wages in Table 30 provide an accurate reflection in their totality of the course of the pay of domestic staff, it was therefore decided to draw up an overall index which could then be applied to all domestic staff.

c) Overall wage index for all domestic staff

In drawing up the overall wage index the same weight was assigned to each series in Table 30. Because the various wage series do not relate to the same time-span, the differential index technique was used. The overall index, with 1920 as the base year, is shown in Table 30 column 23. The same index, with 1939 as the base year, appears in column 24.

If the Brussels wage index for domestic staff is compared with the Belgian index for the hourly wages of unskilled labourers in industry (Table 30 column 35), it is evident that the wages of domestic staff rose more strongly between 1922 and 1925 than the wages of the latter group. It may be that this should be regarded as a compensatory effect for the more moderate wage increases in the initial years after the First World War. Between 1925 and 1932 the two series evolved in parallel, but between 1930 and 1937 the pattern differs markedly. The hourly wages of unskilled industrial workers fell by 24% between 1930 and 1935, subsequently rising between 1935 and 1937 by 22%. The wages of domestic staff only begin to fall in 1931 and the reduction is much less pronounced (9% between 1931 and 1935). No rise occurred between 1935 and 1937; wages remain stable. From 1937 onwards the two categories evolve in concert, with a slight increase.

The main point of difference between the two series is therefore the much greater stability of the nominal wages of domestic staff between 1930 and 1937. This was a period of nominal wage inertia, both in the years of economic decline (1930-1935) and in the years of economic recovery (1935-1937). Given the marked fall in prices in 1930-1935 and the rise in 1935-1937 this means that the real wages of domestic staff evolve anti-cyclically.

Why did the nominal wages of domestic staff fall so little in the depression? The answer to this question may well be complex and calls for a thorough analysis of the labour market, going beyond the scope of this study. As a provisional hypothesis it may be suggested that many people operate in a kind of "money illusion", in the sense that they calculate in nominal rather than real terms. Together with a psychological aversion towards nominal wage-cuts and the particularly well developed personal links between employers and their domestic staff, this may provide a possible explanation for the curious stability of the nominal wages of domestic staff during the depression years.

Is the index that has been constructed on the basis of Brussels data representative for the pay levels over time of domestic staff throughout Belgium? In the absence of wage figures for domestic staff in other regions it is difficult to answer this question. Similarly a comparison of the course of industrial hourly wages in Brussels with macro-economic industrial hourly wages in the country as a whole provides little if any additional insight. In 1932 the Research Unit of the National Bank observed that Brussels wages responded less rapidly to economic fluctuations than wages elsewhere in the country[23]. According to the National Bank, however, this was attributable to the fact that the Brussels industrial structure was dominated by small, craft-type firms, the wages of which were inherently less cyclically sensitive than the wages paid in the large, export-oriented industrial basins of (for example) Liège or Henegouwen.

---

[23] *Le mouvement des salaires en Belgique de 1922 and 1932*, in: "Banque Nationale de Belgique. Bulletin d'Information et de Documentation", vol. 2, 1932, pp. 197-202. Zie ook SCHOLLIERS P., *Loonindexering en sociale vrede. Koopkracht en klassenstrijd in België tijdens het Interbellum*, Brussels, 1985, p. 250.

2. Unit pay of the various categories of domestic staff

On the basis of Brussels figures, an index was constructed in the previous point which, in the absence of an alternative, was taken as representative of the *evolution* of the wages of domestic staff throughout the country. To which absolute wage figures should this index next be coupled? The obvious step is, as far as possible, to draw on the Brussels data presented in Table 30. Before this can be done, however, it needs to be established whether the *level* of Brussels pay was representative for Belgium as a whole. This was done with the aid of the ESC 1937 which, among other things, investigated regional pay variations. In view of the differences in the industrial structure referred to above there is little point in taking pay in industry as the reference point, for which reason pay in the commercial sector was instead taken as the point of departure[24]. The average hourly wage of workers in the commercial sector in Belgium as a whole amounted to BF 3.89 and that of Brussels workers to BF 4.26, or 9.5% more. Precisely the same deviation was established for servants in the commercial sector: an average monthly wage of BF 1,208 for the country as a whole and BF 1,323 for Brussels, or 9.5% higher[25]. On the basis of these figures the pay of Brussels domestic staff has been reduced by 10% to make them representative for Belgium as a whole.

For each occupational category of domestic staff, an indication is provided below of the annual pay that has been used as the base to which the previously constructed overall wage index will be linked. The classification into occupational categories is based on the censuses of 1920 and 1930 (see Table 28). Unless specified otherwise, annual wages have been arrived at by multiplying monthly pay by 12.

a) Stewards, administrators, managers, receivers:

- Men: average wage of male white-collar workers in industry and commerce in Belgium in 1937 = BF 19,165 (see Chapter 2 Table 23 column 8)
- Women: average wage of female servants in industry and commerce in Belgium in = BF 10,052 (see Chapter 2 Table 23 column 8)

b) Special watchmen of goods, yachts, fisheries, woods, etc.:

- Men: 90% of the wage of a nightwatchman in Brussels (Table 30 column 19) in 1928 = BF 10,076

---

[24] The following sectors formed part of the commercial sector in the 1937 census: purchase, sale and renting of industrial and agricultural products, banks, insurance, commercial intermediaries, hotels and cafés, recreation (e.g. cinemas) and personal care (especially hairdressers).
[25] Average Brussels hourly wages and monthly wages: ESC 1937, vol. VI, p. 50. Average Belgian hourly and monthly wages: own calculations, namely a weighted average of the average male and female rates of pay (average male and female pay: ESC 1937, vol. VI, pp. 38 and 40-41; weighting on basis of number of men and women: ESC 1937, vol. VI, p. 37 and 39).

- Women: 70% of males pay = BF 7,053 in 1928

c) Nightwatchmen not with a public authority:

- Men: see b
- Women: see b

d) Servants responsible for the preparation and handling of foodstuffs:

- Men: hourly wage of male workers in the hotel industry in Belgium in (BF 3.64, see ESC , vol. IV, p. 38) x 8 hours x 300 working days = BF 8,736 in
- Women: 90% of the arithmetic mean of the wages of a female cook (Table 30 column 3) and a female cook/maid (column 1) in Brussels = BF 5,805 in 1939

e) Personal servants:

- Men: see d
- Women: 90% of the arithmetic mean of the wages of a chambermaid (Table 30 column 7), a nanny (column 9) and servant (column 11) in Brussels = BF 4,050 in 1939

f) Servants responsible for tending and leading animals:

- Men: see d
- Women: 90% of the wages of a servant in Brussels (Table 30 column 11) = BF 4,050 in 1939

g) Housekeepers, cleaners, charwomen:

- Men: see d
- Women: 90% of the arithmetic mean of the wages of charwomen in Brussels (Table 30 column 13, column 15 and column 17) = BF 5,507 in 1934

h)   Ladies' companions, readers, private stenographer or private secretary:

- Men:see a
- Women: see a

i. Part-time charwomen (not recorded in the censuses):

It has been assumed that for each case of employment the individual concerned worked four hours a day for three days a week and that the hourly wage in 1939 was BF 2.50[26]. This gives an annual level of pay in 1939 for each case of employment of 2.50 x 3 x 4 x 52 = BF 1,560.

3. Wagebill of domestic staff

The wagebill was arrived at as follows:
a) For each occupational category broken down by sex the basic levels of pay, as discussed in the previous point, have been linked to the overall wage index for domestic staff (Table 30 columns 23-24). In this way one arrives at wage series for 1920-1939 by occupational category and by sex.
b) The wage series calculated in a) are multiplied by the numbers estimated in Paragraph 1 for each occupational category. This results in the annual wagebill per occupational category and by sex.
c) Aggregation of the various wagebills in b) provides the total wage and salaries of domestic staff.

The final result of these calculations is shown in Table 31.

SECTION 3. PAY OF BORDER-WORKERS

As discussed in the introductory section, the wagebill has been calculated only for the border-workers employed in France. This has been done because border employment was on a limited scale in other countries and it has been assumed that the remuneration of such work was offset by the wages earned by foreign border-workers in Belgium. The wagebill of Belgian border-workers in France was arrived at by annually estimating their numbers (Paragraph 1) and subsequently multiplying these by a unit level of pay (Paragraph 2).

Paragraph 1. Number of Belgian border-workers in France

There are no annual figures on the number of Belgian border-workers in France. Although data exist for certain years, these are drawn from various sources and often differ considerably. They relate to the total number of Belgian border-

---

[26] In its post-war estimates, the NIS assumes that each case of employment represented on average three half working days (*Het Belgisch nationaal inkomen van 1948 to 1954*, p. 592; *De nationale rekeningen van België 1953-1962*, p. 1144).

workers in France, the number of Belgian border-workers in the Département du Nord, where the majority of Belgian border-workers were employed, or to the number of border-workers in France coming from the province of West Flanders. The various figures that have been found have been brought together in Table 32. This overview clearly reveals the respective differences and inconsistencies in the available statistical material. According to the French census of 7 March 1926, for example, the number of Belgian border-workers in France was 42,000, while the Belgian occupational census of 31 December 1930 records 79,626 such persons, implying a doubling in the numbers of such workers in the second half of the 1920s. By contrast an article in the French "Etudes et conjoncture" claims that the number of Belgian border-workers peaked in 1926-1928 at 100,000 and that in 1930 their numbers were down to just 70,000. Another clear example of disparate figures relates to the number of West Flanders border-workers in 1935: according to the source the estimates vary from 31,227 to 51,500.

The lack of a homogeneous series and the inconsistencies in the available statistical material mean that the ultimate estimates of the number of border-workers are inevitably subject to a large margin of uncertainty. The estimates are in the first place based on the French censuses (1921, 1926, 1931, 1936) and the Belgian occupational census (1930), as these sources are probably the most reliable. Interpolations or extrapolations have been made for the missing years on the basis of information in Table 32, the level of industrial production, the exchange rate, legislation in relation to border employment and the evolution of the number of border-worker cards issued. Before providing the background to the specific estimates, the broad outline to emerge from a literature is discussed, as well as the system of border-worker cards[27].

The number of border-workers rose appreciably in the 1920s. In combination with the shortage of manpower in Northern France resulting from the war and the low French birth rate, the economic boom years swelled the demand for foreign workers. On the Belgian side it was possible to respond to this demand on account of the improved means of transportation and the fact that the border region with France - especially the province of West Flanders - was characterized by low wages and a shortage of local employment opportunities. The increase in the number of border-workers began after the brief economic slump of 1921. The stabilization of the Belgian Franc on 25 October 1926 made it particularly attractive for Belgians to work in France as border-workers since the stabilization - amounting in practice to a substantial devaluation of the Belgian Franc - meant a rise of some 40% in the earnings of border-workers paid in French Francs (see Table 33 column 3).

In due course the French trade unions protested against the invasion of

---

[27] The discussion of border work is based on: *La main-d'oeuvre frontalière dans le Nord de la France*, especially pp. 37-39; LENTACKER F., *o.c.*, especially pp. 275-281; THEYS J., *o.c.*, especially pp. 37-43.

Belgian workers in the Northern France labour market as they considered that the large numbers of Belgians undermined the position of French workers (on account of the downward pressure on wages and the greater docility of the Belgians). Similarly Belgian employers had misgivings about the exodus of their countrymen, especially in the second half of the 1920s, when the boom in Belgium led to a shortage of labour in certain sectors of the economy. The Belgian and French governments consequently concluded an agreement on 4 July 1928, under which a system of border-worker cards was introduced as from the beginning of 1929. Border-worker cards were issued by the mayor of the municipality in which the border-worker in question was domiciled, after which it had to be stamped as valid for a period of two years by the French authorities (*l'Office régionale de la main-d'oeuvre étrangère*). In practice, the introduction of the border-worker card system amounted to a potential protection of the French labour market as the number of border-workers could be officially limited by refusing visas. As will be seen below, the French authorities made grateful use of this facility during the depression of the 1930s.

The depression saw a marked fall in the number of border-workers. Under the Act of 10 August 1932 restrictive measures were introduced in order to protect the French labour market. On 9 May 1935 a Franco-Belgian agreement was concluded which, among other things, provided for the delimitation of the border zone in Belgium. The geographical definition of the border-worker phenomenon naturally served to eliminate those border-workers living outside that zone. Sometime later the French authorities decided to subject the number of foreign workers to a quota under the decree of 3 September 1935. All these protectionist measures and, of course, the fact that the depression reduced the demand for labour by Northern French industry exerted a negative impact on the number of border-workers, as reflected in the number of new border-worker cards declared valid by the Office régionale de la main-d'oeuvre étrangère in Lille (see Table 33 column 2)[28].

The improvement in the international economy and the devaluation of the French Franc on 1 October 1936 saw an increase in French industrial production. Employment opportunities accordingly rose, as reflected in the brisk renewal of border-workers' passes at the end of [29]. In view of the success of devaluation of the French Franc, however, it is questionable to what extent the Belgians remained interested in working in France.

Table 35 contains the estimates for the number of Belgian border-workers. Column 1 shows the results of the French and Belgian counts. The figure for 1930

---

[28] The number of border-workers actually working in France cannot be determined by aggregating the number of border-worker cards declared valid by the French authorities as possession of such a card did not guarantee employment. It is consequently unclear whether the statutory provisions were sometimes evaded by the French employers and Belgian employees in the form of black labour.

[29] THEYS J., *o.c.*, p. 43. The author does not indicate how many new border passes were declared valid by the French authorities.

(79,626), which is based on the Belgian occupational census of 31 December 1930, may be a slight overestimate as it includes both the employed and unemployed border-workers, and has been reduced to 75,000. In 1921 the number of border-workers (16,600 ; French census) is likely to have been down on that in 1920 on account of the economic slowdown. For this reason 20,000 border-workers are assumed to have been in employment in 1920. The figures between 1921 and 1926 (42,000, French census) were filled in by linear interpolation. The number of border-workers continued to rise after 1926, partly on account of the devaluation of the Belgian Franc on 25 October 1926, which made it particulary attractive for Belgian residents to work in France. It has been assumed that the number of border-workers reached a peak in 1928, the final year without border-worker passes; a figure of 80,000 - as recorded in the Belgian occupational census of 1930 - would appear acceptable. Although border-worker passes were compulsory in 1929, it may, given the economic upswing, be assumed that this measure had little impact on the actual numbers. For this reason an employment figure of 80,000 border-workers has been assumed for 1929, with linear interpolation between 1926 and 1928. With reference to 1931 and 1936 the figures of the French census were taken over (55,787 and 45,284 respectively). The intervening years were filled in on the basis of the evolution of the number of border-worker passes issued, industrial output, the French protectionist measures of 1932 and 1935 and information in Table 32. An increase in the number of border-workers to 50,000 has been assumed in on account of the improved conditions in the labour market. On account of the declining output and the unfavourable exchange rate for border-workers, the numbers in 1938 and 1939 were cut by 5,000.

Paragraph 2. Unit remuneration and wagebill

In so far as could be established, no wage series have been drawn up for Belgian border-workers in France. For this reason, the wage figures in the French "Annuaire Statistique", published by the Statistique Générale, the forerunner of the present Institut National de la Statistique et des Etudes Economiques (INSEE), have been used. These annual reports contain the daily wages for 36 male and six female occupations in Paris on the one hand and in the remainder of French towns on the other[30]. The average wages in each department were also specified, although these were not broken down by occupational category. Every five years between 1896 and 1924 and annually from 1924 onwards, all these wages were brought together by the Statistique Générale, which obtained its information from

---

[30] The number of male occupational categories was expanded in 1932 to 43.

the *Conseils de prud'hommes* or from the mayors of the most important towns in each department where no *Conseil de prud'hommes* was established[31].

On the basis of the daily wages of various categories of workers, an average daily wage for the border-workers has been compiled below. The weighting has been based on the sectoral breakdown and sex distribution of the border-workers as shown in the Belgian occupational census of 1930[32]. According to this occupational census, 23.3% of the border-workers were female, the great majority of whom were employed in the textile industry (86.4%). Of the male border-workers 33.6% worked in textiles, 28.9% in the metal industry, 11.0% in construction, 5% in the timber and furniture industry and 21.4% in other industries or in trade. The wage series put together for the border-workers is a weighted average of the daily wages in the rest of France of a weaver (35%), a turner (25%), a bricklayer (10%), a carpenter (5%) and of female workers in the clothing industry (25%)[33]. The results are shown in Table 34 column 1[34].

The daily wages constructed along these lines have been converted in column 2 to annual wages. Statutory working hours in France after the First World War were eight hours per day and 48 hours per week, implying a six-day working week[35]. It has been assumed that people worked 49 weeks per year[36]. At the end of 1936 the 40-hour week was brought in (this was a statutory cut in working

---

[31] COMBE P., *Niveau de vie et progrés technique en France (1860-1939). Contribution à l'étude de l'économie française contemporaine. Postface (1939-1949)*, Paris, 1956, p. 99. According to Combe these wage-series are reliable. The wages in the *Annuaire Statistique* in fact formed the basis for the various French wage-series worked out elsewhere (see for example PHELPS BROWN E.H., BROWNE M.H., *A Century of Pay. The Course of Pay and Production in France, Germany, Sweden, the United Kingdom, and the United States of America, 1860-1960*, London; Melbourne; Toronto; New York, 1968, pp. 364-367; CHADEAU E., *L'économie nationale aux XIXe et XXe siècles*, in : "Annuaire statistique de l'économie francaise aux XIXe et XXe siècles", vol. 1, Paris, 1989, pp. 231 and 236; MITCHELL B.R., *European Historical Statistics 1750-1970*, London, 1978, pp. 72-73.

[32] *OC 1930*, pp. 766-767. Although the sectoral breakdown of the border workers relates to all Belgian border-workers, i.e., also those employed in other neighbouring countries, the numbers working in France were so large (90.3%) that this distribution can be applied to the border-workers in France without undue problem. The fact that the figures from the 1930 occupational census related only to trade and industry is also little source of distortion since border employment in agriculture and forestry was - in contrast to seasonal employment - on a negligible scale (*La main-d'oeuvre belge en France*, p. 43). In 1946 agriculture and forestry accounted for just 2.2% of cross-border employment in France (*Algemeene telling van 30 april 1946 van de grensarbeiders die in Frankrijk gaan werken*, in: "Statistisch Bulletin", vol. 32, 1946, p. 726).

[33] The *Annuaire Statistique* does not provide any female textile wages. The six female wage series all relate to the clothing industry. The average of these wages has been taken.

[34] The wages in the *Annuaire Statistique* relate to 1921 and the period 1924-1939. Figures for the missing years were arrived at by interpolation and extrapolation of the series compiled above on the basis of miner' wages in COMBE P., *o.c.*, p. 101 and 617.

[35] PHELPS BROWN E.F., BROWNE M.H., *o.c.*, p. 207.

[36] Idem, p. 356.

hours without loss of pay)[37]. A five-day working week has consequently been assumed from onwards. After 1936 most workers in France enjoyed several days paid leave. This does not however have any impact on the annual wages, since the workers continued to draw their normal pay while on holiday.

In columns 3 and 4 the employers' statutory social security contributions have been added to the annual wages: from 1922 onwards for industrial accidents only and from 1930 onwards for children's allowances and pensions[38].

In columns 5 and 6 the wages in French Francs have been converted into wages in Belgian Francs. In 1935 and 1936 just 90% of the official exchange rate has been applied, on the grounds that after the devaluation of the Belgian Franc by 28% on 31 March 1935, the consortium of textile manufacturers of Roubaix-Tourcoing creamed off the larger part of the exchange rate benefit for their Belgian employees by cutting their pay by 20% in relation to their French colleagues[39]. After the devaluation of the French Franc on 1 October 1936 a stop was put to these practices. In relation to 1935-1936 the exchange rate has been reduced by just 10% as it is unclear whether the wage reductions also applied outside the textile industry and because the practices applied for only a part of the year (from April 1935 up to the end of September 1936).

Finally, the total wages and salaries of the border-workers has been arrived at in Table 35 by multiplying the numbers gainfully employed (column 3) by the unit pay (column 4).

SECTION 4. PAY OF SEASONAL WORKERS EMPLOYED ABROAD

Since seasonal employment of Belgian residents in countries other than France was on a negligible scale, this section provides estimates for the pay of seasonal workers in France only. The majority of the Belgian seasonal workers were employed in agriculture, especially cereals and sugar-beet cultivation. In addition some were employed (full-time or on the side) in various seasonal industrial activities, e.g. in the sugarmills and chicory drying plants (known as *asten*) or were employed as brickmakers and navies.

The total wagebill of seasonal workers was estimated by multiplying the number of individuals concerned (Paragraph 1) by the annual unit pay. The annual unit pay was arrived at by multiplying the average annual working hours (Paragraph 2) by the average hourly pay (Paragraph 3). The average number of hours worked is highly important because seasonal workers were by definition employed for only part of the year. In determining the unit-pay account was of course taken of possible benefits in kind, such as food and lodging.

---

[37] COMBE P., *o.c.*, p.98.
[38] Idem, pp. 120-121. No account has been taken of the employers' contributions for paid leave (approximately 4% from 1936 onwards) since the paid leave-days have been treated as working days in calculating the annual wages.
[39] LENTACKER F., *o.c.*, pp. 278-279; THEYS J., *o.c.*, p. 111.

Paragraph 1. Number of Belgian seasonal workers in France

No precise figures were ever drawn up for the number of Belgian seasonal workers in France. Information is, however, available on the number of officially recorded border crossings. Mauco shows the number of such crossings by Belgian seasonal workers employed in the agricultural sector in France for the period 1921-1926[40]. Lentacker published figures for the entire inter-war period on the number of Belgian seasonal workers departing for France[41]. Mauco's figures are lower than Lentacker's, averaging around 75%. This is logical because Mauco recorded only the seasonal workers in agriculture while Lentacker recorded all seasonal workers, i.e. also those employed in industry. The two series clearly run in parallel, leading one to suspect that they are drawn from the same source, namely the figures derived from the French immigration posts established at the Belgian border at Feignies and Tourcoing after the First World War.

Does the series for the number of officially recorded entries provide a reliable account of the number of seasonal workers? Two problems arise. In the first place numerous seasonal workers did not remain in France for an uninterrupted period. They would for example return home after the cereal harvest in July/August and go back to France in September/October for the sugar-beet harvest[42]. According to a limited survey conducted by Neels in the early 1920s, among 11 West Flanders seasonal workers from 10 different municipalities in the arrondissement of Bruges, 9 of the 11 made their way to France twice a year[43]. The remaining 2 remained in France permanently from mid-May to November. Since seasonal workers generally cross the border more than once per year, the number of border crossings is, a priori, higher than the number of seasonal workers.

A second source of distortion arises from the fact that numerous seasonal workers crossed the border without reporting to the immigration bureaus. The number of registered border crossings is consequently lower than the number of seasonal workers. If the two distortions offset one another, the number of registered border crossings provides a good approximation of the number of seasonal workers. It may be assumed that this was indeed the case, since the French agricultural census of 1927 concluded that some 45,000 Belgian agricultural workers were employed in French agriculture, of whom 18,822 were residing permanently in France[44]. This implies that some 26,000 Belgian seasonal

---

[40] MAUCO G., *o.c.*, p. 366.
[41] LENTACKER F., *o.c.*, p. 394.
[42] SCHEPENS L., *o.c.*, p. 215.
[43] NEELS G., *De tijdelijke uitwijking naar Frankrijk beschouwd uit het arrondissement Brugge*, in: "De Gids op Maatschappelijk Gebied", vol. 19, 1924, p. 588.
[44] *La main-d'oeuvre belge en France*, p. 43. The pay of the Belgians permanently resident in France must be eliminated: since these workers were French residents, their wages and salaries form part of French, not Belgian, national income.

workers were employed in French agriculture. According to Lentacker the number of border crossings was 31,000 but, as noted above, this figure also includes seasonal workers who earned their living outside agriculture[45]. A figure of just 5,000 seasonal workers not employed in agriculture appears realistic since the literature indicates that the majority of seasonal workers were agricultural labourers.

The suggestion that the number of officially recorded border crossings roughly corresponds with the number of seasonal workers is confirmed by Ronse[46]. This contemporary observer claimed that only half the seasonal workers reported to one of the French immigration bureaus. In view of the fact that most seasonal workers went to France twice a year (see the Bruges survey), the two distortions more or less cancelled one another out. For this reason Lentacker's series has been retained as an indication of the annual number of seasonal workers (see Table 37 column 1).

Three phases may be distinguished in the evolution of the number of seasonal workers. Between 1920 and 1924 the number of Belgian seasonal workers in France averaged around 22,000 a year, with an outlier of 30,000 in 1921 - a figure probably attributable to the high level of unemployment in industry, thus releasing a considerable volume of labour for agriculture. The second period consists of 1925-1931, with an average of 31,600 seasonal workers. This increase may be attributed to the favourable economic conditions, when the traditional shortage of labourers in the comparatively sparsely populated France was accentuated, and even greater numbers of Belgian labourers were recruited than before[47]. Furthermore, as noted in the previous section, a much more pronounced increase in the number of industrial border-workers was also observed in this period. During the final phase (1932-1939) the numbers slipped to an average of 18,500. This was primarily related to the depression, which affected agriculture particularly severely, thus diminishing the demand for labour. For the Belgians there was another adverse factor, namely the protectionist measures introduced in 1932 to discourage the number of foreign seasonal workers[48].

---

[45] LENTACKER F., *o.c.*, p. 394.
[46] RONSE E., *Les formes nouvelles de l'émigration belge*, in : "Revue Catholique Sociale et Juridique", vol. 26, 1921, pp. 146-147.
[47] It is curious that despite the unfavourable working conditions (long hours and lengthy periods away from home), the number of Belgian seasonal workers in France continued to rise during the boom years, when there were more employment opportunities in Belgian industry. It may be that seasonal workers, who were mainly employed in agriculture, had something of an aversion to factory employment. It is also possible that the traditional orientation towards seasonal work in France meant that in certain regions, seasonal workers responded with marked inertia to the improved conditions in the Belgian labour market. Finally, higher wages were paid in France.
[48] LENTACKER F., *o.c.*, p. 211.

Paragraph 2. Average working hours

A characteristic feature of seasonal employment is the fact that the employment relates to only part of the year and that at these times people generally work considerably longer hours than they do in all the year round work. This high intensity of the employment is due to economic and social factors: both the employer and the employee have an interest in highly intensive employment in the months when work is available (e.g. during the harvest period). The employer must find a way of handling the superabundance of work in a short time-span, while the employee needs to earn sufficient income in the spells of employment to bridge the periods of unemployment or underemployment[49].

To begin with, the number of months per year for which Belgian seasonal workers were on average employed in France will be examined below. It will then be established how many days per month were generally worked. The number of working hours per day will then be estimated. Finally these three variables are multiplied, so as to provide an idea of the number of working hours per year. In particular, the estimates have been based on the results of the aforementioned survey by Neels[50] conducted in the early 1920s among 11 seasonal workers from ten different municipalities in the arrondissement of Bruges.

1. Average number of months of employment per year

The number of months that seasonal workers remained in France depended heavily on the nature of the work in question (e.g. agriculture or non-agriculture) and the number of seasons in which they participated (e.g. spring sugar-beet work and/or grain harvest and/or sugar-beet harvest). In Neels' survey, two of the respondents worked in France for six and a half months per year, five workers for six months, two workers three and a half months and two workers three months. On average, therefore, the respondents spent five months in France.

To what extent are the results of this highly limited survey representative of all seasonal workers and the inter-war period as a whole? This is difficult to assess since, as far as could be established, no other inter-war figures have been published on working hours. It was, however, possible to establish how long Belgian seasonal workers generally remained in France at the end of the nineteenth century on the basis of an official enumeration conducted around 1897. This count, which was never published by the government, but the results of

---

[49] Some seasonal workers did of course work in industry between seasons, e.g. in the Walloon coal mines, but the majority remained at home without work (VANDERVELDE E., *L'exode rural et le retour aux champs,* Paris, 1903, pp. 165-166).
[50] C. NEELS, *o.c.*, p. 588.

which were used by Eylenbosch and later Schepens, contains semi-monthly figures for the number of Belgian workers temporarily resident in France[51].

The number ranged from 0 in January/February to 40,176 in the second half of July. If it is assumed that all seasonal workers were in France during the second half of July, the average annual period of residence in France may be calculated. This calculation suggests that seasonal workers spent an average of 42% of the year abroad, roughly corresponding with five months[52]. The average period of residence in France did not therefore change between the end of the nineteenth century and the early 1920s. It has been assumed that this remained the case in the inter-war period.

2. Average number of working days per month

One of the question in Neels' survey was "Do you work on Sundays?" Three seasonal workers replied "yes", two "sometimes", one "at harvest time", one "seldom" and four "no". On the basis of this limited survey, it may be assumed that half the seasonal workers worked on Sundays. It may also be assumed that the workers were all employed on the other days of the week. Taken as a whole, therefore, one arrives at an average of 28 working days per month.

3. Average number of working hours per working day

The same survey suggests that the average number of working hours per working day was around 13. This figure may appear on the high side, but it needs to be borne in mind that the work was concentrated in the summer months and that seasonal workers were required to earn sufficient income during these months to last them the entire year. For this reason the figure from Neels' survey has been applied for all seasonal workers. It may be assumed that the number of working hours remained unchanged during the inter-war period[53].

---

[51] *Onze Belgen die een deel des jaars in Frankrijk verblijven. Verslag op het Congres van Luik in 1898 voorgebracht door G. Eylenbosch, Schrifver van den Belgischen Volkbond*, Ghent, 1898; SCHEPENS L., *o.c.*, pp. 215-217.

[52] By aggregating the semi-monthly figures one arrives at 405,430. If this result is divided by 24, one arrives at the average number of seasonal workers throughout the year (16,893). This result is 42% of the maximum employment (40,176).

[53] A statutory reduction in the number of working hours for agricultural labourers was not introduced until 1947 (COMBE P., *o.c.*, p. 98).

4. Average number of working days per year

Multiplication of the number of working months per year (5) by the number of working days per month (28) and the number of working hours per day (13) results in an average of 1,820 working hours per year, which has been rounded down to 1,800.

Paragraph 3. Average hourly wage and total wagebill

There are no wage series for the Belgian seasonal workers in France. Since the majority of the seasonal workers were employed in agriculture, the French wages paid to agricultural laborers are the most suitable for estimating the total wagebill of the Belgian seasonal workers. In this respect it has been assumed that the seasonal workers were all male and that those employed in the non-agricultural sector earned the same as those in agriculture.

In his well documented study on the living standard in France, Combe complied numerous wage series, including one for agricultural workers. The agricultural series, which relate to France as a whole, are based on the major agricultural surveys conducted in 1910 and 1929 and the wages determined for the purpose of the Acts of 15 July 1914 and 15 December 1922 concerning industrial accident legislation[54]. Combe's series for agricultural workers relates to day labourers and on average Combe provides data every two years (see Table 36 column 1). Three problems arise in using these figures as an indication of the wages received by Belgian seasonal workers:

1. The figures relate to day wages, whereas hourly wages are needed. Combe does not specify the number of working hours to which his daily wages in agriculture relate. It may be assumed that the daily wages were paid in respect of a normal working day of eight hours.
2. Many seasonal workers received benefits in kind such as free housing and food. These benefits must be regarded as part of pay and therefore taken into account[55]. Combe's wage series, however, relates to agricultural workers who received neither food nor lodging from their employers[56]. It is logical to assume that, if an agricultural worker is fed or provided lodgings by his farmer, he would receive a lower cash wage than a worker looking after his own food and lodgings. If it is assumed that the total pay (i.e. cash + any benefits in kind) is always the same, irrespective as to whether part of the pay is in kind, Combe's series can be used without problems.
3. It is unclear whether Combe's series includes employers' social security contributions. It may be that this is not the case. As far as could be established, employers' contributions from 1923 onwards were confined to

---

[54] See Chapter 1.
[55] COMBE P., *o.c.*, pp. 102-103.

industrial accident insurance. It may be assumed this contribution was the same as that for industrial workers, namely some 4% of pay[57].

The daily wages of agricultural workers as drawn from Combe's study are shown in Table 36 column 1. The missing years have been interpolated or extrapolated on the basis of the daily wages of border-workers as estimated in the previous paragraph (columns 2-3). Column 5 takes the employers' social security contributions into account. On the basis of average annual working hours of 1,800 and assuming that Combe's daily wages represent the pay for an eight-hour working day, the average annual pay of Belgian border-workers in France has been estimated in column 6. French yearly wages have been converted into Belgian francs in column 7-8. Finally the total wagebill is arrived at in Table 37 by multiplying the number of persons employed by the unit pay.

---

[56] Idem.

[57] COMBE P., Idem, pp. 120-121. The suggestion that employers' contributions for seasonal workers were confined to industrial accident insurance may be deduced from the fact that in 1948 the total employers' contributions for social security for seasonal workers averaged just 5.6% of pay, while for border-workers the figure was 27.3% (own calculations on the basis of NIS, *Commissie van het Nationaal Inkomen*, pp. 36 and 43).

CHAPTER 4

EMPLOYERS' SOCIAL SECURITY CONTRIBUTIONS[1]

Section 1. Definition of the heading

In the income approach of the National Accounts, figures relating to social security are presented not from the receipts but from the contribution side. Hence one will look in vain for headings such as unemployment payments received, sickness or industrial accident benefits, pensions, child allowances, etc.[2]. The reason for this method is that in the income approach the national product is equated with the sum of all incomes received in return for participation in the production process (pay from employment, entrepreneurial income, return on capital invested, reserved profit, etc.). The national income therefore represents the primary division of income in a country. In principle no account is taken of the secondary distribution of income (i.e. the redistribution of primary income via taxation, social security contributions and transfers). Social security payments are transfers, and consequently must not be included in estimating national income. However, when part of income is spent on contributions towards social security, these payments should be included, because they count as participation in the production process.

Social security contributions have a threefold origin: they derive from employees, from employers, or from government. As previously explained in Chapter 1, employers' social security contributions have been included in the total wages and salaries of paid employees[3]. Government contributions derive from tax receipts, either from direct taxation (income taxes) or from indirect taxation[4]. The direct taxes paid by private persons have already been included under the various income headings (income from paid employment, entrepreneurial income, income from capital), since, in presenting the national income for private persons, it is always the income before payment of direct taxation (the gross income) which is taken into consideration. The direct taxes paid by companies form a separate

---

[1] The authors thank Geert Dancet and Patrick Nackaerts for their help in checking the references for this chapter.
[2] With the exception of pensions and other social benefit payments for employees of the government and some semi-governmental organisations. These are, however, included in national income (see Chapter 1).
[3] See Chapter 1.
[4] It may also happen that government involvement is (partially) financed by loans. The interest on these loans constitutes a debet item in national income (see Chapter 15).

heading in the national income[5]. The same applies to all indirect taxation[6]. Because employers' social security contributions are not included under any other heading, they are dealt with separately in this chapter.

A simple example may perhaps clarify the above theoretical exposition. Suppose that person A works in a factory and earns BF 1,000 gross. He has no other form of income, and pays BF 300 income tax and BF 100 employee's social security contributions. His net income is therefore BF 600. Suppose that in addition his employer pays BF 200 for social security and that individual A receives total unemployment benefits of BF 150 from social security (for example BF 50 from medical insurance and BF 100 as family allowance). A's disposable income is BF 750 (BF 600 net income + BF 150 receipts from social security). However, it is not the disposable income (the income resulting from secondary income distribution) which qualifies for inclusion in the national income but the primary income with the addition of the employer's social security contributions[7]. The contribution of person A to the national product and national income therefore totals BF 1,200 (BF 1,000 gross income + BF 200 employer's social security contribution). In this case the contribution to the national product is higher than the disposable income. Of course the reverse is also possible. Suppose, for example, that individual B is unemployed and has no capital. He receives no kind of income, either for labour, or for capital. He is, however, entitled to unemployment benefit of BF 500. His disposable income is therefore BF 500 and his contribution to the national product is nil.

The employers' social security contributions included in this chapter relate only to the private sector, because employees in the public sector receive social security payments directly from the state, provinces, municipalities or (in some cases) state-owned industries, without making any contributions. These payments can be regarded as a form of deferred wage and as such they are included in Chapter 5 with the pay of government employees[8].

By social security is understood all compulsory welfare measures laid down in the legislation currently in force. If an employer pays premiums voluntarily, for example in order to secure an additional pension for his staff, then those contributions are classified under the heading of salaries and wages[9].

In the inter-war period, Belgium moved from a voluntary to a compulsory system in various branches of social security, namely pensions, family allowances, occupational diseases and industrial accidents. Before the First World War

---

[5] See Chapter 13.

[6] See Chapter 17.

[7] Employers' social security contributions may be regarded as a type of compulsory wage. Since employers' contributions are in line with employees' participation in the production process, they represent remuneration for labour as a factor of production and consequently form part of income from paid employment

[8] *De nationale rekeningen van België 1953-1962*, pp. 1144-1145. See also Chapter 1.

[9] Idem, p. 1144. See also Chapter 1. Voluntary employers' contributions are included in Chapter 6, "Income from Paid Employment: Additions and Adjustments".

compulsory insurance had already been introduced for miners' pensions and for industrial accidents for the vast majority of manual workers, as well as for some white-collar workers. After the Second World War the obligation was extended to sickness and unemployment insurance.

With the introduction of a universal compulsory system of social security on 1 January 1945 (Decree of 28 December 1944), almost all contributions were paid into the coffers of the newly-founded *National Social Security Agency* (Rijksdienst voor Maatschappelijke Zekerheid, RMZ), the *National Miners' Pension Fund* (Nationaal Pensioenfonds voor Mijnwerkers, NPM) and the *Merchant Seamen's Social Security Agency* (Dienst voor Maatschappelijke Veiligheid der Zeelieden ter Koopvaardij, DMVZK)[10]. Before the Second World War there was no centralized system of contributions and there was a jumble of payment offices and officially recognized insurance companies. In order to understand this complicated system a discussion of the legal framework is indispensable[11]. In this discussion attention will be paid in the first instance to employers' contributions.

During the inter-war period employers had to pay contributions for industrial accidents, occupational illness, family allowances and pensions. The insurance premiums against industrial accidents and occupational illness were the full liability of the employers. In the family allowance sector there was a very limited degree of government subsidy, while the pension system was also financed by employees' contributions and government subsidies. The involvement of employers in insurance against sickness and unemployment was minimal. These two branches of social security, which in the period under review were not compulsory, were funded almost exclusively by employees and government. Employers' contributions to workers' annual holidays, which had been introduced in the Act of July 1936, are regarded in accordance with NIS procedure as pay[12]. These contributions are incorporated in gross pay, as presented in Chapter 1.

In the following sections the various components of the statutory employers' contributions are discussed one by one[13]. Because it is impossible to understand the method of reconstruction or the interpretation of the results without a good grasp of the sometimes complex legal provisions, each section begins with a

---

[10] The most important exception is insurance against industrial accidents, which, though compulsory, remained in the hands of private insurance companies and employers' funds even after the Second World War.

[11] The analysis of the statutory framework in this and subsequent sections is based mainly on HAIDANT P., *Précis de législation industrielle et sociale,* Brussels ; Liège ; Paris, 1939; JULIN, A., *Enquête sur les charges sociales de l'industrie,* in "Editions du Comité Central Industriel de Belgique", Brussels, 1933; VELGHE H., *Les lois belges d'assurance et de prévoyance sociales,* Brussels, 1933.

[12] *De nationale rekeningen van België 1953-1962,* p. 1143.

[13] Voluntary employers' contributions - for example, for supplementary pensions - are included with salaries in Chapter 6, "Additions and Adjustments".

description of the legal framework. This is followed by the actual method of reconstruction.

Because of the difference in organization of the pension systems of mineworkers, other manual workers and white-collar workers, the pension contributions for these categories of employees are discussed separately in Sections 2, 3 and 4. Employers' contributions for family allowances are dealt with in Section 5, and those for job-related sickness insurance in Section 6. Finally in Section 7 the premiums for industrial accident insurance are discussed.

Table 38 presents the various components of the statutory employers' contributions[14].

SECTION 2. EMPLOYERS' CONTRIBUTIONS TO MINEWORKERS' PENSIONS

The miners played a leading role in the development of the Belgian pension system. As early as 1840 they set up pension funds, into which employees and employers paid contributions on a voluntary basis. From 1891 onwards the government began subsidizing the pension system, and with the passing of the Act of 5 June 1911, which came into force on 1 January 1912, compulsory pensions insurance for all miners was introduced. Every mine-owner was required to open a pension account for his employees with the *General Savings and Annuity Fund* (Algemene Spaar- en Lijfrentekas, ASLK), either directly, or indirectly via the existing pension funds. Both employers and employees were obliged to make pension payments into this account. The Act of 20 August 1920 led to the setting up of the NPM which provided an umbrella for the operation of the various funds.

Employers' contributions can be found in the annual reports of the NPM (see Table 38, column 1)[15]. These contributions consist of a fixed portion of the wage, a percentage which in the period under review was raised several times[16].

---

[14] In the present national accounts employers' social security contributions are classified under three headings:
    1) Figures derived from RMZ, NPM and HVKZ
    2) Special arrangements for some categories of employees
    3) Industrial accident insurance.
Employers' contributions in the inter-war years fall under the first heading, with the exception of contributions to industrial accident insurance, which are part of item 3). The heading "special arrangements" is either not applicable to the inter-war period or is subsumed in item 1 of this footnote. For a summary of "special arrangements" see *De nationale rekeningen van België 1953-1962*, p. 1145.
[15] The figure for 1920, which relates only to the last quarter, was multiplied by four.
[16] Employers' contributions rose gradually from 2.5% of wages in 1920 to 6.5% after 1 October 1937.

SECTION 3. EMPLOYERS' CONTRIBUTIONS TO MANUAL WORKERS' PENSIONS

The inter-war period can be divided into three periods as regards the pension system for manual workers.

Before 1926 the system was entirely voluntary. However, since 1891 and particularly since the Act of 10 May 1900 pension savings had been encouraged by the government by the granting of subsidies.

The Act of 10 December 1924, which came into force on 1 January 1926, changed the situation from a subsidized voluntary system into a compulsory system for all workers earning less than BF 12,000 per annum (+ BF 1,000 for each child under 16). Every month a payment of BF 3 had to be made for each male worker over 18 both by the employer and by the employee. For male workers under 18 and for all female workers the monthly contribution was BF 1. The employee's pension contribution was deducted from his/her wages and together with the employer's contribution converted into pension stamps which were affixed to special cards and submitted to the ASLK.

A third period was ushered in by the Act of 14 July 1930. This widened the group of those subject to compulsory insurance to all manual workers in paid employment, irrespective of their income, and to self-employed workers with a maximum annual income of BF 18,000. The level of the contribution was now independent of age and sex, but was related to the level of earnings. Both the employer and the employee had to pay approximately 1.33% of the wage earned, with a monthly minimum and maximum contribution of BF 2.50 and BF 12.50 respectively. From an annual wage of approximately BF 10,400 upwards the contribution remained constant[17]. For workers in jobs carrying a high health risk, the contribution was approximately 50% higher[18].

Pension payments were published in the annual reports of the ASLK (see Table 38, column 2). In the period of compulsory insurance, from 1926 onwards, employers' contributions equal one half of total contributions, since employees

---

[17] The Act of 14 July 1930 divided wages into eight classes, according to the frequency of payment (every two weeks or 15 days, weekly, every ten days, etc.), with a corresponding monthly contribution to the pension system. There was fixed contribution for each wage class, so that the basic contribution for the lower limit of the class was higher than for the upper limit. The basic contribution for the middle of each class for both employers and employees was approximately 1.33% of the total wage earned (varying according to class and frequency of payment from 1.29% to 1.38%). The basic contribution at the upper limit of the lowest class, depending on the frequency of payment was between 1.15% and 1.19%, and at the lower limit of the highest class between 1.43% and 1.47%.

[18] Because of the fact that higher pension contributions had to be paid for manual workers in jobs with a high health risk, and the fact that there was a ceiling to contributions for all manual workers above a certain wage (an annual income of approximately BF 10,400, which in the 1930s was close to the average income for manual workers), it is not possible to reconstruct the total wages of manual workers via the total amount of pension payments. Consequently in Chapter 1 salaries were estimated on the basis of wages insured against industrial accidents.

and employers paid the same[19]. In accordance with the methodology set out in Section 1[20], no account was taken of any supplementary voluntary payments. Before 1926 all contributions are voluntary and were consequently not included.

SECTION 4. EMPLOYERS' CONTRIBUTIONS TO WHITE-COLLAR WORKERS' PENSIONS

Before 1926, just as for manual workers, the pension system for white-collar workers was characterized by a voluntary system. A compulsory system was introduced by the Act of 10 March 1925, which came into effect on 1 January 1926[21]. All employees with white-collar status, including temporary government civil servants, had to pay 3% of their earnings to the ASLK towards their future pensions[22]. The employers' contribution was 5%. Both employers' and employees' contributions were calculated on a basis of an annual salary with a ceiling of BF 15,000[23]. The maximum annual compulsory contribution was therefore BF 450 for the employee and BF 750 for the employer[24].

From 1 January 1932 onwards a new Act, passed on 18 July 1930, came into force. The basic contribution of the employer was reduced to 4%, that of employees remained at 3%. The reduction in the overall basic contribution was compensated for somewhat by an increase in the ceiling to BF 18,000. An important innovation was that the ASLK lost its monopoly as an insurer. Henceforth employees could decide for themselves what institution or insurance company the contributions should be paid to: the ASLK, a private insurance company or employers' fund, or the new official *National White-Collar Workers' Pension Fund* (Nationale Kas voor Bediendenpensioenen) which was to be set up. Besides the National White-Collar Workers' Pension Fund, the Act of 1930 also provided for the setting up of the *Benefit Fund for White-Collar Workers* (Toelagenfonds voor Bedienden). The function of this fund was to pay pension

---

[19] Only in 1926, the first year in which the Act on compulsory pensions insurance was in force, was no complete report prepared by the ASLK. However, the total amount of contributions, both compulsory and voluntary, was published. The compulsory employers' contributions for manual workers was estimated, assuming the same proportion of the independently insured - mainly self-employed persons - as in 1927.
[20] Payments by "manual workers not employed by companies", which may be a designation of self-employed manual workers, were also left out of account.
[21] In fact the Act of 10 March 1925 was never implemented on a number of points and was replaced by transitional measures which were renewed annually until the end of 1931. This situation is taken into account.
[22] The Act of 10 March 1925 specified an employee's contribution of 5% for white-collar workers earning over BF 6,000 per annum and 3% for those earning less. However, the Act of 10 June 1926 reduced personal contributions to 3% for all white-collar workers.
[23] This ceiling was raised by BF 500 for each dependent child below the age of 16. The increase for dependent children was abolished by the Act of 18 June 1930.
[24] Where there were no dependent children.

benefits, for a transitional period, to white-collar workers born between 31 December 1861 (for women 31 December 1866) and 1 January 1895[25]. The Benefit Fund for White-Collar Workers was financed partly by an employer's contribution of BF 120 for each white-collar worker employed (irrespective of the age of the employee) and an employee's contribution, which varied from BF 90 for employees born before 1 January 1875 to BF 30 for employees born between 1890 and 1894.

Since all contributions to the compulsory pension system for white-collar workers had to be paid into an ASLK account between 1926 and 1931, employers' contributions could be calculated very simply by multiplying the total payments for employees' pensions (employers' and employees' contributions), which were published in the annual reports of the ASLK, by 5/8 (see Table 39, column 1).

From 1932 onwards employers' contributions are divided between the ASLK, the National White-Collar Workers' Pension Fund and private insurance companies or employers' pension funds. Besides the usual contribution of 4% to one of these insurance bodies, a further sum of BF 120 per employee had to be paid to the Benefit Fund for White Collar Workers. Employers' payments to the ASLK and the National White-Collar Workers' Pension Fund constitute 4/7 of the total contributions (of employers and employees) to these institutions (columns 1 and 2). No precise details are available for payments into private insurance companies or employers' funds. Julin estimates total employers' contributions, excluding those into the Benefit Fund for White-Collar Workers (i.e. the amounts paid into the ASLK, the National White-Collar Workers' Pension Fund and the private insurance companies and employers' funds), at almost BF 130 million, which is approximately double the amount of payments into the ASLK and National White-Collar Workers' Pension Fund combined[26]. For this reason it was assumed that in the period 1932-1939 contributions to private insurance companies and funds were exactly the same as those into the ASLK and National White-Collar Workers' Pension Fund combined (column 3).

Finally employers' contribution to the Benefit Fund for White-Collar Workers were estimated. Total payments into this fund were published in its annual reports. The most important task was to separate the employers' contributions from those of the employees. Employers' contributions amounted to BF 120 for each employee, irrespective of age. Employees' contributions applied only to older employees born before 1895, and reduced progressively the more recently the employee was born. On the basis of the scale of statutory contributions for each year of birth an approximate estimate could be made of the

---

[25] This relates to those white-collar workers who had already paid pension contributions - since they had not reached pensionable age on 1 January 1926, the date on which compulsory pensions insurance came into force - but who because of their age had accumulated insufficient capital to receive a full pension.

[26] JULIN A., o.c., pp. 61-62.

average employee's contribution. In 1932 this was BF 3.7[27]. This amount was reduced annually by BF 2 to BF 23 in 1939 in order to take account of the attainment of pensionable age by the employees liable for the highest contributions. Finally, employers' contributions were determined on the basis of the estimated average employer's contribution and of the published total payments (see column 4).

SECTION 5. EMPLOYERS' CONTRIBUTIONS TO FAMILY ALLOWANCES

The system of family allowances came into existence in Belgium after the First World War on the initiative of employers[28]. The first fund for family allowances was set up in Verviers in 1921 by the industrialist Lechat. This initiative was imitated elsewhere in the country and the number of funds set up either on a regional basis or per branch of industry expanded constantly. The system was a voluntary one (there was no statutory provision), but was encouraged by some municipal and provincial authorities, which had decided that only those companies who had joined a child allowance fund would be eligible for official orders.

A statutory scheme was introduced on 14 April 1928. From then on all industrial companies delivering goods or carrying out work for central government, provinces or municipalities were obliged to pay family allowances to their employees via the funds, which were now given legal status.

The Act of 14 April 1928, which came into force six months after its publication (20 October 1928), operated for only two years. On 4 August 1930 a new Act was passed which obliged all companies in agriculture, industry, commerce and other services to contribute to family allowances on behalf of their employees from 1 January 1931 onwards[29]. For each male employee the sum of BF 0.65 per day, and for each female employee BF 0.35 per day, was payable. At the discretion of the employer, these amounts were paid into the existing fund or into new funds. In addition to these independent primary funds a secondary fund, the *National Settlement Fund for Family Allowances* (Nationale Verrekenkas voor Gezinsvergoedingen), was set up. One function of this fund was to provide partial

---

[27] In estimating this average employer's contribution, allowance was made for younger white-collar workers (born before 1 January 1895) who were exempted from payments into the Benefit Fund for White-Collar Workers.

[28] Besides the works listed in footnote 11, the discussion of the system of contributions for family allowances is based on DE LEENER G., *Les Caisses de compensation des Allocations familiales en Belgique. Leur rôle - législation - leur avenir*, Brussels, 1929; DE LEENER G., *Vingt-cinq années de régime des allocations familiales en Belgique*, Brussels, 1947.

[29] The group of manual workers for whom employers were not required to pay any contribution was limited to resident domestic and personal servants. These employees received family allowances from the newly-founded National Settlement Fund for Family Allowances. Employees of the State, provinces, municipalities, the National Belgian Railway Company (NMBS) and other companies of a public nature received family allowances direct, i.e. without the intervention of a fund.

compensatory assistance from primary funds with a surplus to funds in deficit. The National Settlement Fund for Family Allowances reported annually on its activities, and on those of the scores of primary funds.

No further major changes were made to the system described above during the 1930s. Changes related mostly to the level of benefits and contributions. One exception was the Act of 10 June 1937, which extended the system to the self-employed and employers with effect from 1 January 1938.[30]

From 1931 employers' contributions on behalf of employees were published in the annual reports of the National Settlement Fund for Family Allowances (see Table 40, column 6)[31]. Before 1931 two problems present themselves: the amount of the contributions is unknown and it is debatable whether these amounts should be included.

In Section 1 it was emphasized that under this heading account should be taken only of compulsory payments and that voluntary employers' contributions should be included under pay in Chapter 6, "Income from Paid Employment: Additions and Adjustments"[32]. During the period preceding the first Act on family allowances, payments were in theory voluntary, but some local and provincial authorities restricted work and delivery contracts to companies belonging to a fund. The same applied to central government after the Act of 14 April 1928. A universal compulsory system did not materialize until 1 January 1931. Until the end of 1930 there was therefore a mixed voluntary-compulsory system, so that it is open to debate whether family allowances pre-1931 form part of statutory social security[33]. Because no universal compulsory system existed until the end of 1930, in what follows employers' contributions to family allowances are regarded as voluntary and are consequently included in Chapter 6. However, an estimate of these employers' contributions is given in this chapter.

As has been said, no precise data are available on the scale of contributions before 1931. According to De Leener, payments averaged approximately 2% of the wages of employees belonging to funds[34]. This author also gives the number of employees belonging to funds and the number of funds in 1927 and 1929. In addition he gives the number of new funds in the years 1920-1926. In Table 40 an

---

[30] The statistics relating to the self-employed and the employers are found in the annual reports of the National Mutual Fund for Family Allowances.
[31] *Caisse Nationale de Compensation pour Allocations Familiales. Rapports du Conseil d'Administration et de la Direction*, 10ième exercice (exercice 1940), Annex 4, p. 37. The fall in the employer's contribution in 1935 is due to a reduction in the contribution per employee from 1 January 1935 (Act of 16 January 1935). The doubling of payments between 1935 and 1937 is mainly the result of a sharp rise in the contribution per employee from 1 July 1936 (Act of 28 July 1936).
[32] See below. Voluntary employers' contributions form part of Chapter 6, "Additions and Adjustments".
[33] This discussion has absolutely no repercussions for the level of the national income. It affects only the division into subcategories.
[34] DE LEENER G., *Les caisses,* pp. 89-90; DE LEENER G., *Vingt-cinq années*, p. 49.

estimate is given of employers' contributions on the basis of these sparse data, while also taking account of the Act of 14 April 1928, which came into force only at the end of the year.

SECTION 6. EMPLOYERS' CONTRIBUTIONS TO JOB-RELATED SICKNESS BENEFIT

The Act of 24 July 1927 obliged companies in a number of industries with a high risk of job-related sickness to make payments into the *Contingency Fund* (Voorzorgskas), set up under the Ministry of Industry, Employment and Social Welfare. The repercussions of the Act, which remained in force for the remainder of the inter-war period, were very limited. According to Julin contributions in 1932 totalled only BF 596,607[35]. It was assumed that there was no appreciable change in other years (see Table 38, column 5).

SECTION 7. EMPLOYERS' CONTRIBUTIONS TO INDUSTRIAL ACCIDENT INSURANCE

The statutory framework of industrial accident insurance has already been discussed at length, in Chapter 1[36]. Most employers had taken out insurance with private insurance companies or mutual employers' funds. The premiums paid by them were published in the three-yearly industrial accident insurance reports (see Table 41, column 1). The other employers, both those who paid contributions into the Guarantee Fund and those who were exempted (who are sometimes also called "self-insurers"), remained financially liable in the case of accidents. According to Julin, expenditure resulting from this liability for "self-insurers" amounted to 0.83% of the total wages and salaries paid by the employers concerned in 1926 and 1.10% in 1929[37]. For simplicity's sake the figure of 1% of pay was used, both for "self-insurers" and for employers paying into the Guarantee Fund see column 2)[38].

---

[35] JULIN A., *o.c.*, p. 122.
[36] See Chapter 1.
[37] JULIN A., *o.c.*, p. 17.
[38] The total wages and salaries paid by "self-insurers" and by employers making payments into the Guarantee Fund was estimated in Chapter 1 (see Table 1, columns 5 and 6).

CHAPTER 5

PAY AND PENSIONS OF GOVERNMENT STAFF

SECTION 1. DEFINITION OF THE HEADING

This chapter details the pay and pensions of staff in government employment. More specifically, it deals with employees of central government, of the provinces, the municipalities, free education and some public institutions. These employees are not subject to legislation on social security. They receive a government old-age pension, family allowances and other social benefits free of charge. These costs were not included in the previous chapter on employers' contributions to social security and hence must be included here. Pensions are regarded as a form of "deferred wage".

In reconstructing expenditure on pay and pensions for government staff the following division is used. Central government (Section 2) is divided into the civil service, state education and the military establishment. With provincial and municipal authorities a distinction is made between administrative and teaching staff (Sections 3 and 4). Government subsidies for pay in free education are dealt with separately (Section 5). Finally, following NIS methodology the following public institutions are dealt with: the State Railways/NMBS (Section 6), the Telegraph and Telephone Corporation (RTT), the Postal Services and the Belgian Airwaves Authority (Section 7), and the public companies controlled by the provincial and municipal authorities (Section 8).

The results presented here are the work of Piet Clement. Since his method of reconstruction is given in detail in a seperate publication in this series, he exposition here is limited to a brief summary of his study. For detailed calculations and information on the sources used the reader is advised to use Clement's work[1].

SECTION 2. CENTRAL GOVERNMENT: CIVIL SERVICE, STATE EDUCATION AND MILITARY ESTABLISHMENT: TOTAL PAY AND PENSIONS

Since expenditure on the pay of administrative, teaching and military staff in the employment of the central government is calculated in the same way, these

---

[1] CLEMENT P., *The Growth of a Welfare State in Belgium* (Studies in Economic History, vol. 5, Brussels, 2000).

categories are dealt with jointly here. A distinction is made between wages and salaries on the one hand and pension costs on the other. Following the usual convention the stipends of ministers of recognized religions are included with civil service pay. The state police force occupies a special position because it fulfils both military and civil functions and consequently falls under both the Ministry of Defence and the Ministry of Home Affairs. Two-thirds of the pay of the state police force was included with the civil service, one third with the military establishment. As regards the military establishment not only pay and salaries were included but also expenditure on "benefits in kind", especially food and clothing provided free of charge.

Total expenditure on the pay of central government staff was given in the annual *Accounts of the Audit Office* (Rekenhof). These contain a section entitled "Final Account of the Belgian State Budget", in which an analysis of expenditure in varying degrees of detail is given for each ministerial department. In these final accounts, which are usually published some years after the conclusion of the financial year in question, only expenditure actually incurred is included. Consequently the use of these data is preferable to the figures included in the original budgets, which reflect only projected expenditure. Nevertheless in a number of cases it was necessary to refer for more detailed information to the original budget data, as published in the *Parliamentary Documents of the Chamber and Senate.*

The difficulties in analysing the budget accounts are twofold. In the first place the accounts do not give aggregate figures for staff costs on the one hand and costs of material, investment, social transfers, etc. on the other hand. Because of this the gathering of data on the pay of government staff is very time-consuming. In the second place it is not always clear which budget items are to be regarded as staff costs. Expenditure on staff and materials are regularly combined. In order to remedy this it is necessary to refer to the additional information contained in the comments on the draft budgets and in the reports of the Chamber or Senate committees examining these drafts. From 1934 onwards the budget accounts were better structured; henceforth staff costs were grouped according to ministry.

Expenditure on pay and pensions for staff in the civil service, state education and the military establishment was reconstructed on the basis on a complete analysis of the final accounts of the Belgium state budgets for the years 1920-1939.

As regards pension costs, it should be noted that until the end of 1936 these were included in the accounts as a subcategory of the national debt. A separate pensions budget was not drawn up until 1937. Only service pensions in the strict sense were included with military pensions; disability pensions or pensions awarded as a result of involvement in military action are not included here.

SECTION 3. PROVINCES AND MUNICIPALITIES: CIVIL SERVICE

The administrative apparatus of the provinces and municipalities includes the staff employed by these bodies with the exception of teaching staff (Section 4) and the employees of public companies controlled by provinces and municipalities (Section 8). The staff of the *Public Welfare Committees* (Commissies van Openbare Onderstand, *COO*) are also included with the administrative apparatus of the municipalities.

Paragraph 1. The provinces

A portion of provincial staff were paid directly by central government through the budget of the Ministry of Home Affairs. This expenditure was already included with the administrative apparatus of central government in the previous section. The remuneration and pensions paid by provincial authorities themselves are discussed here.

Wages, salaries and pensions paid by the provinces were calculated on the basis of the data in the *Statistical Yearbooks*[2] and of a budgetary analysis of the province of Brabant. The Statistical Yearbooks give the final accounts of the nine Belgian provinces, but without making a distinction between staff costs and other expenditure. This distinction is of course made in the detailed budget documents of the various provinces. Since a complete analysis of all provincial budgets would be enormously time-consuming, it was assumed that the portion of staff costs in total expenditure was roughly the same for all provinces. Subsequently only the budgets of the province with the highest number of inhabitants namely Brabant, were fully analysed. The total staff expenditure of all provinces was then obtained by dividing the staff costs of Brabant by the total expenditure of Brabant, and multiplying this quotient by the total expenditure of all provinces.

Paragraph 2. The municipalities

The staff costs of the municipalities and the COO's were calculated principally on the basis of the municipal accounts published in the Statistical Yearbooks. This posed three problems: firstly, no distinction was made between staff costs and other expenditure; secondly the Statistical Yearbook up to 1939 includes only the accounts of municipalities with more than 40,000 inhabitants; and thirdly no figures are available on the COO's until 1939.

The latter two problems were solved to a certain degree by the fact that the Statistical Yearbook for 1939 contains more information than previous years. In

---

[2] *Statistisch Jaarboek (van België en Belgisch Kongo).*

1939 all municipal accounts were published, i.e. including the accounts of municipalities with fewer than 40,000 inhabitants. In consequence in the case of 1939 it was possible to calculate the proportion of the expenditure of municipalities with more than 40,000 inhabitants in the total expenditure of all municipalities. This coefficient was subsequently related to the expenditure of municipalities with more than 40,000 inhabitants prior to 1939, so that an approximate estimate was obtained of the total expenditure of all Belgium municipalities for the period 1920-1939. The expenditure of the COO's for the period 1920-1939 was estimated in the same way, namely on the basis of the COO expenditure of municipalities with more than 20,000 inhabitants in 1939.

On the basis of the above calculations it was possible to estimate the total expenditure of the municipalities and the COO's for the period 1920-1939, but the problem remained of how to separate out the staff costs. In the absence of more detailed information, the proportion of staff costs contained in the total costs of municipalities and COO's in the period 1948-1958 was calculated on the basis of NIS data. Subsequently it was assumed that this proportion was the same during the inter-war period.

SECTION 4. PROVINCIAL AND MUNICIPAL EDUCATION (INCLUDING PAY SUBSIDIES)

The staff of provincial and municipal schools were paid by these local government bodies. However, central government also funded part of the pay by awarding the provinces and municipalities pay subsidies. Remuneration paid by provincial and municipal authorities was reconstructed in the same way as remuneration paid to the civil service (Section 3). Central government pay subsidies, however, present a problem because all grants to subsidized education (i.e. provincial, municipal and free education) were included as a single budget item in the Parliamentary Documents (budget of the Ministry of Public Education). For the distribution of the state subsidies between provincial and municipal education on the one hand and free education on the other the postwar ratios were followed (NIS data) and it was hence assumed that the proportion of total pay subsidies received by provincial and municipal education were the same during the inter-war period as in the period 1948-1954. Any errors are of less significance here since they cancel each other out and hence have no influence on the total volume of the national income.

SECTION 5. FREE EDUCATION

Only the pay subsidies of the state for independently organized education in Belgium are included. The greater part of these subsidies were calculated on the basis of the data given in Section 4. In addition the state subsidies to the Catholic University of Louvain and the Free University of Brussels, which can also be found in the budget of the Ministry of Public Education, were included.

SECTION 6. STATE RAILWAYS/NMBS

The salaries, wages, pensions and social security payments relating to railway personnel are summed up in the annual reports of the Belgian State Railways (up to August 1926) and of the NMBS (from September 1926 onwards). Privately run railway lines operating with a government licence, were not included here because they were included with the private sector.

SECTION 7. RTT, THE POSTAL SERVICE AND THE BELGIAN AVIATION AUTHORITY

The salaries, wages, pensions and social security costs of the *telegraphic and telephone services* (RTT[3]), the postal service and the Belgian Aviation Authority - all semi-public companies - are found in the *Accounts of the Audit Office* and in the *Parliamentary Documents*.

SECTION 8. PUBLIC COMPANIES CONTROLLED BY THE PROVINCES AND MUNICIPALITIES

No figures are available on staff costs for these institutions. This is because only relevant profit or loss figures are included in the provincial and municipal budgets, and no summary of income and expenditure. The staff costs of these companies were therefore calculated on the basis of a proportion of total expenditure of all provincial and municipal authorities, which was assumed to be constant. This proportion was determined in line with NIS data for the period 1948-1954[4].

---

[3] The RTT was set up as a semi-public company in 1930. Prior to that date, the telegraphic and telephone services were managed directly by the state.
[4] See Section 3 for the calculation of the total expenditure of the provinces and municipalities.

CHAPTER 6

INCOME FROM PAID EMPLOYMENT: ADDITIONS AND ADJUSTMENTS

In the National Accounts published by the NIS, the main heading "Income from Paid Employment" concludes with a subheading entitled "Additions and Adjustments[1]". This item includes a broad spectrum of adjustments to total wages and salaries as given in the annual reports of the bodies responsible for collecting social security contributions[2].

In the first section a brief summary is provided of the additions and corrections made by the NIS in the 1940s and 1950s[3]. The question whether these corrections are also necessary for the inter-war period is also addressed. The way in which the additions and corrections were obtained for the period 1920-1939 is discussed in the second section.

SECTION 1. CONTENT OF THE HEADING

A first series of adjustments carried out by the NIS relates to the occupational categories for which total wages and salaries are determined on a fixed basis in the annual reports of the RMZ. These are agricultural labourers, fishermen, seamen, and employees paid (partly) in tips (employees in or attached to hotels, cafés, hairdressing establishments in the leisure sector, etc.). The fixed pay on which social security contributions are calculated is much lower than the wages actually earned, so that the NIS makes a rough estimate of the difference between the two amounts[4]. Since in reconstructing the pay of the aforementioned occupational categories in the inter-war period fixed wages were never used, no further adjustments are required in this case.

A second correction includes the benefits in kind accorded mineworkers or workers in the coke-fired blast furnaces. This relates to the value of the coal and

---

[1] *Het Belgisch nationaal inkomen van 1948 tot 1954*, pp. 589-590; *De nationale rekeningen van België 1953-1962*, pp. 1147-1148.
[2] RMZ, NPM and DMVZK. To avoid repetitions in what follows, the designation RMZ refers not only to the RMZ itself but also to the other two, smaller bodies charged after the Second World War with the collection of social security contributions.
[3] NIS, *Commissie voor het Nationaal Inkomen*, pp. 14-16.
[4] As a correction for the pay of agricultural labourers, the NIS takes the amount required to bridge the gap between the contractual wages declared to RMZ on the one hand and the aggregate of wages and salaries estimated as a operating input for self-employed farmers on the other.

coke supplied free to these employees. During the inter-war period mineworkers and related workers also enjoyed this benefit so that a correction is required in this case also.

In addition the NIS includes a number of sums which correspond to financial benefits accorded employees and not contained in the social security statistics. An example of this is double holiday pay[5]. Since these benefits did not exist during the inter-war period no correction is necessary here.

A fourth addition concerns the income of male and female apprentices for whom no social security contributions need to be paid. However, in reconstructing manual workers' pay in the inter-war period these wages were liable for contributions, so that a correction in this case is superfluous[6].

The NIS also takes account of the very small amount paid to prisoners employed either on independent farms or by the *Prison Labour Authority* (Regie van de Gevangenisarbeid). These payments must in principle also be included for the period 1920-1939, since they are not included in the total wages and salaries insured against industrial accidents. However, the amounts involved are so small that this addition was not included for the inter-war period[7].

A sixth adjustment relates to the remuneration paid by international organizations based in Belgium (e.g. the institutions of the *European Community* (EEG) and the *North Atlantic Treaty Organization* (NATO)) to their staff resident in Belgium. During the inter-war period, however, no international organizations were based in Belgium, so that no adjustment was necessary.

Legislation relating to social security determines that social security contributions must be paid on bonuses (e.g. end-of-year bonuses), shares in profit and other benefits accorded employees (e.g. a thirteen month's pay). This additional pay is therefore in principle included in the RMZ statistics. However, it can be assumed that in some cases these sums are not declared. Account must also be taken of pay which has not been declared to the social security authorities.

Voluntary employers' contributions which do not fit into the compulsory system of social security (e.g. payments for group insurance or supplementary pensions) are not included in the RMZ statistics. Since these voluntary contributions can be regarded as a form of wages, they must be included in estimating the national income.

For all the above cases, that is (additional) pay (wrongly) undeclared to the RMZ, shares in profits and bonuses, and for voluntary employers' contributions not fitting into the compulsory system of social security, the NIS uses a general correction factor. The amount corresponding with this correction factor forms the greater part of the subheading "Additions and Adjustments".

---

[5] Normal holiday pay, on the other hand, is included in the social security statistics.
[6] See Chapter 1.
[7] In the period 1948-1954 the total pay of those in detention amounted to only BF 12 million, which amounts to 0.02% of the overall aggregate wages of manual workers (own calculation on the basis of *NIS, Het Belgisch nationaal inkomen van 1948 tot 1954*, pp. 13 and 16).

Is it necessary to make a similar correction for the inter-war period? It is obvious that, despite legal checks, some (additional) pay is not included in the total wages and salaries insured against industrial accidents. This is undoubtedly the case where certain workers who after completing their normal day's work sometimes worked for a second employer. Account must also be taken of the voluntary employers' contributions which fall outside the scope of compulsory social security[8].

Finally, in accordance with the provisions of the standardized system, costs borne by employees for the purchase of working tools and working clothing must be deducted from pay[9]. In the absence of data, the NIS simply makes an estimate of occupational expenses for clothing. These constitute a negative figure in the heading "Additions and Adjustments". It is advisable to include these costs for the period 1920-1939 as well.

SECTION 2. THE ADDITIONS AND CORRECTIONS MADE

In relation to the period 1920-1939, the pay of manual workers and white-collar workers, as calculated in previous chapters, was amended on four points. First the coal and coke provided free of charge to mineworkers and workers in the coke-fired blast furnaces were included. In addition the voluntary employers' contributions not fitting into the compulsory social security system were estimated. The third and by far the most important adjustment concerns the (additional) pay and bonuses not included in the total wages and salaries insured against industrial accidents. Finally account was taken of the occupational costs borne by employees. An overview of the various additions and corrections is given in Table 43.

1. Free coal and coke

The corresponding value of the free coal and coke supplied to mineworkers and workers in the coke-fired blast furnaces was published annually in the *Annales des Mines* (see Table 43, column 1).

---

[8] Explicit account was taken of the thirteen month's pay and end-of-year bonus, which were paid to a considerable number of employees even in the inter-war period. This non-statutory benefit must therefore not be included here.

[9] *A Standardized System of National Accounts*, p. 80. This deduction for occupational expenses is of course superfluous if the expenditure is refunded by the employer.

2. Voluntary employer's contributions not fitting into the compulsory social security system

It is of course impossible to put an exact figure on this category. It was assumed that for the branches of social security for which there was a statutory employers' contribution, no additional voluntary payments were made. This was the case for the whole of the period under review for mineworkers' pensions and for industrial accidents[10], from 1926 onwards for manual workers' and white-collar workers' pensions, in the course of 1927 for occupation-related sickness, from 1931 for family allowances, and finally from 1936 onwards for manual workers' annual holidays[11].

With regard to manual workers' and white-collar workers' pensions before 1926, it was assumed that half the payments into the annuity fund of the ASLK derive from employers (see Table 44, column 1).

The voluntary employers' contribution for family allowances before 1931 was already estimated in Chapter 4. The results can also be found in Table 44 (column 2).

The amount of compulsory employers' contributions to occupation-related illness, which were introduced in 1927, was so small[12] that it was assumed that in the years before legislation was passed no voluntary payments were made.

There was no statutory obligation for unemployment insurance. Since voluntary unemployment insurance was almost exclusively organized from within the trade unions, and the employers were decidedly hostile to this historical source of power, it was assumed that there was no employers' contribution[13].

Similarly, employers were not obliged to pay any contributions towards medical insurance for their staff. Velge estimated voluntary employers' payments at BF 20 million in 1930[14]. In the absence of data for the other years, this amount

---

[10] For some categories of employee there was no statutory protection against industrial accidents (see Chapter 1). The premiums paid by employers who took out voluntary insurance have been included in the total employers' contributions for industrial accidents, since no division is made in the sources between compulsory and voluntary payments.

[11] See Chapter 4. The wage that manual workers continued to receive during their annual holidays forms part of the aggregate wages and salaries insured against industrial accidents in Chapter 1. Consequently it must not be included here.

[12] See Chapter 4.

[13] VANTHEMSCHE G., *De werkloosheid in België: 1929-1940*, Berchem, 1989; GOOSSENS M. et al., *Interwar Unemployment in Belgium,* in: "Interwar Unemployment in International Perspective" (NATO ASI Series D. Behavioural and Social Sciences", vol. 23), EICHENGREEN B., HATTON T.J. (eds), Dordrecht ; Boston ; London, 1988, pp. 296-297. Though employers' unemployment funds were set up here and there, their impact was negligible. On 31 October 1930 639,274 employees in Belgium had joined an unemployment fund. KIEHEL C.A., *Unemployment Insurance. A Development of the Ghent and Liège Systems*, New York, 1932, p. 148.

[14] VELGE H., *Le mouvement social en 1930*, in: "Bulletin de l'Institut des Sciences Economiques", vol. 2, 1931, p. 126.

was linked to the index of the total pay of manual and white-collar workers employed in the private sector in Belgium (Table 44, columns 3 and 4).

Finally the value of the coal supplied free to retired miners or to their widows and orphans was included in this subheading (column 5). The data calculated by Schroeven as part of the reconstruction of national expenditure are mainly based on the annual reports of the NPM[15].

3. Undeclared income of manual and white-collar workers

In principle, the total wage mass of workers, includes all pay of whatever kind. A statutory exception is the pay of employees working for an employer who had not had at least one workman in his employment for at least two months per year[16]. This provision included, for example, manual workers who occasionally (often after their normal day's work) did odd jobs. It is more than likely that some pay of employees who were subject to the industrial accident legislation was also undeclared. Evasion of social security legislation most probably also occurred in the inter-war period, despite the surveillance measures built into the law[17].

There is no indication at all of the amount of the above pay, so that any estimate is bound to be arbitrary in nature. Because this income mostly relates to irregular and occasional work it does however seem plausible to assume that the amount of this pay was greatly influenced by the economic climate. It was assumed that the pay equivalent to 3 hours per week was not declared.

This means 150 working hours per year or 6.25 % of the previously reconstructed total wages of manual and white-collar workers employed in the private sector in Belgium. It was also assumed that moonlighting by the unemployed amounted up to one third of the average wage of a manual worker in the private sector (see Table 45).

4. Occupational costs borne by employees

Regarding the size of this item, which must be deducted from pay, no indications are available. As already mentioned, in the absence of data the NIS simply estimates the occupational costs for clothing[18]. In 1948-1953, these totalled on

---

15   SCHROEVEN C., *Consumer Expenditure in Interwar Belgium*, Chapter 6.
16   See Chapter 1.
17   Idem.
18   The NIS estimate is based on a survey conducted in the Brussels Tram Company. *De nationale rekeningen van België 1953-1962*, pp. 1147-1148.

average 0.6% of the pay of manual and white collar workers subject to the RMZ[19]. Because of lack of data, the same percentage was retained for the inter-war period (see Table 43, column 4).

---

[19] Own calculation on the basis of *Het Belgisch nationaal inkomen van 1948 tot 1954*, pp. 13 and 16.

CHAPTER 7

INCOME FROM ENTREPRENEURSHIP IN AGRICULTURE, HORTICULTURE AND FORESTRY

Section 1. Content of the chapter and principal source

Paragraph 1. Definition of the concept of income from entrepreneurship in the agricultural sector

This chapter deals with the income from entrepreneurship of farmers and market gardeners, and with self-employed income deriving from the exploitation of privately-owned woods.

Income from entrepreneurship is defined here as the difference between the value of gross output on the one hand, and the operating expenses or inputs necessary to achieve this output on the other hand[1].

Because farmers and market gardeners, unlike traders and craftsmen, are taxed at a fixed rate, there is no point in estimating income from entrepreneurship in the agricultural sector on the basis of tax statistics. For this reason the calculation method also used by the NIS, namely the reconstruction of income by deducting estimated inputs from the estimated gross output, was used[2].

In order to determine gross output in agriculture and horticulture it is necessary first of all to calculate total physical output. Gross output is then obtained by subtracting internal intermediate production from total physical output. The latter consists of intermediate products, such as for example sowing-seed and feed grain, in so far as these are produced and used within the agricultural and horticultural sectors, either within the same company or through sale to another agricultural company.

Gross output includes all end-products, both those sold on the market and those consumed by the operator's family (home consumption). In addition gross output in the agricultural sector also includes the intermediate products supplied to other sectors, such as the food or textile industry. Finally it should be noted that the production of non-professional farmers and market gardeners (i.e. the yield of privately-owned vegetable gardens, pigs, poultry, rabbits, etc.) is also included.

---

[1] For a general definition of the concept of "income from entrepreneurship" see Chapter 8, Section 1.
[2] *Het Belgisch nationaal inkomen van 1948 tot 1954*, pp. 600-604 ; *De nationale rekeningen van België 1953-1962*, pp. 1148-1151.

121

Gross output can be calculated in two ways: either from the supply side or from the demand side. In the supply side approach production data are used, while in reconstructing from the demand side output is estimated on the basis of domestic expenditure, with the addition of exports and subtraction of imports. Depending on the availability and the quality of sources, one of these two methods was chosen for each subheading.

In order to find the value of output, gross output must be multiplied by unit prices. Since the ultimate aim is to calculate farmers' income, it is necessary to use *farm-gate prices*, and not market prices, since the margin between these two prices benefits the trader, not the farmer.

The results presented here relating to agriculture and horticulture are the work of Jan Blomme[3]. Since his method of reconstruction is given in detail in a separate publication in this series, the exposition here is limited to a brief summary of his study. The chapter concentrates particularly on the mutual interrelationship of the various aggregates. The principal source material used by Blomme will also be given in all cases. For detailed calculations and information on the sources used the reader is advised to use Blomme's work.

In Table 46 the final results of Blomme's research are given. The various inputs can be found in Table 47 at the end of the third section.

This chapter is organized as follows. After this first introductory section, the gross value of agricultural and horticultural production is calculated in the second section. Then in the third section the inputs in these sectors are dealt with, together with the difference between output and input, i.e. income from entrepreneurship in agriculture and horticulture. Finally in the fourth section income from entrepreneurship from woods exploited privately is estimated. Before beginning a brief discussion of the various subheadings a summary is given of the principal sources used by Blomme.

Paragraph 2. Summary of the principal sources

The principal source material is made up of the general agricultural censuses of 1910, 1929 and 1950. These give a detailed overview of the acreage of the various crops and of quantities of livestock. The agricultural censuses also contain a great deal of interesting information relating to the input of labour, machinery, animal feedstuffs, fertilizers, etc.

In addition to these general censuses, in some years specific censuses were organized by the government, such as for example the agricultural labourers' census conducted as part of the ESC of 1937. Information on employment in agriculture was also derived from the national censuses of 1920 and 1930.

---

[3] BLOMME J., *The Economic Development of Belgian Agriculture, 1880-1980. A Quantitative and Qualitative Analysis*, in: "Studies in Quantitative Economic History", vol. 3, Brussels ; Louvain, 1992.

Another frequently used source is the annual estimates of the government agronomists which appeared in the Statistical Yearbook, in which the acreage and yield of the various crops are given, together with the volume of livestock. It should however be borne in mind that these are estimates, so that the same accuracy cannot be expected from this source as from the censuses.

On more than one occasion, particularly in relation to inputs, the standard work by Bublot on Belgian agriculture between 1846 and 1955 was used[4].

A great deal of information on the most diverse aspects of the agricultural industry can also be derived from the particularly rich archives of the *Belgian Farmers' Federation* (Boerenbond), an influential professional association of farmers and market gardeners.

Where production was estimated on the basis of expenditure, use was made mainly of the budget surveys of 1921 and 1928-1929 and of a number of studies dealing with the problems of food stocks on the eve of the Second World War[5]. Import and export data derive from the statistics on foreign trade.

Agricultural price information was collected by the government from an early date and is consequently available in abundance. Monthly price lists for the most important arable produce, and for butter and eggs, can be found in the *Belgian State Gazette* (Belgisch Staatsblad), while annual livestock prices are published in the Statistical Yearbook.

SECTION 2. GROSS VALUE OF AGRICULTURAL AND HORTICULTURAL PRODUCTION

In calculating the gross output value, a distinction is made between livestock farming, arable farming and market gardening. In the case of livestock farming and horticulture, the figures relate to production per calender year. In the case of arable farming, because of the nature of the available statistics (e.g. lack of data on stock at 31 December) it is only possible to use harvest years.

---

4 BUBLOT G., *La production agricole belge. Etude économique séculaire 1846-1955*, Louvain, 1957.
5 *Une enquête sur la nature et le coût de l'alimentation*, in: "Revue du Travail", vol. 31, 1922, passim; JULIN A., *Résultats principaux d'une enquête sur les budgets d'ouvriers et d'employés en Belgique,* in: "Bulletin de l'Institut International de Statistique", 1934; *Comité National de l'Alimentation (C.N.A.). Deuxième rapport: le régime alimentaire actuel de la population belge, ses caractéristiques et l'influence qu'auraient sur lui les mesures envisagées pout lutter contre les restrictions des importations en temps de guerre*, in: "Bulletin de la Santé Publique", vol. 4, 1939; DE LEENER G., *L'approvisionnement en produits alimentaires de la Belgique*, in: "Bulletin d'Information et de Documentation", vol. 14, 1939; ROGER C., *La politique d'alimentation en Belgique. Volume II: La consommation des denrées alimentaires en Belgique avant la guerre actuelle,* Brussels, 1942. For a critical discussion and incorporation of the budget surveys, see SCHROEVEN C., *Private Consumer Expenditure*, Chapter 2.

Paragraph 1. Livestock production

The principal sources relating to livestock production are the agricultural census of 1929, the annual estimates by the government agronomists in the Statistical Yearbook, and the official slaughtering statistics.

This source material was subjected to a twofold test. In a first, internal test the internal consistency of the various statistics was monitored. In a second external test the previously revised census declarations were compared with an external database, and subsequently adjusted. The method used is based on the compilation of annual animal feedstuff balances. In such a balance the total supply of animal feedstuffs is compared with the requirement of total livestock recorded in the official statistics. The difference becomes a criterion for assessing the underestimate of livestock in the censuses.

In what follows a short description is presented of the principal elements of livestock farming output, mainly the production of meat, dairy products, eggs, wool and changes in the quantity of livestock. Following this, the way in which prices were calculated is explained.

1. Meat production

Figures relating to meat production for most animals were derived from the slaughtering statistics. In this source only the dead weight of the slaughtered animals is given. Since the ultimate aim is to estimate agricultural income, and since farmers usually sell their livestock while still alive, it is the prices of live animals which are important here. For this reason the quantities given were converted with the help of officials coefficients for the ratio of live to dead weight for each animal. In order to take account of clandestine slaughtering, calf production was raised by 5%. Since domestic meat production must be estimated, the total weight of imported livestock was deducted from the official slaughtering figures. The weight of exported livestock was added to the Belgian slaughtering figures. In view of the large number unregistered slaughterings, pork production was not derived from the slaughtering statistics but from the results of the animal feedstuff balances compiled by Blomme. Poultry and rabbit meat production was calculated on the basis of egg and rabbit consumption in the budget surveys.

2. Dairy production

In order to estimate dairy production total milk production was first calculated. The next step was to establish, on the basis of the agronomic literature, the fluctuating proportions of milk intended for human consumption (i.e. end production), for animal feed (i.e. intermediate production within the agricultural sector), for butter production on the farm (i.e. intermediate production within the agricultural sector), and for butter and cheese production in dairies and cheese-making plants (i.e. intermediate production for the food industry). It was also possible to derive conversion coefficients from this literature, which indicate how much milk is required for the production of a particular quantity of butter.

In accordance with the methodology set out at the beginning of this chapter, only milk production was included which was intended for human consumption and for butter and cheese production in dairies and cheese-making plants. Since the butter produced on farms constitutes an integral part of agricultural production the amount of farm butter produced, but not the amount of milk required, was taken into account. The by-products of butter production on the farm - skimmed milk and buttermilk - were included. No account was taken of milk used as animal feed, because this leaves the farm in another form with the value of this milk contained in the value of the livestock.

3. Egg production

Since the numbers of poultry declared in the agricultural census of 1929 are an obvious underestimate, egg production was estimated from the demand side. In the budget surveys egg consumption is expressed in kilograms, and it was therefore necessary to divide the consumption given by the average weight of an egg. The number of eggs obtained in this way was finally multiplied by the export-import balance.

4. Wool production

Wool production was set at 3 kilograms per sheep per annum, excluding lambs.

5. Changes in the numbers of livestock

Fluctuations in livestock numbers form an integral part of agricultural output. The increase in the numbers of livestock is the equivalent of a part of production, while a drop in numbers represents an advance levy on the future production of agricultural businesses. The growth in the numbers of livestock can also be regarded as the production of capital goods which instead of being sold on the market are sold by the farmer to himself. A reduction in the numbers of livestock should in that case be interpreted as the loss of part of the farmer's capital stock. The changes which take place in the numbers of livestock are calculated by the difference between the situation on 31 December in two successive years.

6. Livestock prices

Annual livestock prices (price per kilogram live weight) for all large market towns are published for each type of animal in the Statistical Yearbook. In the first instance provincial prices were calculated for each category of livestock by taking the mathematical average of the prices for all market towns in the relevant province. The national price for each type of animal was then obtained through a weighted average of the provincial price data, with the weighting factors being each province's share in total Belgian numbers of the animal in question during the agricultural census of 1929.

Because production and prices of butter and eggs showed large seasonal variations due to the annual production cycle, a chronological weighting of the provincial prices for these products, published monthly in the State Gazette was first carried out. Next a geographical weighting of the provincial data was carried out, with the weighting factors being the number of cattle or laying-hens in the agricultural census of 1929. The results obtained were finally reduced by 5%, because the prices of butter and eggs in the Belgium State Gazette are market prices, whereas in estimating farmers' income farm-gate prices are required.

Paragraph 2. Arable crop production

As already explained in the first section, the gross output can be reconstructed from both the demand and the supply side. Depending on the availability and the quality of data a decision was taken in the case of each crop to use one of these two approaches.

With the supply side approach the required data are first and foremost the acreages and yields of the various crops. The total agricultural acreage was obtained from the agricultural censuses, to which a number of corrections had however to be made. The amendments made are very much inspired by the method developed by Gadisseur in relation to agricultural censuses before the First World War[6]. Yields are mainly based on the annual estimates of government agronomists in the Statistical Yearbook, and also on information from the archives of the Belgian Farmers' Federation. Intermediate supplies within the agricultural sector, such as for example oats for farmers' horses, or a portion of the harvest used for planting or seeding, were deducted from total physical production.

In reconstructing the gross output from the demand side in the case of end-products (e.g. grain used for bread-making), budget data provided the starting point. For intermediate production intended for the non-agricultural sector (e.g. grain for the beer-brewing or gin-distilling industry) use could in some cases be

---

[6] GADISSEUR J., *Le produit physique de l'économie belge, 1831-1913. Présentation critique des données statistiques* (Ph.D Dissertation, Economics Department, State University of Liège, 1979-1980, 9 vol.).

made of tax statistics. The export-import balance was then added to Belgium's end and intermediate demand from the non-agricultural sector to arrive at national gross output.

Working on the assumption that the bulk of crops were sold a relatively short time after harvesting, only the average price of the last four months of the calender year was taken into account. The Belgian State Gazette publishes monthly market prices for each crop and for each province. A national price was obtained by weighting the provincial prices geographically on the basis of the acreage of each crop in the agricultural censuses. Finally these market prices, in accordance with NIS procedure, were reduced by 5% in order to arrive at farm-gate prices.

Paragraph 3. Horticultural production

Estimating horticultural output is no easy task. Not only does this sector contain an enormous diversity of crops (vegetables, fruit, flowers, tree seedlings), but there is the additional problem that a considerable amount is produced by non-professional gardeners, especially in vegetable growing.

Acreage was calculated for each crop on the basis of the agricultural censuses. In this way the total acreage under cultivation was obtained for each of the following groups of crops: vegetables grown in the open, vegetables under glass, flowers grown in the open, flowers under glass, fruit grown in the open, fruit under glass, mixed crops (e.g. vegetables and fruit) under glass, and tree nurseries. In the case of vegetables grown in the open the acreage was moreover divided into professional and recreational horticulture.

For the period 1933-1939 precise lists were found in the archives of the Belgian Farmers' Federation for each crop with regard to the output of professional market gardeners. These sources indicate that the yield of domestic vegetable growing in vegetable gardens can be put at half that of professional market gardeners.

Since there are no systematic price lists relating to horticultural produce sold on the Belgium market, one must of necessity do with import and export prices.

These prices, together with acreage in the census years, are the only data which give an idea of the output value in the period 1920-1932. No quantitative data are available on yields. Since quantitative indications suggest that average yields in horticulture are fairly stable and since the great variety of produce means there is a good chance that a possible failed harvest in a particular crop is compensated for by surplus yield in another crop, it was assumed that the various yields were the same in the period 1920-1932 as the average yields for 1933-1935.

By multiplying together acreage, yield and price, one obtains the figure for horticultural output.

SECTION 3. INPUTS AND INCOME FROM ENTREPRENEURSHIP IN AGRICULTURE AND HORTICULTURE

Inputs include all expenditure incurred by farmers and market gardeners necessary to achieve the gross output. These inputs consist of rents, the wages of agricultural labourers, fertilizers, animal feedstuffs, planting stock and seed, interest on borrowed operating capital, depreciation, general overheads, and finally indirect taxes minus any subsidies.

The difference between gross output and inputs equals the self-employed income of farmers and market gardeners. This self-employed income is complex in nature (cfr. Chapter 8). It contains a (fictional) wage for the farmer and any members of his family giving assistance, a (fictional) interest payment on operating capital, and where appropriate a (fictional) profit. In fact, income from entrepreneurship consists of a reward for entrepreneurial labour, entrepreneurial management and entrepreneurial risk, and also a return on operating capital. It is impossible, and pointless, to divide income from entrepreneurship into these fictional component parts.

In this section the method of reconstructing the various inputs will be briefly discussed. For the general results of the calculations and for the income from entrepreneurship the reader is referred to the summary Table 46 at the beginning of this chapter. The course of the various inputs may be found in Table 47 at the end of this section.

1. Rents

In order not to confuse income deriving from ownership of land and agricultural buildings with income from agricultural activity proper, the amount of rent is calculated in the system of national accounts on the assumption that all land and agricultural buildings are rented by the farmer concerned. If the latter is in fact the owner of the land and agricultural buildings, then a fictional rent is included as an input. This fictitious rent subsequently reverts as capital income to the farmer and as such is included under Chapter 10, "Rents (receieved or imputed) payable to private individuals).

The rents included here as an input relate to the lease (actually paid or imputed), and to the (actually paid or imputed) rent of agricultural buildings. The rent of the actual residence of the family of the farmer or market gardener does not of course form part of production costs, and consequently is not included here as an input.

Leases were divided into agricultural and horticultural leases. Agricultural leases were in turn subdivided into grazing land, arable land and so called general-purpose land. This last category includes mainly land in the immediate vicinity of the farmhouse, which is mostly let at a lower price together with the agricultural buildings. Working on a rough postwar estimate made by the NIS, it was assumed that 15% of agricultural acreage consisted of general purpose land.

Information on the share in the total acreage of grazing land, arable land, and horticultural land was found in the agricultural censuses and in the estimates of government agronomists. Data on the levels of rents derive from a detailed study in the journal of the NBB, surveys conducted by the Belgian Farmers' Federation, and Bublot's rent index.

The (imputed) expenditure on the rent of agricultural buildings is based on an estimate relating to 1929. For that year the total area occupied by agricultural buildings was multiplied by the average rateable value per m^2. The amount of rent paid for agricultural buildings determined in this way totalled 10.7% of all rent. It was assumed that this ratio remained the same for the whole inter-war period. The total area of agricultural buildings was then estimated on a yearly basis through interpolation and extrapolation of data in the agricultural censuses of 1929 and NIS figures relating to 1950. Multiplication of land rent by 0.107 gives the (imputed) rent for agricultural buildings.

2. Wages of agricultural labourers

The simplest way of calculating the total wages of those employed in agricultural work is to multiply the number of workers by an average annual pay figure. This requires data on the number of agricultural labourers, the average daily wages and the average number of hours worked per year. This information is available for numbers and for daily wages, but not for the average number of hours worked. Given the heterogenous nature of paid employment in agriculture this poses serious problems, since some workers were permanently employed in this sector, and others only in the high season. It was therefore necessary to find some way of expressing the volume of paid agriculture labour in terms of full-time labour units.

The first step was to estimate the number of days' labour required annually to achieve the output for one hectare. In the case of livestock farming it was established how many man-hours were required to care for each type of animal. These estimates, combined with data on the level of livestock numbers and the acreage occupied by each crop, made it possible to calculate the total annual number of man-days worked in agriculture and horticulture. In converting man-days into full-time a working year of 300 working days was assumed.

The second step was to split this total labour input into self-employed labour (farmers/market gardeners and family members assisting) and paid labour (agricultural labourers). In the case of paid labour a further distinction was made between adult male labour, adult female labour and child labour (below the age of 18).

The third step was to obtain the total wages of agricultural labourers by multiplying the number of labour units in each category (men, women and children) by 300 day-wages and totalling the results obtained for each category.

Data relating to labour input per crop and per type of animal were mainly derived from the archives of the Belgian Farmers' Federation. The division of labour input was made on the basis of the agricultural census of 1929, the national censuses of 1920 and 1930 and the ESC of 1937. Daily wages were calculated on the basis of information from the Ministry of Agriculture, the Belgian Farmers' Federation and Bublot.

3. Fertilizers

Only fertilizers purchased outside the agricultural and horticultural sectors are included here as an input. These are mainly nitrate, phosphate and potash fertilizers, together with soil-enrichment agents such as lime. Of course it is also possible for a farmer to buy fertilizers from another farmer or market gardener. For the individual farmer this purchase naturally represents an input, but for the object of this study, the agricultural and horticultural sectors as a whole, this is a zero transaction, since one farmer's expenditure constitutes income for the other[7].

Since the data on the consumption of fertilizers in the agricultural census of 1929 are unreliable, this input was as far as possible reconstructed from the supply side. As regards quantities the main source was the *Annuaire International de Statistique Agricole* and the statistics on foreign trade. Price data were found in the archives of the Belgian Farmers' Federation (for 1932) and in Bublot (price index)[8].

4. Animal feedstuffs

This heading includes imported feedstuffs and residue purchased from some branches of the domestic food industry such as pulp and molasses from the sugar factories and lees from breweries. The value of the by-products of butter production which were returned free of charge by dairies to farmers were included. These are the skimmed milk and buttermilk which were used by the farmers as animal feed. The imputed value of these derivatives is included here because most dairies offered farmers a lower milk price than the open market, but in exchange for this the by-products of the butter production were returned to the latter free of charge. Since in estimating the value of dairy production no account was taken of the lower milk price for supplies to dairies, but the normal market price (minus a distribution margin of 5%) was included, it is logical that the full value should be included for the return of skimmed milk and buttermilk.

---

[7] The same observation is true of feedstuffs, planting stock and seeds.
[8] BUBLOT G., *o.c.*, pp. 390-392.

The quantities of animal feedstuffs imported or purchased outside the agricultural sector were estimated on the basis of the animal feedstuff balances constructed by Blomme. The prices of the various feedstuffs for 1932 derive from the archives of the Belgian Farmers' Federation, and for the other years from Bublot's animal feed-price index. In the case of compound feedstuffs, in order to avoid duplications only the value added resulting from the combination and sale of these products was included. It was assumed that this amounted to 20% of the price of simple feedstuffs.

5. Planting stock and seed

Here, as in the case of fertilizers and animal feedstuffs, only purchases outside the agricultural and horticultural sectors must be included. These purchases are mainly of foreign origin. Because of the small volume of purchases of Belgian seed and planting stock, and in the absence of the necessary data concerning these, only foreign supplies were included.

Since planting stock and seed cannot be isolated in the import statistics, as they form part of larger headings, this source was not used here. The figures included have therefore been reconstructed on the basis of archive material from the Belgian Farmers' Federation (prices and quantities in 1928), an index of the acreage under cultivation (quantities in the other years) and Bublot's price index (prices in the other years).

6. Interest on borrowed operating capital

As has already been explained, income from entrepreneurship in agriculture and horticulture consists in part of a return on the farmers or market gardeners own operating capital, as for example the livestock, agricultural machinery, tools, material and equipment. If this operating capital has been financed with borrowed money, a debt rests on this capital. The interest on this debt must be paid, is an operating cost and must therefore be included. Since income from property (land and buildings) does not form part of income from entrepreneurship but is included in income from capital, the interest on mortgage loans must not be included here as an input.

The outstanding agricultural debt for the period 1920-1930 was estimated on the basis of loans granted by the ASLK and the Raiffeisen Funds of the Belgian Farmers' Federation. The outstanding agricultural loans (excluding mortgage debts) were increased by a factor of 2.5 to take account of credit granted by banks, solicitors, private individuals and firms selling agricultural material, etc. In order to estimate the annual interest due the amount obtained in this way was multiplied by the mortgage interest rate.

As a result of the financial difficulties with which the saving funds of the Belgian Farmers' Federation had to contend during the agricultural depression of the 1930s, it was impossible to use the above method for the depression years. Therefore it is assumed that from 1931 onwards operating capital borrowed formed a constant proportion of total operating capital (12%, by analogy with the period 1928-1930). By multiplying the estimated operating capital by this fixed percentage and also by the mortgage interest rate, one obtains the interest charges on borrowed operating capital which are to be included.

7. Depreciation

The depreciation included as an input relates only to operating capital. This depreciation must be included because income from entrepreneurship consists partly of a return on the self-employed person's own operating capital. The return from property on the other hand, as has already been said, does not form part of this income from entrepreneurship but belongs with income from property. Depreciation on agricultural buildings therefore constitutes a charge on the owner and not on the business. What is included as an input as regards land and buildings are the rents (actually paid or imputed if the farmer is also the owner of the property). These rents have been previously dealt with. To summarize, one can say that as far as operating capital is concerned, depreciation and interest on borrowed capital are included as an input. As far as property is concerned, the rents are included as an overhead.

Of course account is only taken here of those elements in operating capital which are subject to depreciation, namely machinery and material. Other forms of moveable asset such as livestock and liquid funds are therefore left out of account.

Estimates concerning the amount of capital plant and other material were made on the basis of data deriving from Bublot and of the Ministry of Agriculture. The figures obtained were then written off linearly at the rate of 5% per annum.

8. General overheads

This heading forms a heterogenous category of purchases outside the agricultural and horticultural sectors not included elsewhere as a separate item. For example expenditure on energy, repair and maintenance of machinery, insurance, pesticides and vet's fees are classified under general overheads. Expenditure under this heading was obtained on the basis of a number of business accounting studies at the end of the 1930s.

9. Indirect taxation

Only indirect taxes (e.g. transfer duties) must be included as an input, because direct taxes (i.e. taxes on income) form an integral part of income from entrepreneurship in the system of national accounts. The indirect taxes were estimated in the same way as the general overheads, namely on the basis of a number of business accounts.

10. Subsidies

Since subsidies reduce costs for the operator, they are accounted for here as a negative input. In the period under review subsidies were granted only in 1933-1935 and in 1938[9].

SECTION 4. SELF-EMPLOYED INCOME FROM WOODS NOT CONTROLLED BY THE FORESTRY COMMISSION

This section deals with income from entrepreneurship issuing from the exploitation of woods in private ownership. This income mainly concerns forestry. The income deriving from the ownership of these woods, namely the (imputed) rents, are not included here, because they form part of income from capital[10].

The method of reconstruction for this item is given in detail in Table 48, so that only the most important elements of the estimates are discussed here. No information is available on the income from private woods. Only for 1921, 1925, 1930 and 1935 did data appear on the income from and the acreage of woods in government ownership. The total area of forestation (government plus private) is also known for the agricultural census years. On the basis of these data the acreage of forests in private ownership was estimated. In addition it was assumed that the income per hectare for forests in private ownership is the same as that of woods belonging to the government. This income contains earnings from entrepreneurship and a property component. It was assumed that the respective proportions were 2/3 and 1/3 because the NIS arrives at a similar average proportion for the period 1948-1954[11].

---

9   BAUDHUIN F., *Economie agraire,* Louvain, 1945, p. 29.
10 See Chapter 8.
11 In 1948-1954 self-employed income averaged 65.7% of total income from private woods (NIS, *Commissie van het Nationaal Inkomen,* 1955, p. 138).

CHAPTER 8

ENTREPRENEURIAL INCOME OF THE PROFESSIONS, INDEPENDENT TRADERS, CRAFTSMEN AND PARTNERSHIPS

SECTION 1. DEFINITION OF THE HEADING

In this chapter an estimate is made of the income of all self-employed workers and partnerships, excluding entrepreneurial income from agriculture, horticulture and forestry, which was dealt with in the previous chapter. A distinction is made between independent traders and craftsmen (Section 3), the professions (Section 4) and partnerships (Section 5). For the sake of brevity, the designation independent traders and craftsmen is used here for all self-employed workers not engaged in agriculture, horticulture or forestry, and not classifiable as exercising one of the professions. This includes a very heterogenous group of persons, whose income and social status may vary widely. For example, both the small self-employed craftsman and the large industrial proprietor belong in this category[1]. The professions include lawyers, solicitors, physicians, dentists, pharmacists, authors, painters, sculptors, architects, engineers, etc., where the latter practise independently. The term "partnerships" refers to companies which have adopted one of the legal forms provided for in the commercial legislation, with the exception of joint-stock companies[2]. Income from *de facto* partnerships (i.e. partnerships not having a legal form provided for in the commercial legislation), made up of family members or other participants who run a business jointly without a formal partnership contract, forms part of the income of independent traders and craftsmen[3].

Entrepreneurial income includes all income of self-employed persons or partnerships issuing from the economic activity of the enterprise they own. Entrepreneurial income consists of two components, which are difficult to separate from each other: on the one hand remuneration for the labour of the

---

[1] In what follows the category "Independent traders and industrial entrepreneurs" is sometimes used, for example, in taxation statistics. The term "Industrial entrepreneurs" refers in this case to both self-employed persons working alone and to employers.
[2] Partnerships here means partnerships with limited liability (by far the largest group), partnerships forming a single company, simple limited partnerships and cooperative partnerships. *Het Belgisch nationaal inkomen van 1948 tot 1954*, p. 607; *De nationale rekeningen van België 1953-1962*, pp. 1152-53.
[3] *Het Belgisch nationaal inkomen van 1948-1954*, p. 600; *De nationale rekeningen van België 1953-1962*, p. 1152.

entrepreneur and unsalaried members of his family, and on the other return on the capital which the entrepreneur has invested in his enterprise.[4] This capital consists both of company assets financed by the proprietor in setting up his enterprise, and of the funds which have accumulated over the years as a result of the reinvestment of part of the operating surplus in the enterprise (self-financing)[5].

The entrepreneurial income included in the national accounts consists of the difference between the gross trading receipts (i.e. the value of all goods or services sold by the self-employed) and operating costs. These operating costs consist of the wages and salaries of staff, interest on borrowed capital, hire of company premises, depreciation, the purchasing of raw materials and intermediary products, etc.

The following are excluded from entrepreneurial income: the imputed income arising from the ownership of company premises or land, and income from financial assets[6]. This means that if the entrepreneurial activity of a self-employed person or partnership takes place in a building or on land owned by the entrepreneur, a rent or leasehold value is imputed corresponding to the amount the entrepreneur person would have to pay if renting the property. The imputed amount is then treated as an operating cost and deducted from the operating result[7]. In this way the level of entrepreneurial income is not affected by whether or not the proprietor owns the business premises or land. The amount of the imputed rent forms part of Chapter 10, "Rent (Received or Imputed) Payable to Private Individuals"[8]. Income from financial assets, depending on the nature of the assets, is included in Chapter 9, "Interest Payments to the Personal Sector" or Chapter 11, "Dividends, Returns on investments abroad, Bonuses and Grants Accruing to Private Individuals".

---

[4] OECD, *A Standardized System of National Accounts,* Paris, 1958, p. 81.

[5] For this reason there is no separate heading in the breakdown of national income for the reserves set aside by the self-employed, the professions and partnerships. (*Het Belgisch nationaal inkomen van 1948 tot 1954,* p. 600; *De nationale rekeningen van België 1953-1962,* p. 1148). There is, however, a separate category for the reserved profits of joint-stock companies (see Chapter 12).

[6] *Het Belgisch nationaal inkomen van 1948 tot 1954,* p. 600; *De nationale rekeningen van België 1953-1962,* p. 1148.

[7] NIS, *Commissie van het nationaal inkomen,* 1955, p. 139.

[8] NIS, *Het Belgisch nationaal inkomen van 1948 tot 1954,* pp. 277-278. In this respect the NIS's methodology differs from that of the OECD, which states that only *the income from the ownership of land and buildings not employed in the operation of the enterprise are excluded (OECD, o.c.,* p. 81) In his estimates of the national income of Great Britain, Feinstein draws a distinction with regard to the imputed rent of the self-employed and partnerships between agriculture and other entrepreneurial activities: *income from the ownership of farmland and buildings (including the rental income imputed to owner-occupiers of farms) is treated as part of rent and not as income from farming. For other non-corporate enterprises, as for all companies, the imputed income of businesses owning the land and buildings which they occupy is included in trading profits and not under the heading rent* (FEINSTEIN, C.H., *National Income, expenditure and output of the United Kingdom 1855-1965,* in: "Studies in the National Income and Expenditure of the United Kingdom" 6, Cambridge, 1972, p. 38).

Like income from paid employment, entrepreneurial income appears in the national accounts inclusive of direct taxation[9].

As in the NIS's present national accounts, entrepreneurial income for the inter-war period has been calculated on the basis of the statistics relating to income tax, and more specifically trade tax. However, data on the income of partnerships have been available only since 1951, so that for this category a rough estimate only could be made on the basis of postwar coefficients.

Before the method of reconstruction is discussed, a brief survey will be given in the next section of the origin and development of the income tax system in Belgium, and of the fiscal statistics relating to trade tax.

SECTION 2. THE SYSTEM OF INCOME TAX AND THE FISCAL STATISTICS RELATING TO TRADE TAX

In the first paragraph a brief general summary will be given of the principal taxes on income in Belgium in the inter-war period. Next the statistics relating to trade tax will be discussed. Finally the number of independent traders and craftsmen in the fiscal statistics will be compared with their number in the censuses.

Paragraph 1. Income taxes in Belgium during the inter-war period[10]

After the First World War the Belgian tax system was radically changed. The principal innovation was the introduction of a coherent system of income tax (Act of 29 October 1919, supplemented by the Act of 30 August 1920). The former system of direct taxation still dated largely from the period of French occupation at the turn of the nineteenth century and was based more on outward signs of income and wealth (for example, the number of doors and windows) than on actual income. The new system was introduced to accommodate the government's growing financial needs resulting from the First World War, as well as from considerations of justice. The fact was that before the war state income was

---

9 OECD, *o.c.*, p. 81; *De nationale rekeningen van België 1953-1962*, p. 1148.
10 This paragraph is based on DE VISSCHERE F.E., *Het Belgische belastingswezen en zijn grondbeginselen. Een studie over zijn wording en ontwikkeling sedert 1830*, in: "Economisch-sociale bibliotheek. Monografieën", VAN GOETHEM F. and SAP G. (eds), vol. IX, Brussels ; Antwerp ; Louvain ; Ghent, 1935, pp. 109-189, 266-280; LOECKX F., *L'Evolution de l'impôt sur les revenus en Belgique*, in: "Revue Economique Internationale", 1937, passim; PUTMAN, R., *Les impôts directs en Belgique de 1914 à 1940*, in : "Histoires des finances publiques en Belgique", Brussels ; Paris, Institut Belge de Finances Publiques (ed.), vol. I, 1950, pp. 357-541; VANDENDRIESSCHE S., *Evolutie van de Belgische centrale-overheidsuitgaven sinds 1919. Onderzoek naar de determinerende factoren*, in: "Ministerie van Financiën, Documentatieblad", 1977, pp. 80-85, 157-159, 191-194, 222-224.

dominated by indirect taxation, which of course falls more heavily on the lower-income groups (i.e. a regressive tax system)[11].

The main characteristics of the new system of income tax remained largely unaltered during the inter-war period and even after the Second World War[12]. A split tax was levied separately on each category of income: income from business activity (wages, profits) were subject to trade tax[13]; property tax was payable on movable capital assets (deposits, bonds, dividends, etc.); owners were required to pay property or land tax on income from real estate. In addition an extra tax was levied on the total income (the so-called supertax). The trade tax was progressive, with a basic rate varying from 2% for the lowest to 10% for the highest income band.

Between 1920 and 1930 no fundamental changes were made to the direct taxation system. As a reaction to the increasing government deficits in the first half of the 1920s a number of new, relatively unimportant direct taxes were introduced (for example, the tax on betting and gaming imposed by the Act of 28 August 1921) and some existing rates were raised, exemptions reduced or modes of application adjusted. The Acts of 31 December 1925 and 8 June 1926 especially, which were part of the process of monetary reform, meant a significant increase in the tax burden (see Table 50, column 8). The increase in tax receipts is of course also connected with the generally favourable economic climate since the end of 1922, with inflation, and with the progressive nature of some taxes. This is because under a progressive tax system not only nominal but also real tax receipts increase in periods of economic growth and/or inflation, since taxpayers find themselves in higher income bands with a higher basic rate.

Because of the improved state of government finances and the particularly favourable economic climate at the end of the 1920s an Act was passed on 13 July 1930 which introduced a general easing of the tax burden. This reduction was mainly due to the replacement of the *supertax*, based on the declared overall income, by the supplementary personal tax, which was levied on the assumed income determined on the basis of certain indicators (rental value of residence, domestic staff, vehicles, etc.). This supplementary tax, which produced much less for the exchequer than the supertax, was therefore in some senses a return to the pre-war fiscal system (see Table 50, columns 4 and 5).

---

[11] In 1912 the state received BF 261,9 million in indirect taxation as against only BF 75,6 million in direct taxes (PIRARD J., *Le pouvoir central belge et ses comptes économiques 1830-1913*, p. 225).

[12] VAN DEN EYNDE F., *De statistiek inzake inkomstenbelastingen*, in: "Bulletin der Belastingen", vol. 380, 1961, p. 1917.

[13] Social transfers, such as family allowances, pensions paid as part of the statutory pension scheme, allowances for invalids, victims of industrial accidents, the unemployed etc., were not subject to trade tax *(Act of 31 July 1943 , art. 29 (4)*; BAUDHUIN F., *La Belgique en 1936. Les revenus,* in: "Bulletin de l'Institut de Recherches Economiques", vol. 8, 1937, pp. 123-124.

In fact, in the light of the sudden onset of the depression at the end of 1930 this can be seen as a particularly unfortunate measure[14], since the government soon found itself faced with increasing expenditure, for example on unemployment benefit, combined with a reduction in income. The drastic fall in direct taxation receipts (1929: BF 3,602 million, 1932: BF 2,339 million) was, however, not due solely to the adverse effect of the 1930 tax reform on the exchequer, but also to the decline in economic activity and to deflation, which in a system of progressive taxation obviously works to the benefit of the taxpayer. For this reason various measures were taken from 1931 onwards to maintain the level of tax receipts, but without achieving the desired result. Eventually the government was forced to take the exceptional step of levying (supposedly for the year 1933 only) the so-called *national crisis tax*, the fiscal basis of which was approximately the same as that of the split taxes (Act of December 1932 and Royal Decree of 13 January 1933)[15]. Although it was originally envisaged that the national crisis tax would be introduced for only one year, it was also levied in the following years. When the budgetary situation improved with the economic recovery of 1935-1937, the national crisis tax was abolished (Act of 19 June 1937). At the end of 1937, however, a new recession began with its accompanying treasury difficulties, causing the reintroduction of the national crisis tax (Act of 17 June 1938).

Because the additional personal taxation introduced in 1937 had been a failure in revenue terms, it was amended by the Royal Decree of 22 February 1935. Instead of a tax assessment based on certain indicators, there was a return to a tax based on the actual overall income, increasing both the number of taxpayers and the tax yield[16].

As regards entrepreneurial income in the inter-war period, a distinction must be made between the period 1919-1928 and the period 1929-1939. Before 1929 entrepreneurial income was divided into income from labour and income from capital that the proprietor had invested in his business. Trade tax was levied on the first component, while property tax was payable on the second constituent. The

---

[14] DECHESNE L., *La crise financière, conséquence de la réforme fiscale*, in: "Revue économique internationale", 1932, pp. 398-399.

[15] The principal income subject to split taxes, but not to the national crisis tax, was that from dividends.

[16] In 1930 the supplementary personal tax applied to only 27,654 taxpayers (VANDENDRIESSCHE S., *o.c.*, p. 194). In the tax year 1936, 273,439 people paid additional personal tax. Divided by job category this is: 94,760 industrial entrepreneurs and traders, 7,954 agricultural proprietors, 122,374 civil servants and white-collar workers, 15,791 manual workers, 4,531 managers and supervisory directors, 10,469 persons engaged in the professions, 17,560 persons with no business income (those with private incomes) (VAN DER AA E.R., *Studie over het opzetten eener statistiek in de mobiliënbelasting, de bedrijfsbelasting, de nationale crisisbelasting en in de aanvullende personeele belasting aangeslagen inkomsten en van het rendement dezer belastingen (Fiscaal dienstjaar 1945 - Inkomsten verworven in 1944)*, in: "Statistisch Bulletin", vol. 32, 1946, p. 838).

previously mentioned Act of 13 July 1930 put an end to this artificial division. From the tax year 1930 onwards (income acquired in 1929) the whole of entrepreneurial income was subject to trade tax.

Paragraph 2. The fiscal statistics relating to trade tax on natural persons

During the inter-war period the Ministry of Finance did not publish systematic statistics on income tax[17]. However, statistics were compiled for certain years for internal use. Regarding the tax burden on natural persons these statistics provide information by occupational category on the number of taxpayers, their taxable income and tax receipts.[18] Some of these statistics were partially published, mostly in response to a parliamentary question addressed to the Minister of Finance or through the agency of authors with good contacts with the tax authorities, such as Professors Baudhuin, Collin and Mahaim[19].

In one of the journals of the Ministry of Finance it becomes apparent that the tax authorities compiled statistics on the tax burden on natural persons for approximately half the inter-war years, namely for the tax years 1920, 1921, 1923 to 1931, 1933 and 1936.[20] These statistics relate to income earned in 1919, 1920, 1922-30, 1932 and 1935[21]. Sadly, these important sources have not been traced. According to the Ministry of Finance the original statistics are no longer in its possession. They may have disappeared, but it is also possible that they have been deposited in the Belgian National Archives[22]. However, no permission was given to consult the unclassified archives of the Ministry of Finance, and therefore the authors of this study were forced to resort to the fragmentary published information. This relates to incomes earned in 1920, 1922, 1924-1930, 1932 and 1935.

Although the importance of the statistics on trade tax cannot be emphasised too highly - for the reconstruction of certain occupational categories such as the self-employed, employers and those in the professions they are the only source - these inter-war tax documents must be treated with the necessary circumspection, as the additional work caused by the compiling of the statistics was invariably

---

[17] Only receipts for each type of tax were published annually (see Table 50).
[18] Taxable income corresponds with the net income, being the gross income minus operating costs (for example, payment of staff, rental value of the business premises,...).
[19] At the bottom of Table 51 the reader will find the references to the published statistics relating to the tax burden on natural persons. The statistics on corporation tax on company profits are discussed in Chapter 13, "Direct Taxation of Companies of all Legal Forms".
[20] VAN DEN EIJNDE F., *De statistiek inzake inkomstenbelastingen*, pp. 1918-1919.
[21] In what follows, dates always relate to the year in which the income was earned, not the year in which it was taxed.
[22] As long ago as 1961, the original statistics for the tax year 1925 were missing from the archives of the Ministry of Finance, probably as a result of the relocations of the tax authorities during the war (VAN DEN EIJNDE F., *o.c.*, p. 1919).

regarded as incidental by a generally overworked administration. A possible margin of error must therefore be allowed for[23]. Not until after the Second World War were detailed fiscal statistics systematically compiled in Belgium on taxable incomes assessed for trade tax. In contrast to the 1920s and 1930s the NIS has been responsible since the war for the compiling of statistics[24].

In the inter-war fiscal statistics relating to trade tax the active population is subdivided into six occupational categories: manual workers, white-collar workers and civil servants, managers and directors of companies, self-employed farmers, independent traders and industrial entrepreneurs, and the professions. For the first three occupational categories, all of which had a statute of remuneration, trade tax was deducted at source. The other groups, engaged in self-employed occupations, were taxed on the basis of their declared income[25]. Naturally opportunities for tax fraud were greater here than with those in paid employment. In the 1920 and 1922 statistics a group headed "other" is also included, without any description of the content of the group. In Table 51 a general summary is presented of the data found relating to independent traders and industrial entrepreneurs, the professions and the category "other". It is apparent that the scope of the information varies greatly from year to year. In the best case (1935) the number of taxpayers, the tax yield and the taxable income for six income groups are available.

Taxpayers with more than one occupation, so-called *multiple job holders*, were included only once in the fiscal statistics, namely in the category of their main occupation[26]. In that case the taxable income included income from the secondary occupation. What does this method imply for the estimates of self-employed income? Of course, if principal and secondary occupations were in the same professional tax category, for example a smith who also ran an ironmongery business (both occupations come under independent traders and industrial entrepreneurs), no problem arises. It is a different matter if the two or more different occupations belonged to different tax categories, for example a factory

---

[23] *De ontwikkeling van de inkomstenstructuur volgens de belastingstatistieken*, in: "Tijdschrift voor Documentatie en Voorlichting van de Nationale Bank van België", januari 1953, p. 18.

[24] The first set of statistics published by the NIS relates to incomes earned in 1945 (*Statistiek van de belastbare inkomens aangeslagen in de bedrijfsbelasting en in de aanvullende personele belasting (dienstjaar 1946 - inkomsten verworven in 1945)*, in: "Statistisch Bulletin", March 1950, pp. 584-598). Previously the NIS had already worked out statistics relating to the tax year 1945 (income from 1944). However, this was regarded as a trial run and not published (VAN DEN EIJNDE F., *o.c.*, p. 1922).

[25] Arable farmers were taxed at a fixed rate (mainly on the basis on the acreage under cultivation), which resulted in an underestimate of actual incomes (*Le rendement de la taxe professionelle de 1928 à 1935*, in: "Banque Nationale de Belgique. Bulletin d'Information et de Documentation", vol. 13, 1938, p. 15). For this reason entrepreneurial income in agriculture is estimated by a different method than through tax statistics (see Chapter 7).

[26] VAN DEN EIJNDE F., *o.c.*, p. 1928; *L'Evolution de la structure des revenus d'après les statistiques fiscales*, in: "Banque Nationale de Belgique. Bulletin d'Information et de Documentation", vol. 28, 1953, p. 22.

worker also managing a pub. Suppose that the person in question earned BF 10,000 as a factory worker and BF 5,000 as a landlord, then his total income is included among those of manual workers. As a result the income of manual labourers is overestimated by BF 5,000 and that of independent traders and industrial entrepreneurs underestimated by the same amount.

This study works on the premise that if someone performed both a salaried and a freelance job, the salaried job formed the main source of income[27]. It is therefore assumed that the salaried job was the main occupation, and that of running a business secondary. As a result, in fiscal statistics the full occupational income of the multiple job holder, namely the salary and self-employed income, forms part of the taxable income of salaried workers. This assumption implies that no income from paid employment is included in the taxable income of the category of independent traders and industrial entrepreneurs, so that the taxable income of the category of independent traders and industrial entrepreneurs can be regarded in its entirety as entrepreneurial income. A second important implication is that in the salaried tax categories (manual workers, civil servants and white-collar workers, and directors of companies), part of taxable income consists of entrepreneurial income, namely that of multiple job holders.

In estimating entrepreneurial income, one of course takes into account not only entrepreneurial income from principal occupations, but also that from secondary occupations. Since the taxable income of the category independent traders and industrial entrepreneurs does not include entrepreneurial income of multiple job holders with a salaried main occupation, a rough estimate of this income will be made at the end of the section[28]. This income will then be added to other entrepreneurial income, which is estimated on the basis of fiscal statistics, namely entrepreneurial income from a main occupation and that from a secondary occupation, if the main occupation is also a self-employed one in industry or trade.

In principle everyone resident in Belgium with an earned income - as an employee, as a self-employed person or as an employer - was subject to trade tax. That income might be acquired either in Belgium or abroad. Those persons resident abroad but engaged in a business in Belgium, were liable for tax[29]. Minimum amounts were laid down in tax legislation which were exempt from trade tax. In addition the level of the tax threshold was determined by the number of the taxpayer's dependents and the population of his place of residence[30]. More than half the working population earned less than the taxable minimum and hence was not required to pay any trade tax. However, those exempted were nevertheless

---

[27] This is also the opinion of Senator Van Coillie, reporter of the Senate Committee on Economic Affairs (*De Middenstandspost. Weekblad van den Landsbond van den Christelijken Middenstand van België*, vol. 13, no. 10 (6 March 1938), pp. 155-156).

[28] See below.

[29] *Act of 31 July 1943,* Sections 2 and 31.

[30] The tax threshold was higher in the large municipalities and towns because the legislators assumed a positive correlation between the degree of urbanization and life expectancy.

included in the fiscal statistics[31]. The term "taxpayer" in inter-war fiscal statistics therefore refers not to the number of persons who had actually paid trade tax but to the number of people with income liable to trade tax.

According to Van den Eynde the income which the tax authorities calculated for those exempted in compiling the statistics was the taxable minimum, even though they in fact earned less[32]. This implies that the total taxable income in the fiscal statistics is to some extent an overestimate. The Act of 13 July 1930 set the taxable minimum at BF 4,800 for municipalities with less than 5,000 inhabitants, BF 5,600 for municipalities with between 5,000 and 30,000 inhabitants, and BF 7,200 for municipalities with over 30,000 inhabitants. In addition the taxable minimum was increased by at least BF 960 for each dependent family member[33]. However, it is clear from the fiscal statistics for 1935 that for the category of independent traders and industrial entrepreneurs 131,218 of the 547,098 persons liable for tax had a taxable income of less than BF 5,000 (see Table 51). This would imply that all those 131,218 persons lived in municipalities with fewer than 5,000 inhabitants and had no dependents, which seems highly unlikely. For this reason, until there is evidence to the contrary, it will be assumed here that all those liable for tax, including those who paid no trade tax, were included in the statistics with their actual taxable incomes.

As regards the inclusion of persons who paid no trade tax, the 1935 fiscal statistics differ from those of the preceding years. In the 1935 statistics the total number of taxpayers was 3,028,447, as against 3,462,698 in the 1932 statistics[34]. This fall of approximately 434,000 units cannot possibly be attributed to such a large reduction in the working population. On the contrary, the reduction is largely or wholly due to the fact that in 1935 a number of persons with very small incomes were no longer required to complete tax returns and consequently were no longer included in the statistics. However, it must not be deduced from this that in the 1935 fiscal statistics only those taxpayers were included who had actually paid trade tax. In fact, of the 3,028,447 people included in the statistics, 1,514,659 paid trade tax, and 1,513,788 were exempted[35]. If one assumes that the working population was the same in 1935 as in 1932, namely 3,462,698 persons (= the number of persons liable for tax in the 1932 fiscal statistics), then one obtains for

---

[31] In postwar fiscal statistics, compiled by the NIS, this was no longer the case. For industrial workers, traders and the professions only the incomes of those who actually paid tax form part of the statistics (*Statistiek van de belastbare inkomens aangeslagen in de bedrijfsbelasting en in de aanvullende personele belasting (dienstjaar 1946 - inkomsten verworven in 1945)*, p. 586; *Statistiek van de belastbare inkomens aangeslagen in de bedrijfsbelasting en in de aanvullende personele belasting (dienstjaren 1947 en 1948 - inkomens verworven in 1946 en 1947)*, p. 351).

[32] VAN DEN EIJNDE F., *o.c.*, p. 1928.

[33] Act of 13 July 1930, Section 19 (1) and (4).

[34] Sources: see Table 51.

[35] Legislative Chambers, Chamber of Representatives, *Bulletin van Vragen en Antwoorden*, session 1937-1938, 3 March 1938, pp. 292-293.

1935 the figure of 1,948,039 persons who paid no trade tax, of whom 1,513,788 were required to make a declaration of income and were therefore included in the statistics, and 434,251 who were not included. This implies that in 1935 only 44% of the working population paid trade tax.

What are the consequences of this different scheme for the numbers liable for tax and the taxable income of industrial entrepreneurs and independent traders and the professions in 1935? No problem arises in the case of industrial entrepreneurs and independent traders, since they were all required to fill in tax returns[36]. As a result the 1935 statistics are perfectly comparable with those of previous years. This is not, however, the case with the professions. The reduction in the number of those liable for tax in the 1935 statistics (15,505 as against 16,146 in 1932, see Table 51), is at least partly due to the non-inclusion of persons with a small income. The effect on the number of those liable for tax, however, is extremely limited, in view of the fact that the persons omitted numbered only a few hundreds and their income was very low.

Paragraph 3. Numbers of independent traders and industrial entrepreneurs: comparison of the fiscal statistics with the censuses

The reliability of taxable income as a designation of entrepreneurial income is difficult to check, since their are no alternative income figures for the self-employed and employers. It is more than likely that significant tax evasion and avoidance took place, but one can only guess at the extent of evasion and avoidance and its evolution over time[37]. It is, however, possible to investigate in approximate terms whether the number of independent traders and industrial entrepreneurs in the fiscal statistics agrees with the number of operators in the censuses of 1920, 1930 and 1937. It is clear from Table 51 that the number of independent traders and industrial entrepreneurs in the fiscal statistics increased constantly and sharply (from 311,864 in 1920 to 547,098 in 1935). Does this marked rise correspond to reality or must the increase be attributed to the fact that initially not all self-employed persons and employers were included in the statistics, because they escaped the attention of the tax authorities? This hypothesis is not fanciful, since trade tax was introduced only in 1919 and the tax service was only gradually expanded to cope with the increase in its responsibilities[38].

In Table 52 the number of industrial entrepreneurs and independent traders in the fiscal statistics (FS) of 1920, 1930 and 1935 is compared with the number of self-employed persons in industry and trade according to the Industrial and Commercial Census of 1930 (ICC 1930), the Economic and Social Census of

---

36 VAN COILLIE, *o.c.*, p. 156.
37 On the problem of tax evasion and avoidance, see below.
38 See footnote 56.

1937 (ESC 1937), the Occupational Census of 1930 (OC 1930), and the Population Censuses of 1920 and 1930 (PC 1920 and PC 1930)[39]. The results of the censuses have where necessary been converted in such a way that all figures in Table 52 relate to the number of operators whose main occupation is as self-employed persons or employers in trade or industry[40]. In the censuses fishing and transport are regarded as branches of industry[41]. Trade consists of the headings purchasing and sales, banks, insurance, commercial intermediaries, hotels and entertainment[42].

Before proceeding to an analysis of the correspondence between the number of independent traders and industrial entrepreneurs in the FS and the censuses, the question must be asked whether the content of both groups is *a priori* the same. Regarding the FS the question arises as to what occupational category to assign self-employed persons who are not engaged in agriculture, industry or trade, and who cannot be regarded as exercising a profession (for example, hairdressers). These self-employed persons are not included in the ICC, the OC or the ESC[43]. It is highly probable that in the FS of 1920 and 1922 they form part of the unspecified category of "others" (see Table 51)[44]. In subsequent years, however,

---

[39] For a discussion of the censuses see Chapter 2, "Pay of White-Collar Workers in the Private Sector", pp. 4-6.

[40] In order to avoid duplications, *multiple job holders* in the group of self-employed persons in trade and industry (for example, a smith also running an ironmongery business) were included only under their main occupation. *Multiple job holders* whose main occupation was as paid employees, agricultural workers, or practitioners of one of the professions were similarly excluded. At the bottom of Table 52 there is an explanation of exactly how any conversions were made. The most important problem was posed by the ESC of 1937, because this census (with the exception of independent traders without paid staff) provides information on the number of establishments and not on the numbers of self-employed persons. However, it is clear from the ICC of 1930 that the number of establishments was virtually identical with the number of individual proprietors in industry (approximately 221,000 establishments and 223,000 persons with the main occupation of proprietor). Therefore the number of industrial establishments in 1937, with an addition of 2,000 units, was included as indicating the number of proprietors. As regards commercial establishments with salaried staff (35,000 in 1937) it was assumed that their number corresponded with the number of commercial proprietors with paid employees.

[41] However, in the 1920 PC transport is classified under trade. In the PCs of 1920 and 1930 fishing was not part of industry but a separate main heading. For the purposes of comparability with the other censuses, proprietors in the transport sector in the PC of 1920 and self-employed fishermen in the PCs of 1920 and 1930 were transferred to industry.

[42] In the commercial census of the 1937 ESC, a heading entitled "personal care" is also included. This consists mainly of hairdressers. For the purposes of comparability this heading was not retained.

[43] With the exception of hairdressers in the 1937 ESC. In the PC these occupations are included but in the comparative survey in Table 52 they have not been retained.

[44] It is possible that in the FS other occupations were included under the category "others" which could be regarded as unambiguously as industrial or commercial activities. An example would be the self-employed fishermen.

this category no longer occurs. However, one can presume that the tax authorities included these self-employed persons under the heading of independent traders and industrial entrepreneurs, which would imply that this category is somewhat wider than in the censuses. Working on the above assumption, in order to arrive at an homogenous category of independent traders and industrial entrepreneurs in the FS, the category "other" must be included under independent traders and industrial entrepreneurs for the years 1920 and 1922. As a result of this addition the number of independent traders and industrial entrepreneurs rises in the 1920 FS by 30,544 units, so that the adjusted total becomes 342,408.

Because of the probable inclusion in the tax category "independent traders and industrial entrepreneurs" of self-employed persons who did not fall within the scope of the ICC, ESC or OC, the FS figures are *a priori* higher than those of the censuses. On the other hand it is possible that a number of occupational categories were included among self-employed persons which in the FS do not fall under the heading independent traders and industrial entrepreneurs, but under the professions. Examples of this would be exchange brokers, stockbrokers and other financial intermediaries in whose case it is unclear in which category they have been included by the tax authorities.

For the year 1930 the correspondence between the ICC and the OC on the one hand (440,000 people) and the FS on the other (446,000) is particularly satisfying. The higher figure in the FS is perhaps largely due to the inclusion of self-employed persons not actively engaged in industry or trade. The number of self-employed persons in the PC is noticeably higher (486,000). This difference may be due to the fact that a number of multiple job holders with a salaried main occupation characterized themselves in the PC as self-employed, because they associated this with a higher social status[45]. In addition allowance must be made for a general overestimate of the working population in the PC.

There is also a particularly good correspondence between the FS for 1935 (547,000) and the ESC 1937 (534,000). Although no FS was compiled for the year 1937, it is possible on the basis of the figure in ESC 1937 and the difference between the 1930 FS and the 1930 ICC to make an estimate of the number of people liable for tax in the tax category independent traders and industrial entrepreneurs in 1937. Based on the assumption that the difference between the (non-existent) 1937 FS and the 1937 ESC is the same as the difference found in 1930 (6,000 units), one obtains the figure for 1937 of 540,000 persons liable for tax, which is 7,000 less than in 1935.

As for 1920, the only possible comparison is with the PC. The number of operators in the 1920 PC is 53,000 greater than in the 1920 FS. The reason for this discrepancy should be sought not so much in an underestimate of the number of those liable for tax in the 1920 FS, but in an overestimate of the number of

---

[45] The higher PC figure cannot be due to duplications, because in the PC account was taken only of the main occupation given to the census agent.

entrepreneurs in the 1920 PC. The fact is that in 1930 the number of operators in the PC, which was undoubtedly an overestimate, was 40,000 units more than in the FS, which is of the same order of magnitude as the difference in 1920. Consequently one can state that the number of industrial entrepreneurs and independent traders in the 1920 FS is a only a slight underestimate (between 10,000 and 15,000 units). The small number of industrial entrepreneurs and independent traders in the 1920 FS is therefore in the first place a reflection of economic reality, and only to a lesser extent the result of a statistical underestimate.

It is clear from the above exposition that the number of people liable for tax in the FS, with a few adjustments, gives a reliable picture of the evolution of the number of self-employed persons and employers in industry and trade. In Table 53 the number of industrial entrepreneurs and independent traders is given on the basis of the adjusted fiscal statistics. In 1920 and 1922 the category "other" has been included and 15,000 and 8,000 persons respectively were added to compensate for the probable underestimate of the first FS. In 1924 4,000 people were transferred from the professions to industrial entrepreneurs and independent traders[46]. For 1937 the estimate based on the ESC was retained and the missing years were interpolated linearly.

What strikes immediately is the spectacular rise in the number of self-employed and employers in the period 1928-1935. Between 1928 and 1935 the number of industrial entrepreneurs, independent traders and craftsmen increased by approximately 135,000 full-time equivalents, which corresponds to an average yearly rise of 4.1%. Due to lack of data, these figures cannot be compared with the evolution of the total working population, but they can be compared with that of the total population (with an average annual increase of 0.6%)[47]. It is true that in 1920-1928 one can also see an increase in the number of self-employed and employers (approximately 55,000 persons, or a yearly average of 1.9% as against an average annual increase in population of 0.9%), but this rise is not only much smaller but to a large extent attributable to the general increase in the working population[48].

---

[46] The number of people in the professions category in the FS for 1920 may be too high, in the light of a comparison with the figures for the other years (1922: 15,098; 1928: 16,486, see Table 51). It was assumed that in 1924 4,000 persons who in other years were classified with industrial workers and traders were wrongly included with the professions.

[47] Population growth was calculated on the basis of official population figures corrected by Buyst (BUYST E., *An Economic History of Residential Building in Belgium*, passim).

[48] Between 1920 and 1926 the number of workers employed in trade and industry (excluding transport) rose by over 300,000 full-time equivalents, namely from 832,000 to 1,145,000 (GOOSSENS M., *Reconstructie van werkgelegenheidcijfers voor het Interbellum. Methodologie en resultaten*, in: "Workshop on Quantitative Economic History", vol. 87.01, Louvain, 1987, p. B.3b). The number of white-collar workers employed in industry and trade (including private transport) rose between 1920 and 1926 from 91,000 to 133,000 (see Chapter 2, Table 22, column 17).

The enormous increase in the number of self-employed persons between 1928 and 1935 is mainly due to the economic crisis of the first half of the 1930s. Many workers who became unemployed set up small businesses for want of an alternative, often a shop or a pub, which brought about a kind of proletarianization of the self-employed classes[49]. Collin, the particularly perceptive academic and banker who in 1936-1937 was appointed as a Royal Commissioner by the government to report on the problems of the self-employed middle classes, paints a very accurate picture when he writes: *"One may indeed rightly wonder whether this growth in the producing and trading middle class is healthy or a cancerous proliferation. In our opinion the latter view is the correct one. During the Depression years the retail trading sector has been the refuge of all those who had been previously defeated in the economic struggle. White-collar workers who had lost their positions, the unemployed who had no claim to benefits and even large-scale independent traders whose businesses had collapsed, have resorted to running small businesses"*[50]. The causal relationship between the Depression and the increase in the number of small businesses is confirmed if the number of operators between 1935 and 1937 is compared. In this period there was an economic recovery, which was accompanied by a fall or at least a stabilisation in the numbers of self-employed.

SECTION 3. ENTREPRENEURIAL INCOME OF INDEPENDENT TRADERS AND CRAFTSMEN

The entrepreneurial income of independent traders and craftsmen was estimated in four stages, corresponding to the four paragraphs below. The first three paragraphs relate to the entrepreneurial income of independent traders and craftsmen whose entrepreneurial activities in trade or industry were their main occupation. This also includes income from a self-employed secondary occupation in trade or industry if the main occupation is also a self-employed job in trade or industry (for example, main occupation = hairdresser, secondary occupation = chemist). This entrepreneurial income is estimated on the basis of fiscal statistics. For the sake of simplicity all this income is classified under the common denominator *of main occupation*. In the last paragraph a rough estimate is made of the entrepreneurial income issuing from a secondary occupation if the main occupation is salaried (for example, main occupation = factory worker, secondary occupation = pub landlord), as a self-employed agricultural worker, or

---

[49] Between 31 December 1930 and 27 February 1937 the number of workers employed in industry and trade (excluding transport) fell by approximately 100,000, namely from 1,058,000 to 965,000 (GOOSSENS M., *o.c.*, p. B.3b).
[50] COLLIN F., *Verslag nopens den ambachts- en handeldrijvenden middenstand*, Brussels, 1937, pp. 14-15. For a discussion of how Collin's report was produced, see VANDEPUTTE R., *Fernand Collin en zijn tijd*, Tielt, 1985, pp. 121-128.

as a practitioner of a profession. In what follows this income will be referred to under *secondary occupations*.

Based on the fiscal statistics for trade tax the following operations had to be carried out for main occupations:
a) Homogenization of the taxable income for years for which fiscal statistics are available (Paragraph 1).
b) Conversion of taxable income into income actually earned in the years for which fiscal statistics are available (Paragraph 2).
c) Estimate of income actually earned in years for which no tax data are available (Paragraph 3).

Paragraph 1. Homogenisation of taxable income

The taxable business income of the tax category "independent traders and industrial entrepreneurs", as given in Table 51 and Table 54, column 1, does not always cover the same ground. For this reason corrections were carried out in Table 54 in order to homogenize data: for 1920 and 1922 the taxable income of the category "other" will be included, for 1924 a number of people in the "professions" category are transferred to independent traders and industrial entrepreneurs, and for the period 1920-1928 income from business capital invested must be included. First, however, taxable income must be estimated for 1928, 1929 and 1932, the years for which the number of people liable to tax in each income group is known, but not the taxable income.

As is shown by Table 51, no information is provided on taxable income in the fiscal statistics for 1928, 1929 and 1932. This can, however, be easily estimated by imputing an average income to each person liable for tax for each income class, namely the average of the lower and upper limit. That this method produces very reliable estimates (except in the 50,000 to 100,000 income group) is shown by the 1935 statistics. For that year the total taxable income for each income group was divided by the number of those liable for tax, with the following results: 4,500 for the 5,000 and below group, 7,500 for the 5,000-10,000 group, 17,499 for the 10,000-25,000 group, 37,499 for the 25,000-50,000 group, 70,000 for the 50,000-100,000 group, and 249,649 for the over 100,000 group. In the light of these results for 1935, the following averages were included for each income group for 1928, 1929 and 1932: 4,500, 7,500, 17,500, 37,500, 70,00 and 250,000. After multiplying the number of those liable for taxation in each income group by the average incomes given above, and adding the results obtained, one arrives at the total taxable income (see Table 54, column 2).

It has been pointed out previously that the category "other", which occurs only in 1920 and 1922 and of which no further definition is given, probably relates to persons who in subsequent years are classified in the category "independent traders and industrial entrepreneurs"[51]. The taxable income of the category

---

[51] Cf. above.

"other" is therefore added to that of industrial entrepreneurs and independent traders (column 3).

For 1924 a small correction was made in connection with what is undoubtedly too high a number of those exercising professions in that year's fiscal statistics (1922: 15,098, 1924: 19,307, 1928: 16,486, see Table 51). It was assumed that in the year in question 4,000 persons classified in other years with industrial entrepreneurs and independent traders were wrongly included by the tax authorities in the professions. For this reason those 4,000 people were transferred to the industrial entrepreneurs and independent traders, and the average taxable income of the latter category was imputed to them.

The last and most important correction relates to the income from invested business capital. As has already been mentioned in the discussion of income tax, up to and including 1928 entrepreneurial income was divided into two parts[52]. The largest portion was regarded by the legislators as remuneration for work performed by the entrepreneur. This portion was subject to trade tax. In addition a portion of self-employed income was regarded as a return on the capital which the entrepreneur had invested in his business. This portion was liable to property tax. The Act of 13 July 1930 put an end to this division, so that only trade tax was payable on the total entrepreneurial income, i.e. including the return on capital invested. This means that the trade fiscal statistics from 1929 onwards cover a wider field than those in 1920-1928.

For 1920-1928, in order to homogenize the fiscal statistics, the income from business capital invested must be added to income subject to trade tax. Data on income from capital invested were found for the years 1920, 1922, 1924 and 1928 (see Table 55, column 5). However, a problem arises from the fact that these figures relate to the capital invested by the proprietor in agriculture as well as in industry and trade. It was assumed that the share of independent traders and craftsmen in the total income from capital invested is the same as their share in the total income from labour of agricultural entrepreneurs, tradesmen and craftsmen (columns 1-4). Finally an estimate must be made for 1927, the only year for which there are data on income from labour, but not for income from capital invested. Since the income from capital invested for independent traders and industrial entrepreneurs for both 1924 and 1928 totalled 14.3% of income from labour, it was assumed that this was also the case in 1927 (columns 7-9).

Paragraph 2. Conversion of taxable income into actual income

For a wide variety of reasons actually earned entrepreneurial income is higher than taxable income. Some factors relate to tax legislation; others are attributable to tax evasion or avoidance by taxpayers. The great problem is of course that no data are

---

[52] Idem.

available on the income actually earned, so that it is impossible to determine by what percentage this differs from the taxable income. An incidental, but no less important problem is the question whether one should use a constant or variable percentage increase for the period 1920-1939.

The adjustments to be carried out have by definition a particularly high degree of uncertainty. It is true that one can highlight factors which indicate an underestimate of the taxable income as a designation of the income actually earned, and one can also adduce arguments for using a higher coefficient for some years than for others, but this information does not allow one to arrive at precise margins of deviation. As will become apparent, this is in fact equally the case for the present-day estimates of entrepreneurial income by the NIS.

For every year for which tax data are available, a percentage increase based largely on qualitative date will be assumed. Before proceeding to concrete applications a summary will first be given of the most important elements to be taken into account. Subsequently it will be examined by what percentage the NIS raises taxable income from 1948 to the present and what incremental factor Baudhuin uses for some years in the inter-war period.

1. Arguments in favour of increasing taxable income

a) Tax fraud

Tax fraud is a phenomenon found in all ages, and therefore can be assumed to have occurred during the inter-war period. The extent of evasion, however, varies and is determined by various factors, of which the most important are the level of monitoring and possible penalties and the tax burden. In addition it may be assumed that there are more opportunities for fraud in a boom than in a recession.

The tax burden
Measured by present-day standards the tax burden during the inter-war period was exceptionally low. In 1935 independent traders and craftsmen paid an average of only some 5% tax on their business income[53]. However, this should not lead to the

---

53 The tax burden was calculated by dividing the total amount of tax paid by taxable income. For income earned in 1935, BF 132 million in trade tax was paid by industrial entrepreneurs and independent traders (see Table 51). In addition this occupational category was charged BF 73 million supplementary personal tax (VAN DER AA E.R., *o.c.*, p. 838). The amount of national crisis tax paid by industrial entrepreneurs and independent traders is unknown. However, total receipts from the national crisis tax have been published (see Table 50, column 6). On the assumption that the share of industrial entrepreneurs and independent traders in national crisis tax was the same as that of natural persons (36%) in total trade tax, an amount of BF 180 million was obtained. Therefore a total of BF 385 million in direct taxation was paid by industrial entrepreneurs and craftsmen. This amount is 5.2% of taxable business income. However, one must bear in mind that supplementary personal taxation and national crisis tax relate not only to business income but also to total income, hence

premature conclusion that few attempts were made to evade taxes. After all, compared with the tax regime before the First World War, 5% is a heavy tax burden, and it is clear from Collin's report on the middle classes that many self-employed people were utterly convinced that they were paying a great deal in taxation[54]. Was the tax burden greater or less during the other years of the inter-war period? In the absence of data it is difficult to give an exact answer to this question. One can say at any rate that in years when no supertax or national crisis tax was levied (see Table 50), the tax burden was less. As far as it is possible to check, however, the fluctuations in the tax burden were not such as to change the nature of tax evasion behaviour.

Tax monitoring

The taxation reform of 1919-1920 brought about a veritable revolution in the Belgian tax system. It is logical that at the beginning of the 1920s a great deal of income should have escaped the attention of the tax authorities, because there was no tradition of income tax and the tax authorities were not able to cope with their task in the initial period[55]. However, over the years the Ministry of Finance became better staffed and at the same time tax legislation was refined[56]. Undoubtedly the fiscal know-how of civil servants increased constantly. For this reason it seems logical to presuppose a higher percentage of tax evasion for the beginning of the 1920s than for the remaining years of the inter-war period.

The economic climate

The opportunities for tax evasion may be greater in periods of economic growth than at times of recession. For this reason self-employed income in the fiscal statistics of 1922 and 1935 were raised by a smaller percentage than that in the fiscal statistics for other years. The reverse was done in the very prosperous 1928-1930 period.

---

including movable and immovable income. In addition actually earned entrepreneurial income is - partly because of tax evasion - higher than taxable income. A tax burden of 5% on entrepreneurial income can therefore be regarded as a maximum figure.

[54] *"On only one point is there unanimity, namely that taxation is weighing far too heavily on the various businesses. As much as any other citizen, perhaps even more than other citizens, the shopkeeper and trader would breathe a sigh of relief if he had to pay less tax"* (COLLIN F., *o.c.*, p.74).

[55] MAHAIM E., La fortune et le bien-être, in: MAHAIM E. (ed.), "La Belgique restaurée", Brussels, 1926, pp.522.

[56] PUTMAN R., *o.c.*, pp. 444 and 450. F. Baudhuin wrote in 1933 that the number of staff at the Ministry of Finance had risen from 9,800 to 15,200 officials as a result of the application of the new tax legislation since the First World War (BAUDHUIN F., *Essai sur les classes moyennes*, in: "Banque Nationale de Belgique. Bulletin d'Information et de Documentation", vol. 8, 1933, p. 319).

b) Tax avoidance: fictitious remuneration of family members helping in business

As discussed in the first section, entrepreneurial income consists of the difference between gross entrepreneurial income (the value of all goods or services sold by the entrepreneur) and operating costs (wages and salaries, interest on borrowed capital, rent paid or imputed for business premises or land, depreciation, etc.). It was fiscally attractive for entrepreneurs to assign unpaid family members a fictitious remuneration for tax purposes, for example the minimum exempted from all taxes. In this way operating costs were increased and taxable income was reduced, so that less tax was payable.

The fictitious remuneration of family members helping in the business was included in the fiscal statistics under the income of manual workers (or possibly white-collar workers). Since this remuneration was not in fact paid, they belong in the distribution of the national income not with paid employment but form part of entrepreneurial income, which as a result is underestimated in the fiscal statistics.

c) Fixed assessment of taxpayers with no business accounts

In order to facilitate the smoother collection of taxes and to accommodate the complaints of numerous small businesses and their professional associations, who believed that the tax authorities were assigning too high an income to them, it was determined in the Act of 13 July 1930 that from the tax year 1930 onwards (= incomes earned in 1929), self-employed persons who kept no accounts would be taxed at a fixed rate. Their income was determined from then onwards on the basis of a number of indicators which were worked out by the tax authorities in consultation with professional associations. The testimony of tax specialists showed that such a system was much more beneficial to those involved[57]. For this reason a higher coefficient will be used from 1929 onwards.

2. The incremental coefficients of the NIS and Baudhuin

In Table 56 the annual incremental coefficients of the NIS are presented. These coefficients, determined in a very arbitrary manner, are exceptionally high (especially in 1948-1950) and after 1951 very stable.

The increments used by Baudhuin in his estimates of the inter-war national income for industrial entrepreneurs and independent traders are clearly arbitrary (1924: taxable income = BF 6,440 million, Baudhuin's estimate = BF 8,500 million, using a coefficient of 32%; 1935: taxable income = BF 7,372 million, Baudhuin's estimate = BF 9,000 million, as a result of using a coefficient of 22%).

---

[57] See LOECKX E., *o.c.*

3. Incremental coefficients for the inter-war period

Because of relative lack of expertise within the fiscal administration it is advisable to assume a higher incremental coefficient for the inter-war period than after the Second World War. For this reason 60% was maintained as a general incremental coefficient. As is clear from the above exposition this general coefficient needs adjusting for certain years. These adjustments are given in Table 57, where entrepreneurial income actually earned is estimated.

Paragraph 3. Interpolation and extrapolation of the missing years

In Table 58 there is an estimate of entrepreneurial income for the years in which no fiscal statistics are available. The interpolations and extrapolations were made on the basis of the development of private consumption of food, drink, tobacco, clothes, transport (with the exception of trams, buses and railways) and leisure time.

Paragraph 4. Entrepreneurial income of independent traders and craftsmen (secondary occupation)

As was previously indicated, an estimate remains to be made of entrepreneurial income from a secondary occupation if the main occupation is not self-employed work in trade or industry.

Entrepreneurial income from a secondary occupation is obtained by multiplying the number of people involved by an estimated average income. The number of persons with a secondary occupation is known only for 1930 (see Table 59). It was assumed that between 1920 and 1930 their numbers developed in line with the number of main occupations (see Table 60). For the period 1930-1939 the number of persons involved was kept constant. It can be deduced from postwar NIS figures that average income from a secondary occupation was approximately 50% of the average entrepreneurial income of those working as independent traders and craftsmen as a main occupation

SECTION 4. THE ENTREPRENEURIAL INCOME OF THE PROFESSIONS

The entrepreneurial income of the professions was calculated in the same way as that of independent traders and craftsmen, namely on the basis of the fiscal statistics. Here too the data were adjusted upwards to allow for tax fraud. Interpolations and extrapolations for the missing years were made on the basis of the development of the average entrepreneurial income of independent traders and craftsmen and of hourly wages for manual workers. The results of the estimates are given in Table 49, column 4.

SECTION 5. THE ENTREPRENEURIAL INCOME OF PARTNERSHIPS

No data are available on the entrepreneurial income of partnerships for the inter-war period. In fact, tax data on the subject have been compiled only since 1951. The estimates of the NIS show that in 1948-1954 the entrepreneurial income of personal partnerships averaged 7.4% of the entrepreneurial income of independent traders and craftsmen. It was assumed that the inter-war figure was 7% (see Table 49, column 5).

CHAPTER 9

INTEREST PAYMENTS TO THE PERSONAL SECTOR[1]

SECTION 1. DEFINITIONS AND SURVEY OF CONTENTS OF THE THREE CHAPTERS DEALING WITH INCOME FROM PROPERTY ACCRUING TO THE PERSONAL SECTOR

Interest (Chapter 9), rent (Chapter 10) and dividends, bonuses and gifts (Chapter 11) accruing to private persons form, in the terminology of the system of National Accounts, the income from property accruing to the personal sector.

The income from these sources may, however, be either received or imputed[2]. The latter is the case with respect to the imputed interest on the actuarial reserves of life insurance companies, the imputed interest on the services provided free of charge by banks and other financial intermediaries to their clientele and the imputed rent for owners occupying their own houses or tilling their own land.

By the personal sector is understood family households and non-profit making organisations[3], in their capacity as owners of financial assets and of improved or unimproved properties.

As for all components of national income, the income from property is subject to the residence criterion. This means that the incomes accruing to the personal sector ordinarily resident in Belgium are taken into account, irrespective of the origin of those earnings (i.e. at home or abroad). If a Belgian resident - irrespective of nationality - has invested part of his assets abroad, the earnings from that property are added to Belgian national income. Conversely, the income from property owned by private persons who are not ordinarily resident in Belgium and who have invested part of their capital in that country does not form part of Belgian national income but of the country in which they reside.

In relation to the income from property of self-employed persons and partnerships, a distinction is drawn in the standardized system of national accounts between (i) the income from the working capital invested in the individual's own business, and (ii) the income from real estate (land and buildings) and from assets invested outside the individual's own business. The working capital invested in the individual's own business forms part of income from self-employment (Chapters 7 and 8) and is not therefore taken into consideration. On the other hand the second group of incomes does, according to the conventions of the OECD,

---

[1] The authors thank Guido Pepermans for his important contribution to this chapter.
[2] OECD, *A standardized system of national accounts,* pp. 77-78; *De nationale rekeningen van België 1953-196*2, p. 1153.
[3] For example private hospitals and free education establishments.

form part of the property income accruing to the personal sector. This means that the reimbursement for self-financed machinery and equipment is added to entrepreneurial income[4], and that the reimbursement for self-financed industrial buildings is added to property income. Income from savings passbooks, bank deposits, bonds and shares, etc., are also included under the property income accruing to the personal sector since these assets are invested outside the self-employed sector or partnerships.

In order to avoid double-counting, the reimbursement on capital accruing to share companies is not included as these incomes are in turn distributed over the various factors of production of the company in question, or added to the company's reserves. A simple illustration in relation to property investments may help clarify the logic and consistency of this method of operation[5].

If banks or investment companies hold bonds or shares of other companies in their portfolio, they receive a reimbursement on those holdings in the form of interest and dividends. That reimbursement is a reward for the factor of capital, as supplied by the financial institutions in question. In turn these earnings are used to finance the pay of the employees in the institutions in question and the interest paid to own deposit-holders, and to pay dividends to own shareholders, etc.[6]. These factor-incomes form part of national income[7]. If the interest and dividends accruing to the financial institutions were also to be regarded as forming part of national income, income and value added would no longer be equal (the income would be higher), which is impossible by definition.

The distinction between investments made by the personal sector and by financial institutions may be further spelled out by a simple example. Let us assume that private individual A owns a quantity of capital and that he employs that capital productively in company B (meaning that it creates an added value), and that A receives a reimbursement in return. Let us suppose that the invested capital amounts to BF 10 million and the value added realized in consequence to BF 1 million. If, for the sake of simplicity, it is also assumed that the reimbursement paid to each factor of production is equal to the value added which it realizes, A will then receive an income of BF 1 million. If private individual A were no longer directly to invest the same capital of BF 10 million in company B but to purchase bonds in investment company C, which in turn used that sum to invest in company B, one then obtains a different situation. Assuming that the

---

[4] In the agricultural sector the livestock herd needs to be added. Since livestock form part of the farmer's operating capital, the income arising from ownership of livestock must be added to entrepreneurial income and not to income from property.

[5] A similar example can readily be constructed in relation to the income from real estate (i.e. land and buildings).

[6] To avoid undue complications it has been assumed in this example that no corporation tax is payable and that the value added is divided in its entirety over the factors of labour and capital, implying that no profit is added to the reserves.

[7] In so far as accruing to the personal sector.

value added of the capital invested in company B is the same (BF 1 million) and that the rate of interest on the bonds is 8%, investment company C will then receive BF 1 million and pay out 800,000 BF to private individual A. The difference of BF 200,000 is used by C to pay its employees and to distribute dividends to its shareholders. In order to calculate national income a total sum of BF 1 million is once again obtained in this case: BF 800,000 for A and BF 200,000 for the employees and shareholders of C. This total sum is equal to the value added. If the proceeds from the investment by investment company C were also to be added to national income, one would then arrive at a sum on the income side of BF 2 million, compared with an added value of just BF 1 million. In order to avoid double-counts of this kind under the income approach, only the income from capital accruing to the personal sector is counted as part of national income.

Finally it should be noted that the figures shown in Chapters 9, 10 and 11 are the income before taxation. The direct taxation on property income is therefore contained in the figures.

The following forms of interest are dealt with in this chapter[8]:
1) Interest on savings deposits ;
2) Interest on bank deposits ;
3) Imputed interest on the actuarial reserves of life insurance companies ;
4) Interest on government securities ;
5) Interest from a bond loan transacted by companies ;
6) Interest on mortgage loans ;
7) Imputed interest relating to the services provided free of charge by banks and other financial intermediaries.

The interest from the foreign investments of Belgian residents are included in Chapter 11, "Dividends, bonuses and gifts accruing to the personal sector", although they in fact belong in this chapter. This is because the available source material does not permit a division into interest on the one hand and dividends and other income from foreign assets on the other. Needless to say this method of operation does not have any impact on the total income from property or, consequently, on the size of national income[9].

In the case of some of the items above, no direct information is available, either on the interest payments in their entirety or on the proportion of the interest accruing to the personal sector. In these cases it was therefore necessary to work on the basis of the total level of outstanding debt, to which an average rate of interest was then applied. The product arrived at in this fashion was then

---

[8]   For a summary of the contents of Chapter 10, "Rent" and Chapter 11, "Dividends, bonuses and gifts", see the introductory section to those chapters.

[9]   For the same reason the NIS classes the interest on foreign investments under the heading "Dividends, bonuses, gifts", subheading "Income from investments abroad" (*De nationale rekeningen van België 1953-1962*, p. 1155).

multiplied by the proportion accruing to the personal sector. This latter step is the most contestable element in the reconstruction, since, in the absence of data, the share accruing to the personal sector has been determined on the basis of post-war ratios of the NIS - which have in turn often been determined in a comparatively arbitrary way.

Section 2. Interest from savings deposits

The interest payments to the personal sector by the following institutions are examined in turn below[10]:
1) Algemene Spaar- en Lijfrentekas (ASLK) ;
2) Private savings banks ;
3) Municipal savings banks ;
4) Public credit institutions (excluding ASLK).

During the inter-war period the majority of private savings deposits were in the hands of the ASLK, followed by those managed by the private savings banks[11].

Under the NIS's present method of calculation, this heading has also taken account since 1963-1971 of the interest on time deposits and demand accounts with the ASLK and of the interest on the savings securities issued by the private savings banks[12]. The interest on time deposits and demand accounts with the present private savings banks (the successors to the former private *spaarkassen*) are now also included under this heading[13]. The inclusion of these interest payments was necessary since the blurring of the dividing lines between the traditional deposit banks on the one hand and the public credit institutions and private savings banks on the other since the late 1960s meant that the latter also

---

[10] In the absence of data no account has been taken of the interest on loans concluded between private individuals themselves (for example with relatives or friends). An exception consists of the loans granted by private individuals for which a mortgage was concluded. These have been included in Section 7.

[11] Apart from the interest on deposits held with the aforementioned institutions, the NIS also includes under the heading "Interest on savings deposits" the interest on capitalization transactions (Nis, *Commissie van het Nationaal Inkomen*, pp. 247-248). The amounts in question are very small (just 0.1% of the total interest on savings deposits in 1948-1954), and relate particularly to the actuarial reserves of building societies. Since this form of saving was virtually non-existent during the inter-war period, the corresponding subheading has been left out of account (the actuarial reserves of the capitalization companies amounted in 1939 to just BF 1 million, compared with BF 480 million 1947, see the ASLK Annual Report of 1947, p. 39 (*Verslag over de verrichtingen en de toestand van de Algemene Spaar- en Lijfrentekas*).

[12] *De nationale rekeningen van België 1963-1971*, p. 371. It is unclear whether the changes in the NIS methodology commence in 1963 or 1971, or in one of the intervening years.

[13] Communication by Mr. A. Hermans, an official at the NIS, for which the authors express their thanks.

began to carry out banking transactions, as reflected in the change of name of the private "spaarkassen" into "savings banks"[14].

The NIS has therefore opted to base the content of the various subheadings on the type of institution paying the interest and not on the type of deposits on which interest is paid. The various subheadings were, however, named on the basis of the latter criterion, as a result of which the NIS created unnecessary confusion. For example, the heading "Interest on savings deposits" includes all interest paid to the personal sector by the private savings banks and public credit institutions (of which the ASLK is the most important), i.e. including the interest on demand deposits and demand accounts and the interest on savings securities. An exception is formed by the interest on the savings certificates issued by the public credit institutions. Since these financial institutions enjoyed a state guarantee, the interest on the securities issued by them is classified together with the interest on government securities[15]. The heading "Bank deposits" (Section 3) covers only the deposits with deposit banks, including the savings deposits with those institutions.

Possibly because the private savings banks (spaarkassen) and public credit institutions carried out few if any bank transactions during the 1940s and 1950s, the NIS's estimates of national income in that period include only the interest on savings deposits and not on the time deposits and demand accounts with those institutions. Nor was any account taken of the interest on savings certificates issued by the private savings banks (spaarkassen). The NIS makes no reference in its methodology to the reason for the non-inclusion of such interest. Once again this is probably attributable to the limited importance of savings securities.

The NIS's working method, as set out in its methodology for national income between 1948 and 1954, has as far as possible been followed for the inter-war period[16]. This means that the heading "Interest on savings deposits" (Section 2) includes all savings deposits, excluding those held with the deposit banks, while the heading "Interest on bank deposits" (Section 3) includes all deposits held with deposit banks, including the savings deposits.

---

[14] The blurring of the dividing lines in the Belgian financial sector was in particular facilitated by the Royal Decree number 11 of 18 April 1967 and the Mammoth Act of 30 June 1975 (LE BRUN J., *Het juridisch statuut van de spaarbanken*, in: "De Belgische spaarbanken. Geschiedenis, recht, economische functie en instellingen", Tielt, Belgische Spaarbankenvereniging (ed.), 1986, pp. 299-377; RAPORT A., *Vijfentwintig jaar Vereniging Privé-Spaarkassen*, in: "idem", pp. 251-296; VERAGHTERT K., *Van spaarkas tot spaarbank (1940-1975)*, in: "idem", pp. 211-250.

[15] Communication by Mr. A. Hermans, an official at the NIS, for which the authors express their thanks.

[16] NIS, *Commissie van het nationaal inkomen*, pp. 242-251.

Paragraph 1. Interest on savings deposits held with the ASLK

With respect to the interest on savings deposits held with the ASLK, a distinction has, in line with the NIS, been drawn between:
1) Capitalized interest accruing to the personal sector ;
2) Interest paid in the course of the financial year accruing to the personal sector ;
3) Interest on the endowment passbooks of returned servicemen ;
4) Interest on the deposit passbooks of non-profit organisations.

1. Capitalised interest accruing to the personal sector

The annual reports of the ASLK do not make any reference to the sum of capitalized interest. Monthly figures are however published in relation to the deposits, withdrawals and outstanding amounts of the personal sector. These figures are also included in the NBB's "Belgische economische statistieken". This information enables the capitalized interest to be calculated accurately (see Table 61).

The outstanding deposits on 31 December (column 3) contain the capitalized interest. If the outstanding deposits on 30 November (column 1) and the net deposits (= deposits - withdrawals) during the month of December (= column 2) are deducted from this sum, one obtains the capitalized interest (column 4).

As a test for the accuracy of the calculations, the implicit rate of interest on the ASLK deposits (= capitalized interest (average outstanding deposit sum) was compared with the explicit rate of interest for small deposits (= the rate of interest actually applied by the ASLK). The implicit (column 6) and explicit (column 7) rates of interest correspond very closely. The latter is consistently a little higher, which is attributable to the fact that the ASLK paid a higher rate of interest on small than on large deposits[17]. Since all deposits - i.e. including large ones - are taken into account in calculating the implicit rate of interest, the latter is lower than the explicit rate of interest on small deposits.

2. Interest paid in the course of the working year accruing to the personal sector

The ASLK annual reports do not provide any information on the interest paid in the course of the working year. Such interest was for example paid out to private individuals who liquidated their savings accounts in the course of the year. The

---

[17] In 1933-1936, for example, the interest payable on deposits up to BF 20,000 was 3% and from BF 20,000 upwards 2% (*Belgische economische statistieken 1929-1940*, p. 14). This limit of BF 20,000 was in fact high since a manual worker's annual earnings in the period in question were roughly only BF 10,000 (see Table 9 column 3).

NIS figures for the 1948-1954 period suggest that the sums in question are very small (averaging just 1.6% of the capitalized interest)[18].

3. Interest on the endowment passbooks of returned servicemen

As a mark of the nation's gratitude, returned servicemen from the First World War received an endowment under the Act of 25 August 1920 in proportion to their length of service at or behind the front[19]. Under the Act of 10 August 1921 the endowments were credited in passbooks managed by the ASLK on behalf of the State. These deposits attracted 5% interest. Up to the end of 1925, the beneficiaries were only able to withdraw money from their endowment passbook. Under the Act of 9 August 1926 the holders of still current passbooks were permitted to make personal deposits to restore the original balance on their passbooks, apart from the capitalized interest[20]. These deposits were subject to an annual rate of interest of 5%, payable by the Exchequer[21].

The ASLK annual reports do not provide any direct information on the interest paid out on returned servicemen's endowment passbooks. The amount of deposits and withdrawals was, however, published for each year and, from 1927, also the outstanding amounts on 31 December (see Table 62 columns 1, 2 and 3) were published. On the basis of these figures it is possible to calculate the interest. This is done by multiplying the outstanding amount by the rate of interest, which was established by law at 5% throughout the inter-war period.

Before making this calculation, it is necessary to calculate the outstanding savings balance for the period 1921-1926. It has been assumed that the net withdrawals (= withdrawals less deposits) in a given year were spread out evenly over that year. The outstanding balance at the end of year t is then the result of the following formula:

$$S_t = \frac{S_{t+1}}{1.05} + \frac{1/2\ NA_{t+1}}{1.05} + 1/2\ NA_{t+1}$$

where S_t = outstanding amount at 31 December of year t
S_{t+1} = outstanding amount at 31 December of year t+1
NA_{t+1} = net withdrawals during year t+1

---

18 Own calculations on the basis of NIS, *Commissie van het nationaal inkomen*, p. 243.
19 *Annual report ASLK 1939*, pp. 51-52.
20 Example: assume that a returned servicemen had received an endowment after the war of BF 10,000 and that he had withdrawn BF 6,000 from his endowment passbook in 1924, thus leaving a balance of BF 4,000. Under the Act of 9 August 1926 the holder of the passbook was permitted to deposit a maximum sum of BF 6,000, thus returning the balance of the account to BF 10,000.
21 Such deposits were advantageous to the holder since the 5% rate of interest was higher than the market rate of interest (cf. Table 61 column 7).

On the basis of the known outstanding amount at 31 December 1927, it is possible to calculate the balance at the end of the preceding years with the aid of the above formula (column 4).

The average annual balance of year t is then arrived at by taking the average of the balance of 31 December of year t-1 and the balance at 31 December of year t (column 5)[22]. Multiplication of this result by the rate of interest (5%) then gives the interest amount (column 6).

4. Interest on deposit passbooks of non-profit making organisations

Once again no information whatever is available on such interest in the inter-war period. Nor does the NIS have precise data on this item for its post-war estimates, in view of the fact that a constant sum of BF 15 million was recorded for the period 1948-1954[23]. This sum roughly corresponds with 1.5% of the capitalized interest accruing to the personal sector. The same percentage was applied to the inter-war period (see Table 64).

Paragraph 2. Interest on savings deposits held with private savings banks ("spaarkassen")

Belgium had a very wide range of private savings banks (spaarkassen) during the inter-war period, the origins, objects and working methods of which often varied widely[24]. These savings banks may be subdivided into five groups: the savings banks based on the religious/philosophical divisions in society (i.e. the savings banks of socialist cooperatives, Christian workers' savings banks, Catholic agricultural savings banks), savings banks owned by neutral cooperatives, savings banks organized as a company extension, mortgage company savings banks and savings banks attached to deposit banks. No account has been taken here of the interest paid out by the latter group of institutions, as this is included in Section 3 (Interest on bank deposits)[25]. The most important savings banks discussed in this

---

[22] In the case of 1921, the balance at 31 December was taken by way of approximation for the average outstanding amount.
[23] NIS, *Commissie van het nationaal inkomen,* p. 243.
[24] VANTHEMSCHE G., *De Belgische spaarbanken tijdens het Interbellum,* in: "De Belgische spaarbanken. Geschiedenis, recht, economische functie en instellingen", pp. 161-209.
[25] According to Vanthemsche, the savings bank activities of the deposit banks were abolished by law in 1934-1935 (VANTHEMSCHE G., *o.c.*, p. 177). Nevertheless the annual reports of the Banking Commission indicate that the banks were still attracting savings deposits at the end of the 1930s (see for example the *Annual Report of the Banking Commission 1946-1947,* p. 31). These deposits have not, however, been entered under "savings passbooks" but under "bank passbooks", possibly so as to draw a clear distinction for the public with the "savings passbooks" of the private savings banks.

section are the Catholic agricultural savings banks organized by the Belgian Farmers Association and the savings banks attached to mortgage companies.

After the Second World War all private savings banks were subjected to the supervision of the *Central Small Savers Office* (Centraal Bureau voor Kleine Spaarders, CBKS). This institution was set up under the Act of 7 December 1934 and the Royal Decree of 15 December 1934 with a view to protecting the deposits of small savers against the consequences of the crisis in the Belgian financial system[26]. During the depression a number of banks and savings banks - especially those affiliated to the Catholic Farmers Association and the socialist workers' movement - had been confronted with serious liquidity and solvency problems.

In its post-war estimates the NIS uses figures derived from the CBKS, since this institution centralized all information on the private savings banks[27]. For the inter-war period an alternative source had to be found, firstly because the CBKS was not established until the end of 1934, and secondly because not all private savings banks were initially subject to the supervision of the CBKS[28]. On the basis of Vanthemsche's work, it was possible to estimate the total outstanding savings deposits in each year[29]. It has been assumed that all deposits were held by the personal sector. The total outstanding level of deposits was then multiplied by a rate of interest in order to obtain the interest payments.

In his study on the Belgian savings banks during the inter-war period, Vanthemsche has accumulated as much information as possible on the savings deposit balances. For most savings banks he has been able to recover figures for all or at least a large number of years. In the case of the savings banks for which Vanthemsche did not publish figures for all years the balances in the missing years were interpolated or extrapolated on the basis of the known years or on the basis of the movements in the balances of other savings banks for which information was available. The result of Vanthemsche's investigative work and the interpolations and extrapolations are shown in Table 63 (column 1-6). The total amount of savings deposits of the savings banks for which information was available (column 7) was augmented by 5% in order to take account of the

---

[26] LE BRUN J., *o.c.*, pp. 302-304 and 354-355; VAN DER WEE H., VERBREYT M., *Mensen maken geschiedenis. De Kredietbank en de economische opgang van Vlaanderen*, Tielt, 1985, p. 77; VAN DER WEE H., TAVERNIER K., *De Nationale Bank van België en het monetaire gebeuren tussen de twee wereldoorlogen*, Brussels, 1975, pp. 270-271; VANTHEMSCHE G., *o.c.*, pp. 180-194.

[27] NIS, *Commissie van het nationaal inkomen*, p. 243. Under the Act of 30 June 1975 the CBKS was dissolved and the supervisory function with respect to the private savings banks was transferred to the Banking Commission (LE BRUN J., *o.c.*, p. 355).

[28] This depended on the legal status of the savings bank in question. In 1935 only two savings banks were subject to CBKS supervision; in 1939 the number had risen to nine (VANTHEMSCHE G., *o.c.*, p. 194).

[29] VANTHEMSCHE G., *o.c.*, pp. 197-199.

deposits of the savings banks for which no figures were recovered for any year (columns 8 and 9)[30].

Although Vanthemsche does not indicate anywhere the time of the year to which his figures relate, it may be assumed that in most cases this is the end of the calender year. For this reason the annual average balance of year t was taken as the average of the balance in year t - 1 and that in year t (column 10)[31].

The series obtained in this way was then multiplied by an average rate of interest[32]. Since no figures could be found for the rates of interest paid by private savings banks, it was assumed that these were 0.5% higher than that paid by the ASLK (column 11), on the grounds that it may reasonably be assumed that the rate of interest paid by the private savings banks was higher than that paid by the semi-government ASLK, which was under State guarantee. The savings banks, which enjoyed no such protection, would only had been able to attract the necessary savings by offering a higher rate of interest.

Paragraph 3. Interest on savings deposits held with municipal savings banks

During the inter-war period there were three savings banks subject to the supervision of the local municipal executive. These were in Doornik, Nijvel and, to the end of 1929, in Aalst. The deposits held with these banks, which were very small, were published in the Statistical Yearbook. The same applies to the relevant rates of interest. The interest payments calculated on the basis of these figures are shown in Table 64 (column 3).

Paragraph 4. Interest on savings deposits held with public credit institutions (excluding ASLK)

Apart from the ASLK, a number of other semi-government financial institutions attracted savings deposits from the personal sector. The amounts in question were, however, very small, since these bodies attracted the majority of their working

---

[30] This relates primarily to savings banks organised as an extension of companies and the savings banks of the smaller mortgage companies (by contrast the savings banks of the large mortgage companies have been included in Vanthemsche's study, see Table 63 column 6). Since the deposits held with these savings banks were comparatively unimportant a 5% increase appears justified.

[31] For 1920 the outstanding amount at 31 December was used to approximate the average balance.

[32] This method of calculation contains a minor inaccuracy arising from the fact that the interest added at the end of a given year may not be included in the interest-bearing balance for the same year. However, since the average rate of interest is known with no greater precision, there would be little point in attempting to refine the calculation any further. This observation also applies to the other headings for which interest payments have been estimated by multiplying the outstanding level of deposits by an average rate of interest.

capital from other sources[33]. The total interest payments accruing to the personal sector are shown in Table 64 column 4. The calculations are based on the annual reports of some of these institutions. The share of interest payments accruing to private individuals has been determined on the basis of the NIS's post-war figures[34].

SECTION 3. INTEREST ON BANK DEPOSITS ACCRUING TO THE PERSONAL SECTOR

As noted earlier, this heading includes all interest payments on deposit accounts (including savings deposits) with deposit banks, in so far as these accrued to the personal sector.

First of all the annual level of outstanding deposits has been estimated for each category. The various outstanding amounts have then been multiplied by their respective rates of interest. Finally the share accruing to the personal sector of the interest payments arrived at in this way has been estimated.

With respect to the outstanding amounts, figures are available from 1935 onwards in the annual reports of the Banking Commission, the body responsible for supervising the bank system in Belgium since that year[35]. Before 1935 the

---

[33] In order of importance, the main semi-government financial institutions in Belgium were: The *Algemene Spaar- en Lijfrentekas* (ASLK, established in 1865), The *Gemeentekrediet van België* (established in 1860) and the *Nationale Maatschappij voor Krediet aan de Nijverheid* (NMKN, established in 1919). The ASLK's main working funds consisted of private savings deposits. The interest on these deposits was stated in paragraph 1. The Gemeentekrediet, whose main function consists of lending to lower levels of government (i.e. the provinces and municipalities), is largely financed by the issue of bonds and savings certificates, most of which are placed with the public. The NIS regards these savings certificates issued by the Gemeentekrediet as forming part of the public debt. In so far as they accrue to the personal sector, the interest payments on these savings certificates have consequently been included in section 5 ("Interest on government securities"). By contrast the interest on ordinary savings deposits held with the Gemeentekrediet have been included in this section. In the inter-war period the amounts in question were, however, very small. The NMKN is concerned with the provision of corporate finance, especially the granting of investment credits. The NMKN largely obtains its working funds by issuing bonds and savings certificates. Since the NMKN operates under a state guarantee, the NIS classifies these securities as part of the national debt (more specifically as part of the loans guaranteed by the State; see NIS, *Commissie van het nationaal inkomen*, p. 259). In so far as these bonds and savings certificates are held by the public, the relevant interest has been included in section 5. While it is true that the NMKN also attracts time deposits from private individuals, the amounts in question are so small that the NIS has disregarded them in its post-war calculations. On account of their very small scale these amounts have also been disregarded for the inter-war period.

[34] NIS, *Commissie van het nationaal inkomen,* pp. 245-247.

[35] The Banking Commission was established by Royal Decree 185 of 9 July 1935 (DURVIAUX R., *La banque mixte. Origine et soutien de l'expansion économique de la Belgique*, in: "Université Catholique de Louvain, Collection de l'Ecole des Sciences Economiques", vol. 33, Brussels, 1947, pp. 195-200 ; VAN DER WEE H., TAVERNIER K., *o.c.*, pp. 297-303.

necessary information was found in a number of publications dealing with the banking sector as a whole[36].

In calculating the interest on bank deposits the NIS draws a distinction between[37]:
- demand accounts and time deposits of no more than one month ;
- deposit passbooks (= savings deposits) ;
- time deposits of more than one month.

Until 1951, however, the annual reports of the Banking Commission draw no distinction between demand accounts and time deposits of no more than one month on the one hand and deposit passbooks on the other. Since the two groups of deposits were subject to different rates of interest, a breakdown is desirable. According to NIS figures, based on the annual reports of the Banking Commission, the outstanding balances on deposit passbooks amounted to 12.1%, 12.9%, 14% and 15.1% of the total outstanding amount of deposit passbooks, demand accounts and time deposits of no more than one month in the period 1951-1954[38].

It has been assumed that this share during the inter-war period was 10%. Figures published by the ASLK for 1938 indicate this proportion to be broadly correct, at least in the late 1930s. In 1938 the ASLK compiled a survey of saving in Belgium. According to that survey, savings deposits in the bank sector amounted to BF 1,249 million[39], equal to 8.6% of the total of deposit passbook accounts, demand accounts and time deposits of no more than one month (BF 14,592 million) according to the annual report of the Banking Commission.

Columns 1-5 of Table 65 show how the outstanding amounts of the various kinds of deposits were calculated. Despite the fact that these amounts derive from various sources, the series finally obtained (columns 3-5) exhibit a plausible pattern[40]. Since these figures relate to the end of the year, the annually outstanding amount in year t was set at the average of the outstanding amount on 31 December of year t-1 and the outstanding amount on 31 December of year t (columns 6-8)[41].

The rate of interest on time deposits with a term of more than one month has been taken as the interest on six-month time deposits (column 9). The figures for

---

[36] DURVIAUX R., *o.c.*, p. 121; EYSKENS G., *La bourse et les banques en 1931*, in: Bulletin de l'Institut des Sciences Economiques", vol. 3, 1932, p. 160 ; VAN DER WEE H., TAVERNIER K., *o.c.*, pp. 432-433.
[37] NIS, *Commissie van het nationaal inkomen*, p. 250.
[38] Own calculations on the basis of NIS, *Commissie van het nationaal inkomen*, p. 250.
[39] *ASLK Annual Report 1947*, p. 37.
[40] With the exception of the negative figure arrived at in 1920 for time deposits of more than one month (column 1 minus column 2).
[41] For 1920, the sum at 31 December 1920 was used to approximate the average outstanding amount.

1920-1925 relate to a large Brussels bank[42], those for 1929-1940 to all Belgian banks[43]. The interest rate for 1926-1928 was arrived at by applying the trend-corrected interpolation technique to these figures. It has been assumed that the interpolated series followed the same path as the yield on the 3% perpetual state loan[44].

With respect to the deposit passbooks, the same rate of interest was taken as that paid by the private savings banks, namely the ASLK rate of interest plus 0.5% (column 10)[45].

Demand accounts and time deposits with a term of no more than one month were assumed to pay the same rate of interest. Figures on the interest paid on demand deposits were found for 1920-1925 (for a large Brussels bank) and for 1929-1940 (for all Belgian banks)[46]. The period 1926-1928 was filled out using the trend-corrected interpolation technique. It has been assumed that the interpolated series followed the same path as the private discount rate for commercial paper (column 11)[47].

After multiplying the various deposit amounts by their respective interest rates, the total interest payments were obtained (columns 12-15). Finally it needs to be established what percentage of this total accrued to private individuals[48]. The NIS assumes that the personal sector share was 75%[49]. In the absence of alternative figures this percentage was also adopted for the inter-war period (column 16).

SECTION 4. IMPUTED INTEREST ON THE ACTUARIAL RESERVES OF LIFE INSURANCE COMPANIES

For statutory and commercial reasons companies engaged in life insurance business maintain reserves enabling them to meet their obligations to

---

[42] DURVIAUX R., *o.c.*, p. 122. The author does not specify the name of the bank; it was probably the Société Générale or the Banque de Bruxelles.
[43] *Belgische economische statistieken 1929-1940*, p. 14.
[44] The average yield on this state loan amounted to 5.77% in 1925, 6.64% in 1926, 5.01% in 1927, 4.61% in 1928 and 4.54% in 1929 (own calculations on the basis of monthly figures in *Belgische economische statistieken 1919-1928*, p. 36; *Idem 1929-1940*, p. 75).
[45] Cf. above.
[46] DURVIAUX R., *o.c.*, p. 122; *Belgische economische statistieken 1929-1940*, p. 14.
[47] The average private discount rate for commercial paper was 5.44% in 1925, 6.28% in 1926, 4.05% in 1927, 4.06% in 1928 and 4.30% in 1929 (*Belgische economische statistieken 1919-1928*, p. 4; *Idem 1929-1940*, p. 9).
[48] By the personal sector is meant persons residing in Belgium (including unincorporated businesses) or non-profit making organisations. The interest payments not accruing to the personal sector go to (share) companies or abroad.
[49] NIS, *Commissie van het nationaal inkomen*, p. 251.

policyholders at all times[50]. These reserves, known as actuarial reserves, should not be confused with ordinary reserves, which correspond with the reserved (or undistributed) profits accumulated over time. Reserved profits appear on the liability side of the balance sheet of any kind of joint stock company (i.e. not just insurance companies) and form the subject of a separate chapter in this volume (Chapter 12, "Company transfers to reserve".

To some extent, the actuarial reserves in the life insurance sector represent an asset of the body of policyholders in relation to the insurance company, in the sense that the (generally annual) insurance premium paid by the policyholder does not correspond with his risk of death or chance of reaching a certain age but is generally the same amount in each year. In principle the premium demanded by the insurance company should correspond with the risk covered - a risk that corresponds with the chance that the policyholder will die or reach a certain age. Since that risk rises over time, the policyholder should in fact pay a higher premium with age. A gradual increase in the premiums payable over time could, however, dampen the willingness of the public to take out life insurance, for which reason the insurance companies tend to level out the premiums. In the early years of the policy the equalized premium will lie above the corresponding risk, so that part of the premium collected (namely that part of the premium that exceeds the insurance risk and the insurance costs) needs to be set aside each year in the form of reserves[51].

In fact the actuarial reserves belong to the policyholders and may be regarded as a form of saving. Consequently the interest on these reserves also accrues to the policyholders and is included in this chapter. The relevant rate of interest on the actuarial reserves is not the market rate but a technical or actuarial rate of interest subject to statutory limitation. This rate of interest seldom varies over time and is commonly imposed by the government.

Since the actuarial reserves relate to life insurance, it may be assumed that the underwriters and/or beneficiaries of the policies are private individuals[52]. The interest on the actuarial reserves may, therefore, be included in this chapter in their entirety.

---

[50] Life insurance may be divided into three categories:
 - life assurance: in the event of the death of the policyholder, the insured sums are paid out to a person (or persons) specified in the policy;
 - endowment insurance: the insured sums are only paid out if the policyholder is still alive at the date agreed in the policy;
 - mixed life insurance: the insured sums are payable either on death or upon expiry of the period agreed in the policy.
 (VANDEPUTTE R., *Handboek voor verzekeringen en verzekeringsrecht,* Antwerp, 1969, pp. 18-19.)
[51] VANDEPUTTE R., *Idem*, p. 36.
[52] NIS, *Commissie van het nationaal inkomen*, p. 263.

The interest on actuarial reserves included in this chapter relate only to voluntarily taken out insurance. By contrast, the interest paid on the actuarial reserves of statutory pension funds (i.e. pension funds arising from the application of the pension legislation) form part of Chapter 14 "Income from property and entrepreneurial income accruing to the government".

In calculating the interest on actuarial reserves a distinction was drawn according to the statutory framework in which insurance companies operate[53]:
- companies subject to supervision under the Act of 25 June 1930 (= private companies) ;
- institutions whose operation is governed by special legislation (= semi-government institutions: principally the ASLK; the remainder are negligible[54]) ;
- employers' welfare institutions (= pension funds established by certain companies with the object of providing staff with a supra-legal pension).

The ASLK's actuarial reserves were published in its annual reports (see Table 66 column 1). These are the reserves at 31 December. To arrive at the annual average actuarial reserve of year t, the weighted average was taken of the reserve at 31 December of year t-1 and that on 31 December of year t (column 2). In 1920-1921 the actuarial technical rate of interest was 3%, and from 1922 onwards 4%[55]. Multiplication of the average actuarial reserve by the rate of interest results in the imputed interest payments.

With respect to the private insurance companies the actuarial reserves from 1932 were published in the official annual report on the operation of private life insurance companies[56]. This report is the consequence of the Act of 25 June 1930, under which such companies came under government supervision. On account of the absence of statutory control for the period 1920-1931 no data are available for the body of private life insurance companies. It has been assumed that the ratio between the actuarial reserves held by the ASLK and those held by the private companies in 1920-1931 was the same as in 1932. The actuarial reserves of the

---

53 *Idem,* pp. 263-264.
54 The NIS also takes into account the Nationale Maatschappij voor Kleine Landeigendom (NIS, *Commissie van het nationaal inkomen,* pp. 265-266). The actuarial reserves of this institution, which was established in 1935, were however so small in the post-war years (BF 3 million in 1947, BF 20 million in 1948, and BF 0.4 million imputed interest in 1948) that it was decided not to incorporate this company in the inter-war period.
55 Royal Decree of 6 September 1910, *ASLK Annual Report 1921,* p. 64; 1929, p. 47. The rate of interest paid by the ASLK remained at 4% after the Second World War (NIS, *Commissie van het nationaal inkomen,* p. 265).
56 *Rapport sur l'Exécution de la loi du 25 juin 1930 relative au contrôle des entreprises d'assurances sur la vie pendant l'année X, présenté aux chambres législatives par Monsieur le Ministre du Travail et de la Prévoyance Sociale,* Brussels, Ministère du travail et de la Prévoyance Sociale, appears annually.

ASLK have consequently been multiplied by a factor of 8.7 (column 4). The further calculation of the imputed interest was done in the same way as for the ASLK, with the difference that the actuarial rate of interest amounted not to 4% but 3.5% (columns 5 and 6)[57].

No information is available on the actuarial reserves of employers' welfare institutions in the inter-war period. In 1948-1954 these reserves averaged 7% of the reserves of insurance companies subject to government supervision. For the inter-war period it was assumed that this share was 5% (column 7). For the further calculation, reference is made to the method discussed for the ASLK figures (columns 8 and 9).

SECTION 5. INTEREST ON GOVERNMENT SECURITIES ACCRUING TO THE PERSONAL SECTOR

If one likes to know the interest accruing to private persons resident in Belgium, only the national internal debt has to be taken into account. Once the interest on the total national internal debt is known, the proportion accruing to private persons can then be calculated.

The internal public authority debts consists of :
- central government debt ;
- provincial and local authority debts ;
- loans guaranteed by the state ;
- inter-urban association debts ;
- colonial debt.

There is only information available on the central government debt and the provincial and local authority debts. Since the other elements are of minor importance, only the interest on the central government and the provincial and local authority debts respectively were calculated. A small increment coefficient was then applied to this interest in order to take into account the missing elements.

The interest paid out on the central government debt for the period 1929-1939 can be found in the "Belgische economische statistieken, 1929-1940". For the period 1920-1928, only the annual outstanding debt and the interest rate on new issues are available[58]. The yearly interest rate on the outstanding debt was calculated by taking an average of the interest rates on all new issues over the ten immediate preceding years. By multiplying the (known) outstanding debt by the average (estimated) interest rate, the interest paid out was arrived at.

---

[57] NIS, *Commissie van het nationaal inkomen,* p. 264. It is unclear why the legislator imposed a different actuarial rate of interest on the private insurance companies from that applying to the ASLK.
[58] DAVIN L.E., *La dette publique de 1919 à 1939,* p. 335.

The interest paid out on the provincial and local authority stocks is more difficult to reconstruct. The "Belgische economische statistieken 1929-1940" include, for the years 1929-1940, the outstanding provincial and local authority debts with the *Municipal Credit Association of Belgium* (Gemeentekrediet van België) other financial institutions and the public. The interest paid out was calculated on the basis of the outstanding debt and using as an interest rate the average interest rate on all new issues over the ten immediate preceeding years[59]. For the period 1920-192 figures are neither available on the interest paid out nor on the outstanding debt. The only figures available figures are the annual repayments of the indebtness (capital + interest) of local authorities with more than 40,000 inhabitants. It was assumed that there was a constant ratio between interest paid out by all provincial and local authorities and the indebtedness of those local authorities with more than 40,000 inhabitants. The average ratio for the period 1929 to the end of 1939 was calculated.

The interest on central government and provincial and local authority debts was increased in order to take into account the remaining elements of the total internal public authority debt (loans guaranteed by the state, inter-urban association debts, colonial debt). An increment coefficient which rose from 1.11 to 1.25 between 1920 and 1939 was therefore used. This coefficient is based on a relative increase in the remaining components in comparison to the central government and provincial and local authority debts for the period 1948 to 1954.

Finally, the proportion of the total interest on the internal public authority debt accruing to the personal sector had to be determined. The following considerations however were taken into account. In 1948 50% of the internal public authority debt was with private persons. It was assumed that this was also the case for 1939. It was further assumed that the proportion of the internal public authority debt with private persons gradually declined in the second half of the 1930s. This was because at that time part of the population had expressed its lack of confidence in Belgium's financial system by choosing to convert their financial assets into paper money or by transferring them abroad. At the same time the financial institutions were able to buy public stock on favourable terms in the second half of the 1930s. In the light of all these considerations the proportion of the interest on public authority stocks accruing to private persons was estimated at 60% for the period 1920-1934, and allowed a linear decline from 60% to 50% for the period 1934-1939.

The figures on this section can be found in column 1 of Table 68.

---

[59] VAN AUDENHOVE M., *Geschiedenis van de gemeentefinanciën*, p. 108.

SECTION 6. INTEREST FORM A BOND LOAN TRANSACTED BY COMPANIES[60]

The volume of the interest paid out can be found in :
- Fiscal statistics on capital gains tax (1920-1928) ;
- Belgian economic statistics published by the National Bank of Belgium (1929 to 1940).

The proportion accruing to private persons was assumed to decrease linearly from 40% in 1920 to 30 % in 1940.
The figures on this section can be found in column 2 of Table 68.

SECTION 7. INTEREST ON MORTGAGE LOANS ACCRUING TO PRIVATE PERSONS[61]

The interest on mortgage loans accruing to the personal sector was estimated as follows. To begin with the total outstanding amount of mortgage loans was calculated, after which the proportion of the loans granted by private persons was determined. Finally the sums arrived at were multiplied by the mortgage rate of interest.

The estimate of total mortgage debt is based on the mortgage registration statistics, which in turn have been calculated on the basis of the arrangement fees[62]. The figures for mortgage registrations show the annual amount of new loans (see Table 67 column 1). In order to calculate the total amount of outstanding debt on the basis of these figures, it is necessary to have some idea about the average life of mortgage loans. According to Génin, who was one of the most senior officials at the Ministry of Finance, the average life of a mortgage loan granted to private persons was five years. Both principal and interest charges were due at maturity. Moreover, he estimated that private individuals granted 40 % of total mortgage lending[63]. The outstanding debt was multiplied by the interest rate to arrive at the annual volume of mortgage interest charges. The results of these calculations are shown in Table 67.

---

[60] Together with section 7 "Interest on mortgage loans accruing to private persons", the content of this section forms a single heading in the national accounts of the NIS.
[61] For more information, see BUYST E., Het inkomen uit onroerend vermogen toevloeiend aan particulieren, België: 1920-1939. In : "Workshop on Quantitative Economic History", Research Paper 94.01, Louvain, 1994, pp. 15-17.
[62] *Belgische economische statistieken 1919-1928,* p. 23; *Idem 1929-1940,* p. 142. The amount of mortgage registrations was arrived at by dividing the sum of arrangement fees by the percentage arrangement rate (e.g. arrangement fees of BF 300 and a rate of 0.3% indicates mortgage registrations totalling BF 100,000).
[63] GENIN E., *Les prêts hypothécaires en Belgique et leur destination,* in : "Bulletin de l'Institut des Sciences Economiques", vol. 4, 1933, pp. 261-262.

Finally it should be emphasized that the amounts included in this section relate only to loans for which a mortgage was taken out and on which mortgage arrangement fees were consequently paid. Within the informal networks of relatives and friends, loans were of course granted that were not subject to any mortgage. It may, however be assumed that the amounts in question were small, as the mortgage arrangement fees were very low (ranging from 0.2% to 0.4%[64]), so that the costs of a mortgage for a creditor did not match up to the costs associated with the risk of insolvency on the part of the debtor[65].

SECTION 8. IMPUTED INTEREST RELATING TO SERVICES PROVIDED FREE OF CHARGE BY BANKS AND OTHER FINANCIAL INTERMEDIARIES

This interest is defined as the difference between the return on capital investments by financial intermediaries (savings banks, deposit banks, insurance companies) and the interest paid out by these bodies. A part of this interest accrues to private persons. Given that it is not possible to calculate precisely the imputed interest for the inter-war period, is was supposed that the ratio between imputed and paid interest in the inter-war period was the same as that after 1945.

The figures can be found in Table 68.

---

[64] *Belgische economische statistieken 1919-1928,* p. 23; *Idem 1929-1940,* p. 142.
[65] Nor does the NIS take any account of the interest on informal loans for which no mortgage was concluded.

CHAPTER 10

RENTS (RECEIVED OR IMPUTED) PAYABLE TO PRIVATE INDIVIDUALS

SECTION 1. DEFINITION OF THE HEADING

This chapter contains an estimate of income from real estate (buildings and land) payable to private individuals. This includes not only the sums actually received for the leasing to others of property which may or may not be built upon. A rent figure, the so-called imputed rent, is also estimated for owners who live or work on their own property, despite the fact that in reality no financial transaction has taken place[1]. The reason for this method of proceeding is an obvious one: if no attribution were made, there would be an artificial rise in national income in the case of a relative increase in the numbers of tenants and landlords in society and an artificial fall in the case of a relative increase in the number of owners using their own property. Yet this change in the pattern of ownership has no effect on the volume of goods and services produced by society as a whole.

A simple example featuring two extreme situations may perhaps demonstrate even more clearly why it is necessary to assign a rent figure for owners who do not let out their property, but use it themselves. In situation A there is an extremely unequal pattern of ownership: all buildings and land are the property of a single individual X, who lets them out to the rest of society. X's rental income of course constitutes part of the national income. Suppose that the same stock of buildings and land is redistributed in such a way that each individual owns the house and land which he/she occupies or works on. In such a society there is no question of any financial transaction regarding rents and leases. If in determining GNP only actually paid rents and leases were to be taken into account, there would be a sharp drop in GNP in the transition from situation A to situation B. Yet no fewer goods and services are produced in situation B than in situation A; there has simply been a redistribution of wealth. Such anomalies are avoided by taking account of imputed rents and leases in the three approaches to GNP (production, income, expenditure).

The rent which is taken into account in this case is a net amount. One can assume that the owner is responsible for depreciation, the larger part of maintenance costs and, if there is a mortgage charge on the property, the mortgage interest payable. Consequently these charges are deducted from the gross rent, i.e.

---

[1] OECD, *A standardized system of national accounts*, p. 82; *De nationale rekeningen van België 1953-1962*, p. 1154.

the rent actually received or imputed. In contrast to the arrangements in certain other countries, taxes on property[2] are traditionally not deducted from the gross rent in the Belgian national accounts. These taxes are regarded by the NIS as direct taxes, which implies that they must be included among factor incomes, in this case from real estate[3].

In theory all (imputed) rental and lease income payable to private individuals (families, charitable institutions, private limited companies) must be included under this heading. This income refers to both dwellings, industrial premises, buildings belonging to charitable institutions (including private hospitals and private education buildings), and agricultural and forestry land. The income from such buildings and land payable to joint-stock companies must not be withheld, since the (imputed) rental income of joint-stock companies, like all their other income, is paid out to their shareholders and directors in the form of dividends and bonuses, or added to the company's reserves after the deduction of expenses (for example, salaries). If this (imputed) rental income were also included under this heading there would be duplication. The same applies to the government's (imputed) rental income. This in fact forms part of Chapter 14 *"Income from property and entrepreneurial income accruing to the government"*.

However, in making a concrete estimate of (imputed) rental incomes it is in most cases impossible to make a distinction between private individuals and non-private organisations. For this reason a number of assumptions must be built in, as the NIS does explicitly or implicitly in the post-war national accounts.

In the first place it is assumed that all residential buildings are private property. This leads to an overestimate of individuals' rental income, since a portion of the housing stock is let by companies, by social housing corporations with central government support, such as the *National Society for Low-Cost Housing* (Nationale Maatschappij voor Goedkope Woningen en Woonvertrekken (NMGW)), or by municipal councils and by the *Public Welfare Commissions* (Commissies voor Openbare Onderstand (COOs)) under municipal control, which were at the time responsible for official poor relief. However, the overestimate of private rental income is limited in extent, because the greater part of the housing stock in Belgium was in private hands during the inter-war period.

As regards industrial buildings the NIS assumes for the sake of simplicity that they are all owned by joint-stock companies[4]. As a result the private (imputed)

---

[2] For a survey of direct taxes in Belgium in the inter-war period, see Chapter 8.

[3] *Het Belgisch nationaal inkomen van 1948 tot 1954*, p. 611. If taxes on the income from real estate were to be regarded as an indirect tax, the net rent would be reduced by the amount of tax paid. On the other hand indirect taxes (Chapter 17) increase as a result, so that the level of national income remains unchanged.

[4] For 1949 and 1954 the NIS made a distinction between the gross income from buildings, depending on whether these were industrial or other types of building. Industrial buildings represent 16.5% of the total income from improved land (NIS, *Commissie van het Nationaal Inkomen*, pp. 277-278).

rental income is underestimated, since a large number of industrial buildings (tradesmen's workshops, factories of family businesses) are in private hands.

On the other hand it is assumed that all commercial buildings belong exclusively to private individuals. As a result the (imputed) rental income of joint-stock companies such as banks, insurance companies, department stores and suchlike is erroneously included. In the absence of factual evidence, the NIS assumes that the overestimate of rental income for commercial buildings is more or less offset by the underestimate for industrial buildings.

It is assumed that all agricultural land and buildings belong exclusively to private individuals, which is a reasonable assumption. In the case of woodlands a distinction can be made between government-owned and privately-owned woods.

As in the methodology of the NIS's, this chapter is subdivided in three headings: the (imputed) gross rent for improved properties (Section 2), unimproved properties (Section 3), the charges (depreciation, maintenance, mortgage interest), and finally the net rent, which is derived from the sum of the first two components minus the charges (Section 4).

The final results of the estimates are shown in Table 69.

SECTION 2. GROSS RENT FROM IMPROVED PROPERTIES

In estimating gross rent a distinction was drawn between dwellings and commercial buildings on the one hand and agricultural buildings on the other. As discussed in Section 1 of this chapter, is was assumed that all commercial and agricultural buildings were owned by private individuals and that the industrial buildings belonged to the corporate sector. The gross rent from agricultural buildings was calculated in Chapter 7. What follows relates to dwellings and commercial buildings.

Gross rent was estimated on the basis of three sets of data : the average (imputed) rent income per household in 1935 (Paragraph 1), a rent index for the inter-war period (Paragraph 2) and the annual number of households (estimated by Buyst on the basis of the population censuses and the Registers of Births, Deaths and Marriages)[5].

Paragraph 1. The average rent income per household in 1935

The average rent in 1935 was estimated from land registry particulars. In Belgium owners are assessed not in terms of the value of their property, but on the estimated income derived from it. This income, known as *cadastral income*, is adjusted from time to time by the *Land Registry Board* (Bestuur van het Kadaster)

---

5   BUYST E., *o.c.*, passim.

by means of a large-scale revision operation in which the entire stock of property is charted and an estimate is made of the income derived from its use, either actually received or imputed. During the inter-war period only one such excercise took place, the implementation of which took six years (1930-1935). The estimate of cadastral income was based on the rents in 1927-1930. The (imputed or actual) rental value of alle property in 1935 is therefore expressed in 1927-1930 prices, with the exception of government buildings, as these were exempt from taxes. The cadastral income was converted into 1935 prices on the basis of the rent index (cfr. infra, Paragraph 2).

Two adjustments were made to the total cadastral income. To begin with, the income from industrial buildings was deducted, as it was assumed that these did not accrue to the personal sector. The cadastral income was then converted into gross rent, since the cadastral income is a net figure that was arrived at by the Land Registration Board by deducting a fifth from the estimated gross income for maintenance and repairs. The cadastral income was therefore increased by 25% to arrive at total gross rent. This sum was finally divided by the number of households, resulting in the average gross rent in 1935. It was consequently assumed that the number of dwellings and commercial buildings corresponded with the number of households. As a result, an average gross rent of BF 3,577 in 1935 was arrived at.

Paragraph 2. A rent index for inter-war Belgium

Until recently virtually no research was carried out into the evolution of property rents in the 1920s and 1930s. In his 1955 study on the housing market in Belgium Leeman compiled price indices for three cities (Brussels, Ghent and Huy)[6]. However, this covers only a small number of dwellings: 16 middle-class properties and six working-class properties let by private individuals and ten working-class properties let by the National Association for Low-Cost Housing, a social housing association supported by government.

In the 1970s, as part of research into prices and earnings, two studies were published by researchers of the Free University of Brussels with rent data for the nineteenth and twentieth centuries: Avondts and Scholliers studied Ghent domestic rents and Van Den Eeckhout and Scholliers published figures relating to the city of Brussels[7].

---

[6] LEEMAN A., *De woningmarkt in België (1890-1950)*, in: "Katholieke Universiteit te Leuven. Reeks van de School voor Economische Wetenschappen", vol. 50, Kortrijk, 1955, p. 70.

[7] AVONDTS G., SCHOLLIERS P., *Gentse prijzen, huishuren en budgetonderzoeken in de 19e en 20e eeuw*, in: "Centrum voor Hedendaagse Sociale Geschiedenis. De Gentse textielarbeiders in de 19e en 20e eeuw", dossier 5, Brussels, 1977, pp. 53-152; SCHOLLIERS P., VAN DEN EECKHOUT P., *De Brusselse huishuren: 1880-1940*, in: "Centrum voor Hedendaagse Sociale Geschiedenis. Lonen en prijzen in België in de 19e en 20e eeuw", dossier 1, Brussels, 1979.

The Ghent data published by Avondts and Scholliers could not be retained for the compilation of a Belgian rent index during the inter-war period, because they go only up to 1925[8]. The Brussels rent index however covers the entire inter-war period and consequently was used as a starting point for the reconstruction of a Belgian index[9]. It relates to the rents of dwellings let by the Brussels Public Welfare Committees.

Because the figures published up to now on rents were insufficient to allow a reliable rent index for Belgium to be compiled as part of the national accounts, unpublished data of the Public Welfare Committees in cities as Antwerp, Ghent, Leuven and Liège were compiled and these were combined with the figures of Scholliers for Brussels in order to arrive at a representative rent index for the whole of Belgium. The results of this research are presented in Table 70. For more details on the reconstruction method of this index, the reader is referred to the studies of Henau and Buyst on the subject[10].

The rent index was then linked to the average gross rent in 1935 (Paragraph 1) and multiplied by the annual number of households as calculated by Buyst (cfr. infra) to provide an approximation of the housing stock (Table 71).

SECTION 3. GROSS RENT FROM UNIMPROVED PROPERTIES

This section relates to gross income from agricultural and forestry lands. In the former case the estimates were based on the rents, which were previously estimated as part of the charges in calculating agricultural income (Chapter 7). It was assumed that of the total rentals, 90% related to land and 10% to commercial buildings (Table 72). The estimate of the rent from forestry lands was also discussed in Chapter 7.

SECTION 4. CHARGES AND NET RENT

The charges to be deducted from gross rent consist on the one hand of depreciation and maintenance (by owners only) and on the other of interest charges on

---

8   The Ghent rent index covers the period 1796-1925. It was compiled on the basis of 332 dwellings which were let by the predecessors of the Public Welfare Committees (77% of the dwellings), the city of Ghent (14%) and the Catholic Church (9%). AVONDTS G., SCHOLLIERS P., *o.c.*, pp. 56-57.

9   In the work of Van Den Eeckhout and Scholliers two indices are combined: the first from 1800 to 1914, the second from 1914 to 1940.

10 HENAU A., *De Belgische huishuren gedurende het Interbellum*, in: "Workshop on Quantitative Economic History", vol. 91.01, Leuven, 1991; BUYST E., *Het inkomen uit onroerend vermogen toevloeiend aan particulieren: België, 1920-1939*, in: "Workshop on Quantitative Economic History", vol. 94.01, Leuven, Table 5.

mortgages, where the latter were entered into to buy land or buy buy or build a dwelling.

Paragraph 1. Depreciation and maintenance costs

Estimates of the depreciation of improved properties are presented in Chapter 10. No statistical information is available for the inter-war years that allows a calculation of maintenance costs for improved properties. Between 1953 and 1961 maintenance costs on average amounted up to 17% of gross rent. Given that 1930 resembled the 1950's very closely regarding rent legislation, allowing market forces to a large extent to determine rents, total maintenance costs by owners and tenants in 1930 were put at 17% of the gross rent for that year. Maintenance costs by proprietors only were estimated at 60 % of that total. The maintenance costs for the remaining years were calculated by linking the 1930 figure (proprietors only) to a cost index and to an index of the number of dwellings (i.e. gross rent in constant prices). The cost index consists of two variables : wages in the construction industry (75%) and prices of construction materials (25%)[11].

The results obtained probably overestimate the maintenance costs in the 1920's as it may be assumed that owners who were letting rather than living in their properties themselves will have cut maintenance costs to the bone at this time of severe rent restrictions[12]. For this reason the maintenance costs by proprietors for the period 1920-1927 have been reduced by 30%. Over the period 1928-1930 this adjustment coefficient was gradually scaled back to 0% (Table 73 column 2).

Paragraph 2. Mortgage interest

No statistical information is available on aggregate mortgage interest charges, although details do exist on mortgage rates and the number of new mortgage contracts. Mortgages granted by individual persons were assumed to have an average term of five years; both principal and interest charges were due at maturity. Mortgages granted by financial institutions were assumed to have an average term of seven years; a seventh of the debt was assumed to be paid off each year. In this way it was possible to calculate the annual level of outstanding mortgage debt. It was further assumed that mortgage debt granted by individual persons and private financial institutions, 50% was entered into for building or purchasing dwellings or land (since mortgage debts taken out for other purpose must obviously not be taken into account). For public financial institutions this ratio was increased up to 90%[13]. For every category of lenders (private

---

11 BUYST E., *Residential Building...*, pp. 91-92.
12 For more details, see BUYST, E., *o.c.*, pp. 222-224.
13 For more information, see BUYST, E., *Inkomen...*, pp. 15-28.

individuals, private financial institutions and public financial institutions) the outstanding debt was multiplied by the interest rate. By doing so we arrived at the annual volume of mortgage interest charges (Table 73 column 2).

Table 73 shows the total volume of charges. These have been deducted from gross rent in Table 69 to obtain net rent.

CHAPTER 11

DIVIDENDS, RETURNS ON INVESTMENTS ABROAD, BONUSES AND GRANTS ACCRUING TO PRIVATE INDIVIDUALS[1]

SECTION 1. DEFINITION OF THE HEADING AND DISCUSSION OF THE SOURCES

Paragraph 1. Definition of the heading

Together with interest (Chapter 9) and rent income (Chapter 10), the income in this chapter forms the income from property. As in the two preceding chapters, only those sums have been taken into account that were imputed to private persons resident in Belgium, i.e. sums accruing to companies or paid abroad have been excluded[2]. The figures shown include direct taxes.

A distinction has been drawn between:
- Dividends paid by Belgian companies principally trading in Belgium (Section 2)
- Dividends paid by Belgian companies principally trading in the colonies or abroad (Section 3)[3]
- Income from investments abroad (Section 4)
- Directors' bonuses (Section 5)[4]
- Corporate grants to households and to non-profit organisations serving households (Section 6).

---

[1] The statistical material for this chapter was largely assembled by Guido Pepermans. He also made a major contribution towards the reconstruction method, for which the authors express their thanks.
[2] The personal sector is taken as meaning households and non-profit organisations. The reason why only the income accruing to private individuals resident in Belgium has been included, is discussed in the introduction to Chapter 9, "Interest accruing to the personal sector".
[3] Between 1908 and 1960 Belgium was the colonial authority in the Belgian Congo. In addition Belgium was granted a mandate over Ruanda-Urundi (the present Ruanda and Burundi) by the League of Nations in 1923. The latter two areas, which had formed part of the German colonies in East Africa until the war, became independent in 1962.
[4] It may be debated whether the bonuses for the managing and supervisory directors of a company should be regarded as property income or income from employment. The standardized system of the OECD does not make any explicit reference to this distinction. In the national accounts of the NIS they are treated as income from property. For the sake of consistency with present Belgian data, directors' profit-shares have therefore been treated in this volume as an element of income from property.

Apart from the dividend payments of foreign companies principally trading abroad, the heading "Income from investments abroad" comprises all other forms of income from property invested abroad, such as interest on foreign state securities[5], interest on bank deposits abroad and rent income from property located abroad. This item therefore also includes income which in fact belongs in Chapter 9 (interest) or in Chapter 10 (rent). Since the available sources do not permit any breakdown into the various components of income from property invested abroad, they have been brought together in this chapter.

For the sake of completeness this chapter should also contain a heading with respect to the dividends paid out by foreign companies established in Belgium. Such companies were, however, in Belgium on only a very limited scale during the inter-war period, so that the dividends they paid out may be disregarded[6].

The results of the estimates are shown in Table 74.

Paragraph 2. Discussion of the sources

The estimates in this chapter are based on two sources: the return-on-capital statistics for Belgian and Congolese joint-stock companies compiled by the National Bank of Belgium (NBB) and fiscal data relating to financial assets taxation.

1. The return-on-capital statistics of the National Bank of Belgium

From 1927 onwards the NBB collected statistics on the profitability of Belgian and Congolese joint-stock companies. These tables, which appeared in the *Belgische Economische Statistieken*, are based on the balance sheets and profit and loss accounts published in the annexes to the *Belgian State Gazette* and in the *Bulletin officiel du Congo belge*[7].

According to Belgian company law, all joint-stock companies (i.e. public limited companies and partnerships limited by shares) were obliged to file their balance sheet and profit and loss account each year with the office of the clerk of the commercial court where the company seat was located[8]. This had to be done

---

5   With the exception of interest on colonial loans, which form part of Chapter 9.
6   Foreign companies were represented on a significant scale in the inter-war period only in the Antwerp port area (e.g. General Motors, Ford and Bell Telephone). The mass influx of foreign companies in Belgium did not take place until the 1960s. The post-war national accounts of the NIS do not take any account of the dividends paid by the Belgian branches of foreign companies since these could, according to the Ministry of Finance, be disregarded. NIS, *Commissie van het Nationaal Inkomen*, p. 197.
7   *Belgische Economische Statistieken 1919-1928*, pp. 19-22; *Idem 1929-1940*, pp. 160-187.
8   *Belgische Economische Statistieken 1929-1940*, p. 160.

no later than 14 days after adoption of the balance sheet by the annual general meeting of shareholders[9]. Joint-stock companies were subsequently required to submit these documents to the Belgian State Gazette which then published a summary of the balance sheet and the profit and loss account in its annexes no later than ten days from the date of filing with the court.

In principle the NBB's return-on-capital statistics cover all joint-stock companies under Belgian law, i.e. companies with their company seat in Belgium, irrespective as to where the business itself was carried out, as well as joint-stock Congolese law. The balance sheets of the latter companies were published in the annexes to the Belgian State Gazette - if they had a seat in Belgium - or in the Bulletin officiel du Congo belge.

The tables do not include foreign companies with an establishment in Belgium[10], and the majority of the companies of a public or semi-public nature[11]. Needless to say the statistics do not include those companies which, despite the statutory requirement, had not filed their balance sheets. A number of companies - especially smaller ones whose shares were not traded on the stock exchange - failed to comply with the filing and publication requirement. This was because they risked incurring no more than a fine, which was generally not collected[12]. Despite this limitation the NBB assumed that the majority of joint-stock companies were included in the figures[13].

The companies have been divided in the return-on-capital statistics into 42 industries. From 1935 onwards a breakdown was also provided according to the principal location of commercial activity (in Belgium, the Belgian Congo or abroad).

The following particulars are included in the tables for each industry: number of companies (total number, number profit-making, number loss-making), paid-up

---

[9] There was generally an interval of several months between the closing date of the financial year and the date on which the balance sheet and profit and loss account was adopted by the annual general meeting of shareholders.

[10] Notwithstanding the fact that foreign companies were also required to publish their balance sheet and profit and loss account in the annexes of the Belgian State Gazette.

[11] The accompanying text specifically states that the National Belgian Railway Company (NMBS), the National District Railway Company (Nationale Maatschappij voor Buurtspoorwegen (NMVB), the Municipal Credit Association of Belgium (Gemeentekrediet van België) and the National Low-Cost Housing Association (Nationale Maatschappij voor Goedkope Woningen) were not included *(Belgische Economische Statistieken 1929-1940*, p. 160). In addition a comparative survey of the various sub-headings indicated that the General Savings and Annuity Fund (Algemene Spaar- en Lijfrentekas, ASLK) and the Telegraph and Telephone Company (Regie van Telegraaf en Telefoon, RTT) were not included in the return-on-capital statistics. The following were, however, included in the tables: the National Bank of Belgium, the National Industrial Credit Association (Nationale Maatschappij voor Krediet aan de Nijverheid, NMKN) and the Bank of Belgian-Congo *(Idem*, p. 160).

[12] *Idem*, p. 160.

[13] *Idem*.

capital, the net result (the total profit of the companies operating at a profit, the total loss of the companies operating at a loss and the balance of the two figures)[14], the profit distributed to shareholders, the bond debt and the amount of bond coupons[15]. The distributed dividends and bond coupons are gross figures. They therefore contain the direct tax on movable property income to which the holders of securities were subject. From 1936 onwards the reserves were also published[16].

The information from the return-on-capital statistics of relevance for this chapter naturally consists of the distributed dividends, as well as the net operating results. On the basis of the latter figures a rough estimate will be made of the corporate grants to households and non-profit organisations serving households. Directors' bonuses will be estimated on the basis of dividend payments.

The statistics published by the NBB contain annual figures arrived at by aggregating the (unpublished) monthly tables. Up to and including 1932 the balance sheet data were included in the table of the month in which the balance sheet was published in the Belgian State Gazette. Most companies' financial year ran to 31 December. Since a few weeks or months tended to elapse between the compilation of the balance sheet and its publication (i.e. after approval by the general meeting of shareholders and deposition with the office of the clerk of the commercial court), a considerable number of data included in the return-on-capital statistics of year X in fact relate to financial year X-1.

From 1931 onwards the method was revised to some extent: the criterion for inclusion was no longer the publication data in the Belgian State Gazette but the date on which dividend coupons became payable[17]. Where that date was unknown the date of approval of the balance sheet by the general meeting was used as the criterion for inclusion. For the years from 1931 onwards, therefore, the observation also applies that the majority of the figures in the return-on-capital statistics for year X relate to corporate activities in year X-1.

Calculations by the NIS on the return-on-capital statistics for 1953 indicate that in that year roughly 75% of the published profits and distributed dividends corresponded with the balance sheets for the previous year and 25% with the balance sheets completed for the year of profit publication or dividend payment[18]. In the absence of other data it has been assumed that this breakdown also applied to the inter-war period. The amount of profits or the dividends arising from the economic activity in year t will therefore be arrived at by taking 75% of the

---

[14] For a description of the net result in the profitability statistics, see Chapter 12, "Reserved Profits of Corporations".
[15] From 1933 the amount of coupons paid out by private companies was not just shown but also the amount of the coupons on bond loans issued by the government. See Chapter 15, "Interest on the government debt".
[16] See Chapter 12.
[17] *Belgische economische statistieken 1929-1940*, p. 161.
[18] NIS, *Commissie van het Nationaal Inkomen*, p. 188.

published profit or the dividends distributed in year t+1 together with 25% of those published or distributed in year t[19].

The return-on-capital statistics provide the basic material for the figures reconstructed in this and also the following chapter on reserved profits. Since these statistics commenced only in 1927 and do not provide any information on income from investments abroad, these data had to be drawn from a different source, namely figures relating to the taxation on income from non-property sources.

2. Fiscal data relating to the financial assets tax

a) Characteristics of the financial assets tax

As a result of the Act of 29 October 1919, supplemented by that of 3 August 1920, Belgium received a totally new system of income tax[20]. One of the new taxes was levied on the earnings from financial assets[21]. In principle all income on movable property in respect of which the creditor or debtor resided in Belgium was taxed[22]. A Belgian resident (either a private individual or a company) which had invested all or part of his or its assets abroad was therefore liable to pay tax to the Belgian Exchequer. Similarly a foreign resident who owned Belgian shares, bonds or savings deposits, etc., was liable to Belgian tax. The treatment below is confined to the financial assets taxation on dividends paid by Belgian companies or on the financial assets taxation on earnings obtained abroad.

Tax was payable to the Belgian tax department on all dividends distributed by Belgian companies, irrespective as to whether the shares in the company were

---

[19] In its post-war calculations of national income the NIS has proceeded along the above lines in estimating the reserved profit but not in estimating dividends. In the case of dividends the figures are not converted into the year in which the dividends were realized (i.e. the activity year) but are assigned to the year of payment (i.e. year of the profitability statistics). This is an inconsistent method of approach, which has been avoided for the inter-war years, by assigning both dividends and reserved profits to the activity year.

[20] For a discussion of the features of the new tax systems see Chapter 8, "Entrepreneurial income of the professions, independent traders, craftsmen and partnerships".

[21] The statutory provisions in relation to the movables tax are set out in detail in PUTMAN R., *Les impôts directs en Belgique de 1914 à 1940*, in: "Histoire des finances publiques en Belgique", Brussels; Paris, Institut Belge de Finances Publiques (ed.), vol. I, 1950, pp. 374-376, 428-429, 431-432, 452-453, 484-495.

[22] *Idem*, p. 426. Initially the earnings from foreign assets invested in Belgium by non-residents were also taxed. With a view to attracting foreign investment these earnings were exempted from tax under the Act of 13 July 1930 (*Idem*, pp. 428-429, 486). No tax was payable in respect of certain forms of income from government stocks (*Idem*, pp. 374-375). Under the Act of 13 July 1930 the interest on savings deposits held with the ASLK were also exempted in so far as the amount of interest did not exceed BF 100 (*Idem*, p. 429). Under the same Act tax was also no longer payable on the interest of sums invested with the Deposito- en Consignatiekas (*Idem*, p. 429).

owned by private individuals living in Belgium or abroad or by another domestic or foreign company. The tax rate was initially 10% but was increased repeatedly over the years to 22% in 1939[23]. With a view to promoting the rationalization of Belgian industry the Acts of 23 July 1927, 2 July 1931, 23 July 1931 and the statutory order of 22 August 1934 laid down that the shares in companies that merged were temporarily exempted from tax on financial assets[24].

The interests on investments abroad accruing to private individuals or companies resident in Belgium were initially taxed at 2%[25]. Such tax was levied not just on earnings from financial assets (e.g. dividends and interest) but also on property income (rent). In 1925 and 1930 the tax rates were increased to 5% and 6% respectively[26]. In order to avoid double taxation, bilateral agreements were concluded with certain countries (Luxembourg, France, Italy and the Netherlands), under which (among other things) Belgian residents who had invested all or some of their assets in those countries and had paid local taxation were wholly or partially exempted from taxation in Belgium[27].

b)   The fiscal statistics relating to income subject to financial assets tax

The figures on the income subject to financial assets tax are incomplete for the inter-war period and it is difficult to make any judgement about the quality of the available material[28]. Reliable fiscal statistics were not systematically published by the NIS until after the Second World War[29].

The available fiscal information for the inter-war period has been published in various sources, as shown at the bottom of Table 75. For the years 1920-1922 the figures have been drawn from the reply by the Ministry of Finance to a parliamentary question[30]. The same figures as well as figures for 1923 were

---

[23]   *Idem*, pp. 452-453, 492 and 495. According to Baudhuin the tax rate in the mid-1930s was 24.2% (BAUDHUIN F., *La Belgique en 1936. Les revenus*, in: "Bulletin de l'Institut de Recherches Economiques", vol. 8, p. 131 ; BAUDHUIN F., *La Belgique en 1937. Les finances belges en 1937*, in: "Idem", vol. 9, p. 115).
[24]   PUTMAN R., *o.c.*, p. 488.
[25]   *Idem*, p. 491. The tax rate on earnings abroad was set at this very low level in Belgium because these earnings had already been taxed abroad.
[26]   *Idem*, p. 491 (Act of 31 December 1925 and 13 July 1930).
[27]   *Idem*, p. 427 (double taxation agreement with the Grand Duchy of Luxembourg on 9 March 1931, with France on 16 May 1931, with Italy on 11 July 1931 and with the Netherlands on 20 February 1933).
[28]   Cf. below.
[29]   VAN DER AA, E.R., *Studie over het opzetten eener statistiek der in de mobiliënbelasting, de bedrijfsbelasting, de nationale crisisbelasting en in de aanvullende personeele belasting aangeslagen inkomsten en van het rendement dezer belastingen (Fiscaal dienstjaar 1945 - Inkomsten verworven in 1944)*, in: "Statistisch Bulletin, vol. 32, no. 9-10 (September - October 1946), pp. 835-857.
[30]   This concerns figures for the fiscal years 1921-1923. The incomes in these figures were earned

published by Mahaim. In relation to 1923, 1924, 1925 and 1927 information was found in the numerous articles and books by the Louvain professor Fernand Baudhuin, who evidently had good contacts with officials at the Ministry of Finance. In addition fiscal data on the income from financial assets obtained in 1927-1938 were included in two articles published in the journal of the National Bank of Belgium.

The fiscal data of relevance in this chapter are divided into sections on dividends (Sections 2 and 3) and the earnings on investments abroad (Section 4). In the case of dividends the fiscal information will also be compared with the data on the return-on-capital statistics.

SECTION 2. DIVIDENDS DISTRIBUTED BY BELGIAN COMPANIES PRINCIPALLY TRADING IN BELGIUM

As in the case of the post-war national accounts of the NIS, the dividends accruing to private individuals in the inter-war period have been estimated on the basis of the rate of return statistics for Belgian joint-stock companies[31]. One of the elements included in these statistics is the aggregate dividends paid out. The figures in the rate of return statistics, however, had to be adapted for the following reasons:
1) According to the principles of national accounts earnings must be assigned to the year in which they are earned. The information in the rate of return statistics which, as discussed earlier, relates to the year of publication of the balance sheet or to the year of payment of dividends, must consequently be converted to the activity year. This conversion was handled as follows: the amount of dividends arising from economic activity in year t was estimated by taking 75% of the dividends specified in the rate of return statistics of year t+1 and adding to this 25% of the dividends in the statistics for year t[32].
2) The rate of return statistics do not draw a distinction until 1935 between companies principally trading in Belgium, companies principally trading in the Belgian Congo and companies principally trading abroad. No such breakdown was provided in the return-on-capital statistics for 1927-1934; all companies are instead grouped together. For these years the total pay-out of dividends had therefore to be split into dividends assigned to companies principally trading in Belgium (this section), and the dividends paid out by companies principally trading in the Belgian Congo or abroad (Section 3). This breakdown was conducted on the basis of fiscal statistical data.

---

in 1920-1922. In the ensuing analysis the annual figures consistently relate to the year in which the incomes were earned.
[31] NIS, *Commissie van het Nationaal Inkomen*, pp. 187-196; *De nationale rekeningen van België 1953-1962*, p. 1155. Up to and including 1946 the rate of return statistics were drawn up by the NBB, and from 1947 by the NIS (*Belgische economische statistieken 1941-1955*, vol. 1, p. 41).
[32] Cf. above.

191

3) No return-on-capital statistics were drawn up for the period 1920-1926. Fiscal data have been drawn on for these years.

Both the return-on-capital statistics and the fiscal data cover the total amount of dividends paid out. Since only the dividends accruing to private individuals resident in Belgium are taken into consideration, the dividends payable to non-residents or companies should be deducted from the aggregate pay-out. No information is available on the share of private individuals. In order to compensate for underregistration we leave the data unchanged.

Table 75 column 5 shows the amount of dividends paid by Belgian companies principally trading in Belgium according to the return-on-capital statistics for 1935-1939. The dividends paid out by Belgian companies principally trading in the colonies or abroad is shown for the same period in column 7[33]. Column 9 shows the total amount of dividends paid out by all Belgian companies according to the profit and loss statistics for 1927-1939. In columns 6 and 10 the figures have been converted to the activity year according to the method described above[34]. Since the return-on-capital statistics for the period 1926-1934 provide information only on the total amount of dividends paid out, the share of the dividends paid out by the companies principally trading in Belgium needs to be estimated for these years. This estimate is conducted on the basis of the known ratios in the return-on-capital statistics for 1935-1939 and the ratios in the fiscal statistics. Before proceeding to this estimate, the figures in the return-on-capital statistics are compared with the information in the fiscal statistics.

The amount of dividends paid out by Belgian companies according to the fiscal statistics is shown in Table 74, column 1 (principal trading activity in Belgium), column 2 (principal trading activity abroad or in the colonies) and column 3 (total). As may be seen from the available information, a comparison can only be drawn with the return-on-capital statistics for 1927 and 1935-1938. The results of this comparison are disappointing. In 1927 the total amount of dividends paid out according to the fiscal statistics are 9% higher than that according to the information on the basis of the return-on-capital statistics (column 3 versus column 10). In 1935-1938 the situation is reversed and the total figure on the basis of the return-on-capital statistics is appreciably higher than that in the fiscal statistics (19% in 1935, 19% in 1936, 21% in 1937 and 37% in 1938).

No satisfactory explanation has been found for this discrepancy. No evaluation of the reliability of the figures is made in the sources in which the fiscal data are published. As far as the provisions concerning financial assets taxation are concerned, little changed in a statutory sense during the period under review. One factor that may have played a part is the fact that the shares of companies

---

[33] Belgian companies are taken in this context as including companies according to Congolese law.
[34] For the activity year 1926 the total amount of dividends paid out (column 10) was equated with the total amount of dividends paid out in the return-on-capital statistics of 1927 (column 9).

entering into a merger were temporarily exempted from financial assets taxation as a result of the Acts of 23 July 1927, 2 July 1931, 23 July 1931 and the statutory order of 22 August 1934, which were introduced with a view to rationalizing Belgian industry[35]. Since a wave of mergers took place in certain industries as a result of the depression in the 1930s, the amount of non-taxable dividends may well have increased in this period. Nevertheless it is improbable that this factor alone was responsible for the marked discrepancies between the fiscal and return-on-capital statistics[36].

The share of the dividends paid out by Belgian companies principally trading in Belgium in relation to dividends paid out by all Belgian companies is shown in column 4 (fiscal statistics) and column 11 (return-on-capital statistics). In the case of the years for which both sets of figures exist (1935-1938) the share in the fiscal statistics is higher in 1935, 1937 and 1938 and a little lower in 1936. In terms of the order of magnitude, however, the two series may be said to correspond reasonably well. For this reason use was made of the information in the fiscal statistics in order to estimate the share in 1926-1934 of the dividends paid out by Belgian companies principally trading in Belgium in relation to the dividends paid out by all Belgian companies.

In 1927 the share in the fiscal statistics was 73.1%. It has been assumed that this share was the same in the return-on-capital statistics. For 1926 the share was arrived at by linear interpolation of the shares in the fiscal statistics of 1925 and 1927. The share in the intervening years of 1928-1934 has been filled in as follows. First, the share of Congolese companies in the total dividends paid out by all companies listed in the return-on-capital statistics was calculated for the period 1927-1935. For the years 1927 and 1935 the remainder of dividends paid out was then compared to the percentages in columns 4 and 11 in Table 75. On the basis of the difference found for these two years an interpolation was carried out for the intervening years applying the compound annual growth rate. Subtracting now the resulting series and the share of Congolese companies from the total dividends paid out by all companies resulted in the percentages listed in column 12.

By multiplying the total amount of dividends paid out by the ratios determined in this way, one arrives at the amount of dividends paid out by the companies principally trading in Belgium in 1926-1934 (column 13).

In the absence of return-on-capital statistics, the figures from the fiscal statistics have been used for the period 1920-1925.

Column 14 brings together the amount of dividends paid out by Belgian companies principally trading in Belgium for the entire 1920s and 1930s.

---

[35] Cf. above.

[36] Baudhuin also notes the major discrepancies between the return-on-capital and fiscal statistics. While he rules out tax fraud as a possible cause of the lower amounts in the fiscal statistics, he nevertheless gives preference to the figures in the return-on-capital statistics. BAUDHUIN F., *Les finances belges en 1938,* in: "Bulletin de l'Institut de Recherches Economiques", vol. 10, p. 124. The notion that the tax figures have not been distorted by tax fraud would appear a plausible hypothesis since the tax was levied at source (= by the company paying the dividends).

SECTION 3. DIVIDENDS PAID OUT BY BELGIAN COMPANIES PRINCIPALLY TRADING IN THE COLONIES OR ABROAD[37]

The sources and methodology of this section are nearly identical to those in the previous section, so that the discussion can be kept very brief. The results of the estimates have been brought together in Table 76.

For the years for which only the total amount of dividends paid out is known, the share of the dividends paid out by the companies principally trading in the colonies or abroad was of course arrived at by taking account of the share estimated in the previous section of the dividends paid out by the companies principally trading in Belgium (see column 4).

As far as the share of the dividends accruing to private individuals is concerned, no information was again found on these securities for the inter-war period. This meant that the percentage figure adopted with due caution by the NIS (15%) for the period 1948-1954 has necessarily been taken for the 1920s and 1930s[38]. The fact that this percentage is so low may be attributed to the fact that the Belgian companies operating in the colonies or abroad were largely subsidiaries of Belgian portfolio companies, such as the Société Générale.

SECTION 4. EARNINGS FROM INVESTMENTS ABROAD

As noted earlier, this section covers not just the dividends paid out by foreign subsidiaries principally active abroad that accrued to private individuals resident in Belgium but also all other forms of earnings from assets invested abroad, such as interest on foreign government loans, interest on bank deposits abroad and rent income on real estate located abroad, in so far as these earnings accrued to private individuals residing in Belgium[39].

Fiscal data only are available on these earnings, and that for just 12 years (see Table 77 column 1)[40]. The missing years were filled in on the basis of the evolution of the dividends paid up by Belgian companies principally trading in the colonies or abroad (columns 2-4).

The earnings from investments abroad are without question severely underestimated in the fiscal statistics. While it is true that these earnings were

---

[37] Belgian companies are taken here also to include companies according to Congolese law.
[38] NIS, *Commissie van het Nationaal Inkomen*, pp. 201-203.
[39] Cf. above.
[40] In the post-war national accounts of the NIS the earnings from investments abroad are estimated on the basis of figures in the balance of payments (NIS, *Commissie van het Nationaal Inkomen*, pp. 203-206; *Het Belgisch nationaal inkomen van 1948 tot 1954*, pp. 612-613; *De nationale rekeningen van België 1953-1962*, pp. 1155-1156). Since the balance of payments was drawn up in Belgium from 1948 onwards only (in fact for the Belgian/Luxembourg Economic Union), a different source had to be found for the inter-war period.

subject to financial assets tax, the tax authorities were only able to check them efficiently if such earnings were repatriated via a Belgian bank. Where that was not the case - for example if the beneficiary encashed his dividend or bond coupon abroad, of if the earnings were not repatriated at all (i.e. if the proceeds were reinvested abroad) - it was possible to evade tax. On the basis of indications in Baudhuin's estimates of national income, the fiscal data were increased by 50% to allow for evasion (columns 5 and 6).

Baudhuin also bases his estimates of the property incomes from abroad on figures in the fiscal statistics, which he then increases in order to allow for fraud (1923: 414 increased to 600 = 45% increase[41]; 1927: 1,160 increased by 650 = 1,810 = 56% increase[42]; 1935: 800 increased by 400 = 1,200 = 50% increase[43]; 1936: 917 increased to 1,200 = 31% increase)[44]. If these incremental percentages were simply adopted as they stand with interpolation or extrapolation for the unspecified years this would lead to distorted results as Baudhuin's increases were not logically worked out and the various percentages derived above are the result of the fact that Baudhuin consistently wished to work with rounded off figures. Since no evidence whatever was found of an increased or reduced level of tax evasion in any part of the inter-war period, preference was given to a single incremental percentage for the entire period. Baudhuin's estimates suggest that 50% is a defensible figure.

Finally the share accruing to private individuals in the total sum of property income derived from abroad needs to be determined. In the absence of information on this aspect the same share has been taken as that used by the NIS in its post-war estimates, namely one third (column 7)[45].

SECTION 5. DIRECTORS' BONUSES

Directors' bonuses relate to shares in the profit distributed to members of the managing and supervisory boards of companies. The amount of directors' bonuses is therefore related to corporate profits. The share of the profits distributed in the form of directors' bonuses may either be laid down in the articles of association or be determined at the general meeting of shareholders.

No statistics on aggregate bonuses were published for the inter-war period[46].

---

[41] BAUDHUIN F., *Quel est le revenu actuel de la Belgique ?*, in "Banque Nationale de Belgique. Bulletin d'Information et de Documentation", vol. 2, p. 54.
[42] BAUDHUIN F., *Le revenu national en 1930*, in: "Idem", vol. 5, p. 375.
[43] BAUDHUIN F., *La Belgique en 1936. Les revenus*, in: "Bulletin de l'Institut de Recherches Economiques",vol. 8, p. 131.
[44] BAUDHUIN F., *Les finances belges en 1938*, in: "Idem", vol. 10, p. 125.
[45] NIS, *Commissie van het Nationaal Inkomen*, pp. 206-207.
[46] The amount of directors' fees is not included in the inter-war return on capital statistics. It is of course possible to estimate the fees on the basis of a detailed analysis of the balance sheets and profit and loss accounts of a sample of companies, but this would be extremely time-consuming.

Although the trade tax statistics include a heading on the earnings of managing and supervisory directors in companies, these figures relate to a broader category of earnings as they cover not just the shares in the profit but also the remuneration of higher executive personnel in semi-government institutions, such as the National Bank of Belgium, and the remuneration arising from contracts of employment for managers of private companies (e.g. deputy managers and directors)[47].

The estimate of the directors' bonuses paid in the inter-war period is based on the assumption of a link between the amount of fees and the amount of dividends paid out. It has also been assumed that all bonuses paid out by Belgian companies go to Belgians, and that there are no Belgian managing directors in foreign companies. According to the NIS, the ratio between bonuses and dividends paid out by Belgian companies in 1948-1954 averaged 13.9%[48]. It has been assumed that this ratio amounted to 15% in the inter-war period. On the basis of this assumption the amount of bonuses has been estimated in Table 78 (columns 1-4).

By way of a cross-check, the earnings of managing and supervisory directors subject to trade tax is shown in column 5[49]. The comparison of the two sets of figures is disappointing. In the early twenties the figures in the fiscal statistics are lower than the estimates of the bonuses, despite the fact that the fiscal figures cover a wider heading of earnings. The inconsistency between the two series is probably attributable to both the inadequate method for estimating the bonuses and to a possible underestimation of the fiscal data in the early 1920s. Such an underestimate is plausible since trade tax was not introduced until after the First World War and the tax department in the early years was possibly underresourced and lacked the experience to identify evasion efficiently. At any event this comparison indicates that the amounts of the bonuses, calculated either on the basis of the return-on-capital statistics or as shown in the fiscal statistics, need to be treated with due caution[50].

---

[47] BAUDHUIN F., *Prix, consommation et revenu national*, in: "Bulletin de l'Institut de recherches économiques et sociales", vol. 13, p. 422.
[48] Own calculation on basis of *Commissie van het Nationaal Inkomen*, pp. 192, 200 and 211. The NIS figures are based on the return-on-capital statistics, which, after the Second World War, also included the amount of bonuses.
[49] For a discussion of professional tax and the statistics on the earnings subject to that tax see Chapter 8, "Entrepreneurial earnings of the professions, traders, craftsmen and partnerships".
[50] The inadequacy of the estimate of bonuses does not, however, have any effect on the size of national income because an overestimate of the bonuses results in an equally large underestimate of reserved profits (Chapter 12). Conversely, an underestimate of the bonuses corresponds with an equally large overestimate of reserved profits.

Section 6. Corporate Grants

All corporate grants to households or non-profit organisations serving households need to be entered under this heading, with the exception of the bonuses paid to company employees[51]. The larger part of this heading relates to donations to charities or to private individuals in so far as the latter donations could not be regarded as pay[52].

No information whatever is available on the size of corporate grants during the inter-war period. This applies equally to the NIS's post-war estimates, in which corporate grants were set at 2% of the net profit of Belgian companies[53]. In the absence of an alternative and for the sake of continuity with the post-war figures the same method has been applied. The results of the estimate, as conducted in the following chapter on reserved profits[54], are shown in Table 78 column 6[55].

---

[51] *A standardized system of national accounts*, Paris, 1958, p. 78. Bonuses are remuneration over and above the pay stipulated in the contract of employment, which are paid out by some companies to their staff as a share in the profit. In principle they are included in Chapter 1 or Chapter 6.
[52] *De nationale rekeningen van België 1953-1962*, p. 613.
[53] *Idem*, p. 613; *Het Belgisch nationaal inkomen van 1948 tot 1954*, p. 1156.
[54] See Chapter 12.
[55] It may be noted that as in the case of directors' bonuses, an overestimate or underestimate of corporate grants does not affect the level of national income since this has a corresponding effect in the opposite direction on reserved profits.

CHAPTER 12

RESERVED PROFITS OF CORPORATIONS

SECTION 1. DEFINITION OF THE HEADING

By reserved profits of corporations is meant those company profits not distributed in any form or other[1]. These reserved profits are defined as being after taxation and also after the necessary provisions for depreciation have been made[2]. They are therefore net amounts.

The figures relate to companies trading within Belgian territory. This means that the non-distributed profits of foreign companies operating in Belgium form part of Belgian national income and that the additions to reserves realized by Belgian companies abroad or in the colonies do not form part of Belgian national income[3].

The additions to reserves included in this chapter stem from (private) joint-stock companies and public corporations. These are discussed in turn in Sections 2 and 3. With respect to the self-employed and partnerships it has been assumed that the income was fully distributed, without any additions to reserves[4].

Table 79 sets out the results of the estimate. As may be seen from the table, the reserved profits are sometimes negative. In these circumstances part of the reserves built up in previous years will be drawn down, other items in shareholders' equity will be drawn upon or the business will resort to borrowing.

The standardized system of the OECD states specifically that profits arising for example from a revaluation of inventories or from inadequate depreciation are to be excluded[5]. As a logical consequence this also means that if the accounting profits are officially depressed by (for example) the undervaluation of liabilities, undervaluation of assets or excessive depreciation, these accounting profits should

---

[1] The distributed profit may take the form of dividends to shareholders, directors' bonuses, staff bonuses, grants to households and non-profit organisations serving households, and direct taxation). The distributed profits are included in Chapter 11, "Dividends, directors' bonuses and donations" and Chapters 1 and 6 (bonuses). Corporation tax is discussed in Chapter 13.
[2] NIS, *Commissie van het Nationaal Inkomen,* p. 212; *De nationale rekeningen van België 1953-1962*, p. 1156.
[3] *Idem.*
[4] NIS, *Commissie van het Nationaal Inkomen,* p. 212. The earnings of the self-employed and unincorporated businesses form part of Chapter 8, "Entrepreneurial earnings of the professions, independent craftsmen, traders and partnerships".
[5] *A standardized system of national accounts*, Paris, 1952, p. 79.

be increased. Undervaluation of the bookkeeping profits is particularly attractive in boom times. By transferring part of the actually realized profits to hidden reserves, less corporation tax becomes payable and the amount of dividends due to shareholders can be kept limited. Conversely it can be interesting to overestimate the bookkeeping profit in times of recession or, in the event of a deficit, to present the bookkeeping loss as less than it is in reality. Among other things such practices may be prompted by the desire to retain the confidence of shareholders and the external world (clients and suppliers) in the company.

The reserved profits can be estimated on the basis of fiscal data or on the basis of an analysis of the balance sheets and profit and loss accounts of the companies in question. Whether the requirements of the standardized system are complied with will therefore depend heavily on the quality of both kinds of sources. The latter in turn depends on the legislation on corporation tax and the statutory provisions concerning company accounting procedures. Until the introduction of the Act on accounting procedures and the annual accounts of enterprises of 17 July 1975, the provisions in Belgium were exceptionally general and vague. As will be seen from the following section, the quality of the available source material is consequently highly doubtful, as reflected in the very large differences in reserved profits depending on the source one uses. The estimates of the saving of corporations that have ultimately been entered must therefore be interpreted with due caution.

SECTION 2. NON-DISTRIBUTED PROFITS OF JOINT-STOCK COMPANIES[6]

In Paragraph 1 below the reserved profits have been estimated according to the method used in the post-war accounts of the NIS. This method is based on the return-on-capital statistics of the National Bank of Belgium (NBB)[7]. In principle these figures include all joint-stock companies under Belgian or Congolese law. In Paragraph 2 two the results of the NIS method are compared with alternative figures.

Paragraph 1. Estimate according to the NIS method

The saving of corporations is estimated indirectly in the national accounts of the NIS[8]. The point of departure is total net profit. By this is meant total profit less

---

[6] The statistical material for this chapter was largely assembled by Guido Pepermans, for which the authors expres their thanks. The author is also greatful to him for his major contribution towards the method of reconstruction.

[7] For a discussion of the return-on-capital statistics see Chapter 11, "Dividends, returns on investments abroad, directors' bonuses and grants to private individuals".

[8] NIS, *Commissie van het Nationaal Inkomen*, pp. 213-228; *Het Belgisch nationaal inkomen van 1948 tot 1954*, p. 614; *De nationale rekeningen van België 1953-1962*, p. 1156.

depreciation and the tax payable by the company. The net profit is estimated on the basis of the NBB's return-on-capital statistics. Distributed profits are then deducted from the net profit figure. Distributed profits, defined as the sum of dividends, directors' and staff bonuses, were largely estimated in the previous chapter[9].

1. Net profit

Four problems arise in estimating total net profit:
1) As noted in the previous chapter, net profits in the return-on-capital statistics relate to the year of publication of the balance sheet or the year of payment of dividends[10]. Since earnings must be attributed to the year in which they were realized under the standardized system of national accounts, the figures in the return-on-capital statistics must be converted to the activity year[11]. As with dividends this was done as follows: the net profit arising from the economic activity in year t was estimated by taking 75% of the net profit noted in the return-on-capital statistics for year t+1 and adding to that 25% of the net profit in the statistics for year t[12].
2) The return-on-capital statistics do not draw a distinction until 1935 between Belgian companies trading primarily in Belgium and Belgian or Congolese companies trading primarily abroad. No such breakdown is provided in the return-on-capital statistics for the period 1927-1934; all enterprises are included in the same set of statistics. Since the additions to reserves realized by Belgian companies in the colonies or abroad do not form part of Belgian national income[13], they need to be deducted from the overall figures.
In the absence of any figures, it was also assumed that the saving of Belgian companies trading primarily in Belgium took place solely in Belgium. Conversely it has been assumed that the saving of Belgian companies trading primarily in the colonies or abroad took place wholly in those parts of the world[14].

---

9   Dividends and directors' bonuses were estimated in Chapter 11. The figures relating to dividends are largely based on the return-on-capital statistics. The figures for directors' bonuses were roughly estimated by assuming a fixed relationship between the sum of dividends and the amount of directors' fees. Figures on donations were included in the previous chapter but are based on estimates in this chapter. Staff bonuses have also been estimated in this chapter.
10 See Chapter 11.
11 *A standardized system of National Accounts*, passim.
12 See Chapter 11.
13 See introduction to this chapter.
14 The former assumption results in an overestimate of the saving by corporations in Belgian national income and the second to an underestimate. It has been assumed that the two errors more or less cancel one another out.

A related problem is the fact that the return-on-capital statistics include only Belgian companies. This heading needs, however, also to include the reserved profits of foreign companies with establishments on Belgian soil[15]. No figures are, however, available on this aspect. Since very few foreign companies were represented in Belgium in the 1920s and 1930s, the saving of these enterprises has been put at zero[16].

3) No return-on-capital statistics were compiled for the period 1920-1926. The total net profits for these years has instead been approximated (see below).
4) According to the NIS the reserved profits are underestimated in the return-on-capital statistics[17]. In view of the fact that the post-war return-on-capital statistics used by the NIS do not differ substantively from those in the inter-war period, it may be assumed that the saving by corporations in the latter statistics also underestimate the true figure. An upward correction has consequently been made (see below).

The total net profit of Belgian companies trading primarily in Belgium that concluded the financial year with a positive result is shown in column 1 of Table 80[18]. Column 2 shows the total net loss of enterprises with a negative operating result. The figures in columns 1 and 2 have been drawn directly from the return-on-capital statistics. By offsetting the two series against one another one obtains the net result of all Belgian companies trading primarily in Belgium (column 3). In column 4 these net results have been converted to the activity year along the lines described above. Columns 5-7 show the net profit, the net loss and the net result of all Belgian companies, i.e. both those primarily trading in Belgium and those primarily trading in the colonies or abroad, as derived from the return-on-capital statistics[19]. The conversion to the activity year has been conducted in column 8.

Column 9 shows the share of the saving of Belgian companies primarily trading in Belgium in relation to the saving of all Belgian companies in 1935-1939. This series corresponds well with column 10, which shows the ratio between the dividends paid out by Belgian companies primarily trading in Belgium and the dividends paid out by all Belgian companies in 1927-1934. These

---

[15] See introduction to this chapter.
[16] Similarly, in the absence of figures, the post-war national accounts of the NIS do not take any account of the saving by the Belgian establishments of foreign companies. NIS, *Commissie van het Nationaal Inkomen*, p. 230. Multinational cooperations did not establish themselves in Belgium on a large scale until the 1960s (see Chapter 11 footnote 6).
[17] *Het Belgisch nationaal inkomen van 1948 tot 1954*, p. 614; *De nationale rekeningen van België 1953-1962*, p. 1156.
[18] As noted previously, the term "net" relates to the fact that in calculating the operating result, account has already been taken of depreciation and corporation tax liabilities.
[19] Belgian companies are also taken as including companies under Congolese law.

figures were calculated in the previous chapter[20]. If it is assumed that the ratios for the dividends also apply to the saving by corporations, the saving of Belgian companies primarily trading in Belgium in 1927-1934 (column 11) is obtained by multiplying the reserved profits of all Belgian companies (column 8) by the percentages in column 10.

As noted earlier, no return-on-capital statistics were drawn up for the period 1920-1926. Nor are any alternative figures (e.g. fiscal statistics) available for these years that might indicate the level of reserved profits. There was, consequently, no alternative to approximating the saving of corporations. This was done on the basis of the pattern of dividends paid out in 1920-1926 and the ratio between dividends and net profit in 1927-1939.

The ratio between net profit and dividends may be specified as follows:
- If net profits rise, the amount of distributed dividends also increases. Conversely, dividend pay-outs fall with a reduction in net profits.
- The volatility of net profits is significantly greater than that of dividends. In general net profits tend to rise proportionately more than dividend pay-outs in years of economic upswing, while in adverse economic years the fall in net profits is much more pronounced than the drop in dividend pay-outs.
  In view of the fact that the dividends are subject to a certain inertia, the amount of net profits in the worst years of the depression (1931-1934) is lower than the dividend pay-outs. This means that the reserved profits in these years are negative.

There is therefore a clear correlation between net profits and dividends, subject to the proviso that the dividends/net profits ratio rises as the economic situation worsens (see column 13).

Net profits in 1920-1926 were estimated on the basis of the above considerations and the known sum of dividend pay-outs. In 1927-1929 - three decidedly favourable years - the ratio between dividends and net profits averaged 60%. It has been assumed that this ratio was the same for the the period 1920-1926 (column 14). By dividing the known amount of dividends by the ratios determined in this way one arrives at the reserved profit (column 15). Needless to say these estimates are subject to a reasonably high measure of uncertainty, which finds its origin in the comparatively arbitrary determination of the dividends/net profits ratio. The profit figures (i.e. both net profits and the later reserved profits) for 1920-1926 need therefore to be treated with due caution.

According to the NIS, the net profits as derived from the return-on-capital statistics have been underestimated. The NIS reaches this conclusion for the 1951-1953 financial years by comparing the balance sheets as published in the Belgian State Gazette and, consequently, also in the return-on-capital statistics with the balance sheets approved by the tax authorities with a view to determining cooperation tax[21]. The net profit figures in the fiscal statistics are 49%, 39%, and 23% higher than in the return-on-capital statistics in 1951, 1952 and 1953 respectively. The NIS was unable to provide any explanation for these major variances, as an analysis of the factors possibly responsible for these differences (such as depreciation, valuation of stocks and tax provisions) did not provide any satisfactory answer[22].

It may be that certain forms of expenditure relating to goods with a longer probable economic life than one year and which should consequently be regarded as capital expenditure (e.g. office requisites, certain machines and vehicles) were carried in some profit and loss accounts as general expenses whereas the tax department, correctly, treated them as investments[23].

Unorthodox accounting practices of this kind need to be viewed in the light of the inadequate legislation on company accounting procedures, which left enterprises with a large measure of freedom in drawing up their balance sheet and profit and loss account[24]. Although the Acts of 25 May 1913 and 30 November 1935 required all joint-stock companies annually to publish a balance sheet and profit and loss account in which the necessary depreciation had to be made, the law provided no indications as to how this should be done. No clear guidelines were drawn up concerning depreciation and the valuation of stocks, etc., until the Act of 17 July 1975 on accounting procedures and the annual accounts. From that

---

[20] See Chapter 11.

[21] Companies were required to draw up a fiscal balance sheet for the tax authorities in which account was taken of the fiscal regulations with respect to depreciation, the valuation of assets and liabilities, operating charges, etc. These fiscal balance sheets, which often differed markedly from those published in the Belgian State Gazette, were not published. A comparison between the two sets of balance sheets became possible in the 1950s onwards because the tax authorities filled in a statistical sheet for each company from that time onwards, which was then submitted to the NIS, which in turn incorporated these into overall anonymous results. The first year for which overall statistics were drawn up was 1951. NIS, *Commissie van het Nationaal Inkomen*, pp. 218-227.

[22] The difference between commercial depreciation and that accepted by the tax department, for example, was just 2.4% (*Idem*, pp. 222-223). Similarly the fact that trade tax, which was included as an operating cost, is not the same in the accounting balance sheet (in the form of a tax provision deriving from the profit recorded in year t) and the fiscal balance sheet (trade tax paid in tax year t on profits realized in year t-1) cannot possibly explain the difference in net profits (*Idem*, pp. 225-226).

[23] *Idem*, pp. 218-219. If these expenditures are wholly attributed to the year of purchase this has a negative effect on the net profit in that year.

[24] The lack of uniformity in corporate accounting procedures has been described by the accounting expert Gilis as "une véritable anarchie". GILIS H., *Le bilan dans la société anonyme. Etude juridique, économique, financière et comptable,* Brussels ; Renaix, 1927, p. 36. See also NEUMANN H., *De l'intérêt d'une présentation claire des bilans et comptes de pertes et profits des S.A. et la nécessité d'une réforme du régime actuel,* in: "Revue de la Banque", vol. 5-6, 1950, pp. 250-274.

date onwards, enterprises had much less room for manoeuvre to manipulate their operating results[25].

In order to take account of the presumable underestimation of net profits in the return-on-capital statistics, the figure was increased by the NIS by 35% in each year[26]. Since the inter-war return-on-capital statistics were drawn up in virtually the same way as those after the war, it may be assumed that the net profit figures in the 1920s and 1930s were also underestimated. In the interest of continuity with the post-war figures, the net profits as derived from the return-on-capital statistics were therefore also increased by 35% for the inter-war period (see Table 80 columns 17 and 18)[27].

2. Reserved profits

The reserved profit was arrived at by deducting the distributed profit from total net profit (see Table 81). The distributed profit consists of the dividends paid to shareholders, directors' and staff bonuses and corporate grants to households and non-profit organisations serving households.

Dividends were estimated in the previous chapter. The figure required at this point is the total sum of the distributed dividends, i.e. not just the dividends paid to private individuals. In contrast to Chapter 11, however, no account has been taken of the dividends paid out by foreign companies and by Belgian companies primarily training abroad, since only the additions to reserve by Belgian companies primarily trading in Belgium have been included.

As discussed in the previous chapter, the amount of directors' bonuses has been set at 15% of the amount of dividends[28].

---

25   The operating results could for example be manipulated via depreciation. Many companies wrote off their assets in the operating results: in favourable years too much was written off, meaning that the net profit was artificially depressed, while in lean years too little or nothing was written off so that the operating results looked better than they really were (HANON DE LOUVET C., *Analyse et discussion de bilans,* Brussels, 1944, p. 103).

26   The NIS arrived at this percentage in the following manner. In 1951, 1952 and 1953 net profits according to the fiscal data were 49%, 39% and 23% lower respectively than in the return-on-capital statistics (see above). For 1954 the NIS put the difference at 20%. The average for these four years is 33%. This percentage was increased to 40% in order to allow for tax fraud. Finally this 40% was reduced to 35% because companies were able to appeal against the net profit figures arrived at by the tax department (*Commissie van het Nationaal Inkomen,* pp. 226-227). The use of an unvarying incremental factor is of course unsatisfactory since the above figures relating to 1951-1953 indicate that the percentage discrepancy between the net profit figures in the fiscal statistics and the return-on-capital statistics clearly varied from year to year.

27   The fact that the net profit figure as derived from the return-on-capital statistics is underestimated is clearly evident from the return-on-capital statistics for 1936-1940, which include the total reserves. By deducting the reserves for year t from the reserves for year t-1, one obtains the reserved profits in year t (cf. below). Table 82 column 6 reveals that the reserved profit according to this method is consistently negative in 1937-1939, which is highly improbable.

28   See Chapter 11.

In line with the NIS, donations were assumed to be equal to 2% of the net profit[29].

The NIS's estimates of staff bonuses are based on indications in the return-on-capital statistics[30]. The latter do not, however, provide any information on the bonuses paid in the 1920s and 1930s. In 1948-1954 bonuses averaged 2.0% of net profit[31]. It has been assumed that this percentage was the same in the inter-war period.

Paragraph 2. Comparison with alternative figures

The estimates of the reserved profit according to the NIS method is compared with various alternative figures in Table 82. Column 1 shows the additions to reserve as estimated in the previous paragraph. Column 2 shows the profit on which corporation tax was payable. On the basis of these fiscal data (1926 and 1930) or alternatively on an intuitive basis (1936-1938), Baudhuin drew up rough figures for additions to reserve for certain years in the context of his national income estimates (column 3). Finally, savings by corporations has been calculated in columns 4-6 on the basis of the "reserves" item in the return-on-capital statistics of 1936-1940.

The enormous discrepancies between the various series is immediately apparent. Efforts are made to provide an explanation below for some of these discrepancies, but in some cases this was impossible. In fact the inadequate quality of the figures is inherent in the concept of saving by corporations, in the sense that additions to reserve are a residual item, to which no cash flow figures correspond. If the inadequate legislation with respect to the procedures for drawing up the profit and loss account and balance sheet is added, it is scarcely surprising that the figures should vary widely depending on the source used[32].

With the exception of 1930 and 1931, the fiscal figures are considerably higher than those arrived at by the NIS method. Among other things this is attributable to the fact that the concept of reserved profits differs in the two series, in that the fiscal figures for reserved profits include not just the actual additions to reserve but also the directors' and staff bonuses and donations[33]. A second important cause of the higher figures in the fiscal statistics is related to the fact that the latter do not take any account of the losses incurred by certain companies, as

---

[29] *Het Belgisch nationaal inkomen van 1948 tot 1954*, p. 613; *De nationale rekeningen van België 1953-1962*, p. 1156.
[30] NIS, *Commissie van het Nationaal Inkomen*, p. 227.
[31] Own calculation on basis of *Idem*, p. 228.
[32] *L'évolution de la structure des revenus d'après les statistiques fiscales*, p. 21.
[33] NIS, *Commissie van het Nationaal Inkomen*, p. 222. Dividends, however, do not form part of the fiscal additions to reserve; nor have corporation tax payments been included, as the latter could be charged as an operating expense. PUTMAN R., *Les impôts directs en Belgique de 1914 à 1940*, p. 501.

tax is only levied on profits[34]. By contrast the figures based on the NIS method do include negative additions to reserve, i.e. the drawing down of capital. During the worst years of the depression (1931-1934) the inroads made into capital even exceeded the amount of capital added to the reserves, thus resulting in a net negative reserved profit. Despite the major differences between the fiscal statistics and the data based on the NIS method, a comparison of the two series nevertheless clearly shows that the trend is the same (an annual increase between 1926 and 1929 and an annual decrease between 1930 and 1935, followed by a rise in 1936).

In order of magnitude, Baudhuin's estimates in column 3 correspond exceptionally well with the estimated 1930 figure, but far less with the estimates for other years[35]. For the final years of the inter-war period, reserved profits can also be estimated on the basis of the "reserves" item, which was included in the return-on-capital statistics from 1936 onwards (column 4). By deducting the reserves of year t-1 from the reserves in year t, one obtains the reserved profit in year t. Finally column 5 shows the reserved profits in 1937-1939 which are negative in two out of three years. The fact that these figures are negative - when in fact the worst of the depression was over - confirms the supposition on the part of the NIS that the return-on-capital statistics underestimate net profits.

SECTION 3. UNDISTRIBUTED PROFITS OF AUTONOMOUS PUBLIC INSTITUTIONS

This heading includes the additions to reserve of the semi-government institutions of a commercial nature and the intercommunal enterprises[36]. The semi-government institutions nearly all operated in the financial sector, while the intercommunal companies were primarily active in the energy sector (i.e. the production and distribution of electricity, gas and water). The undistributed profits of these institutions - of which the additions to reserve of the ASLK accounted for the bulk - form only a very small item in national income (averaging 0.1% in 1920-1939).

As far as possible the figures on reserved profits were taken directly from the annual reports of the institutions in question[37]. This was possible for most semi-government enterprises (see Table 83 columns 1-3). It may be noted that the National District Railways Company (Nationale Maatschappij van Buurtspoorwegen, NMVB) recorded negative additions to reserve in the early 1920s and 1930s, meaning that the company was drawing down part of its equity

---

34 The fiscal legislation did, however, allow the losses recorded by a company in year t-1 or year t-2 to be deducted from the taxable profits in year t. Idem, p. 510.
35 BAUDHUIN F., *Le revenu national en 1930*, p. 374.
36 *De nationale rekeningen van België 1953-1962*, p. 1156.
37 The list of the relevant institutions was found in NIS, *Commissie van het Nationaal Inkomen*, p. 229.

capital[38]. The table also reveals that a number of public financial institutions came into being in the second half of the 1930s (see column 3). These provide an illustration of government intervention in the financial sector as a reaction to the crisis of the Belgian financial system in the mid-1930s.

In the case of the autonomous public institutions for which no or only incomplete annual reports were found, a rough estimate was made. The post-war annual reports indicate that the additions to reserve of these institutions were minimal in the extreme. For the inter-war period they have been put at 5% of the undistributed profits of the ASLK (column 4).

The additions to reserve of the inter-communal enterprises are also minimal. During the period 1948-1954 they amounted to just 5.9% of the reserved profits of semi-government institutions[39]. With reference to the inter-war period it has been assumed that the additions to reserve of the inter-communal enterprises amounted to 6% of the undistributed profits of the ASLK (column 5)[40].

---

[38] In contrast to the other institutions, where the reserved profits form a single heading in the profit and loss account, the figures for the NMVB are not so easily calculated, in that the annual reports for the company indicate that each district line enjoyed a large measure of independence. If a particular line recorded an operating surplus, that surplus (after payment of dividends and bonuses) was directly transferred to an account in the Reserve Fund or the Provision Fund. If a line was operating at a deficit, the latter was funded by drawing on the accumulated reserves of the line in question in the Reserve Fund or the Provision Fund. If these reserves were exhausted, the deficit was funded through an Advances account. In both cases the capital of the NMVB was drawn down. If a line that had been making a loss returned to profitability its Advances account was first cleared off and, if there was then still a sum remaining, the latter would be transferred to the account of the line in question in the Reserve Fund or the Provision Fund. It is clear that in order to determine the reserved profits of the NMVB, the Reserve Fund, Provision Fund and Advances account need all three to be taken into account. The reserved profit becomes the result of the following calculation:
Reserved profit in year t =
(Reserve Fund year t - Reserve Fund year t-1)
+ (Provision Fund year t - Provision Fund year t-1)
- (Advances year t - Advances year t-1).

[39] Own calculation on the basis of NIS, *Commissie van het Nationaal Inkomen*, p. 229.

[40] This 6% was not calculated on the total additions to reserve of the semi-government institutions since the inclusion of the NMVB would have meant negative figures for 1920-1923, which is highly unlikely.

CHAPTER 13

DIRECT TAXATION OF COMPANIES OF ALL LEGAL FORMS

SECTION 1. DEFINITION OF THE HEADING

This chapter estimates the direct taxes paid by companies - both joint-stock companies and partnerships - established on Belgian soil[1]. The direct taxes levied on private individuals are not shown in a separate heading as they are already included in the factor payments: for the purposes of calculating national income, pay, entrepreneurs' earnings and property income accruing to the personal sector are all gross amounts inclusive of direct taxes.

The OECD standardized system states that direct taxes must be assigned to the year in which the tax is charged and not therefore to the year in which the income on which the tax was levied was realized or to the year in which the tax was paid[2]. It is, however, not always clear whether the fiscal data relate to levied or paid taxes, so that it is possible that the OECD's recommendations are not always adhered to.

Under the Belgian tax system, the year in which taxes are levied is designated as the "financial" or "taxation" year. A financial year commences on 1 January of year t and ends some time in year t+1[3]. The direct taxes levied in financial year t relate in principle to incomes earned in year t-1.

The direct taxes to which companies were subject are[4]:
1. Corporation tax or trade tax on reserved company profits (Section 2).
2. The financial securities tax payable on the earnings from financial assets received by companies established in Belgium (Section 3).
3. The land tax on industrial buildings and land owned by companies (Section 4)[5].

---

[1] *A standardized system of national accounts*, Paris, 1958, p. 83; *Het Belgisch nationaal inkomen van 1948 tot 1954*, p. 615; *De nationale rekeningen van België 1953-1962*, pp. 1156-1157.
[2] *A standardized system*, p. 48.
[3] The financial years 1920-1934 concluded on 31 October of the following year. The financial years 1935-1939 ended respectively on 30 September 1936, 31 July 1937, 31 May 1938, 31 March 1939 and 31 March 1940 (*Belgische Economische Statistieken 1919-1928*, p. 81; *Belgische Economische Statistieken 1919-1940*, p. 146).
[4] For a survey of the direct taxes during the inter-war period see Chapter 8, "Entrepreneurial income of the professions, independent traders, craftsmen and partnerships".
[5] In the standardized system of the OECD land and analogous taxes (such as the national crisis tax on real estate) are regarded as indirect taxes (*Het Belgisch nationaal inkomen van 1948 tot 1954*,

4. From 1933 onwards the national crisis tax (Section 5)[6].

In the absence of data it was only possible to make rough estimates. With one exception, namely the trade tax in 1930, the tax authorities failed to publish any figures whatever with respect to the direct taxes paid by companies. Although figures were published for the total tax receipts for each form of taxation (i.e. trade tax, financial securities tax, land tax and national emergency tax) these figures related to both the personal sector and companies.

The results of the estimates are shown in Table 84.

SECTION 2. TRADE TAX

Trade or corporation tax was levied on that element of profits not distributed in the form of dividends[7]. If for example a company concluded its financial year with a surplus of BF 100,000, of which BF 40,000 was distributed to shareholders (= distributed profit) and BF 60,000 was added to the reserves (i.e. undistributed or reserved profit), only the BF 60,000 was subject to trade tax. The BF 40,000 paid out in dividends was subject to financial securities tax, but the latter tax was charged not to the companies but the shareholders.

The trade tax on reserved company profits was estimated in three steps:
1. Estimate relating to the 1930 tax year on the basis of fiscal data on corporation tax (Paragraph 1).
2. Estimate relating to the tax years for which only the fiscally reserved profits are known (1921, 1927 and 1929-1937) (Paragraph 2).
3. Estimate with respect to the tax years for which neither the tax paid nor the fiscally reserved profits are known (1920, 1922-1926, 1938-1939) (Paragraph 3).

Paragraph 1. Estimate for the 1930 tax year

Solely for the 1930 tax year, the tax department published a figure for the trade tax paid by companies. In response to a parliamentary question, the Minister of

---

p. 618). They do not consequently form part of national income (net national product at factor cost). The NIS, however, adds these taxes to the direct taxes in the Belgian national accounts which, for reasons of continuity, has also been done for the inter-war period. Whether land and related taxes are regarded as direct or indirect taxes makes no difference in estimating the net or gross national product at market prices since this variable includes the indirect taxes.

[6] As far as can be established the supertax and supplementary poll tax did not apply to companies but only to private individuals.
[7] PUTMAN R., *Les impôts directs en Belgique de 1914 à 1940*, p. 378.

Finance advised on 7 July 1932 that the figure was BF 246 million[8]. The trade tax payable by the personal sector amounted to BF 587 million, so that the total trade tax in 1930 tax year came to BF 833 million[9]. In an issue of the *Direct Taxation Bulletin* published by the Ministry of Finance in 1943, a survey is provided of the direct taxation receipts since 1920, in which a figure for the trade tax in the 1930 tax year of BF 986 million is given, i.e. 18.4% more than the figure announced by the Minister of Finance[10]. The accompanying text to both sources provides no indication of the reason for this discrepancy. It may be that the figure provided by the Minister in 1932 was a provisional one which was subsequently revised. Protracted disputes between the tax department and various taxpayers concerning the level of the latter's taxable income meant that the definitive tax receipts were often not determined until a number of years after the end of the tax year in question.

On account of the possibly provisional nature of the figure for corporation tax given by the Minister of Finance, the amount in question has been increased. In doing so it has been assumed that the (presumed) underestimation was the same for the trade tax paid by companies as that paid by the personal sector. The figure for companies (246 million) was consequently increased by 18.4%, thus arriving at a figure of BF 291 million for 1930 (see Table 85 column 1).

Paragraph 2. Estimate of the tax years for which the fiscally reserved profits are known

It was noted in the previous chapter (Saving of corporations) that figures were available for a number of years for the reserved profits of companies subject to trade tax[11]. The available figures are shown in Table 85 column 2. A comparison of the trade corporation tax paid in the 1930 tax year, namely BF 291 million (which relates largely to the profits realized in 1929), with the fiscally reserved profits, namely BF 3,648 million, suggests an average tax rate of 8.0%. Is this a realistic figure? The Act of 16 July 1930 indicates that the rate of trade tax varied according to the level of income from around 5.0% for profits of below BF 60,000 to 9% for profits in excess of BF 200,000[12]. An average tax rate of 8.0% is therefore certainly plausible.

---

[8] The trade tax for the 1930 financial year relates to the profits shown in the balance sheets for the year ending 31 December 1929 or in the course of 1930, depending on whether or not companies' accounting year corresponded with the calendar year.
[9] Legislative Chambers, Senate, *Bulletin van Vragen en Antwoorden*, session 1935-1936, 5 March 1936, p. 571.
[10] Ministry of Finance, *Bulletin van de Directe Belastingen*, vol 181, 1943, p. 68.
[11] See Chapter 12.
[12] Act of 13 July 1930, Section 28. See also PUTMAN R., o.c., p. 513.

For the remaining years it has been assumed that the average tax rate was again 8%. In the 1920s the rate of corporation tax varied, depending on the level of reserved profits, between 5% and 10%, which roughly corresponds with the higher percentages reported for the 1930s[13]. Multiplication of the fiscally reserved profits by 8% results in the corporation tax paid (Table 85 column 4).

A number of criticisms can be levelled against this method of approach. In the first place the various tax rates do not always relate to the same income brackets (in the 1920s these were lower than in the 1930s). Furthermore it may be argued that the average tax rate was less than 8% in the depression years since the profits were generally well below those in 1929 (1930 tax year) and consequently subject to lower tax rates (applying to the lower income brackets). The necessary data for refining the above working method are, however, not available. In addition, the fact that corporation tax in 1935 according to the method described was just 15% of that in 1930 (BF 45 million as against BF 291 million) demonstrates that the effects of the depression on the tax receipts are largely reflected in the figures.

Paragraph 3. Estimate for the financial years for which the fiscally reserved profits are unknown

For those years in which no figures were published for the reserved profits subject to corporation tax (referred to below as "fiscally reserved profits"), the corporation tax was estimated on the basis of the evolution of saving by corporations as reconstructed in the previous chapter (referred to below as "commercially reserved profits")[14].

The years 1922-1926 were filled in on the basis of the corporation tax as estimated in the previous section in 1921 and 1927 and the evolution of the commercially reserved profits in 1921-1927 (column 5)[15]. This was done on the basis of the trend-corrected interpolation technique. Corporation tax in the 1927 tax year was estimated along analogous lines. For the years 1938 and 1939 the corporation tax in 1937 (BF 87 million) was linked to the course of commercially reserved profits.

No figures are available for the commercially reserved profits in the 1920 tax year (i.e. the reserved profits in 1919), so that the working method described above could not be applied. Corporation tax in 1920 was estimated on the basis of the total trade tax (personal sector and companies) in 1920 and 1921 and the corporation tax in 1921.

---

[13] PUTMAN R., *o.c.*, p. 513.
[14] For the sake of simplicity it has been assumed that the reserved profits in year t were subject to corporation tax in year t+1.
[15] The reasons why the commercially reserved profits differ from the fiscally reserved profits were discussed in Chapter 12, "Reserved Profits of corporations", pp. 8-9.

Section 3. Financial securities tax

The financial securities tax payable by companies relates in particular to the dividends they received on their shareholdings. Both participating interests in other Belgian share companies and in foreign or colonial share companies were subject to financial securities tax. The figures do not include the financial securities tax deducted at source by companies in respect of dividends paid to shareholders[16], since the financial securities tax did not have to be paid by the companies distributing the dividends but by the private individuals or companies receiving those dividends as shareholders.

No figures are available on the financial securities tax paid by companies. Similarly the share ownership of companies is unquantified. The financial securities tax paid by companies could only be estimated roughly on the basis of the evolution of the total financial securities tax-take (i.e. paid by the personal sector, companies and abroad; see Table 86 column 1). According to the NIS estimates, an average of 20.1% of the total revenues from financial securities tax between 1948 and 1954 came from companies[17]. It has been assumed that this figure was 20% in the 1920s and 1930s (column 2).

Section 4. Land tax

Similarly no figures are available on the land tax levied on commercial property and premises. As in the case of the financial securities tax, the land tax owing by companies was estimated on the basis of the total receipts (from the personal sector and companies) from this tax (Table 86 column 3). In this respect it was assumed that 15% of the total receipts derived from companies (column 4). This percentage, which must be regarded as a very rough estimate, was arrived at on the basis of post-war ratios.

According to NIS estimates, 16.5% of the total income from improved properties consisted in 1949 and 1954 of industrial buildings and 83.5% of other buildings (dwellings, agricultural buildings, commercial buildings)[18]. Industrial buildings consist primarily of premises owned by companies but can also refer to premises owned by private individuals, such as craftsmen. Correspondingly, the group of "other buildings" consists primarily of premises owned by private individuals but also includes a certain amount of real estate owned by the companies, such as the real estate patrimony owned by banks, department stores and insurance companies. In the absence of other data the NIS has assumed that

---

16 NIS, *Commissie van het Nationaal Inkomen*, p. 236.
17 The highest percentage was 21.3% in 1948, and the lowest 19.1% in 1951 (own calculations on basis of NIS, *Commissie van het Nationaal Inkomen*, p. 238 ; *Belgische economische statistieken 1941-1950*, vol. II, p. 133; *Idem 1950-1960*, vol. II, p. 243).
18 NIS, *Commissie van het Nationaal Inkomen*, pp. 277-278.

the income from industrial buildings owned by private individuals is equal to the income from other buildings owned by companies[19]. In this way 16.5% of the income from improved properties accrues to companies. The share of companies in total land tax is, however, lower, as this tax was levied not just on improved but also unimproved properties (especially agricultural land and wooded areas). On the basis of the assumption that the unimproved properties were totally owned by the personal sector, one arrives at an average share of 14.5% for companies in the total land tax in the period 1948-1954[20]. For the inter-war period this was rounded off at 15%.

SECTION 5. NATIONAL CRISIS TAX

The national crisis tax was introduced in 1932 and essentially applied to all income, including that of companies. Income from the ownership of shares was, however, exempt[21]. As with most other direct taxes, only overall figures were published for the national emergency tax and no separate figures are available for the tax paid by companies. Since the reserved profits formed the most important element for companies in the payment of the national emergency tax, the latter has been estimated on the basis of the evolution of the trade tax payable on reserved profits.

In 1949 companies paid BF 2,120 million in national crisis tax and BF 1,750 in trade tax[22]. The national crisis tax payable by the corporate sector therefore amounted to 21% more than their trade tax. It has been assumed that this figure was 20% in the inter-war period. The national crisis tax paid by companies has been estimated by multiplying the trade tax paid by companies by 120% (see Table 84 column 4). Since the national crisis tax was abolished between 19 June 1937 and 17 June 1938, the trade tax was multiplied by just 60% for these years.

---

[19]   NIS, *Commissie van het Nationaal Inkomen*, pp. 239 and 278.
[20]   Own calculation on the basis of NIS, *Commissie van het Nationaal Inkomen*, pp. 277-278. Example for 1948: Total income from real estate = BF 21 billion (buildings) + BF 3.0 billion (land) = BF 24 billion. Company buildings = 16.5% of BF 21 billion = BF 3.5 billion. BF 3.5 billion/BF 24 billion = 14.4%.
[21]   PUTMAN R., *o.c.*, p. 401.
[22]   NIS, *Commissie van het Nationaal Inkomen*, pp. 236 and 239.

CHAPTER 14

INCOME FROM PROPERTY AND ENTREPRENEURIAL INCOME ACCRUING TO THE GOVERNMENT

As in the method of the NIS, income from property and entrepreneurial income accruing to the government is subdivided into two main headings: imputed net rent (Section 1) and interest, dividends, rent income, profits and losses (Section 2).

SECTION 1. IMPUTED NET RENT[1]

In line with the NIS, account has only been taken of the imputed rent of buildings belonging to public authorities and equivalent bodies, in so far as these buildings are used by civil administrative agencies or are intended for education and health care[2]. No account has been taken of the buildings made available for the army or a government corporation, or of historic buildings, monuments and museums, etc. The income from the letting to private individuals of buildings or land owned by the government forms part of Section 2.

The imputed net rent (= gross rent less maintenance costs and depreciation) was estimated in the same way in the inter-war period as the NIS's post-war estimates[3]. The starting point for the exercise was provided by the Inventory of State Property on 31 December 1935. In this inventory the value of the State property covered by this heading is put at BF 6.92 billion. The construction of a series of values for the whole inter-war period was carried out in chapter 16. The series of the stock of public buildings used in that chapter consist, however, of values at the end of each year, while the NIS bases the calculation of imputed rent on mid-year values. The values of the stock of public buildings in chapter 16 thus first had to be recalculated on a mid-year basis[4]. Following the NIS, the imputed net rent has been set at 3.5% of the value of the property[5]. As the series of public property is expressed in 1936-38 prices, the resulting series of imputed net rent is expressed in 1936-38 prices as well. Imputed net rent in current prices was

---

[1] The authors thank Michelangelo van Meerten for assembling a part of the statistical material for this section.
[2] NIS, *Commissie van het Nationaal Inkomen*, p. 1157.
[3] NIS, *Commissie van het Nationaal Inkomen*, pp. 285-286.
[4] The mid-year values were calculated as the average of the values at the end of the previous and the current year.
[5] *De nationale rekeningen van België, 1953-1962*, p. 1157.

215

obtained by multiplying the series in 1936-38 prices by the index building costs and dividing the outcome by 100. The results of the estimates are shown in Table 87.

Section 2. Interest, Dividends, Rent Income, Profits and Losses

This heading covers dividends, interest and other forms of income collected by government agencies or equivalent bodies (e.g. agencies concerned with the compulsory system of social security, and municipal public welfare committees) by way of compensation for invested capital. This income was increased by the positive (or reduced by the negative) result of any economic activity exercised by the government in the corporate sector[6]. The latter applies for example in the inter-war period to the majority of the railway network, which was directly operated by the State until 23 June 1926 (when the NMBS was established), the operation of the telephone and telegraph services until 19 July 1930 (when the RTT was established) and the post office (owned by the State throughout the inter-war period).

A distinction has been drawn between the central government (Paragraph 1), the statutory pension funds (Paragraph 2) and other government (Paragraph 3).

Paragraph 1. Central Government

The sums included under this heading were arrived at by the systematic screening of the "Final Accounts of the Budget of the Belgian State" published in the *Books of the Audit Office* (Boeken van het Rekenhof)[7]. From 1923 onwards these accounts were published in highly detailed form. The published information for 1920-1922 is summary in nature, so that it has sometimes been necessary to resort to rough estimates for these years.

As far as the intervention of the central government in the losses of government enterprises or semi-government corporations is concerned, the problem arises as to whether these should be recorded as negative entrepreneurial income or as a subsidy in Chapter 17. Clearly, the concept of "loss" for a public enterprise is open to interpretation and can give rise to highly varying estimates according to the importance attached to the concept of "subsidy". In its methodological notes published in the Statistical Yearbook of 1963, the NIS states that in principle it regards a priori state intervention as a subsidy and a posteriori state intervention as a loss[8]. Nevertheless the NIS has not always stuck to this rule, for all the sums which the State currently assigns to the NMBS are recorded in the

---

[6] *De nationale rekeningen van België, 1953-1962*, p. 1157.
[7] For a discussion of these final accounts see Chapter 5, "Pay and pensions of government staff".
[8] *De nationale rekeningen van België 1953-1962*, p. 1157.

national accounts as negative entrepreneurial income, including the monies included in the state budget[9]. For the sake of simplicity, all negative balances of government or semi-government enterprises financed with the aid of public monies have been entered as negative entrepreneurial income in the inter-war period. The subsidies included in Chapter 17 relate only to private companies.

Table 88 shows all income from property and entrepreneurship accruing to the central government, with the exception of the sums relating to the railways, post office, telegraph and telephone. The first three columns relate to interest on loans granted by the government, columns 4-6 to entrepreneurial income and the share in the operating profit of government or semi-government corporations, and column 7 shows the dividends paid on shares in government ownership.

Table 89 shows the amounts relating to the railways[10]. Until the Act of 23 June 1926, the larger part of the Belgian railway network was directly operated by the State. Where operating income exceeded operating expenditure, the surplus accrued directly to the State, while deficits were made good by the government. For the period 1923-1926 the *Books of the Audit Office* provide both the receipts and the expenditure, while for 1920-1922 they show just the receipts. Figures do however exist for the total expenditure by the railways, post office, telegraph and telephone service (see Table 91 column 6). The balance in 1920-1922 has been calculated in Table 91 for these three sectors as a whole.

As part of the public finance reforms, the State railways were converted into the NMBS on 23 June 1926[11]. The State owned a large part of the shares in the new company and moreover had an entitlement to 50% of any profits[12]. Straight after formation, the NMBS was radically rationalized which, in combination with the favourable economic situation, resulted in exceptionally good operating results (see Table 89 columns 4 and 5). From 1933 onwards the government provided subsidies to enable the company to charge reduced fares for certain categories of users (e.g. ex-servicemen and families with large numbers of children).

The current income and expenditure of the post office and the telegraph and telephone agency are shown in Table 90. As noted previously the overall total has been calculated for 1920-1922 together with that of the State railways (see Table 91 columns 5-7). The latter Table also shows the total figures for the heading.

---

9 Communication by Mr. Modart, NIS official.
10 The figures relate solely to current income and expenditure, not to capital income and expenditure.
11 See Chapter 15.
12 DELORY F., *Les finances des chemins de fer belges*, in: "Histoire des finances publiques en Belgique", Brussels; Paris, Institut Belge de Finances Publiques (ed.), vol. III, pp. 118-120, 133.

Paragraph 2. Statutory pension funds, interest on actuarial reserves

This paragraph deals with the interest on the actuarial reserves of the pension funds or of companies that built up funds as part of the statutory system of social security[13]. In line with the NIS a distinction has been drawn between the statutory pension funds and the industrial accident insurance funds[14].

The final results of the estimates are shown in Table 92. The interest on the actuarial reserves included in this paragraph average 0.24% of national income. Column 4 reveals that the share rose especially in the early 1930s. Of the total interest on actuarial reserves those of the statutory pension funds average 69.4% and those of the industrial accident insurance funds 30.6%.

1. Interest on actuarial reserves of statutory funds

As noted earlier, this heading only includes the interest on actuarial reserves of the pension funds established as part of the statutory system of social security[15]. The majority of the statutory pension funds were administered by the *General Savings and Annuity Fund* (ASLK). This semi-government agency had a monopoly over the collection of contributions and payment of pensions for manual workers[16]. To the end of 1931 the ASLK exercised a comparable monopoly over white-collar workers' pensions[17]. From 1932 onwards white-collar workers were able to choose their statutory pension fund: the ASLK, the National Fund for White-collar Workers' Pensions (Nationale Kas voor Bediendenpensioenen (NKB) or a private insurance company. Miners' pensions were administered partly by the ASLK and partly by the National Miners' Pension Fund (Nationale Pensioenfonds voor Mijnwerkers (NPM)).

The total actuarial reserves of all the pension funds were published only for 1938, namely in the savings survey drawn up by the ASLK for that year[18]. The figures relate to the actuarial reserves on 31 December (Table 93 column 1). In the ASLK annual reports, the chapter devoted to the Annuity Fund sets out the evolution of the capital accumulated in the ASLK's Interest Fund pursuant to the pension acts. These figures, which roughly correspond with the actuarial reserves

---

[13] For an explanation of the way in which interest on actuarial reserves has been handled see Chapter 9, "Interest payments to the personal sector".
[14] NIS, *Commissie van het Nationaal Inkomen*, pp. 267-271.
[15] The interest on the actuarial reserves of life insurance companies, by contrast, form part of Chapter 9, "Interest payments to the personal sector".
[16] See Chapter 4, "Employers' social security contributions".
[17] Idem.
[18] *Annual Report ASLK 1947*, p. 28.

of the ASLK's pension funds, also show the situation at the end of the year[19]. The size of the Interest Fund has been published for all years (column 4). The actuarial reserves of all the pension funds were estimated on the basis of the known figure for 1938 and the evolution of the Interest Fund and the ASLK.

In 1938 the Interest Fund and the ASLK accounted for 82% of the total actuarial reserves of all pension funds or, conversely, the total actuarial reserves corresponded with 122% of the Interest Fund. It has been assumed that this percentage remained constant during the period 1932-1939. The percentage may well have been somewhat lower during the period 1920-1931, as all white-collar workers' pensions were administered by the ASLK in those years. The incremental factor for this period has been set at 110% (column 5). By multiplying the size of the Interest Fund by the incremental factor in each year one arrives at the actuarial reserves of all the pension funds (column 6). Since these figures relate to the end of the year, the average annual amount in year t was obtained by taking the arithmetic average of the actuarial reserves at 31 December in year t-1 and those at 31 December in year t (column 7). The sum obtained in this way was then multiplied by the technical rate of interest provided for under the Act of 3.75%[20] (column 8).

2. Interest on the actuarial reserves of industrial accident insurance funds

The majority of the industrial accident insurance was in the hands of private insurance companies and employers' funds. In addition the *Industrial Accidents Insurance Fund* (Rentekas voor Arbeidsongevallen) came under the ASLK.

The interest on the actuarial reserves was estimated along the same lines as the pensions. The total definitive actuarial reserves for 1938 were published in the survey of savings drawn up by the ASLK (Table 94 column 1)[21]. For the remaining years there are the provisional actuarial reserves of the private insurance companies and employers' funds (column 2)[22] and the definitive actuarial reserves of the ASLK (column 3)[23]. The evolution of the sum of the two series (column 4) was linked to the known total figure for 1938. In this way one arrives at an estimate of all definitive actuarial reserves at the end of the year

---

[19] From a bookkeeping point of view the Interest Fund forms the countervalue to the actuarial reserve, the security reserve and the other technical or statutory reserves. The size of the Interest Fund is therefore an approximation, although on the high side, of the actuarial reserve (NIS, *Commissie van het Nationaal Inkomen*, pp. 268-269). This factor does not however detract seriously from the method of reconstruction, since the amounts in the Interest Fund were applied for their evolution, not for their absolute value.

[20] NIS, *Commissie van het Nationaal Inkomen*, p. 268.

[21] *Annual Report ASLK 1948*, p. 45.

[22] *Reports on Industrial Accidents*. For example the *Report for 1933-1935*, pp. 37, 39 en 48).

[23] *Annual Reports ASLK*.

(column 5). The annual average of these actuarial reserves (column 6) and the amount of interest (column 7) were calculated in the same way as that for the old-age pensions[24].

Paragraph 3. Other government

This paragraph refers in the first place to the municipalities and also to the provinces and the Public Welfare Committees. The latter were responsible for official poor relief and were organized at municipal level. This paragraph includes all income from property and entrepreneurship, with the exception of the imputed rent for the buildings owned by other government and employed by the latter for its own use (e.g. town halls, municipal and provincial schools and COO hospitals). The net rent income from buildings and land let to private individuals therefore do form part of this heading.

The final results of the estimates are presented in Table 95. The total figures form an average of 0.59% of national income. The municipal incomes form the largest part of these totals (an average of 84.2%). The average share of the incomes accruing to the Public Welfare Committees and the provinces were 14.1% and 1.7% respectively.

1. Municipalities

The figures were estimated on the basis of the municipal accounts published in the Statistical Yearbook. The income from property and entrepreneurship collected by the municipalities appear under the heading "Municipal property and charges" or "Municipal enterprises or equivalent services". In the case of both headings the balance between current income and current expenditure has been calculated[25]. The income from property relates in particular to the letting of municipal land and buildings to the personal sector. The charges relate to the services supplied by the municipalities for which the user was asked to make some payment. The municipal enterprises and equivalent services operated mainly in the gas, electricity and water sectors and were generally organised in the form of intercommunal enterprises.

With the exception of 1939, aggregate municipal accounts were not published in the inter-war period, although the accounts of all municipalities with over

---

[24] In line with the NIS a technical rate of interest of 3.75% was also applied to the actuarial reserves of the industrial accident insurance funds.
[25] This working method is the same as that applied by the NIS in its post-war calculation of national income. The same applies to the income from property and entrepreneurship of the COOs and the provinces. NIS, *Commissie van het Nationaal Inkomen*, pp. 296-298.

40,000 inhabitants were included each year in the Statistical Yearbook[26]. In his study of municipal finances, Van Audenhove has aggregated these accounts for the 14 municipalities that had over 40,000 inhabitants throughout the inter-war period[27]. The estimates of property and entrepreneurial income are based on the 1939 figures (all municipalities), the evolution of which in the remaining years was linked to the figures for the 14 municipalities with over 40,000 inhabitants.

For the heading "Municipal property and charges", the aggregated municipal accounts for 1939 included both income and expenditure (see Table 96 columns 1-2). The accounts of the municipalities with over 40,000 inhabitants only show income as a separate category for this item (column 4). It has been assumed that the balance (of income and expenditure) of all the municipalities follow the same pattern as the income of the municipalities with over 40,000 inhabitants. The evolution of column 4 was linked to the balance of all the municipalities in 1939 (column 3). The result of this calculation is the net figure for all municipalities in 1920-1939[28].

With respect to the heading "Municipal enterprises or equivalent services", both the aggregate accounts in 1939 and the accounts of the municipalities with over 40,000 inhabitants include income and expenditure figures (columns 6-7 and 9-10). The evolution of the balance of the municipalities with over 40,000 inhabitants (column 11) was linked to the balance of all the municipalities in 1939 (column 8), thus arriving at the balance for all municipalities for the entire period in column 12[29].

---

[26] For the period 1937-1939 the Statistical Yearbook also published the accounts of municipalities with at least 5,000 inhabitants. *Statistisch Jaarboek*, vol. 62, 1940, pp. 168-174; *Idem*, vol. 63, 1941, pp. 154-155.

[27] VAN AUDENHOVE M., *Geschiedenis van de gemeentefinanciën*, in: "Gemeentekrediet van België. Driemaandelijks Tijdschrift", vol. 35, 1981, pp. 214-215. The number of municipalities with over 40,000 inhabitants rose between 1920 and 1939 from 15 to 23. 14 municipalities had over 40,000 inhabitants throughout the period in question (Anderlecht, Antwerp, Borgerhout, Bruges, Brussels, Elsene, Ghent, Liège, Malines, Ostend, Schaarbeek, Sint-Gillis, Sint-Jans-Molenbeek and Verviers). The figure for the municipality of Laken in 1920 was also included since that municipality was merged with Brussels in 1921. The 14 municipalities in question plus Laken accounted for 1,464,235 inhabitants in 1920 (19.8% of the Belgian population). In 1939 the figure was 1,465,663 (17.5% of the Belgian population).

[28] The sharp rise between 1933 and 1934 is probably attributable to the discontinuity in the accounts of the municipalities with over 40,000 inhabitants, since the "Other receipts" heading in these accounts fell from 1933 to 1934 from BF 348 to 90 million. These figures strongly suggest that part of the income from property and charges was entered under "Other receipts" until 1934.

[29] The income and expenditure figures for the municipal enterprises also contain discontinuities, which may be due to accounting shifts (namely the rise in income in expenditure between 1926 and 1927, and especially the fall in income and expenditure between 1935 and 1936). The impact on the balance in 1936 appears negligible, while the increase in the balance between 1926 and 1927 may be too pronounced.

2. Public Welfare Committees

Apart from municipal grants, a substantial proportion of the Public Welfare Committee's income came from their property, namely the letting of land and buildings to the personal sector. The aggregate accounts of the Public Welfare Committees were not, however, published in the Statistical Yearbook until 1941[30], so that the net income from property in the inter-war period had to be estimated indirectly. It has been assumed that this net income evolved in the same way as the net income from municipal property and the municipal charges. The evolution of those figures was then linked to the known balance in 1941.

The current income and expenditure relating to property in 1941 are shown in Table 96 columns 14-15. The balance in 1941 (column 16) amounted to 31.2% of the balance of income and expenditure of municipal property and charges in 1941 (column 3). This ratio has been multiplied in column 18 by the net income from municipal property and charges in 1920-1939 (column 5). The result is an estimate of the net income from property of the COOs in 1920-1939.

3. Provinces

The income from property and entrepreneurship of the provinces was notably limited in the inter-war period. The net income was estimated on the basis of the headings "Property and charges" and "Provincial enterprises and equivalent services" in the provincial accounts, which were published in the Statistical Yearbook.

The current income from property and charges was included under a separate heading for all years (see Table 97 column 1). Current expenditure, however, was not shown separately until 1944. In the period 1944-1953 current expenditure averaged 67% of income. It has been assumed that this percentage was the same in the inter-war period (column 2). The balance of income and expenditure is shown in column 3.

With respect to the provincial enterprises, separate figures were not included in the accounts until 1939 (columns 4-5). On the basis of the assumption that the net income from the provincial enterprises evolve in the same way as the balance of the municipal enterprises, the balance of the provincial enterprises has been estimated in column 7.

---

[30]   *Statistisch Jaarboek*, vol. 66, 1944, p. 155.

CHAPTER 15

INTEREST ON THE PUBLIC DEBT

SECTION 1. DEFINITIONS AND SUMMARY OF CONTENTS

Paragraph 1. Why is the interest on the public debt deducted from national income?

In the standardized system of national accounts of the OECD, the interest on the public debt is by convention regarded as an income transfer[1], on the grounds that the debt is assumed to be used for consumer purposes (e.g. the payment of wages and salaries to government personnel, the payment of unemployment benefits, costs of heating, lighting and routine maintenance of government buildings). This assumption is undoubtedly not entirely correct, since a part of the government debt has its origin in capital expenditure (e.g. road construction, the building of schools and hospitals and port infrastructure). It is however impossible to determine the extent to which the revenue raised from public loans is used for consumer purposes or in order to build up the level of public property.

On the other hand, the standardized system of national accounts implicitly assumes that all private debts are employed for investment purposes. In contrast to the interest on the public debt, the interest on private debt is consequently regarded not as a transfer but at an added value. This assumption too is only partly true, since a proportion of the private debts are entered into in order to finance consumer spending. An obvious example is consumer credit. As in the case of government, however, it is in many cases virtually impossible to tell whether a private loan is used to finance current or capital expenditure.

The interest payments on the public debt are explicitly or implicitly counted in various headings as a positive contribution to national income. As far as the interest accruing to households and non-profit institutions is concerned, the amounts paid out are explicitly included in Chapter 9 "Interest payments to the personal sector". The interest accruing to share companies form part of their corporate receipts, which are in turn implicitly distributed over the various factor incomes (pay, dividends, interest on borrowed capital, rent and reserved profits). Since it is assumed by convention that the interest on the government debts is a transfer and because the amounts paid out have been entered elsewhere, an

---

[1] NIS, *Commissie van het Nationaal Inkomen*, p. 300; OECD, *A standardized system of national accounts,* pp. 52 and 80.

adjustment needs to be made here in order to avoid double-counting. This adjustment amounts to the deduction from national income of the total interest on the public debt.

A similar adjustment in respect of private debt would be superfluous, since it has been assumed that this debt was entered into for productive purposes. The interest on the private debt, the payment of which was also regarded in the above heading as a positive contribution to national income, must consequently be treated as a factor income.

The debt of the semi-government institutions forming part of the corporate sector (e.g. the National Belgian Railway Company (NMVB), the Telegraph and Telephone Company (RTT)) are equated in the OECD's standardized system of national accounts with the private debt[2]. This means that it has been assumed that this debt is employed for productive purposes and that the interest payments should not be deducted in calculating national income. The same applies to the debts of inter-communal companies[3].

It cannot be emphasized enough that the approach recommended by the OECD rests on convention[4]. It would undoubtedly be more logical not to include the interest on the full public debt under this heading, but only the interest on that part of the debt with which consumer spending is financed. On the other hand it would also be more correct for the interest on the private consumer debt correspondingly to be entered as a negative adjustment item.

In order to remain consistent with the methodology of the NIS, which is based on the recommendations of the OECD, and also because the available source material does not permit a distinction to be drawn between consumer and capital expenditure debt, the total public debt has been regarded in this study as consumer debt and the total private debt as productive. This implies that the total interest on the public debt has been treated in this chapter as a negative item in order to neutralize the government interest payments counted elsewhere.

The public debt taken into consideration in this chapter consists of the State debt and that of lower levels of government (i.e. provinces and municipalities). The interest payments are estimated respectively in Sections 2 and 3 and the results shown in Table 98.

---

[2] *A standardized system,* p. 80.
[3] For an overview of the inter-communal companies that placed bond issues in the capital market during the inter-war period, see VAN AUDENHOVE M., *Geschiedenis van de gemeentefinanciën,* pp. 107-108).
[4] In fact the treatment of the interest on the public debt as a transfer arises from an assumption with respect to the production approach. The added value of the government sector is defined in the standardized system as the sum of the compensation of government personnel and the imputed rent on government buildings. *De nationale rekeningen van België 1953-1962,* pp. 1137-1138. In contrast to the private sector, therefore, the reimbursement paid on borrowed capital is not - with the exception of buildings - regarded as added value for the government sector.

Paragraph 2. Definition of the public debt

The public debt in Belgium is generally divided into the direct and the indirect public debt[5]. By direct public debt is meant the debt of the State in the narrow sense. This debt is directly spent by the Belgian State. The indirect State debt comprises the loans taken out by public utilities and semi-government enterprises or by autonomous funds coming under the aegis of the government, the servicing (= interest payments + redemption of capital) of which has been undertaken by the State.

Generally speaking such loans are concluded for a specific purpose, a familiar example in the Second World War being the loans for the *Roads Fund* (Wegenfonds). By contrast the loans entered into by seven semi-government institutions or enterprises, the servicing of which is handled by the organizations themselves, are not regarded as part of the public debt. If for example the NMBS, RTT or other institutions for the public benefit place a bond loan on the capital market on which they themselves repay the capital and interest, the outstanding capital of such a loan does not form part of the public debt but of the debt of semi-government institutions[6].

Since the indirect public debt differs little if at all from the direct public debt in substantive terms, the two are dealt with together below[7]. It is, furthermore, often difficult to draw a distinction in the statistics on the public debt[8].

The interest to be included in this chapter covers that on the direct national debt and that on the indirect public debt, in so far as the latter was not concluded for the benefit of semi-government enterprises of a commercial nature[9].

During the inter-war period the indirect debt consisted in large part of loans entered into by funds established after the First World War with a view to

---

5   *Belgische economische statistieken 1929-1940*, p. 147 ; TIMMERMANS A., *La dette publique*, in: "Université de Louvain. Institut des Sciences Economiques Appliquées. Collection du Centre de Recherches en Economie et Gestion des Entreprises", vol. 15, Courtrai, 1958, p. 141.

6   The interest on this debt must not be deducted from national income. Cf. above.

7   The difference between direct and indirect public debt is largely a formal one: the direct public debt arises as a result of direct resort by the State to the money or capital market, while in the case of the indirect public debt the resources are mobilized by the State through other channels (e.g. autonomous funds).

8   The debt of the State towards the National Bank of Belgium, with respect to the withdrawal of German Marks, for example, is treated in some years as part of the direct debt and in others as part of the indirect debt. (*Belgische economische statistieken 1929-1940*, pp. 147-149). In the case of the figures found on the interest burden of the public debt no distinction whatever is in fact drawn between the direct and indirect debt. Cf. below.

9   NIS, *Commissie van het Nationaal Inkomen*, p. 300; *De nationale rekeningen van België 1953-1962*, p. 618. An example of such a loan concluded during the inter-war period is that raised by the Nationale Kredietkas ten behoeve van de Middenstand. DAVIN L.E., *La dette publique de 1919 à 1939*, dans: "Histoire des finances publiques en Belgique", Brussels; Paris, Institut Belge de Finances Publiques (ed.), vol. II, 1954, p. 295.

compensating the victims of war damage[10]. The interest on these loans should without any doubt be included in this chapter.

Another significant element of the indirect public debt during the inter-war period consisted of the preference shares issued by the NMBS. This indirect debt arose in 1926 as a result of the monetary reforms and stabilization carried out by the government in that year under the direction of Minister Emile Francqui[11]. One of the most important objectives of Francqui's monetary reforms was the consolidation of the large volume of floating debt which the government had built up during and after the war. This floating debt placed the national currency under strong pressure and constituted a continual threat to monetary stability. The consolidation of the floating debt largely took the form of a partial privatization of the State Railways. Until 1926 the State Railways, which exploited the larger part of the Belgian Railway network, was fully in the hands of the government. Under the Act of 23 July 1926 the State Railways were converted into the National Belgian Railways Company. This company was under the control of the State, which had a majority on the governing board. The capital was set at BF 11 billion, corresponding with the value of the assets. This was represented by 10 million ordinary shares of BF 100 each (BF 1 billion) and 20 million preference shares of BF 500 each (BF 10 billion). The State held the ordinary shares, while the preference shares were placed at the disposal of the Fund for the Redemption of the National Debt (Fonds tot Delging van de Openbare Schuld)[12]. On the same day as the formation of the NMBS (23 July 1926) it was decided to consolidate the floating debt by means of a compulsory conversion. The holders of treasury bonds were obliged to convert their short-term government securities. One of the possibilities they were offered was to convert their treasury bonds into preferential NMBS shares, thus giving them a stake in the new company[13]. The term "share"

---

[10] In 1921, 1922 and 1923 these funds issued three lottery-loans each of BF one billion under the name of *Lottery-loan Devastated Regions* (Lotenlening Verwoeste Gewesten) (DAVIN E., *o.c.*, p.36 VRANCKEN F., SEULEN E., *Financement et liquidation de la première guerre mondiale*, in: "Histoire des finances publiques en Belgique", vol.II, 1954, pp.24-25 ; *Belgische economische statistieken 1929-1940*, pp.148-149.

[11] In connection with the monetary reforms and the establishment of the NMBS, see: DAVIN L.E., *op. cit.*, pp. 306-314; JANSSENS V., *De Belgische frank. Anderhalve eeuw geldgeschiedenis*, Antwerp; Amsterdam, 1976, pp. 200-203; VANDENDRIESSCHE S., *o.c.*, pp. 70-73; VAN DER WEE H., TAVERNIER K., *De Nationale Bank van België en het monetaire gebeuren tussen de twee wereldoorlogen*, Brussels, 1975, pp. 175-178.

[12] The Fund for the Redemption of the National Debt was established by the Act of 7 June 1926. One of the tasks of this fund consisted of reducing the National Debt, especially in the short term (DAVIN L.E., *o.c.*, pp. 305-306. VANDENDRIESSCHE S., *o.c.*, p. 71 VAN DER WEE H., TAVERNIER K., *o.c.*, p. 174).

[13] Over BF 4 billion in treasury certificates were converted into preferential NMBS shares (BF 4,192 million according to FRANCK L., *La stabilisation monetaire en Belgique*, Paris, 1927, p. 161; BF 4,238 million according to JANSSENS V., *o.c.*, p. 201; BF 4,374 million according to VAN DER WEE H., TAVERNIER K., *o.c.*, p. 177). The conversion operation was a total success and, together with the devaluation of the BF on 25 October 1926, ushered in a boom for the Belgian economy.

is somewhat misleading, since the shares provided an entitlement to a fixed annual interest of 6%, irrespective of the NMBS's operating results[14]. In view of the fact that the State accepted responsibility for the guaranteed interest and the later redemption of the preference shares, these shares may in fact be equated with the consolidated government debt. For these reasons they have been included in the official statistics of the public debt[15] and the interest payments also need to be included in this chapter.

The statistics on the national debt generally draw a distinction between short and medium-term debt (floating debt) and long-term debt (consolidated debt). The short and medium-term debt consisted primarily of treasury bonds and certificates, and the long-term debt of bonds[16].

Finally the national debt may be divided into domestic and foreign debt. With respect to the latter, a distinction is drawn between the loans raised on foreign capital markets and inter-governmental debt. The latter arose as a result of the advances received by Belgium during and immediately after the First World War from the United States, Great Britain, France and the Netherlands[17]. The redemptions of and interest payments on the inter-governmental debt came to a halt with the Hoover Moratorium of June 1931[18].

Paragraph 3. Definition of local government debt

Constitutionally, Belgium was a centralized nation during the inter-war period, although the municipalities had a comparatively high degree of autonomy. At intermediate level were the nine provinces, whose autonomy used to be limited. There was no question of a federalized state structure with regions and

---

[14] After the conversion of the national debt in 1935 the rate of interest was 4% (DAVIN L.E., *o.c.*, p. 321). Apart from the fixed-interest payment of 6% the owners of preference shares were entitled to half the net profit (VAN DER WEE H., TAVERNIER K., *o.c.*, p. 175).

[15] *Belgische economische statistieken*, pp. 147-149.

[16] *Idem.*

[17] Under Article 232 (3) of the Treaty of Versailles, Germany was required not just to pay war reparations but also the redemption and interest on the advances received by Belgium up to 11 November 1918. This means that Germany was substituted for Belgium with respect to the war advances. The US Congress, however, refused to ratify the Treaty of Versailles, so that Belgium remained the direct debtor with respect to the United States (VANDENDRIESSCHE S., *o.c.*, p. 108). With respect to the debts entered into after the war to finance reconstruction, and also in respect of the loans granted by the Netherlands arising from the internment costs of Belgian soldiers during the war, however, the Belgian State remained the direct debtor. For a survey of the intergovernmental debts see DAVIN L.E., *o.c.*, pp. 295-299; VANDENDRIESSCHE S., *o.c.*, pp. 108-109.

[18] The Hoover moratorium also meant that Germany was no longer obliged to pay reparations. The cessation of the redemptions and interest payments on the intergovernmental debt did not, however, mean that this debt had officially been cancelled. For this reason these debts still appear in the official surveys of the national debt, although they are never taken into account in assessments of the state of the government debt (VANDENDRIESSCHE S., *o.c.*, p. 208).

communities in the inter-war period; this only arose after the constitutional reforms of 1970, 1980, 1988 and 1993[19]. The term "local government debt" therefore refers to the debt of the municipalities and provinces.

Local government debt consists of two major components: on the one hand the debt held with the *Municipal Credit Association of Belgium* (Gemeentekrediet van België) and on the other the debt arising from the direct resort to the capital market by the municipalities and provinces. During the inter-war period only the large municipalities and some of the provinces placed bond loans on the capital market[20]. Private individuals were also permitted to subscribe to most of these loans. The small municipalities raised their loans with the Gemeentekrediet, a semi-government financial institution in which the municipalities were the main shareholders, established in 1860 with the principal objective of providing the municipalities and provinces with credit. The municipalities and provinces that raised bond issues independently could also take up loans with the Gemeentekrediet. The latter obtained its working funds mainly from the issue of bonds and treasury certificates, most of which were placed with the public.

SECTION 2. INTEREST ON THE STATE DEBT

For the period 1929-1939 the interest payments on the State debt were published in the "Belgische Economische Statistieken" of the NBB, under a heading entitled "State Debt Charges"[21]. For the period 1920-1928 data were found in the master's dissertation by Michiels, based on unpublished information of the Ministry of Finance[22]. Michiels' figures correspond closely with those of the NBB, which also obtained its information from the Ministry of Finance. The period 1929-1939 is first discussed in detail below, followed by a more summary treatment of the years 1920-1928.

---

[19] The Constitution of Belgium currently provides for three Regions (Flanders, Wallonia and Brussels) and four Communities (Dutch-speaking, German-speaking and the bilingual Brussels Dutch/French Community).
[20] During the period 1918-1939 bond loans were issued only by the provinces of Antwerp and East Flanders. The municipalities that raised funds directly in the capital market were Aalst, Anderlecht, Antwerp, Bergen, Bruges, Brussels, Charleroi, Dinant, Elsene, Etterbeek, Ghent, Halle, Kortrijk, Laken, La Louvière, Liège, Louvain, Malines, Oostend, Schaarbeek, Sint-Gillis, Sint-Joost-ten-Node and Verviers. These were generally small loans taken up on an ad hoc basis (e.g. shortly after the First World War, when many municipalities ran into financial problems). Only Antwerp, Brussels, Ghent and Liège systematically issued bond loans of any size. In 1928 Antwerp even raised a loan for 10 million dollars in the foreign market. As far as can be established this was the only loan placed abroad by local government. For a chronological survey of the bond loans see *Belgische economische statistieken 1929-1940*, pp. 64-67; VAN AUDENHOVE M., *o.c.*, pp. 107-108.
[21] *Belgische economische statistieken 1929-1940*, pp. 151-152.
[22] MICHIELS J., *Kritische periodes in de evolutie van de rijksschuld: 1926* (Unpublished master's dissertation, Economics Department KUL., 1983, p. 32.

In its figures for 1929-1939, the NBB draws a distinction between the interest on the domestic debt and that on the outstanding debt in the foreign market. Figures are also provided for both categories on the interest on the consolidated debt and the interest on the short and medium-term debt. Since the NBB published separate figures for these four elements of the government debt in connection with the redemption of the debt on the one hand and interest payments on the other, there is no doubt that the figures shown in Table 99 columns 1, 2, 6 and 7 relate solely to the interest payments.

The explanatory text does not state anywhere whether the figures relate solely to the direct public debt or to the direct and the indirect public debt. From a comparison with alternative figures for the period 1933-1939, however, it is evident that the interest on the indirect public debt is totally or as least largely included in the figures of Table 99. This alternative source is the return-on-capital statistics, which were also published in the NBB's Belgische Economische Statistieken[23]. From 1933 onwards these include not just data on the financial results of the private enterprises but also information on the coupons paid out on government securities (see Table 99). A distinction is drawn between domestic State loans, Congo loans, provincial and municipal loans (= solely when loans were raised directly in the capital market, i.e. excluding the loans from the Gemeentekrediet) loans issued by various bodies (= loans by institutions of public benefit), foreign State loans and the foreign loan placed by the City of Antwerp. Since these figures relate to coupons, the figures naturally concern the consolidated debt only.

With the exception of 1936, the interest on the domestic consolidated debt (Table 99 column 1) is higher for all years than the amount of the coupons on domestic State loans (Table 100 column 1)[24]. Among other things the difference is probably attributable to the fact that the interest on the preferential shares of the NMBS in Table 100 more than probably form part of the heading "Coupons of loans issued by various bodies", whereas in Table 99 they may have been included in the interest on the domestic consolidated debt. It was noted previously that these shares form part of the public debt, and that the interest paid out on that debt must consequently be included here[25].

The statistics on the charges on the public debt also include figures entitled "Charges without associated capital" (Table 99 columns 3 and 4). The accompanying text indicates that these are charges for which no corresponding capital is entered in the national debt. In addition the text indicates that these charges include the interest on a number of loans entered into by institutions for the public benefit, for which the State has undertaken to pay the interest, as well

---

[23] *Belgische economische statistieken 1929-1940*, pp. 160-182.
[24] The comparatively high figure for 1936 in the return-on-capital statistics (BF 1,202 million in 1936 compared with BF 948 million in 1935 and BF 1,032 million in 1937) casts doubt on the reliability of the figure for 1936.
[25] Cf. above.

as a number of subsidies[26]. It is impossible to determine from this information whether these figures should be included and, if so, to what extent. If the data relate to part of the indirect public debt they need to be included[27], but if they are related to the debt of semi-government institutions of a commercial nature they fall outside the scope of this chapter. Ultimately it was decided to record the figures in this chapter, as it was possible that the comparatively high charges without associated capital (column 3) in the years 1935 and 1936 were the result of the relatively low interest payments on the domestic consolidated debt (column 1), which would then mean that the figures in columns 1 and 3 were not totally homogeneous.

By adding columns 1, 2, 3 and 4 in Table 99 one obtains the interest on the total domestic public debt (column 5).

As noted, the figures in columns 6 and 7 relate to the foreign debt. Two problems arise in this respect: firstly, the interest on the inter-governmental debt is not included in the figures and, secondly, there is the problem of the exchange rate.

Direct figures on the interest payments on the inter-governmental debt were not found anywhere. The statistics on the charges payable on the public debt as published by the NBB do, however, contain a heading entitled "other charges". This heading relates not just to the inter-governmental debt but to certain other loans (see Table 101 column 1). In addition, the figures cover not just the interest payments but also the capital redemptions. In order to arrive at the interest payments on the inter-governmental debt, an estimate is first made of the charges (= interest payments + redemption of capital) on the non-inter-governmental debt. After deduction of this estimate one arrives at the charges on the inter-governmental debt. The share of interest charges is then established. Multiplication of this share by the charges results in the interest charges on the inter-governmental debt.

As discussed earlier, the redemptions of and interest payments on the inter-governmental debt were suspended as a result of the Hoover Moratorium of June 1931[28]. This is confirmed by the statistics on the outstanding volume of government debt, or at least for the debts vis-à-vis the US and British governments; from 1931 the outstanding amount of these loans remains constant[29]. The Hoover Moratorium did not, however, evidently affect the amounts borrowed by Belgium from the Netherlands to cover the internment costs of Belgian forces during the First World War[30]. This debt, which was subject to

---

[26] *Belgische economische statistieken 1929-1940*, p. 151.
[27] Unless the debt was entered into on behalf of semi-government institutions of a commercial nature (cf. above).
[28] Cf. above.
[29] *Belgische economische statistieken 1929-1940*, pp. 148-149.
[30] Belgium no longer had any debts vis-à-vis the French State from 1926 onwards (VANDENDRIESSCHE S., *o.c.*, pp. 108-109).

5% interest, continued to be redeemed after 1931, until it was fully repaid in 1937[31].

The above information is clearly confirmed by the figures in Table 101 column 1. Up to and including 1931 the figures include the charges on the inter-governmental debt vis-à-vis the United States and Great Britain, the charges on the inter-governmental debt vis-à-vis the Netherlands and other charges that do not relate to the inter-governmental debt. From 1932 onwards there are no longer any charges on the debt to the United States and Great Britain, and from 1938 the debt towards the State of the Netherlands had been repaid. For the period 1938-1940, therefore, the figures relate exclusively to charges not connected in any way with the inter-governmental debt. These charges are extrapolated to the preceding years in column 2[32]. Column 3 indicates the charges on the inter-governmental debt. In columns 4-7 the interest is calculated on the inter-governmental debt vis-à-vis the Netherlands. For the period 1929-1939 it was impossible precisely to determine the interest charges on the total inter-governmental debt. It has been assumed that the share of interest payments in the total charges on the inter-governmental debt was the same as the share of the interest charges in the total charges of the foreign consolidated debt excluding the inter-governmental debt (columns 8-10). Column 11 therefore shows the interest on the inter-governmental debt.

With respect to the interest on the total foreign debt (Table 99 column 9) the problem arises of the exchange rate. From 1929 up to and including 1935 the interest payments have been valued on the basis of the official currency parities of 25 October 1926 and 31 March 1935. From 1936 onwards the interest charges have been estimated on the basis of the exchange rates on the date of payment[33]. For the period 1936-1939 the figures drawn from the NBB can therefore be taken as they stand. The same applies to 1929-1930 since the exchange rate of the currencies in which the foreign debt of the Belgian State was denominated was the same in these years as in 1926[34]. On 20 September 1931 sterling left the gold

---

31 *Belgische economische statistieken 1929-1940*, pp. 148-149.
32 The results in column 2 have not been taken into account in calculating the interest charges on the domestic public debt. In the first place it is unclear whether or not the figures should be counted, while secondly the figures contain both interest payments and capital redemptions. Finally it may be noted that these are comparatively small amounts, so that any errors arising from the mistaken non-inclusion of this item are minor.
33 *Belgische economische statistieken 1929-1940*, p. 151.
34 During the inter-war period, Belgium's foreign debts (in order of importance in 1933) were held in dollars, French francs, sterling, guilders, Swiss francs and Swedish kroner (own calculation on basis of *Belgische economische statistieken* 1929-1940, pp. 148-149). After the devaluation of the BF on 25 October 1926, the exchange rates vis-à-vis the most important foreign currencies were: BF 35.96 to the dollar, BF 175 to the pound sterling and BF 14.45 to the guilder (JANSSENS V., *o.c.*, pp. 428-430). Between 25 October 1926 (when the BF was devalued) and 20 September 1931 (when the pound left the gold standard) only the value of the French franc changes (from BF 1.33 on 25 October 1926 to BF 1.41 on 25 June 1928 = date of stabilization of the FF). No correction was, however, made for the years 1929-1930 for this increase in value of the FF since the debt in FF

standard. Between 1931 and March 1935 the value of sterling vis-à-vis the BF fell by 40.8%[35]. In the statistics on the interest payments on the foreign debt, however, the debt in sterling remained valued at the pre-September 1931 parity of the pound, meaning that the figures are too high. The same applies to the interest payments on the dollar debt from April 1933, the date on which the US dollar left the gold standard and floated[36].

Table 99 column 10 contains an adjustment coefficient for the interest payments on the foreign debt in 1931-1934[37]. This coefficient indicates the weighted exchange rate of the foreign currencies in which the Belgian State had debts vis-à-vis the exchange rate on 25 October 1926. The weighting factors were adjusted each year and are based on the share of each currency in the total outstanding foreign debt[38].

Multiplication of column 9 by the adjustment coefficient in column 10 results in the interest charges on the total foreign debt valued at the exchange rates prevailing at the time of payment of the interest (column 11). Needless to say the figures in column 11 are heavily influenced by the variable pattern of exchange rates (e.g. the fall in the interest charges in 1933-1934 was largely caused by the devaluation of the dollar, the rise in charges in 1935 by the devaluation of the BF and the fall in 1936-1939 largely by the successive devaluations of the French Franc[39].

As noted previously, the interest charges on the public debt for the period 1920-1928 have been ascertained by Michiels (Table 99 columns 5 and 9)[40]. No separation has been made between the interest on the consolidated debt and the interest on the floating debt. With respect to the interest on the domestic debt Michiels notes that the interest charges have been included in the figures without

---

during those years was extremely small. The debt in FF rose particularly in the course of the 1930s (with new loans in 1932, 1933 and 1935, see *Belgische economische statistieken 1929-1940*, pp. 65-66 and 148-149).

[35] The average exchange rate of sterling on the Brussels stock exchange evolved as follows: BF 125.87 in 1932, BF 118.98 in 1933, BF 108.20 in 1934 and BF 103.68 in 1935 (first three months) (JANSSENS V., *o.c.*, p. 428).

[36] During the last eight months of 1933 the average exchange rate of the dollar in Brussels was BF 25.69. From 31 January 1934 there was a fixed parity of BF 21.24 to the dollar. This new parity was 40.9% lower than that before 19 April 1933 (JANSSENS V., *o.c.*, p 429).

[37] No adjustment is required for 1935 since the interest charges for that year have been valued at the devalued exchange rate for the BF of 31 March 1935. As a result of the devaluation the Belgian Franc fell by 28%.

[38] Excluding the intergovernmental debt vis-à-vis the United States and Great Britain from 1932 onwards.

[39] The French franc was devalued by 25% on 1 October 1936. There were further devaluations on 21 July 1937 and 12 November 1938. At the end of 1938 the value of the French franc vis-à-vis the BF was just 41.9% of its value after the devaluation of the BF on 31 March 1935 (JANSSENS V., *o.c.*, p. 429).

[40] MICHIELS J., *o.c.*, p. 32.

showing the corresponding capital. As far as the foreign debt is concerned, no indication is provided as to whether the interest on the inter-governmental debt forms part of the figures in column 9. The close correspondence between the 1928 and 1929 figures indicates that the inter-governmental debt does in fact form part of the foreign debt.

SECTION 3. INTEREST ON LOCAL GOVERNMENT DEBT

As noted earlier, the debt of the municipalities and provinces consists of two large components: on the one hand the debt of the Gemeentekrediet and on the other the debt from public issues of bond loans[41].

There are no direct figures on the total interest charges on local government debt. The annual outstanding volume of debt was, however, published for the years 1929-1939, while the amount of interest and annuities paid out by the municipalities with over 40,000 inhabitants was published for the entire inter-war period. In addition there is a chronological list of the public issues of bond loans by municipalities and provinces with, for each issue, the amount of the loan, term of the loan and the rate of interest. On the basis of this information it was possible to estimate the interest charges on local government debt[42].

For the period 1929-1933 the NBB annually published the outstanding local government debt in all its components (see Table 102 columns 1-8)[43]. The interest paid out was estimated by multiplying the total outstanding amount (column 9) by the average rate of interest (column 10).

For the period 1929-1935 the rate of interest was set at 5% and in 1936-1939 at 4%. 1936 forms a break because the interest rates were consolidated in that year (see below). The interest rates have been selected on the following grounds. From a survey of the direct issues of new bond loans by municipalities and provinces in 1919-1935, it is evident that, taking account of the size and term of the loans, the weighted average rate of interest of the outstanding amount in 1929-1935 of the loans issued in 1918-1935 amounted to approximately 5.5%[44]. It has been

---

[41] Cf. above.
[42] For the period 1933-1939 the return-on-capital statistics also include the amount of coupons paid out on provincial and municipal loans (see Table 100 column 3). These figures are, however, confined to loans quoted on the Brussels stock exchange. Since it is unclear whether all the local government bond loans were quoted on the Brussels stock exchange these figures were not included. With reference to the loans taken out with the Gemeentekrediet it was difficult to calculate the outstanding debt on account of the old fashioned nature of this institution's bookkeeping at that time (VAN AUDENHOVE M., *o.c.*, vol. 36, 1982, p. 105).
[43] *Belgische economische statistieken 1929-1940*, pp. 158-159.
[44] Own calculations on basis of VAN AUDENHOVE M., *o.c.*, pp. 107-108. The term of the loans ranged from 1 to 66 years. In order to calculate the annual outstanding volume of loans issued since 1918, it was assumed that no capital was redeemed during the life of a loan, meaning that the redemption of the capital was repaid in its entirety on the due date. On the basis of this assumption

assumed that the Gemeentekrediet charged the municipalities and provinces the same rate of interest on its loans. This percentage was then reduced by 0.5% to make allowance for the loans issued before 1918. No information is available on those loans but it may be assumed that the rate of interest was lower than that on the loans issued during the inter-war period. In 1936 the overwhelming majority of outstanding local government loans were consolidated[45]. In the case of loans subject to a rate of interest of over 4.5%, the interest was reduced to 4%. The interest rate on new loans issued in 1936-1939 was (with one exception) also 4%[46].

The total outstanding volume of local government debt is not known for the period 1920-1928, so that a different method of reconstruction had to be sought for these years. The interest charges were estimated on the basis of the accounts of the municipalities with over 40,000 inhabitants. These accounts, which were published annually in the Statistical Yearbook, include a heading under ordinary expenditure of *"Interest service and amortisation of permanent debts and loans"* (Dienst van intrest en amortisatie der gevestigde schulden en leningen). Ordinary expenditure includes an item *"Redemption of debts and loans"* (Aflossing van de schulden en leningen) The amortization under the first of these headings relates to annuities, since these always contain an element of interest payment and an element of capital redemption. It has been assumed that the total interest burden on local government debt evolved in parallel with the interest charges and annuities of the municipalities with over 40,000 inhabitants (column 12)[47]. In 1929 the ratio between the two variables was 65% (column 13). By dividing the interest charges and annuities of the municipalities with over 40,000 inhabitants by 0.65, one arrives at the total interest burden on the local government debt (column 14).

---

the weighted average rate of interest on the outstanding capital of the loans issued since 1918 evolved as follows in 1920-1935:
        1929 : 5.60%   1931 : 5.40%   1933 : 5.50%
        1930 : 5.42%   1932 : 5.44%   1934 : 5.50%

[45] This conversion took place as part of a general conversion of government stock in 1935-1936. In relation to the conversion of the local government debt, see *Belgische economische statistieken 1929-1940*, p. 69; VAN AUDENHOVE M., *o.c.*, vol.37, 1983, pp. 44-45.

[46] In the period 1936-1939 the municipalities and provinces placed only one loan with a rate of interest other than 4%, namely a loan issued by the city of Liège in 1939 at 4.5% (VAN AUDENHOVE M., *o.c.*, vol. 36, 1982, p. 108.)

[47] For the evolution of the number of municipalities with over 40,000 inhabitants dose between 1920 and 1939, see footnote 30 of Chapter 14.

CHAPTER 16

DEPRECIATION

The reconstruction of national income by means of the income approach ultimately leads to the aggregation of all income components to form an estimate of net national product at factor cost. After adding indirect taxes and deducting subsidies one obtains net national product at market prices. In order finally to arrive at gross national product at market prices, depreciation needs to be added (cf. below, General Conclusions).

The arrangement of this chapter is as follows. Following a general introduction dealing with the definition and reconstruction problems of depreciation, Section two examines the estimates of the DULBEA and NIS for depreciation in the post-war period. Section three deals with the reconstruction of depreciation in the period 1920-1939.

The results presented here are the work of Michelangelo van Meerten. Since his method of reconstruction is given in detail in a seperate publication in this series, the exposition here is limited to a brief summary of his study. For detailed calculations and information on the sources used, the reader is advised to use Van Meerten's work[1].

Section 1. Definition and Reconstruction Problems

Depreciation is defined as *the sums debited against operating revenues with the object of providing for the charge or loss which arises in connection with the deterioration in the value of fixed assets during the accounting period due to wear, normal obsolence and damage*[2]. This reflects the fact that capital goods have a finite economic life[3], depending on the one hand on the annual wear and tear resulting from use in the production process and from the destruction of capital goods by fire and similar such factors and, on the other, on technical obsolescence resulting from the appearance on the market of technically superior substitutes.

---

[1] VAN MEERTEN M.A., *Capital Formation in Belgium, 1900-1995*, (Studies in Economic History, vol. 6, Louvain, 2003).
[2] OECD, *A Standardized System of National Accounts*, p. 78.
[3] An exception to this rule is made in the National Accounts for certain infrastructural capital goods such as roads which are assumed to have an infinite economic life on account of maintenance and repairs. These capital goods are consequently left out of account in calculating depreciation. *Idem,* pp. 66 and 79.

At first glance it would seem logical to estimate depreciation on the basis of balance sheet figures supplied by the corporate sector and the government, with the aid of which the gross investments in capital assets were calculated for the inter-war period[4]. For a number of reasons, however, the depreciation figures shown in the profit and loss accounts of the corporate sector and the government provide a poor measure for depreciation in the national accounts.

In the first place the depreciation recorded by companies is, in contrast to that in the National Accounts, dependent on the state of the economy and the accounting policies of the companies in question[5]: generally speaking, depreciation is higher in a boom and lower in a recession[6]. Secondly, the scale of depreciation is, for bookkeeping purposes, influenced by the tax legislation on depreciation[7]. Finally, no uniform basis for calculating depreciation existed throughout the inter-war period: companies calculated depreciation on the basis of both historical cost and the replacement value of capital goods, whereas only the latter provides a valid basis for calculating the scale of depreciation[8].

The most suitable method for reconstructing depreciation is formed by the *Perpetual Inventory Model* (PIM), which establishes the relationship between the gross and net stock of capital goods on the one hand and the investments, decommissioning and depreciation on the other[9]. On the basis of the PIM an initial

---

[4] See VAN MEERTEN M.A., *o.c.*

[5] Under accounting theory depreciation should be calculated before determining the balance sheet and profit and loss account. In practice, however, the level of depreciation is influenced by companies' financial results and by the distributions of profit sought by the shareholders and managers of the company. See MOREAU L., *Le Bilan des Sociétés par Actions, Le Compte des Résultats, Interprétation & Unification*, Brussels, 1919, p. 198: "*Une pratique vicieuse et encore admise par certaines administrations est celle du non-prélèvement d'amortissements au cas de résultats précaires*". See also: HANON DE LOUVET C., *Analyse et Discussion de Bilans*, Brussels, 1944, pp. 103-104; Groupe d'études de la comptabilité nationale, *Premiers éléments d'une comptabilité nationale de la Belgique, 1948-1951*, Brussels 1954, p. 159; KAHN B., *Depreciatie*, NIS, Brussels 1961, pp. 3 and 4.

[6] During the inter-war period companies were required by law to draw up their balance sheet and profit and loss account "*dans lesquelles les amortissements nécessaires doivent être faits*" (see art. 75 of the "code de commerce", WAUWERMANS P., *Manuel Pratique des Sociétés Anonymes*, Brussels, 1924, p. XXXIV.). In practice companies were left totally free under law to calculate depreciation.

[7] During the inter-war period the fiscally permitted level of depreciation failed for a long time to take account of the rise in the replacement value of capital goods, while the fiscal legislation after the Second World War increasingly encouraged accelerated depreciation.

[8] Even where companies consistently applied the replacement value of the capital goods in question, that value could vary considerably. It should also be noted that some companies either failed explicitly to include depreciation in the profit and loss accounts or took no account whatever of depreciation. The latter applied to the majority of government agencies throughout the inter-war period.

[9] See for example WARD M., *The measurement of Capital*, Paris, OECD, 1976, pp. 56-59.

estimate can be made of the gross stock of capital goods at constant prices, which can in turn be used to calculate depreciation, given the average expected life of the capital goods. The initial estimate of the gross stock of capital goods does, however, depends on the availability of figures on annual gross investment in the past[10].

SECTION 2. THE POST-WAR ESTIMATES BY DULBEA AND NIS

Although both the DULBEA group and the NIS recognized the aforementioned objections towards using balance sheet depreciation figures, they nevertheless used the depreciation recorded in the fiscal balance sheets of limited liability companies in estimating national income in the post-war period[11]. The DULBEA group arrived at the conclusion that the size of depreciation calculated on the basis of the fiscal balance sheets for 1953 corresponded closely with the figures in the input-output table drawn up for that year, but that the annual fluctuations in depreciation in the fiscal balance sheets were implausible[12]. The annual course of depreciation was therefore calculated by working on the basis of the average annual growth in depreciation over the period 1948-1955.

It was next assumed that the method for calculating depreciation by companies was based on the historical cost of capital goods. For the purposes of correctly converting the depreciation at historical cost into replacement values at constant prices, information was required on the years of construction of the capital goods to which the depreciation related. In other words, figures were required on the gross investments out of which the stock of capital goods had been built up[13]. Since no data were available on investment prior to 1948 and DULBEA also lacked any direct information on the age-structure of the stock of capital goods, it was assumed for the sake of simplicity that in 1947 the companies had revalued all the capital goods pre-dating 1939 still in their possession at 1947 replacement values, under the Act of 20 August 1947, while the investments in 1940-1947 were left out of account[14]. The DULBEA subsequently reached the

---

10   This is because the gross stock of capital goods at a particular point in time consists of capital goods procured in the preceding years. On the basis of an average life of capital goods of say 40 years, this means that the oldest capital goods in the capital stock will be 40 years old. In order to reconstruct the stock of capital goods, one therefore needs to have at one's disposal a series of gross investments going back 40 years.
11   See KAHN B., *o.c.*; *De Nationale Rekeningen van België 1953-1962*, pp. 1158-1159.
12   KAHN B., *o.c.*, pp. 4-5; the fact that the annual fluctuations in depreciation in the fiscal balance sheets were not plausible, is related to the aforementioned objection of the cyclical sensitivity of the depreciation recorded in corporate balance sheets.
13   On the basis of the aforementioned PIM, estimates could then be made of the stock of capital goods and the depreciation at constant prices.
14   See KAHN B., *o.c.*, pp. 3-4; in this way the need to estimate the losses of capital goods due to the Second World War was also avoided.

237

conclusion that 16% of the total depreciation related to buildings and 84% to plant and equipment[15]. The conversion into replacement values at constant prices was effected with the aid of price-index figures for the construction industry and for plant and equipment.

In estimating depreciation for the period 1953-1962, the NIS worked along almost the same lines as DULBEA, except that fiscal depreciation figures were available for a large proportion of the companies from the annual production statistics[16]. On the basis of the revaluations already employed by DULBEA in 1947, the NIS continued the calculations with the PIM, in which respect it was assumed that the average life expectancy was 30 years for buildings and 10 years for plant and equipment. The ratio between the depreciation of buildings and that of plant and equipment was deemed to be equal to the ratio of the investment in buildings on the one hand and that in plant and equipment on the other. In the case of industries for which the NIS did not have annual production statistics, it calculated the depreciation on the basis of the comparative ratio between added value and depreciation in comparable industries for which annual production statistics were available. Finally, the NIS calculated depreciation for a number of industries, such as agriculture and posts, telegraph and telephone, on the basis of figures directly supplied by these industries, while the depreciation for dwellings was estimated as part of the rental calculations[17].

SECTION 3. ESTIMATE OF DEPRECIATION DURING THE INTER-WAR PERIOD

The drawbacks towards using the depreciation stated in corporate balance sheets were examined in the first section of this chapter. It was noted in Section 2, however, that DULBEA nevertheless observed that the total volume of depreciation as calculated on the basis of balance sheet depreciation figures corresponded well with the results obtained with their input-output table.

Both DULBEA and NIS had corporate fiscal balance sheet data at their disposal for the post-war period. For the inter-war period, by contrast, only the balance sheets published by limited liability companies are available[18]. Since the published balance sheets were presented at the annual meeting of shareholders and were drawn up with actual or prospective shareholders in mind, the published distribution of the profit over depreciation and other components could sometimes

---

[15] *Idem*, p. 5.
[16] *De Nationale Rekeningen van België 1953-1962*, p. 1158. The NIS estimated depreciation as part of its estimate of national product by means of the production method.
[17] *Idem*, p. 1159.
[18] During the inter-war period limited liability companies were required by law to publish their balance sheets and profit and loss accounts. The published balance sheet were, however, a highly abridged version of the balance sheets submitted for tax purposes. See VAN MEERTEN M., *o.c.*, chapter 1, for a more detailed account of the legislation relating to balance sheets during the inter-war period.

differ from that shown in the fiscal balance sheets. Furthermore, no explicit reference was made to depreciation in many of the balance sheets published in the inter-war period. As a result the balance sheet depreciation figures of the inter-war period are much less suited to estimating the size of total investment than those in the post-war period[19].

With respect to the post-war period, DULBEA noted that the balance sheet depreciation figures were not suitable for estimating the annual level of depreciation, while the comparatively marked cyclical fluctuations during the inter-war period make it even more unlikely that the balance sheet data can be used to provide a plausible estimate of the annual level of depreciation[20]. On the basis of these considerations the balance sheet depreciation figures were not considered suitable as a basis for calculating depreciation during the inter-war period.

In the absence of available (investment) data for Belgium in the pre-inter-war period, a direct reconstruction of depreciation according to the aforementioned PIM, on the basis of investment series in the pre-inter-war period, could not be carried out[21]. The initial estimate of depreciation and the associated capital stock in the inter-war period needed therefore to be conducted along different lines, as discussed below. In line with the working method employed for the reconstruction of gross investment, three categories of capital goods were distinguished: dwellings, other buildings and plant and equipment[22]. With respect to the latter two categories of capital goods, namely other buildings and plant and equipment, a further distinction was drawn between the private sector and the government. One exception in this respect was formed by the agriculture, forestry and fisheries sector, the depreciation for which had already been calculated as part of the reconstruction of gross investment in this sector during the inter-war period, which figures could therefore be taken over as they stood[23].

Paragraph 1. Depreciation of dwellings

On the basis of the number of dwellings during the inter-war period as calculated by Buyst and the average cost price per dwelling during the base period 1936-

---

[19] In addition, the lack of input-output tables for the inter-war period means that no check is possible on the depreciation figures in the same way as that done in the post-war period.
[20] The estimate of the annual level of depreciation during the inter-war period would moreover have been seriously complicated by the revaluation of the fixed assets noted in the balance sheets as permitted by the Minister of Finance in 1927, particularly since far from all companies incorporated this permitted revaluation in their balance sheets.
[21] For an initial estimate of the capital goods stock in for example 1919, one needs an investment series going back at least as far as the expected economic life of the pre-1919 capital goods.
[22] See VAN MEERTEN M., *o.c.*, chapter 2.
[23] *Idem,* Chapter 4.

1938, a direct calculation could be made of the capital stock of dwellings[24]. It was assumed that the average expected economic life of residential dwellings was 150 years and that dwellings were depreciated on the straight-line method (Table 103a). The annual depreciations in 1936-1938 prices[25] were subsequently converted into current prices with the aid of the price index for housing costs[26].

Paragraph 2. Depreciation of other buildings in the private sector[27]

In the absence of direct estimates of the capital stock of other buildings during the inter-war period, it was decided to conduct a reconstruction based on estimates of the level of depreciation in Belgium in the post-Second World War period.

The initial data on post-war depreciation were found for 1948 in the reconstruction of the national accounts made by the *Groupe d'Études de la Comptabilité nationale of the Université Libre de Bruxelles*[28]. From 1950 onwards estimates of the post-war capital stock were published by the Planning Office[29]. On the basis of these data an initial estimate was made of the capital stock of other buildings in 1938 by the following method.

In the first place it was assumed that the Belgian capital stock had recovered in 1947 from the extremely low level of investment and the capital destruction during the Second World War and had returned to the 1938 level - or in other words that the depreciation in 1948 would not differ significantly from that in 1939[30].

---

[24] These figures have been taken from BUYST E., *An Economic History of Residential Building in Belgium between 1890 and 1961*, Table II,9 and Annex Table 1.
[25] Calculated at 1/150th of the housing stock in the preceding year.
[26] For more information, see BUYST E., *Inkomen...*, Table 4.
[27] With the exception of agriculture, forestry and fisheries. Other buildings in this sector are included in the total depreciation at current prices and at 1936-1938 prices in Table 106.
[28] Groupe d'études de la Comptabilité nationale, *Économie belge et Comptabilité nationale, 1948-1954*, Brussels, 1955, pp. 78 and 161. The Committee's original estimates differ in various respects from the drafts of the National Accounts, see *Idem*, pp. 66-70. With the aid of the figures in Appendix 4 of the aforementioned publication of the Committee from 1955, pp. 155-166, it was possible to correct the estimates and bring them into line with the draft National Accounts.
[29] DE BIOLLEY T. ; GILOT, A., *The capital stock of the Belgian economy: evaluation and analysis*, Brussels 1987.
[30] The depreciation in year "t" are related to the capital stock at the end of year "t-1". The assumption that the depreciation related to the capital stock in 1938 would not differ significantly from that related to the capital stock in 1947 is not self-evident. According to Carbonelle the total production of the Belgian industry and transport sector in 1948 was slightly higher than that in 1937 (see CARBONELLE C., *Recherches sur l'Évolution de la Production en Belgique de 1900 à 1957*, in: "Cahiers économiques de Bruxelles", vol.3, 1959, p. 358). As the Marshall Plan got under way, total output grew strongly in 1949 and 1950. On the basis of the scale of production in 1948 and the growth figures in 1949 and 1950 it appears likely that production in 1947 was lower than in the Second World War. This would mean that the scale of depreciation in 1939 would be underestimated

The depreciation figures published by the *Groupe d'études de la comptabilité nationale* have been separated into the private sector and the public sector. The breakdown into the various categories of capital goods was calculated as follows. In the case of the private sector it was assumed that the ratio between the depreciation of other buildings on the one hand and that of plant and equipment on the other would be the same as the ratio between the investments in both categories of capital goods[31]. The depreciation obtained for 1948 was then converted into 1936-1938 prices on the basis of the building costs indexed for other buildings[32]. It was next assumed that the average life expectancy of other buildings during the inter-war period was 40 years[33]. Since, as noted in the previous section, an average life expectancy for other buildings of 30 years was applied in the post-war period, the depreciation in 1939 was equated to three-quarters of the depreciation calculated for 1948 in 1936-1938 prices. The value of the capital stock of other buildings in 1938 at 1936-1938 prices was then obtained by multiplying the depreciation for 1939 by 30[34].

In order to calculate the capital stock of "other buildings" at 1936-1938 prices for the years 1919-1937 and for 1939, two data series were required: the annual gross investment and the annual retirement of written off capital goods[35]. The figures in relation to the annual gross investments per capital good had become available[36], but a further assumption needed to be made for the annual retirement of capital goods. It was assumed that the retirement of other buildings amounted to 90% of the average gross investment in 1925-1935[37]. The capital stock in 1936-1938 prices could now be calculated for the period 1919-1937 by reducing the

---

if it were equated with that in 1948. On the other hand the depreciation for 1939 has been somewhat overestimated under the method suggested here since the DULBEA group's estimates for the post-war depreciation also include depreciation for the agricultural sector, whereas these were counted separately for the inter-war period.

31   This assumption is also employed by the NIS. Cf. below.
32   See VAN MEERTEN M., *o.c.*, Chapter 2.
33   Standardized life expectancy derived from MADDISON A., *Dynamic Forces in Capitalist Development, A Long-Run comparative View*, Oxford 1991, pp. 143 and 281. The standardized life expectancy for "other buildings" of 40 years used by Maddison may be on the high side. Hanon de Louvet cites a survey into the life of capital goods carried out by a group of engineers in Breslau (year not specified), in which the longest average life expectancy of industrial buildings used came to 36.1 years; another survey to which he refers carried out by the Comité Central Industriel de Belgique in 1924 even arrived at an average life expectancy of just 20 years; see HANON DE LOUVET C., *o.c.*, pp. 107-110. With respect to these surveys it is, however, questionable to what extent the life expectancies in question related to real life expectancies or to (shorter) fiscal and accounting life expectancies. The effect of a shorter life expectancy on depreciation is analysed later in this chapter.
34   Since the depreciation in year "t" is related to the capital stock in year "t-1".
35   Under the assumption that only completely written off capital goods were retired from the capital stock, in other words that the retirements followed a rectangular pattern.
36   See VAN MEERTEN M., *o.c.*, passim.
37   Ten percent of the gross investment was regarded as lost due to the First World War.

capital stock of 1938 each year by the gross investment and increasing it by the retirement, while for 1939 the capital stock of 1938 was augmented by the gross investment and reduced by the retirement[38]. The annual depreciation in 1936-1938 prices was then calculated by dividing the capital stock at the end of the preceding year by the average life expectancy of other buildings of 40 years. The series obtained in 1936-1938 prices was finally converted into current prices with the aid of the index for the building costs of other buildings available for the inter-war period (Table 103b).

Paragraph 3. Depreciation of plant and equipment in the private sector[39]

The reconstruction of the depreciation on plant and equipment in the private sector was, with the exception of a few minor variations, conducted along the same lines as that described above for other buildings[40]. In the first place the average life expectancy for plant and equipment during the inter-war period was estimated at 15 years[41]. The depreciation for 1948 converted into 1936-1938 prices with the aid of the price index for plant and equipment was therefore multiplied by two-thirds in order to obtain depreciation for 1939[42]. In contrast to the "other buildings" a number of data on the retirement of plant and equipment in the

---

[38] According to the Perpetual Inventory Model:
$GK_t = GK_{t-1} + GI_t - R_t$
in which:
GK_t is equal to the gross capital stock at the end of year "t";
GK_{t-1} is equal to the gross capital stock at the end of year "t-1";
GI_t is equal to the gross investment in year "t";
R_t is equal to the retirement in year "t".

[39] With the exception of the agriculture, forestry and fisheries sector. The depreciation on plant and equipment in this sector is included in the total depreciation at current prices and in 1936-1938 prices in Table 104.

[40] As in the case of the depreciation of other buildings, the assumption that depreciation in 1939 did not differ significantly from that in 1948 very probably entailed an underestimation of the actual depreciation in 1939. On the other hand the depreciation in 1939 was overestimated since the estimates for 1948 also included the depreciation in the agricultural sector, whereas this was counted separately in the inter-war period.

[41] Standardised life expectancy based on MADDISON A., *o.c.*, pp. 143 and 281. The Breslau engineers quoted by Hanon de Louvet also arrived at a somewhat lower average life expectancy for plant and equipment: 12.5 years for the metal industry, an average of 13.6 years for 33 types of equipment in light manufacturing and an average of 14.2 years for 6 categories of machinery in daytime production. In its survey of 1924 the Comité central Industriel de Belgique arrived at an average life expectancy of between 7 and 10 years; see HANON DE LOUVET C., *o.c.*, pp. 107-110. The effect of a shorter life expectancy on depreciation is examined later in this chapter.

[42] This multiplication by two-thirds arises from the fact that a depreciation period of 15 years was assumed for the inter-war period, whereas the post-war figures were based on a shorter depreciation period of 10 years.

private sector were available, in that the decommissioned plant and equipment in 1937 related to the fully written off gross investments in plant and equipment in 1922. It was assumed that the remaining pre-1914 gross investment in the interwar period amounted to 80% of the average gross investment in plant and equipment during the period 1925-1935[43]. On the basis of these assumptions the depreciation of plant and equipment could be calculated in both 1936-1938 and current prices.

Paragraph 4. Depreciation in the public sector

In the case of public sector an initial estimate of the stock of "other buildings" was derived from the values provided by the Inventory of State property on 31 December 1935[44]. The value of State property covered by this heading amounted to BF 6.92 billion[45]. The calculation of depreciation was conducted along the same lines as described above for other buildings of the private sector. In the first place the 1935 stock value was converted into 1936-38 prices by means of the index of building costs of other buildings. In contrast to other buildings of the private sector the life expectancy of public buildings was put at 66.7 years[46]. On the basis of this assumption, the gross investment data for the years 1920-1939[47], and a retirement of other buildings amounting to 90% of the average gross investment in 1925-1935, depreciation of public buildings could be calculated in both 1936-38 and current prices.

An initial value for 1935 of the stock of public equipment was obtained by assuming a ratio of public buildings to equipment of 10 to 1[48]. Depreciation could be calculated along the same lines as for plant and equipment of the private sector, by assuming an average life expectancy of 15 years[49].

---

[43] It was assumed that 20% of the plant and equipment was lost during the First World War.
[44] See NBB, *Belgische Economische Statistieken, 1929-1940*, pp. 437-441.
[45] No account has been taken of the buildings made available for the army or of historic buildings, monuments and museums, nor of land, roads, infrastructure, etc.
[46] This corresponds to the depreciation rate of 1.5 per cent applied to the post-war period by the NIS: NIS, *Commissie van het Nationaal Inkomen*, pp. 285-286.
[47] These data were calculated from CLEMENT, P., *The Growth to a Welfare State, a History of Public Finance in Belgium 1830-1940* (Studies in Economic History, vol. 5, Brussels, 2000).
[48] This corresponds to the outcomes for 1953 compiled by the Planning Office, taking into account the inclusion by the Public Office of roads and the like, see DE BIOLLEY T.; GILOT A., *o.c.*, Appendix 3.1 - 3.10.
[49] The data on gross investment were calculated from CLEMENT, P., *Op. cit.*.

Paragraph 5. Total depreciation

The results of the reconstruction of depreciation as discussed in the preceding sections are shown in Tables 103a, 103b and 104.

The reconstruction of depreciation during the inter-war period rests on a large number of assumptions. The most important of these were formed by the assumed average life expectancy of the two categories of capital goods, "other buildings" and plant and equipment, of 40 and 15 years respectively[50]. It was noted above that the life expectancies cited by Hanon de Louvet for the inter-war period were lower than those used in this reconstruction. The NIS also employed lower average life expectancies of 30 and 10 years respectively for the post-war period. A shorter life expectancy for the capital goods means that the latter must be written off over a shorter period, meaning that the depreciation is higher. Recalculation of the depreciation on the basis of life expectancies of 30 years for "other buildings" and 10 years for plant and equipment does indeed generate depreciation averaging 24.6% more than shown in Tables 105 and 106[51].

---

[50] 66.7 years for public buildings.
[51] Expressed as a percentage of national income under the expenditure approach the difference amounts to 2.2%.

CHAPTER 17

INDIRECT TAXES AND SUBSIDIES

In order to move from Gross National Product at factor cost (GNP_f) to Gross National Product at market prices (GNP_m) (cf. below, General Conclusion), indirect taxes need to be added to BNP_f and subsidies deducted. Indirect taxes are discussed in Section 1 and subsidies in Section two. Each section commences with a definition of the heading, after which the figures are presented.

SECTION 1. INDIRECT TAXES

Paragraph 1. Definitions

1. General distinction between direct and indirect taxes

The distinction between direct and indirect taxes broadly amounts to the fact that direct taxes relate to income or property whereas indirect taxes relate to the commercial traffic in goods and services. Indirect taxes are levied in relation to a particular activity (e.g. transactions, consumption or transfer)[1].

2. Indirect taxes according to the standardized system of the OECD

Under the standardized system of the OECD, indirect taxes are defined as taxes assessed on goods and services and chargeable as a business cost. Also treated as indirect taxes are the taxes levied on the ownership of use of certain durable consumer goods such as motor vehicles[2]. The text of the standardized system continues with a summary of the main categories of indirect taxes: customs and excise duties sales taxes, motor and other licence duties[3], entertainment duties and betting taxes[4], etc.

---

[1] MOESEN W., VAN ROMPUY V., *Inleiding tot de openbare financiën*, Louvain; Amersfoort, 1985[3], pp. 115-117.
[2] OECD, *A standardized system of national accounts,* pp. 80-81.
[3] In the accounts of the Belgian State (Accounts of the Audit Office) road tax comes under direct taxes. In accordance with the recommendations of the OECD, however, they are treated in this study as a direct tax.
[4] The taxes on the organization of lotteries and betting are treated by the OECD as indirect taxes.

Where there is a state monopoly over the production distribution of certain consumer goods, such as tobacco or alcohol, the monopoly profits are treated as an indirect tax[5]. Since no such monopolies existed in Belgium during the inter-war period, this provision does not apply.

Finally the standardized system notes that real estate taxes are included among indirect taxes except "in those cases where the existence of such taxes may be considered as merely a particular administrative procedure for the assessment and collection of income taxes, as will often be the case with taxes levied on the value of farm and buildings"[6].

3. Indirect taxes in the national accounts of the NIS

The NIS has largely adopted the OECD's definition, except that real estate taxes are regarded as a direct tax[7]. On the other hand the NIS classifies certain retributions paid to the state (for example retributions relating to the inspection of weights and measures, pilotage and towage charges) or paid to certain semi-government agencies (for example the payments collected by the National Agency for the Sale of Agricultural and Horticultural Products) as indirect taxes[8].

Whether these retributions should be regarded as indirect tax is a matter of some debate, as they relate to the provision of a service by the government and the payment for that service cannot be regarded as a tax in so far as the amount of the retribution does not exceed the cost price of the service in question. In many cases, however, the charge made exceeds the cost price, in which case the difference between the two sums amounts to an indirect tax. Since it is impossible to distinguish the cost price from the fiscal element in the retributions, retributions of a predominantly fiscal nature are treated in their entirety as indirect tax while those with little if any fiscal element are treated in their entirety as a remuneration for the service in question.

Paragraph 2. Indirect taxes during the inter-war period

For the sake of continuity with the post-war figures, an attempt has been made to include the same or at least comparable taxes during the inter-war period as the

---

The taxes paid by the participants in lotteries and gambling on the profits from such activities are classed under income or direct taxes (OECD, *o.c.*, p. 81).

5   *Idem*, pp. 79-80.
6   *Idem*, p. 81.
7   *De nationale rekeningen van België 1953-1962*, p. 1159; *Het Belgisch nationaal inkomen van 1948 tot 1954*, p. 611.
8   *De nationale rekeningen van België 1953-1962*, p. 1159. C. Modart, an official at the NIS, provided a list of retributions that are classified as indirect taxes.

NIS. For the period 1923-1939 the tax receipts are shown in detail in the final accounts of the Belgian State as published in the *Accounts of the Audit Office* (Rekenhof)[9]. For the period 1920-1922 the final results show overall receipt categories only. The amount of the most important indirect taxes was, however, published in a series of articles by Vandendriessche[10]. In the case of the more minor taxes an estimate was made on the basis of the known sum in 1923 and the overall tax receipts in 1920-1923.

Table 105 provides a survey of the various indirect taxes. The most important of these are customs duties and statistical duties[11] (averaging 25.1% of the total indirect taxes), excise and other special consumption taxes (20.7%)[12], registration and transfer[13] (13.2%), stamp duty and equivalent taxes[14] (35.0%).

With the establishment of the Belgo-Luxembourg Economic Union (BLEU) on 23 March 1921, the customs borders between the two countries were abolished and import duties on products from third countries were levied jointly. After deduction of the collection costs, the proceeds from these duties were divided between Belgium and Luxembourg on the basis of the respective populations in these countries[15]. The final accounts of the Belgian State shows a heading for certain years entitled "Balance on the joint receipts with the Grand Duchy of Luxembourg", arising from this agreement (see Table 105 column 10).

The proceeds from indirect taxes are determined not just by the evolution of the general price level and the state of the economy, but are also heavily affected

---

[9] For a discussion of the final accounts, see Chapter 5, "Pay and pensions of government personnel". The tax receipts are entered under the government funds account. The non-collectible taxes and the repayment of incorrectly collected taxes (= negative item, see Table 105 column 11) are reflected in "Stray items and repayments".

[10] VANDENDRIESSCHE S., *Evolutie van de Belgische centrale-overheidsuitgaven sinds 1919. Onderzoek naar de determinerende factoren*, pp. 145-233.

[11] The statistical duties were introduced under the Act of 31 December 1925, with a view to covering the costs associated with mechanizing the computations of the trade statistics. The amount in question was however small (CRISPIELS J., *Les droits de douane et d'accise de 1914 à 1940*, dans : "Histoire des finances publiques en Belgique", Brussels; Paris, Institut Belge de Finances Publiques (ed.), vol. I, 1950, p. 613).

[12] The most important excise and other special consumption taxes during the inter-war period were those on beer (26.6% of the total receipts in 1930), wine (26.5%), tobacco (19.1%), alcohol (12.1%), brandy (5.2%) and sugar and sugar syrup (4.1%) (Statistical Yearbook, vol. 55, 1933, p. 131).

[13] Registration rights were levied on official deeds drawn up by notaries, bailiffs, and courts, etc. (GENIN E., *Les impôts sur la circulation juridique des biens en Belgique après 1914*, dans: "Histoire des finances publiques en Belgique", p. 549. A familiar example consists of the registration fees associated with the purchase of real estate.

[14] Stamp duty and equivalent taxes were levied on a wide range of products, services and transactions. Most of these were transfer taxes (for a survey of the content, legislation and method of collection of these taxes, see GENIN E., *o.c.*, pp. 581-192. On 1 January 1971 the majority of the stamp duties and equivalent taxes were abolished and replaced by value added tax.

[15] J. CRISPIELS, *o.c.*, pp. 606-607.

by the relevant legislation. The latter applies especially to the proceeds from stamp duty and equivalent taxes - the main transfer taxes during the inter-war period[16]. As a result of the Act of 28 August 1921, 10 August 1923 and 2 January 1926 and the Royal Decrees of 2 and 3 March 1927, the taxable base was extended, certain rates were increased and the inspection possibilities tightened up. The consequences of these measures is clearly reflected in the figures in column 4. In 1930 a number of stamp duties were abolished and certain rates reduced, resulting in a 36% reduction in the revenues[17]. In the course of the 1930s, the tax rates were regularly increased on account of the government's rising financing requirements in the Depression, which again is clearly discernible in the receipts.

SECTION 2. SUBSIDIES

Paragraph 1. Definition

Subsidies are defined in the standardized system of the OECD and in the methodology of the NIS as grants given by public authorities to producers, with the exception of capital transfers. Subsidies tend to offset costs to the producers and may be regarded as negative indirect taxes[18].

As noted earlier, the problem arises with respect to loss-making public corporations as to whether the sums assigned by the government to these corporations should be regarded as negative entrepreneurial income or as a subsidy[19]. For the sake of consistency with what was determined in the chapter on the government's entrepreneurial income, these sums have not been shown as a subsidy.

Paragraph 2. Subsidies during the inter-war period

In the final accounts of the Belgian State, subsidies are entered under the expenditure budgets of the various ministerial departments (e.g. agricultural subsidies under the budget of the Ministry of Agriculture). The various subsidies are broken down into the leading sectors in Table 106. For the period 1920-1922, the accounts were not drawn up in sufficient detail to enable the subsidies to be distilled, for which reason the 1923 sum has been taken for these years.

---

[16] GENIN E., *o.c.*, pp. 587-591.
[17] Since the Great Depression did not hit Belgium until the end of 1930, the fall in the proceeds from stamp duties and equivalent taxes is attributable to only a minor extent to the slowdown in economic activity.
[18] OECD, *o.c.*, p. 81; *De nationale rekeningen van België 1953-1962*, p. 1160.
[19] See Chapter 14.

GENERAL CONCLUSION

BELGIAN NATIONAL INCOME, 1920-1939

INTRODUCTION

The aim of this study was to reconstruct Belgian National Income for the period 1920-1939. This has been done in Chapters 1-17, in which an estimate of the annual income between 1920 and 1939 has been presented for each income category on the basis of the NIS-methodology (ESER79).

The component results are brought together in this concluding chapter resulting in a detailed databank on the development of National Income between 1920 and 1939 (Section 1). Next an attempt is made to give a first interpretative view on the databank: in Section 2 the *nominal growth* in National Income in the inter-war period is examined while Section 3 concentrates on the structural shifts in the income-series during the period 1920-1939. For a thorough analysis of Belgian National Income during the inter-war period however we refer the reader to a more detailed study by the members of the Leuven Workshop on Quantitative Economic History[1].

SECTION 1. BELGIAN NATIONAL INCOME, 1920-1939, THE DATABANK

The results of the reconstruction work presented in Chapters 1-17 are brought together in Table 107 in 20 main headings. For a more detailed table reference is made to Appendix 1.

Table 107 contains three component results[2]: Net National Income (NNI) or Net National Product at factor cost (NNPf), Gross National Income (GNI) or Gross National Product at factor cost (GNPf) and finally Gross National Product at market prices (GNPm). Net National Income or Net National Product at factor cost consists of the sum of the factor reimbursements as calculated in Chapters 1-17. In Gross National Income or Gross National Product at factor cost allowance is made for depreciation. If, finally, indirect taxes and subsidies[3] are taken into account - indirect taxes are not paid out to the factors of production but do have a bearing on the market prices of the goods produced - the result is Gross National

---

[1] See the introduction of this study.
[2] Based on the technical variants of the concept of GNP. VAN ROMPUY P., et al., *Inleiding tot de economie*, p. 283 ff.
[3] Subsidies are regarded under the system of National Accounts as negative taxes.

Product at market prices, which can also be calculated by means of the production and expenditure approaches (cf. Introduction).

In the economic analysis, the term National Income refers to both Net National Product at factor cost and Gross National Product at market prices (cf. Introduction). If the concern is with the income distribution of the population, use of the concept Net National Income is indicated; if on the other hand the interest is primarily in measuring the performance of the overall economy, the term Gross National Product at market prices is used. Since National Income has essentially been calculated in this study as an approximation of GNP, the term NI refers exclusively to this variable in the remainder of this chapter.

Graph 1 illustrates the course of National Income between 1920 and 1939 in nominal terms. Since the inter-war period was characterised by marked price fluctuations, GNP in nominal terms is not a particularly usable parameter for the real evolution of the Belgian economy during this turbulent period. As noted in the introduction of this study, E. Buyst calculated a *BNP-deflator* that allows the nominal series to be transposed in real terms[4].

GRAPH 1

Belgian GNP, 1920-1939 (nominal terms, in 1000 BF)

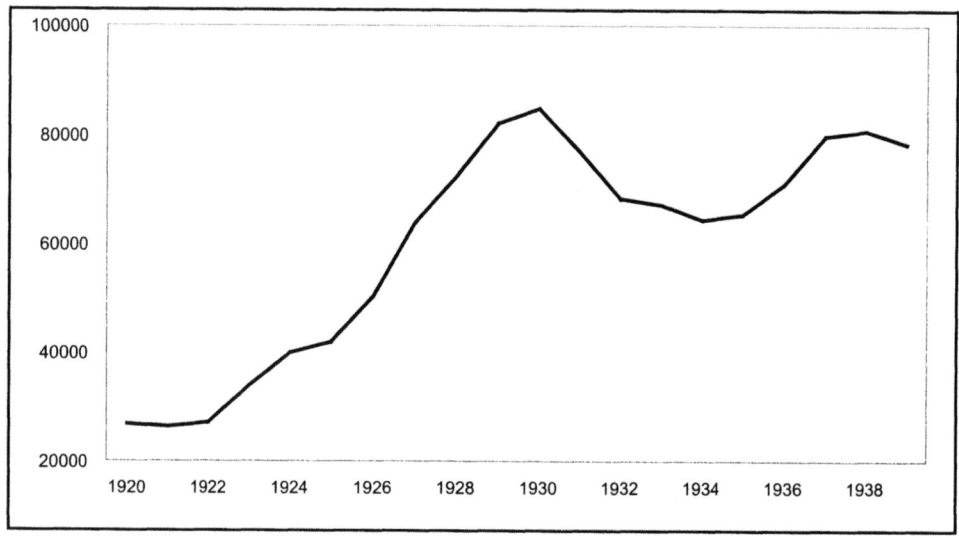

Source: Table 107

---

[4] BUYST, E., *New GNP Estimates*, p. 372.

SECTION 2. THE STRUCTURE OF BELGIAN GROSS NATIONAL PRODUCT, 1920-1939

The share of the various income categories in GNP is shown in Table 108. First, the share of "Income from employment" - in other words the sum of the first ten headings of Table 108 - is examined. This share averaged 68% of GNP during the period 1920-1939. Within this category the earnings of private sector employees - categories 1-4 in Table 108, cf. Graph 2 - were easily the most important, averaging 28% of GNP during the inter-war period. Nevertheless the share of these categories fluctuated significantly between 1920 and 1939, touching 31% in 1921 and a low of 26% in 1926. In the late 1920s the share increased again to loose ground in the 1930s. In view of the fact that the depression bore most heavily on these income groups - the number of unemployed rose by 95,000 units between 1920 and 1931 and a further 92,000 between 1931 and 1933, causing the rate of unemployment to rise from 4% in 1930 to 12% in 1931 and 20% in 1932[5] - this trend should come as no surprise.

GRAPH 2

Share of total income from employment in GNP, 1920-1939

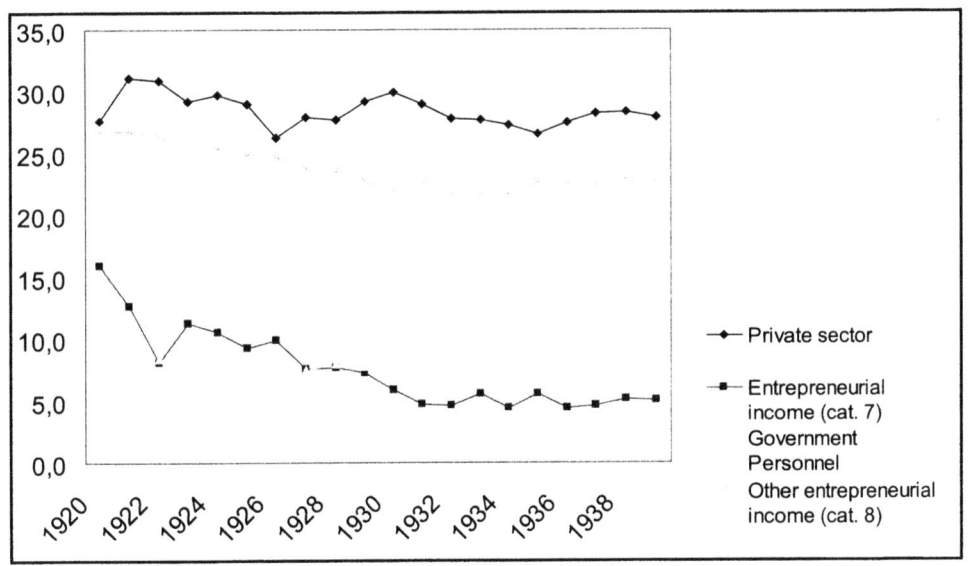

Source: Own calculations on basis of Table 108.

---

[5] GOOSSENS M., *De Belgische arbeidsmarkt tijdens het Interbellum*, in: "Tijdschrift voor Economie en Management", vol. 33, 1988, p. 110.

Within the group of earnings from employment, "Entrepreneurial income of independent traders (including partnerships) and the professions" averaged 21% and 1% (or 22% jointly) during the inter-war period. This share also fluctuated, but in contrast to the share of employees in the private sector, entrepreneurial income exhibited a more clearly downward path. Only in the late 1930s did the share move upwards again, undoubtedly reflecting the hopes of many unemployed persons that they might earn a little extra income as small independent businessmen and traders during the difficult depression years[6]. In contrast to entrepreneurial income, the share of the wages and salaries of government personnel in 1920-1939 exhibits an almost continuously upward trend. On average this share amounted to 8%, but between 1920 and 1939 it rose from 7% to 10% in 1939. The slight declines evident during this 20-year period coincide not by accident with boom periods in the economy, when conditions of employment in the private sector were unquestionably more attractive than those in the public sector. Conversely, the share of the income of government employees clearly rose at the times of recession in the early and late 1930s. This clearly reflects the advent of Keynesian-inspired government policies that were aimed at taking on more employees in recession years and which was not to reach its peak until the 1970s. Finally, independent income from agriculture represented an average of 7.50% of National Income during the inter-war period. The trend was, however, unmistakably downward: in 1921 the share was still as high as 16%, in 1926 it had already slipped to 10%, in 1930 it was down to 6% and on the eve of the Second World War it amounted to just 5%. The greatest decline therefore took place during the 1920s. This confirms the hypothesis formulated elsewhere, namely that the major shakeout of manpower in the agricultural sector took place during the boom years of the 1920s[7].

Within the group of "private sector employees", a significant structural shift took place between 1920 and 1939 (Graph 3): the share of the total wages and salaries of manual workers (averaging 20% between 1920 and 1939) in GNP fell slowly but surely in favour of white-collar workers (averaging 5%). This trend was to continue in full cry after the Second World War. The share of income of domestic staff and border and seasonal workers was minimal throughout the period (averaging 1.5% and 1% respectively), but clearly increased during the depression years. Here again it may be assumed that this form of employment offered an interim solution for the thousands of unemployed persons in the heavily affected industrial sectors. Finally, the expansion of social security during the inter-war period exerted a positive impact on the earnings of all categories of employees in the private sector: the share of employers' social security contributions rose from 0.5% of GNP in 1920 to 1.5% in 1939 (Graph 4).

---

[6] See in this connection also Chapter 8 of this study, which examines the rapid increase in the number of self-employed persons during the depression years.
[7] GOOSSENS M., *o.c.*, p. 115.

GRAPH 3

Share of income from employment of employees in the private sector in GNP, 1920-1939

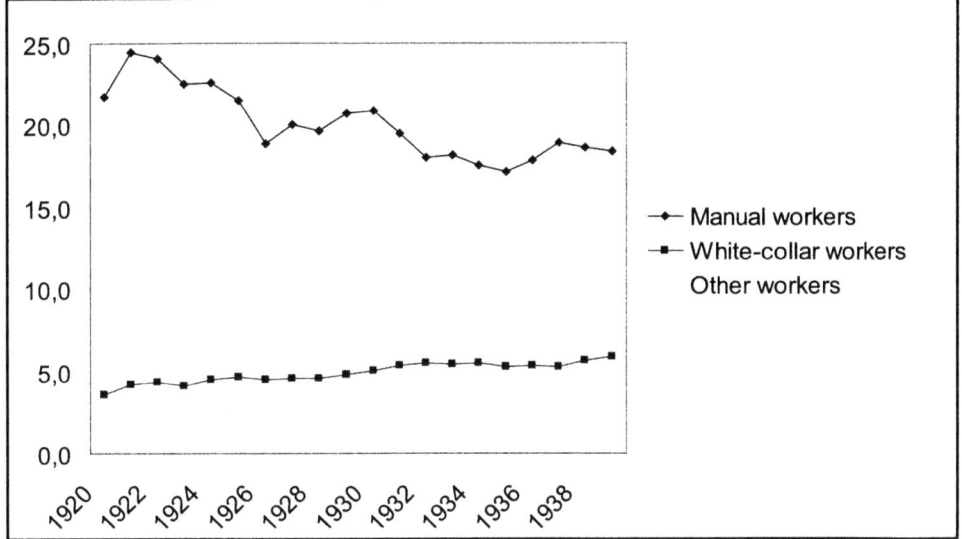

Source: Own calculations on basis of Table 108.

GRAPH 4

Share of employers' social security contributions in GNP, 1920-1939

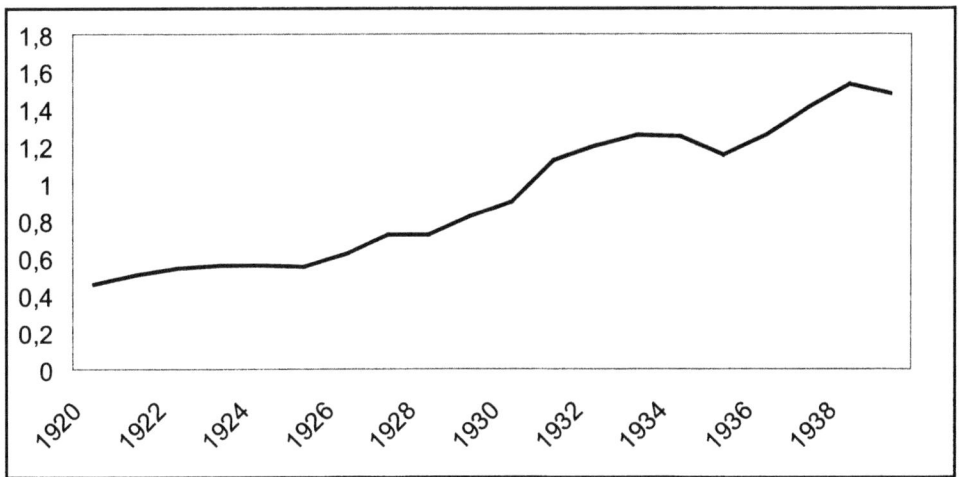

Source: Own calculations on basis of Table 108.

After income from employment, "Income from capital accruing to the personal sector" represented the largest share in GNP during the inter-war period: the share of income from rent, interest and dividends, bonuses and donations rose doubled from 12% in 1920 to 24% in 1934. Thereafter it declined somewhat (Graph 5).

GRAPH 5

Share of income from capital accruing to the personal sector in GNP, 1920-1939

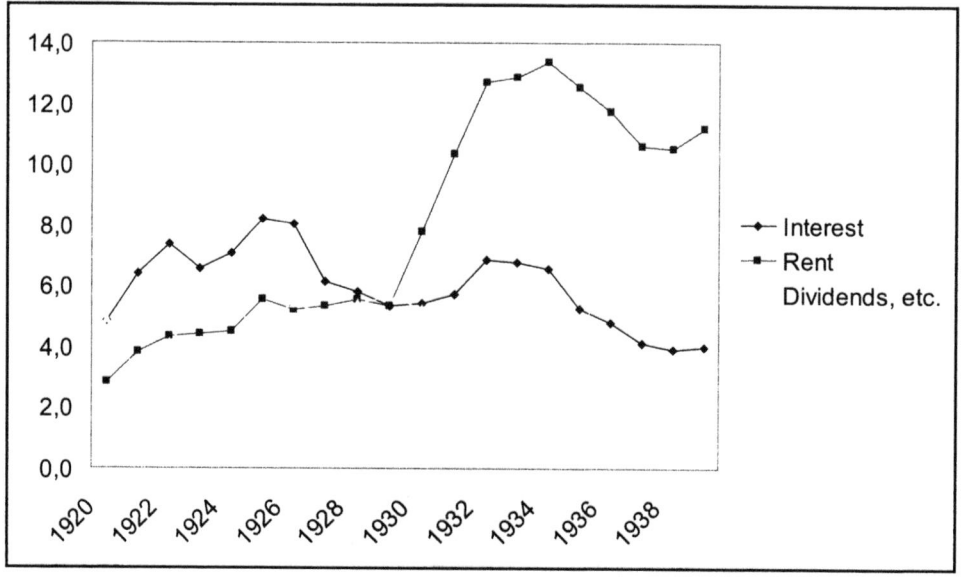

Source: Own calculations on basis of Table 108.

The rapidly increasing share of rent income stands out particularly: this rose from 3% in 1920 to 13% in 1934. Thereafter the share slipped back slightly, but in 1939 still amounted to 11% or four times the share in 1920. Not unexpectedly, the income from risk-free capital on the one hand - i.e. interest - and risk-bearing capital on the other - dividends and bonuses - evolved inversely: in boom periods the share of interest fell in favour of dividends and bonuses, while during the depression years the pattern was reversed.

The direct contribution of companies in the formation of National Income consists of the headings "Saving by corporations", "Direct taxation" and "Depreciation" which, during the inter-war period, amounted to 1.3%, 0.5% and 7.1% of National Income or 9% collectively (Graph 6). In particular, the fluctuations in the share of savings by corporations provide a good indicator of overall economic trends during the inter-war period.

GRAPH 6

Share of companies in the formation of GNP, 1920-1939

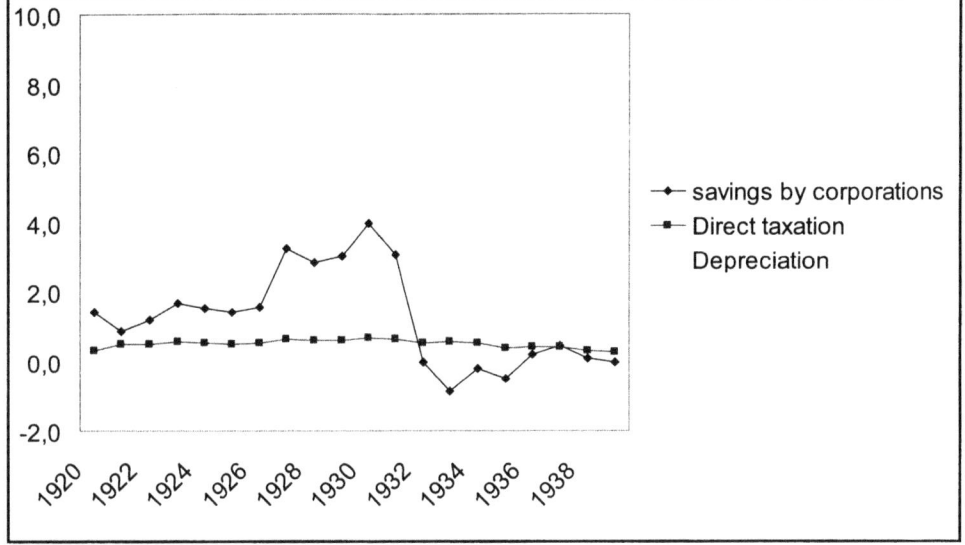

Source: Own calculations on basis of Table 108.

Finally, the share of government revenues consists of the headings "Indirect taxes" and "Property income", which respectively averaged 7.1% and 1.4% of GNP during the inter-war period, or 8,5% together. During this period the share of the public sector in National Income remained fairly limited, but after the Second World War the rapid increase in the public sector share in GNP was to evolve into one of the most characteristic features of the economic structure. Finally it should be noted that the "Interest on the government debt" fell rapidly in prosperous years during the 1920s, before increasing again during the depression years of 1930s (Graph 7).

GRAPH 7

Share of government revenues in GNP, 1920-1939

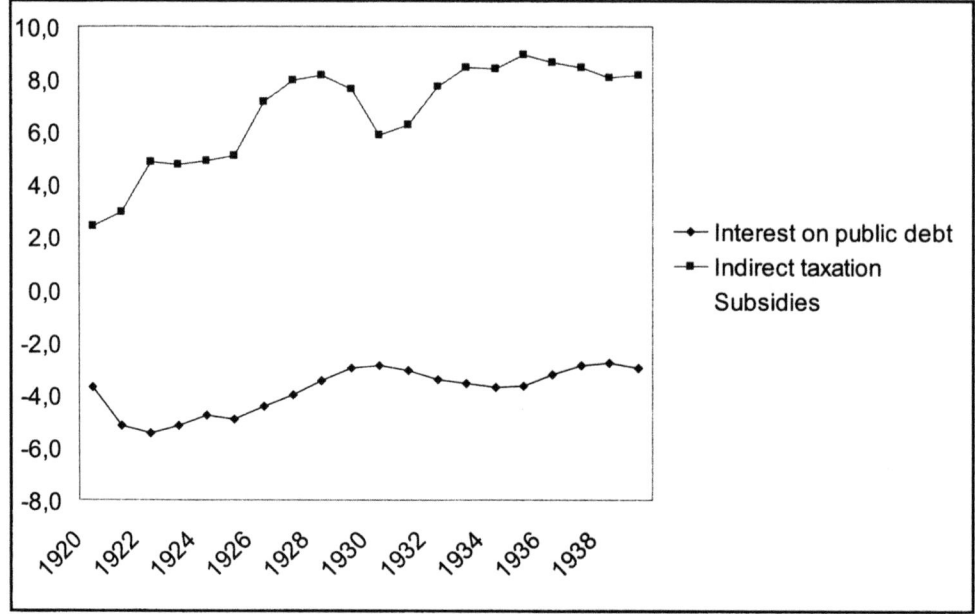

Source: Own calculations on basis of Table 108.

ANNEX 1

Belgian national income in nominal terms, 1920-1939 (in 1 000 000 BF)

	1920	1921	1922	1923	1924	1925	1926	1927	1928	1929	1930	1931	1932	1933	1934	1935	1936	1937	1938	1939
1. INCOME FROM PAID EMPLOYMENT																				
1.1. Wages and salaries of employees subject to the social security provisions																				
1.1.1. Manual workers (including seamen)	5808	6429	6507	7628	9003	9006	9457	12781	14224	17003	17697	14983	12311	12177	11291	11189	12643	15083	15064	14413
1.1.2. White-collar workers	952	1098	1167	1387	1796	1934	2274	2907	3295	3968	4307	4112	3779	3662	3538	3469	3802	4224	4577	4642
Total 1.1.	6760	7527	7674	9015	10799	10940	11731	15688	17519	20971	22004	19095	16090	15839	14829	14658	16445	19307	19641	19055
1.2. Wages and salaries of employees subject to certain social security provisions																				
1.2.1. Domestic staff and servants	369	375	376	474	526	619	674	848	936	1142	1320	1318	1255	1237	1202	1190	1184	1179	1203	1215
1.2.2. Border workers	85	76	98	155	204	219	301	608	831	923	986	729	626	625	597	615	747	724	630	388
1.2.3. Seasonal workers employed abroad	55	82	58	58	99	116	146	216	254	263	278	249	187	85	145	164	217	202	151	93
Total 1.2.	509	533	532	687	829	954	1121	1672	2021	2328	2584	2296	2068	1947	1944	1969	2148	2105	1984	1696
1.3. Employers social security contributions	122	134	147	188	223	230	312	460	521	673	763	857	820	843	805	749	892	1124	1234	1162
1.4. Others employees not subject to the general social security provisions																				
1.4.1. Central government: administrative apparatus (incl. ministers of religion): total wages, salaries and pensions	311	368	381	398	469	532	584	766	1010	1049	1178	1172	1078	1018	1013	999	1082	1279	1376	1351
1.4.2. Central government: state education: total wages, salaries and pensions	30	38	36	38	53	64	69	131	151	159	181	184	174	168	167	165	186	198	224	221
1.4.3. Central government: military apparatus: total wages, salaries and pensions	498	418	536	551	441	487	507	657	848	888	1027	1081	988	909	926	876	1011	1149	1287	1892
1.4.4. Provinces and municipalities:(incl. Public Welfare Committees (COO)): administrative apparatus	201	210	242	236	319	364	385	475	545	636	778	806	767	776	692	657	644	697	751	737
1.4.5. Municipal,provincial&independent education	218	258	254	257	358	407	452	615	878	880	997	995	933	918	907	854	957	1002	1103	1107
1.4.6. National Belgian Railway Company																				
1.4.6.1. Wages and salaries	511	621	608	682	956	1033	1231	1484	1592	1883	1909	1746	1537	1383	1328	1216	1306	1452	1482	1387
1.4.6.2. Pensions and social security charges	8	8	15	17	20	22	77	135	214	246	289	312	302	307	312	303	380	399	426	436
Total 1.4.6.	519	629	623	699	976	1055	1308	1619	1806	2129	2198	2058	1839	1690	1640	1519	1686	1851	1908	1823
1.4.7. Telegraph & Telephone Companyi(RTT), Post Office, Airways, Radio & Television Agency																				
1.4.7.1. Wages and salaries	128	162	161	166	204	242	277	363	458	484	579	597	564	513	488	474	503	530	605	598

1.4.7.2. Pensions and social security charges	8	10	10	10	12	14	20	32	42	49	60	61	63	61	57	55	59	61	67	76
Total 1.4.7.	136	172	171	176	216	256	297	395	500	533	639	658	627	574	545	529	562	591	672	674
1.4.8. Public corporations under local government control																				
1.4.8.1. Wages and salaries	25	26	30	33	41	45	49	63	69	83	97	101	96	99	112	109	91	90	98	100
1.4.8.2. Pensions and social security charges	6	6	8	8	10	11	12	16	17	21	24	25	24	25	28	27	23	23	25	25
Total 1.4.8.	31	32	38	41	51	56	61	79	86	104	121	126	120	124	140	136	114	113	123	125
Total 1.4.	1944	2125	2281	2396	2883	3221	3663	4737	5824	6378	7119	7080	6526	6177	6030	5735	6242	6880	7444	7930
TOTAL 1.	9335	10319	10634	12286	14734	15345	16827	22557	25885	30350	32470	29328	25504	24806	23608	23111	25727	29416	30303	29843
2. ENTERPRENEURIAL INCOME OF THE SELF-EMPLOYED AND PARTNERSHIPS																				
2.1. Agriculture, horticulture and forestry	4257	3329	2181	3812	4216	3862	4963	4865	5578	5960	4999	3667	3185	3737	2876	3689	3111	3674	4137	4004
2.2. Professions	327	334	414	484	562	578	671	743	859	959	1005	977	951	929	906	885	933	1016	1027	1044
2.3. Traders and craftmen																				
2.3.1. As main occupation	5867	5794	5786	6868	8258	8480	10153	12435	13929	15306	15139	14043	12103	11872	11386	12164	13159	14759	15309	14576
2.3.2. As secondary occupation	495	489	488	580	697	716	857	1049	1175	1291	1277	1141	946	889	818	839	914	1032	1070	1019
Total 2.3.	6362	6283	6274	7448	8955	9196	11010	13484	15104	16597	16416	15184	13049	12761	12204	13003	14073	15791	16379	15595
2.4. Partnerships	445	440	439	521	627	644	771	944	1057	1162	1149	1063	913	893	854	910	985	1105	1147	1092
TOTAL 2.	11391	10386	9308	12265	14360	14280	17415	20036	22598	24678	23569	20891	18098	18320	16840	18487	19102	21586	22690	21735
3. INCOME FROM PROPERTY ACCRUING TO THE PERSONAL SECTOR																				
3.1. Interest																				
3.1.1. Saving deposits and capitalized interest	72	126	136	151	174	207	214	240	308	376	433	423	539	463	462	417	396	423	439	431
3.1.2. Bank deposits	105	125	150	179	268	387	514	413	457	532	485	363	346	314	270	174	146	144	133	107
3.1.3. Insurance contracts	4	5	6	7	9	12	15	18	23	31	41	51	60	67	75	84	95	106	117	127
3.1.4. Government funds	640	800	930	1000	1050	1070	1080	1080	1110	1010	1060	1090	1200	1290	1340	1140	1230	1340	1340	1410
3.1.5. Corporate debenture loans	77	103	123	143	155	181	192	147	182	211	265	330	408	405	358	362	365	329	262	236
3.1.6. Mortgage loans	37	59	88	120	160	201	259	321	370	456	558	547	555	553	491	403	333	281	267	261

3.1.7. Imputed interest related to services free of charge by banks and other financial intermediaries	360	460	560	615	995	1375	1765	1695	1740	1780	1765	1600	1570	1460	1225	845	830	665	610	560
Total 3.1.	1295	1678	1993	2215	2811	3433	4039	3914	4190	4396	4607	4404	4678	4552	4221	3425	3395	3288	3168	3132
3.2. Rent (received or imputed)																				
3.2.1. Improved properties	1079	1269	1425	1832	2117	2529	2835	3382	4220	5117	7761	8903	9549	9551	9470	9058	9108	9227	9370	9580
3.2.2. Unimproved properties	357	427	524	552	680	893	1088	1598	1706	1748	1669	1665	1629	1446	1308	1236	1364	1538	1502	1559
3.2.3. Charges	-686	-691	-772	-890	-1013	-1091	-1298	-1571	-1912	-2460	-2830	-2635	-2502	-2368	-2180	-2102	-2144	-2300	-2400	-2377
Total 3.2.	750	1005	1177	1494	1784	2331	2625	3409	4014	4405	6600	7933	8676	8629	8598	8192	8328	8465	8472	8762
3.3. Dividends, bonuses and donations																				
3.3.1. Dividends paid by Belgian companies trading in Belgium	850	510	725	1264	1360	1300	1740	2027	2519	3142	2931	2222	1876	1844	1827	2201	2844	3293	3248	2741
3.3.2. Dividends paid by Belgian companies trading abroad	24	9	18	39	64	75	98	112	122	112	110	75	50	49	52	74	107	131	122	82
3.3.3. Income from investments abroad	255	173	215	207	284	325	466	580	683	675	714	523	379	396	449	459	451	480	357	238
3.3.4. Bonuses	152	86	127	229	268	270	359	416	500	584	550	408	332	326	326	404	533	625	609	493
3.3.5. Corporate grants to households & non profit making institutions serving households	28	17	24	42	45	43	58	91	101	121	136	99	42	29	39	45	70	86	79	65
Total 3.3.	1309	794	1109	1782	2021	2013	2721	3226	3925	4634	4442	3327	2679	2644	2692	3182	4004	4615	4415	3618
TOTAL 3.	3354	3477	4279	5491	6616	7777	9385	10549	12129	13435	15649	15664	16033	15825	15511	14799	15727	16368	16055	15512
4. SAVINGS BY CORPORATIONS																				
4.1. Undistributed profits of companies limited by shares	383	230	326	569	612	585	783	2059	1988	2396	3257	2290	-24	-623	-171	-361	88	329	41	-50
4.2. Undistributed profits of autonomous public corporations	-1	-4	-1	-2	3	7	5	14	58	100	120	57	11	49	50	44	48	44	47	46
TOTAL 4.	382	226	325	567	615	592	788	2073	2046	2496	3377	2347	-13	-574	-121	-317	136	373	88	-4
5. DIRECT TAXES PAID BY COMPANIES	82	125	134	193	216	211	277	408	426	495	564	487	354	388	334	245	305	352	258	221

6. INCOME FROM CAPITAL AND ENTERPREUNIAL INCOME ACCRUING TO THE GOVERNMENT																			
6.1. Imputed rent	113	121	126	146	170	171	203	235	254	302	324	294	269	247	235	240	271	335	373	363
6.2. Interest, dividends, profits																				
6.2.1. Central government	-46	20	186	197	48	243	77	704	627	768	428	90	75	94	160	155	207	278	212	209
6.2.2. Interest on actuarial reserves of pension funds	19	21	24	28	32	35	41	52	66	84	106	133	164	191	210	228	248	270	296	323
6.2.3. Other government	52	74	91	105	122	152	160	223	309	303	289	326	271	330	532	531	515	544	525	481
Total 6.2.	25	115	301	330	202	430	278	979	1002	1155	823	549	510	615	902	914	970	1092	1033	1013
TOTAL 6.	138	236	427	476	372	601	481	1214	1256	1457	1147	843	779	862	1137	1154	1241	1427	1406	1376
7. INTEREST ON PUBLIC DEBT	-997	-1368	-1482	-1749	-1915	-2057	-2247	-2555	-2527	-2474	-2464	-2361	-2329	-2407	-2410	-2402	-2288	-2296	-2244	-2327
NET NATIONAL INCOME (NNI) or NET NATIONAL PRODUCT AT FACTOR COST (NNPf)	23684	23401	23625	29529	34999	36749	42926	54282	61813	70436	74312	67199	58426	57220	54898	55077	59950	67226	68556	66356
8. DEPRECIATION	2430	2130	2100	2690	2910	2950	3740	4340	4660	5440	5540	4810	4620	4300	4150	4520	4920	5860	5790	5710
GROSS NATIONAL INCOME (GNI) or GROSS NATIONAL PRODUCT AT FACTOR COST (GNPf)	26114	25531	25725	32219	37909	39699	46666	58622	66473	75876	79852	72009	63046	61520	59048	59597	64870	73086	74346	72066
9. INDIRECT TAXATION	648	778	1311	1614	1945	2139	3572	5082	5899	6245	4957	4803	5254	5665	5414	5830	6124	6714	6485	6363
10. SUBSIDIES	-4	-4	-4	-4	-4	-4	-2	-2	-14	-13	-15	-8	-9	-19	-42	-63	-67	-49	-69	-131
GROSS NATIONAL PRODUCT AT MARKET PRICE (GNPm)	26758	26305	27032	33829	39850	41834	50236	63702	72358	82108	84794	76804	68291	67166	64420	65364	70927	79751	80762	78298

TABLES

TABLE 1

Wagebill of manual workers employed in enterprises in industry, trade and other service sectors (in BF millions)

year	(1)	(2)	(3)	(4)	(5)	(6)	(7)	(8)	year
1920	3.707	-24	-183	271	104	287	434	4.595	1920
1921	4.182	-28	-228	279	105	320	460	5.092	1921
1922	4.675	-31	-278	228	88	341	308	5.331	1922
1923	5.713	-39	-369	234	84	413	348	6.384	1923
1924	6.988	-50	-486	233	70	501	404	7.660	1924
1925	7.087	-52	-529	198	68	502	370	7.644	1925
1926	8.396	-64	-669	183	64	592	450	8.952	1926
1927	10.418	-82	-883	206	72	628	631	10.990	1927
1928	12.008	-97	-1078	180	76	589	597	12.275	1928
1929	14.987	-125	-1421	136	83	575	648	14.882	1929
1930	16.072	-138	-1605	95	84	598	323	15.429	1930
1931	13.380	-118	-1404	19	65	494	212	12.649	1931
1932	10.938	-119	-1203		53	391	-79	9.979	1932
1933	9.710	-126			47	392	-21	10.002	1933
1934	8.955	-135			41	361	-42	9.179	1934
1935	9.050	-156			35	365	-31	9.263	1935
1936	10.581	-204			34	425	-68	10.768	1936
1937	12.661	-271			33	516	121	13.060	1937
1938	12.491	-267			30	510	127	12.891	1938
1939	11.633	-249			25	481	251	12.142	1939

(1) Total insured wagebill (Report 1939-1940-1941, p. 13).
(2) Insured wagebill in vocational training schools, municipal services and certain branches of special agriculture (Table 3 column 8).
(3) Correction for insured white-collar workers (Table 4 column 7).
(4) Wagebill of workers not insured against industrial accidents (Table 6 column 5).
(5) Wagebill of non-insured manual workers for which contributions are made to the Guarantee Fund (Table 7 column 5).
(6) Wagebill non-insured manual workers whose employers were exempted from contributing to the Guarantee Fund (Table 8 column 3).
(7) Correction for wagebill above maximum wage and below minimum wage (Table 9 column 10).
(8) Total wagebill of manual workers in private enterprises = (1)+(2)+(3)+(4)+(5)+(6)+(7).

261

TABLE 2

Comparison between total insured wagebill (manual workers plus white-collar workers) in the Reports and the Industrial Accident Statistics (in BF millions)

year	(1)	(2)	(3)	(4)
1921	4.183	4.135	-48	-1,1%
1922	4.675	4.708	34	0,7%
1931	13.381	13.496	116	0,9%
1937	15.123	15.592	469	3,1%
1938	15.053	16.646	1.593	10,6%
1939	14.206	14.553	347	2,4%

(1) Wagebill in the Reports (Report 1939-1940-1941, p. 13).
(2) Wagebill in the Statistics (Statistics 1922, vol. II pp. 540-541 (with reference to 1921 and 1922); 1931, p. 90; 1937, vol. I, p. XXI and vol. II, p. XXX; 1938-1939-1940, pp. 29, 161 and 213).
(3) Absolute difference = (2) - (1).
(4) Relative difference = (3) x 100 ÷ (1).

TABLE 3

Wagebill of insured persons employed in vocational training schools, municipal services and certain branches of special agriculture (in BF millions).

year	(1)	(2)	(3)	(4)	(5)	(6)	(7)	(8)	year
1920	3.707						9	24	1920
1921	4.182		1		14		10	28	1921
1922	4.675	1	1		16	12	12	31	1922
1923	5.713		2	18	18		15	39	1923
1924	6.988		2		22		20	50	1924
1925	7.087		2		28		21	52	1925
1926	8.396		3		29		26	64	1926
1927	10.418		4		35		34	82	1927
1928	12.008		4		44		41	97	1928
1929	14.987		6		52		53	125	1929
1930	16.072	5	6		66	51	59	138	1930
1931	13.380		5	61	72		51	118	1931
1932	10.938		14		61		48	119	1932
1933	9.710		22		57		47	126	1933
1934	8.955		28		57		49	135	1934
1935	9.050		37		58		54	156	1935
1936	10.581		53		65		69	204	1936
1937	12.661	75	75	107	82	89	89	271	1937
1938	12.491		74		107		88	267	1938
1939	11.633		69		105		82	249	1939
					98				

(1) Total insured wagebill (Report 1939-1940-1941, p. 13).
(2) Known insured wages in vocational training schools (Statistics 1922, vol I, pp. 79-80; 1931, p. 88; 1937, vol II, p. 70).
(3) Estimated insured wages in industrial training schools = on basis of (1) and (2). The ratio of (2),(1) in 1922, 1931 and 1937 was established by linear interpolation for the intervening years and the resultant series was multiplied by (1).
(4) Known insured wages in municipal services (source : see (2)).
(5) Estimated insured wages in municipal services = on basis of (1) and (4). Method analogous to (3).
(6) Known insured wages in branches of special agriculture already counted elsewhere (e.g. horticulture and floristry) (Statistics 1922, vol.1, pp. 60-62; 1931, pp. 70-73; 1937, vol. II, pp. 54-56).
(7) Estimated insured wages in branches of special agriculture already counted elsewhere = on basis of (1) and (6). Method analogous to (3).
(8) Estimated insured wages in vocational training schools, municipal services and branches of special agriculture already counted elsewhere = (3)+(5)+(7).

TABLE 4

Wagebill of insured manual workers: adjustment for the insured domestic staff (1920-1932) (in BF millions)

year	(1)	(2)	(3)	(4)	(5)	(6)	(7)	(8)	year
1920	3.707			183	4,9%	4,9%	183	3.524	1920
1921	4.182					5,4%	228	3.955	1921
1922	4.675					5,9%	278	4.397	1922
1923	5.713					6,5%	369	5.345	1923
1924	6.988					7,0%	486	6.502	1924
1925	7.087					7,5%	529	6.558	1925
1926	8.396					8,0%	669	7.727	1926
1927	10.418					8,5%	883	9.535	1927
1928	12.008					9,0%	1.078	10.930	1928
1929	14.987					9,5%	1.421	13.566	1929
1930	16.072					10,0%	1.605	14.466	1930
1931	13.380					10,5%	1.404	11.976	1931
1932	10.938			1.203	11,0%	11,0%	1.203	9.734	1932
1933		9.710	1.882					9.710	1933
1934		8.955	2.000					8.955	1934
1935		9.050	2.023					9.050	1935
1936		10.581	2.156					10.581	1936
1937		12.661	2.462					12.661	1937
1938		12.491	2.562					12.491	1938
1939		11.633	2.573					11.633	1939

(1) Insured wagebill of manual workers + white-collar workers with the same risk of industrial accidents as manual workers (Report 1939-1940-1941, p. 13).
(2) Insured wagebill of manual workers (Report 1933-1934-1935, p. 72; 1936-1937-1938, p. 76; 1939-1940-1941, p. 76).
(3) Insured wagebill of white-collar workers (Report 1933-1934-1935, p. 74; 1936-1937-1938, p. 78; 1939-1940-1941, p. 78).
(4) Estimate of insured wagebill of white-collar workers with the same risk of industrial accidents as workers in 1922 and 1932: see text.
(5) Estimated share of white-collar workers' pay in (1) : 1920 and 1932 = (4) ÷ (1).
(6) Estimated share of white-collar workers' pay in (1) : 1920 and 1932 = (5); 1921-1931 = linear interpolation of (5).
(7) Estimate of insured wagebill of white-collar workers with same risk of industrial accidents as manual workers + voluntarily insured white-collar workers = (1) x (6).
(8) Insured wagebill of manual workers : 1920-1932 = (1)-(7); 1933-1939 = (2).

TABLE 5

Problem of the insured white-collar workers: attempt at solution by alternative estimate of the insured manual workers' and white-collar workers' pay

year	(1)	(2)	(3)	(4)	(5)	(6)	(7)	(8)	(9)	(10)	(11)	(12)	(13)	(14)	year
1931	-8,7%	0,7%	12,4%	-8,8%	-16,9%				11.771	13.381	1.610		94,9	105,5	1931
1932	-2,9%	0,4%	20,2%	1,7%	-0,8%				9.785	10.938	1.152		87,3	80,9	1932
1933	-4,3%	0,3%	18,8%	-2,1%	-6,0%			9.710				1.883	92,4	81,2	1933
1934	-4,4%	0,3%	20,5%	2,1%	-2,1%	-7,8%	-1,7%	8.955				2.000	88,6	82,9	1934
1935	8,9%	0,4%	18,9%	7,3%	16,6%	1,1%	3,1%	9.050				2.023	101,3	85,4	1935
1936	11,0%	0,4%	12,9%	2,6%	14,0%	16,9%	0,3%	10.581				2.156	103,8	95,5	1936
1937	5,4%	0,3%	10,7%	-2,4%	3,3%	19,7%	5,7%	12.661				2.462	103,8	106,1	1937
1938	0,7%	0,1%	12,8%	-3,2%	-2,4%	-1,3%	-4,6%	12.491				2.562	98,7	97,8	1938
1939			15,6%			-6,9%	-4,4%	11.633				2.573		95,5	1939

(1) Growth of hourly wage in industry according to CASSIERS I., Une statistique, p. 73.
(2) Growth of Belgian population (Statistical Yearbook for Belgium and Belgian Congo, vol. 74, 1953, p. 32).
(3) Rate of unemployment (100% unemployment only) of workers in industry according to GOOSSENS M., Reconstructie van werkgelegenheidscijfers voor het Interbellum, p. B5.
(4) Growth rate of employment of manual workers in industry (own calculations on basis of (3) namely growth of 100-(3) (= rate of employment)).
(5) Estimated growth of wagebill of workers in industry = (1)+(2)+(4).
(6) Observed growth in insured wagebill of all manaul workers = growth of (8).
(7) = (6)-(5).
(8) Insured wagebill of manual workers (in BF millions) (Report 1933-1934-1935, p. 72; 1936-1937-1938, p. 76; 1939-1940-1941, p. 76).
(9) Estimated insured wagebill of manual workers (in BF millions) on basis of (8) and (5); 1932 : 9 710 + (100 - 0.8) = 9 785; 1931 : 9 785 + (100 - 16.9) = 11 77).
(10) Observed insured wagebill of manual workers + white-collar workers (in BF millions) (Report 1931-1931-1932, p. 233).
(11) Estimated insured wagebill of white-collar workers (in BF millions) = (10)-(9).
(12) Observed insured wagebill of white-collar workers (in BF millions) (Report 1933-1934-1935, p. 74; 1936-1937-1938, p. 78; 1939-1940-1941, p. 78).
(13) Index of industrial production: weighted quantities. 1930 = 100 according to CARBONELLE C., Recherches sur l'évolution de la production en Belgique de 1900 à 1957, p. 358.
(14) Export index: value of exports divided by index of wholesale prices, 1930 = 100 (Belgian Economic Statistics 1929-1940, pp. 240 and 359).

TABLE 6

Wagebill of workers not protected against industrial accidents, 1910-1931 (in BF millions)

Year	(1)	(2)	(3)	(4)	(5)	Year
1910	52.938	40.000	80.000			1910
1920	59.521	35.457	70.914	3.814	271	1920
1921	61.389	34.168	68.336	4.084	279	1921
1922	69.301	28.708	57.416	3.968	228	1922
1923	73.978	25.481	50.961	4.583	234	1923
1924	79.172	21.896	43.793	5.313	233	1924
1925	83.805	18.699	37.398	5.304	198	1925
1926	88.953	15.147	30.293	6.034	183	1926
1927	90.704	13.938	27.877	7.379	206	1927
1928	95.068	10.927	21.854	8.253	180	1928
1929	100.673	7.059	14.118	9.608	136	1929
1930	104.226	4.607	9.214	10.338	95	1930
1931	109.453	1.000	2.000	9.704	19	1931

(1) Number of companies insured with recognized private insurance companies or with collective funds (Report 1939-1940-1941, p. 12).
(2) Number of companies with non-insured manual workers : 1910 and 1931 = own estimate; 1920-1930 : interpolation on basis of (1).
(3) Estimate of number of non-insured manual workers = (2) x 2.
(4) Annual pay of non-insured workers = weighted average of hourly wage of manual workers in industry in companies with less than 5 workers in February 1937 (BF 3.80) x incremental factor for 1937 as a whole (1.043) x working year (2,400 hours) x industrial hourly wage index. Sources: Hourly wage: own calculation on basis of ESC 1937, vol. II, p. 98; vol. IV, p. 59. Incremental factor: own calculation on basis of Belgian Economic Statistics 1929-1940, p. 199. Industrial hourly wage index: CASSIERS I. Une statistique, p. 73).
(5) Wagebill of non-insured workers (in BF millions) = (3) x (4) ÷ 1 000 000.

TABLE 7

Wagebill of non-insured manual workers for whom payments made to Guarantee Fund
(in BF millions)

year	(1)	(2)	(3)	(4)	(5)	year
1920	3.269	327.682	27.307	3.814	104	1920
1921	3.349	309.384	25.782	4.084	105	1921
1922	3.683	266.630	22.219	3.968	88	1922
1923	2.984	220.752	18.396	4.583	84	1923
1924	2.508	159.063	13.255	5.313	70	1924
1925	2.752	153.564	12.797	5.304	68	1925
1926	2.427	126.792	10.566	6.034	64	1926
1927	2.325	116.904	9.742	7.379	72	1927
1928	2.061	121.218	9.206	8.253	76	1928
1929	2.061	121.218	8.671	9.608	83	1929
1930	1.854	97.620	8.135	10.338	84	1930
1931	1.756	80.942	6.745	9.704	65	1931
1932			6.000	8.859	53	1932
1933			5.500	8.599	47	1933
1934			5.000	8.234	41	1934
1935			4.500	7.869	35	1935
1936			4.000	8.571	34	1936
1937			3.500	9.512	33	1937
1938			3.000	10.021	30	1938
1939			2.500	10.089	25	1939

(1) Number of companies making payments to the Guarantee Fund (Report 1921-1922-1923, p. 173; 1924-1925-1926, p. 197; 1927-1928-1929, p. 219; 1930-1931-1932, p. 235).
(2) Sum of proportional premiums in the Guarantee Fund (same source as (1)).
(3) Non-insured workers for whom payments made to Guarantee Fund: 1920-1931: total proportional premiums (1) ÷ premium per worker (BF 12), with the exception of 1928-1929 (unreliable figures): linear interpolation between 1927 and 1930; 1932-1939: own estimate.
(4) Annual pay (see Table 6 column 4).
(5) Wagebill of non-insured manual workers for whom payments made to Guarantee Fund (in BF millions) = (2) x (3) ÷ 1,000,000.

TABLE 8

Wagebill of non-insured manual workers whose employers were exempted from contributing to the Guarantee Fund (in BF millions)

year	(1)	(2)	(3)
1920		3.934	287
1921		4.387	320
1922		4.674	341
1923		5.654	413
1924		6.856	501
1925		6.876	502
1926	592	8.113	592
1927		10.084	628
1928		11.429	589
1929	575	14.089	575
1930		14.652	598
1931		12.071	494
1932		9.536	391
1933		9.563	392
1934		8.777	361
1935		8.863	365
1936		10.309	425
1937		12.511	516
1938		12.351	510
1939	481	11.635	481

(1) Known wagebill of non-insured manual workers whose employers were exempted from contributing to the Guarantee Fund: 1926 and 1929: JULIN A., op. cit., pp. 12 and 14; 1939 : Statistics 1938-39-1940, p. 259.
(2) Adjusted wagebill for insured manual workers (Table 9 column 11).
(3) Estimated wagebill of non-insured manual workers whose employers were exempted from contributing to the Guarantee Fund = on basis of (1) and (2).
The ratio (1)÷(2) in 1926 has been multiplied by (2) in 1920-1925. The ratio (1)÷(2) in 1926, 1929 and 1939 has been interpolated on a linear basis for the intervening years and the resultant series multiplied by (2).

TABLE 9

Adjustment of insured wagebill for wagebill above maximum wage and wagebill below minimum wage
(in BF millions)

year	(1)	(2)	(3)	(4)	(5)	(6)	(7)	(8)	(9)	(10)	(11)	year
1920	39,7	1,85	4.432	730	4 000	961	1.080	12,4%	3.500	434	3.934	1920
1921	42,5	1,98	4.745	730 / 1 500	4 000 / 7 300	980	1.095	11,7%	3.927	460	4.387	1921
1922	41,3	1,92	4.611	1.500	7 300	881	943	7,1%	4.366	308	4.674	1922
1923	47,7	2,22	5.325	1.500	7 300	1.166	1.242	6,6%	5.306	348	5.654	1923
1924	55,3	2,57	6.174	1.500	7 300	1.439	1.529	6,3%	6.452	404	6.856	1924
1925	55,2	2,57	6.163	1.500	7 300	1.226	1.296	5,7%	6.506	370	6.876	1925
1926	62,8	2,92	7.011	1 500 / 2 500	7 300 / 12 000	1.443	1.528	5,9%	7.663	450	8.113	1926
1927	76,8	3,57	8.574	2.500	12 000	2.059	2.196	6,7%	9.454	631	10.084	1927
1928	85,9	4,00	9.590	2.500	12 000	1.963	2.071	5,5%	10.833	597	11.429	1928
1929	100,0	4,65	11.164	2.500	12 000 / 20 000	2.175	2.280	4,8%	13.441	648	14.089	1929
1930	107,6	5,01	12.013	2.500	20 000	2.418	2.472	2,3%	14.329	323	14.652	1930
1931	101,0	4,70	11.276	2.500	20 000	1.978	2.013	1,8%	11.858	212	12.071	1931
1932	92,2	4,29	10.293	3 650	20 000	1.348	1.337	-0,8%	9.615	-79	9.536	1932
1933	89,5	4,16	9.992	3 650	20 000	1.401	1.398	-0,2%	9.583	-21	9.563	1933
1934	85,7	3,99	9.568	3 650	20 000	1.314	1.308	-0,5%	8.819	-42	8.777	1934
1935	81,9	3,81	9.143	3 650	20 000	1.225	1.221	-0,4%	8.894	-31	8.863	1935
1936	89,2	4,15	9.958	3 650	20 000	1.359	1.350	-0,7%	10.376	-68	10.309	1936
1937	99,0	4,61	11.052	3 650	20 000	1.744	1.761	1,0%	12.390	121	12.511	1937
1938	104,3	4,85	11.644	3 650	20 000	1.927	1.947	1,0%	12.224	127	12.351	1938
1939	105,0	4,88	11.722	3 650	20 000	1.852	1.893	2,2%	11.384	251	11.635	1939

(1) Index of industrial hourly wage according to CASSIERS I., op. cit., p. 73.
(2) Weighted average of hourly wage for male and female manual workers in industry and commerce. February 1937 (= BF 4.42) on basis of ESC 1937, vol. IV, p. 49 and 77; vol. V, pp. 38 and 54-61. Incremental coefficient for full year 1937 (4.3%) on basis of Belgian economic statistics, 1929-1940, p. 199.
(3) Weighted average annual wage of male and female manual workers in industry and commerce = hourly wage x 2,400 (300 days x 8 hours) = (2) x 2,400.
(4) Statutory minimum: Act or Royal Decree of 27/08/1919 (in force from 07/09/1919), 07/08/1921 (in force from 14/08/1921), 03/08/1926 (in force from 21/08/1926), 18/06/1930 (in force from 01/01/1932).
(5) Statutory maximum: Act or Royal Decree of 27/08/1919 (in force from 07/09/1919), 07/08/1921 (in force from 14/08/1921), 03/08/1926 (in force from 21/08/1926), 15/05/1929 (in force from 01/07/1929).
(6) Insured wagebill of mine workers in BF millions (Report).
(7) Actually earned wagebill of miners in BF millions (Statistical Yearbook of Belgium and the Belgian Congo, data drawn from the General Mining Industry Council).
(8) Percentage difference between insured wagebill of miners and actually earned wagebill of miners = incremental factor = (7)-(6) ÷ (6).
(9) Insured wagebill of all manual workers in BF millions (total insured wagebill according to Industrial Accidents Report - insured wagebill in vocational training schools, municipal services and certain branches of special agriculture - correction for insured white-collar workers, see Table 1 columns 1, 2, 3).
(10) Adjustment of insured wagebill of all manual workers for wagebill above maximum wage and wagebill below minimum wage (in BF millions) = (8) x (9).
(11) Adjusted insured wagebill of all manual workers (in BF millions) = (9) + (10).

TABLE 10

Wagebill of homeworkers (in BF millions)

year	(1)	(2)	(3)	(4)	(5)	(6)	(7)	(8)	(9)	(10)	(11)	year
1910	141.456											
1920				81.171					4.432	2.384	194	1920
1921				76.785					4.745	2.553	196	1921
1922				72.637					4.611	2.481	180	1922
1923				68.712					5.325	2.865	197	1923
1924				65.000					6.174	3.321	216	1924
1925				61.488					6.163	3.315	204	1925
1926				58.166					7.011	3.772	219	1926
1927		20.332	37,0%	55.023	610.095	30,0	48,1	62,4%	8.574	4.613	254	1927
1928		21.091	39,6%	53.241	652.810	31,0	47,3	65,4%	9.590	5.159	275	1928
1929		20.730	42,3%	49.034	632.822	30,5	47,7	64,0%	11.164	6.006	295	1929
1930	45.497	20.446	44,9%	45.497	583.030	28,5	49,3	57,8%	12.013	6.463	294	1930
1931		18.489	47,6%	38.841	619.492	33,5	66,8	50,2%	11.276	6.202	241	1931
1932		17.544	50,3%	34.903	1.234.381	70,4	154,8	45,5%	10.293	5.661	198	1932
1933		14.848	52,9%	28.054	1.267.166	85,3	159,2	53,6%	9.992	5.356	150	1933
1934		13.413	55,6%	24.129	1.170.043	87,2	153,1	57,0%	9.568	5.451	132	1934
1935		12.497	58,3%	21.453	1.057.882	84,7	146,8	57,7%	9.143	5.272	113	1935
1936		14.281	60,9%	23.444	1.230.975	86,2	155,2	55,5%	9.958	5.531	130	1936
1937	25.569	16.256	63,6%	25.569	1.444.933	88,9	165,9	53,6%	11.052	5.922	151	1937
1938		19.828	66,2%	29.934	1.717.365	86,6	172,8	50,1%	11.644	5.836	175	1938
1939		22.592	68,9%	32.789	2.178.369	96,4	167,9	57,4%	11.722	6.732	221	1939

(1) Total number of homeworkers according to industrial censuses (IC 1910, vol. VI, p. 156-157 ; IC 1930, pp. 1420 and 1434-1437 ; ESC 1937, vol. I, p. 88).
(2) Number of pension contributions by homeworkers (ASLK, Annual Reports).
(3) Estimate of ratio between pension contributions of homeworkers in relation to total number of homeworkers (1930 and 1937: (2),(1); 1930-1937 : Linear interpolation of the ratios in 1930 and 1937 (= annual increase of 2.7%); 1927-1930 and 1938-1939: annual increase of 2.7%).
(4) Estimate of total number of homeworkers: 1920-1926: interpolation between 1910 and 1927 at a constant downward rate; 1927-1939: (2) x (3).
(5) Total pension contributions (employers' contribution + employees' contribution) of homeworkers (ASLK, Annual Reports).
(6) Average pension contribution of homeworkers = (5) ÷ (2).
(7) Average pension contribution of manual workers (own calculation on basis of ASLK, Annual Reports).
(8) Ratio of average pension contribution of homeworkers in relation to average pension contribution of manual workers = (6) ÷ (7).
(9) Average yearly wage of manual workers in industry and commerce (Table 9 column 3).
(10) Estimate of annual wage of homeworkers. 1920-1932: (9) x 0.55 ; 1933-1939: (9) x (8).
(11) Estimate of wagebill of homeworkers (in BF millions) = (4) x (10) ÷1 000 000.

TABLE 11

Wagebill of fishermen and seamen (in BF millions)

year	(1)	(2)	(3)	(4)	(5)	(6)	(7)	year
1910	1.406							1910
1920		1.526	39,7	6.166	9		12	1920
1921		1.538	42,5	6.600	10		12	1921
1922		1.550	41,3	6.414	10		12	1922
1923		1.562	47,7	7.408	12		14	1923
1924		1.574	55,3	8.588	14		16	1924
1925		1.586	55,2	8.573	14		16	1925
1926		1.598	62,8	9.753	16		18	1926
1927		1.610	76,8	11.927	19		22	1927
1928		1.622	85,9	13.341	22		25	1928
1929		1.634	100,0	15.530	25		29	1929
1930	1.646	1.646	107,6	16.711	28	1.884	31	1930
1931		1.612	101,0	15.686	25		30	1931
1932		1.579	92,2	14.319	23		27	1932
1933		1.545	89,5	13.900	21		26	1933
1934		1.511	85,7	13.310	20		25	1934
1935		1.477	81,9	12.719	19		24	1935
1936		1.444	89,2	13.853	20		26	1936
1937	1.410	1.410	99,0	15.375	22		29	1937
1938		1.410	104,3	16.198	23		31	1938
1939		1.410	105,0	16.307	23		31	1939

(1) Number of workers in the fishing industry in census years (OC 1910, vol. II, p. 1414; OC 1930, pp. 752-753; ESC 1937, vol. I, p. 87).
(2) Estimate of number of workers in the fishing industry = linear interpolation of (2)
(3) Index of industrial hourly wage according to CASSIERS I., op. cit., p. 73.
(4) Estimate of average annual wage of workers in the fishing industry = average hourly wage in the fishing industry in February 1937 (BF 6.14) x augmentation factor for all of 1937 (1.034) x working year (2,400 hours) x index of industry hourly wage.
Sources: hourly wage in February 1937: ESC 1937, vol. IV, p. 48; incremental factor: own calculation of Belgian economic statistics 1929-1940, p. 199 ; index of industry hourly wage: see (3).
(5) Estimate of wagebill of workers in the fishing industry
(in BF millions) = (2) x (4) ÷ 1,000,000.
(6) Number of seamen in 1930 according to PC 1930, p. 749.
(7) Estimate of wagebill of seamen (in BF millions) = (6) x (4) ÷ 1,000,000.

TABLE 12

Pay of manual workers employed in the private sector in Belgium (in BF millions)

year	(1)	(2)	(3)	(4)	(5)	(6)	year
1920	4.595	194	461	9	12	5.271	1920
1921	5.092	196	539	10	12	5.849	1921
1922	5.331	180	530	10	12	6.063	1922
1923	6.384	197	546	12	14	7.152	1923
1924	7.660	216	537	14	16	8.443	1924
1925	7.644	204	564	14	16	8.442	1925
1926	8.952	219	592	16	18	9.798	1926
1927	10.990	254	656	19	22	11.942	1927
1928	12.275	275	758	22	25	13.354	1928
1929	14.882	295	723	25	29	15.954	1929
1930	15.429	294	713	28	31	16.496	1930
1931	12.649	241	665	25	30	13.611	1931
1932	9.979	198	617	23	27	10.844	1932
1933	10.002	150	574	21	26	10.775	1933
1934	9.179	132	560	20	25	9.915	1934
1935	9.263	113	514	19	24	9.932	1935
1936	10.768	130	519	20	26	11.462	1936
1937	13.060	151	562	22	29	13.824	1937
1938	12.891	175	556	23	31	13.675	1938
1939	12.142	221	536	23	31	12.952	1939

(1) Pay of manual workers in private enterprises (Table 1 column 8).
(2) Pay of homeworkers (Table 10 column 11).
(3) Pay of agricultural workers (Table 47 column 2).
(4) Pay of fishermen (Table 11 column 5).
(5) Pay of seamen (Table 11 column 7).
(6) Total pay of manual workers in the private sector in Belgium (in current prices) = (1)+(2)+(3)+(4)+(5).

TABLE 13

Pay of white-collar workers in the private sector: simplified table (in BF millions)

year	(1)	(2)	(3)	year
1920	750	135	885	1920
1921	873	149	1.022	1921
1922	944	150	1.094	1922
1923	1.133	171	1.304	1923
1924	1.476	213	1.689	1924
1925	1.596	222	1.818	1925
1926	1.884	253	2.137	1926
1927	2.416	315	2.731	1927
1928	2.750	348	3.098	1928
1929	3.319	410	3.730	1929
1930	3.603	438	4.040	1930
1931	3.418	416	3.834	1931
1932	3.122	380	3.501	1932
1933	3.025	368	3.393	1933
1934	2.916	354	3.271	1934
1935	2.863	348	3.210	1935
1936	3.141	381	3.522	1936
1937	3.507	425	3.932	1937
1938	3.799	460	4.259	1938
1939	3.849	466	4.315	1939

(1) Pay of white-collar workers included in the industrial and commercial censuses (i.e. white-collar workers employed in industry, commerce, the financial sector and the entertainment sector) = Table 25, column 19.
(2) Pay of white-collar workers not included in the industrial and commercial censuses (i.e. white-collar workers employed in the health-care sector, by professionals, and in the cultural/academic sector, etc.) = Table 26, column 11.
(3) Total pay at current prices = (1) + (2).

TABLE 14

Employment, unemployment and total workforce of white-collar workers and manual workers in positions of authority according to the ICC 1930

	Employment			Unemployment			Workforce			Unemployment %		
	Male	Female	Total	Male	Female	Total	Male	Female	Total	Male	Female	Total
Fishing	11	2	13	6	0	6	17	2	19	35,3%	0,0%	31,6%
Mines (1)	9.820	180	10.000	68	1	69	9.888	181	10.069	0,7%	0,6%	0,7%
Quarries	1.768	161	1.929	35	2	37	1.803	163	1.966	1,9%	1,2%	1,9%
Metal	22.998	4.004	27.002	652	74	726	23.650	4.078	27.728	2,8%	1,8%	2,6%
Ceramics	1.618	300	1.918	64	4	68	1.682	304	1.986	3,8%	1,3%	3,4%
Glass	1.515	263	1.778	70	3	73	1.585	266	1.851	4,4%	1,1%	3,9%
Chemicals	10.508	2.715	13.223	218	40	258	10.726	2.755	13.481	2,0%	1,5%	1,9%
Food	6.982	1.934	8.916	160	47	207	7.142	1.981	9.123	2,2%	2,4%	2,3%
Textiles	6.628	2.309	8.937	217	46	263	6.845	2.355	9.200	3,2%	2,0%	2,9%
Clothing	2.327	2.633	4.960	58	92	150	2.385	2.725	5.110	2,4%	3,4%	2,9%
Construction	2.944	719	3.663	275	19	294	3.219	738	3.957	8,5%	2,6%	7,4%
Wood and Upholstery	2.277	822	3.099	91	17	108	2.368	839	3.207	3,8%	2,0%	3,4%
Hides and Leather	1.928	746	2.674	59	14	73	1.987	760	2.747	3,0%	1,8%	2,7%
Tobacco	871	245	1.116	28	9	37	899	254	1.153	3,1%	3,5%	3,2%
Paper	1.132	321	1.453	12	8	20	1.144	329	1.473	1,0%	2,4%	1,4%
Books	1.654	655	2.309	47	12	59	1.701	667	2.368	2,8%	1,8%	2,5%
Art and Precision Work	2.486	1.071	3.557	143	36	179	2.629	1.107	3.736	5,4%	3,3%	4,8%
Transport	7.938	462	8.400	460	48	508	8.398	510	8.908	5,5%	9,4%	5,7%
INDUSTRY TOTAL	85.405	19.542	104.947	2.663	472	3.135	88.068	20.014	108.082	3,0%	2,4%	2,9%
Purchasing and sales	27.306	24.573	51.879	1.020	690	1.710	28.326	25.263	53.589	3,6%	2,7%	3,2%
Banking	23.281	3.818	27.099	590	66	656	23.871	3.884	27.755	2,5%	1,7%	2,4%
Insurance	4.460	1.434	5.894	92	29	121	4.552	1.463	6.015	2,0%	2,0%	2,0%
Commercial intermediaries	6.133	1.795	7.928	262	48	310	6.395	1.843	8.238	4,1%	2,6%	3,8%
Hotels	994	1.521	2.515	219	114	333	1.213	1.635	2.848	18,1%	7,0%	11,7%
Entertainment	510	327	837	105	19	124	615	346	961	17,1%	5,5%	12,9%
COMMERCE TOTAL	62.684	33.468	96.152	2.288	966	3.254	64.972	34.434	99.406	3,5%	2,8%	3,3%
Unclassified				474	158	632						
INDUSTRY/COMMERCE TOTAL	148.089	53.010	201.099	5.425	1.596	7.021	153.514	54.606	208.120	3,5%	2,9%	3,4%

Sources:
- Employment in industry: IC 1930, pp. 1342-1343 (excluding transport = own calculation: see text)
- Employment in commerce: IC 1930, pp. 1478-1479.
- Unemployment: OC 1930, pp. 758-759.

Remarks:
- Unemployment = only full unemployment. For information: total of partially unemployed 3,519 (2,518 in industry, 992 in commerce, 9 unclassified).
- Workforce = employed + unemployed.
- Percentage unemployment = unemployed : workforce x 100.
- (1) Mines = adjusted figure, since the figure in the census (4,238 white-collar workers) is undoubtedly too low. The figure has been adjusted on the basis of the number of manual workers, the number of white-collar workers and the proportion of manual workers to white-collar workers in the mines according to the industrial censuses of 1910, 1930 and 1937.

TABLE 15

Employment, unemployment and total workforce of white-collar workers and manual workers in positions of authority according to the ESC 1937

Sector	Employment			Unemployment			Workforce			Unemployment %		
	Male	Female	Total	Male	Female	Total	Male	Female	Total	Male	Female	Total
Fishing	112	1	113	0	0	0	112	1	113	0,0%	0,0%	0,0%
Mines (1)	11.941	146	12.087	169	0	169	12.110	146	12.256	1,4%	0,0%	1,4%
Quarries	2.253	157	2.410	78	5	83	2.331	162	2.493	3,3%	3,1%	3,3%
Metal	25.277	3.631	28.908	1.313	90	1.403	26.590	3.721	30.311	4,9%	2,4%	4,6%
Ceramics	1.929	247	2.176	88	8	96	2.017	255	2.272	4,4%	3,1%	4,2%
Glass	2.003	261	2.264	133	8	141	2.136	269	2.405	6,2%	3,0%	5,9%
Chemicals	11.843	2.528	14.371	449	77	526	12.292	2.605	14.897	3,7%	3,0%	3,5%
Food	9.751	2.164	11.915	399	95	494	10.150	2.259	12.409	3,9%	4,2%	4,0%
Textiles	9.554	2.384	11.938	434	70	504	9.988	2.454	12.442	4,3%	2,9%	4,1%
Clothing	2.767	2.562	5.329	112	108	220	2.879	2.670	5.549	3,9%	4,0%	4,0%
Construction	4.251	518	4.769	523	23	546	4.774	541	5.315	11,0%	4,3%	10,3%
Wood and Upholstery	2.567	658	3.225	135	22	157	2.702	680	3.382	5,0%	3,2%	4,6%
Hides and Leather	2.258	666	2.924	86	23	109	2.344	689	3.033	3,7%	3,3%	3,6%
Tobacco	847	227	1.074	43	14	57	890	241	1.131	4,8%	5,8%	5,0%
Paper	1.516	421	1.937	65	20	85	1.581	441	2.022	4,1%	4,5%	4,2%
Books	2.729	749	3.478	115	28	143	2.844	777	3.621	4,0%	3,6%	3,9%
Art and Precision Work	1.906	723	2.629	249	43	292	2.155	766	2.921	11,6%	5,6%	10,0%
Transport	5.194	400	5.594	663	61	724	5.857	461	6.318	11,3%	13,2%	11,5%
INDUSTRY TOTAL	98.698	18.443	117.141	5.054	695	5.749	103.752	19.138	122.890	4,9%	3,6%	4,7%
Purchasing and Sales	31.675	28.763	60.438	1.431	1.147	2.578	33.106	29.910	63.016	4,3%	3,8%	4,1%
Banking (*)	16.323	2.534	18.857									
Insurance (*)	5.468	1.879	7.347									
Commercial intermediaries (*)	7.148	2.031	9.179	3.684	457	4.141	35.143	8.429	43.572	10,5%	5,4%	9,5%
Hotels (*)	1.171	904	2.075	(*)	(*)	(*)	(*)	(*)	(*)		(*) (*)	(*)
Entertainment (*)	1.349	624	1.973									
COMMERCE TOTAL	63.134	36.735	99.869	5.115	1.604	6.719	68.249	38.339	106.588	7,5%	4,2%	6,3%
INDUSTRY/COMMERCE TOTAL	161.832	55.178	217.010	10.180	2.310	12.468	172.001	57.477	229.478	5,9%	4,0%	5,4%

Sources:
- Employment in industry: ESC 1937, vol. I, p. 87; vol. II, pp. 8-27 (excluding transport = own calculation: see text)
- Employment in commerce: ESC 1937, vol. III, pp. 54-55.
- Unemployment: ESC 1937, Census of Unemployed, pp. 55-59 and pp. 163-167.

Remarks:
- Employment = only white-collar workers in operational establishments were included. White-collar workers in establishments where production was suspended (898 employees in industry; in commerce there was no suspended production) were not counted.
- Unemployment = only full unemployment of those who have previously worked. Hence no account was taken of unemployed white-collar workers who had not yet been employed (the number of unemployed persons who had not yet worked and who listed themselves as white-collar workers totalled 1,272).
- Workforce = employed + unemployed.
- Percentage unemployment = unemployed : workforce x 100.
* In respect of the number of unemployed persons in the purchasing and sales, banking, insurance, commercial intermediaries, hotels and entertainment sectors, only the total figures were published.

TABLE 16

Estimate of white-collar workers and manual workers in positions of authority in industry and commerce on 31 december 1920: men

	1910			1930			1920		
	PC10	ICC10	(ICC-PC)/PC (a)	PC30	ICC30	(ICC-PC)/PC (b)	PC20	CORR.20	EST20 (c)
Fishing	24	152	533,3%	23	11	-52,2%	61	240,6%	208
Mines	4.291	5.724	33,4%	6.235	9.820	57,5%	4.525	45,4%	6.581
Quarries	1.618	1.833	13,3%	1.893	1.768	-6,6%	1.297	3,3%	1.340
Metal	10.558	11.192	6,0%	25.422	22.998	-9,5%	13.519	-1,8%	13.280
Ceramics	594	897	51,0%	1.414	1.618	14,4%	532	32,7%	706
Glass	1.023	1.025	0,2%	1.909	1.515	-20,6%	1.026	-10,2%	921
Chemicals	2.632	3.485	32,4%	8.976	10.508	17,1%	2.940	24,7%	3.667
Food	3.915	5.648	44,3%	6.160	6.982	13,3%	3.746	28,8%	4.825
Textiles	4.197	5.240	24,9%	7.580	6.628	-12,6%	3.787	6,1%	4.020
Clothing	911	1.125	23,5%	1.216	2.327	91,4%	967	57,4%	1.522
Construction	1.986	1.791	-9,8%	3.723	2.944	-20,9%	2.145	-15,4%	1.815
Wood and Upholstery	981	1.316	34,1%	1.811	2.277	25,7%	1.310	29,9%	1.702
Hides and Leather	716	1.263	76,4%	1.354	1.928	42,4%	1.014	59,4%	1.616
Tobacco	208	628	201,9%	567	871	53,6%	397	127,8%	904
Paper	666	689	3,5%	1.090	1.132	3,9%	758	3,7%	786
Books	590	1.003	70,0%	1.384	1.654	19,5%	673	44,8%	974
Art and Precision Work	731	463	-36,7%	2.394	2.486	3,8%	888	-16,4%	742
Transport	9.492	6.578	-30,7%	14.695	7.938	-46,0%	10.971	-38,3%	6.765
INDUSTRY TOTAL	45.133	50.052	10,9%	87.846	85.405	-2,8%	50.556		52.376
Purchasing and Sales	17.945	16.337	-9,0%	24.268	27.306	12,5%	18.143	1,8%	18.466
Banking	8.241	7.620	-7,5%	29.141	23.281	-20,1%	17.547	-13,8%	15.122
Insurances	5.329	5.017	-5,9%	8.015	4.460	-44,4%	5.907	-25,1%	4.424
Commercial Intermediaries	15.272	4.974	-67,4%	29.209	6.133	-79,0%	14.670	-73,2%	3.929
Hotels	1.479	512	-65,4%	2.967	994	-66,5%	2.275	-65,9%	775
Entertainment	723	215	-70,3%	953	510	-46,5%	608	-58,4%	253
COMMERCE TOTAL	48.989	34.675	-29,2%	94.553	62.684	-33,7%	59.150		42.968
INDUSTRY/COMMERCE TOTAL	94.122	84.727	-10,0%	182.399	148.089	-18,8%	109.706		95.345

280

Sources:
- PC 1910, vol. IV, pp. 210-232.
- ICC 1910, vol. VIII, pp. 72, 398-400, and 440-442.
- PC 1930, vol. V, pp. 188-193.
- ICC 1930, pp. 1342-1343 and 1478-1479.
- PC 1920, vol. III, pp. 232-252 and 566-580.
- Transport = own calculation: see text.

Remarks:
- The most important discrepancy between the PC and the ICC is due to commercial travellers. In the PC they are classified among commercial intermediaries (in 1910: 9,032; in 1920: 5,496; in 1930: 22,196 men). In the ICC almost all commercial travellers fall under the sector in which they operate. Only those commercial travellers selling on behalf of more than one employer are classified as commercial intermediaries. This also explains why in the PC white-collar workers are represented relatively more strongly in commerce, and in the ICC in industry.
(c) Estimate 1920 = (1 + CORR. 20) x PC20
with CORR. 20 = (a+b) ÷ 2.

281

TABLE 17

Estimate of white-collar workers and manual workers in positions of authority in industry and commerce on 31 december 1920: women

	1910			1.930			1920		
	PC10	ICC10	(ICC-PC)/PC (a)	PC30	ICC30	(ICC-PC)/PC (b)	PC20	CORR.20	EST20 (c)
Fishing	0	0	0,0%	2	2	0,0%	4	0,0%	4
Mines	13	2	-84,6%	264	180	-31,8%	307	-58,2%	128
Quarries	15	13	-13,3%	233	161	-30,9%	55	-22,1%	43
Metal	350	320	-8,6%	4.926	4.004	-18,7%	1.564	-13,6%	1.351
Ceramics	21	12	-42,9%	314	300	-4,5%	55	-23,7%	42
Glass	63	23	-63,5%	286	263	-8,0%	133	-35,8%	85
Chemicals	157	160	1,9%	2.362	2.715	14,9%	548	8,4%	594
Food	712	356	-50,0%	2.320	1.934	-16,6%	1.037	-33,3%	691
Textiles	520	277	-46,7%	2.789	2.309	-17,2%	918	-32,0%	625
Clothing	1.097	913	-16,8%	2.344	2.633	12,3%	1.173	-2,2%	1.147
Construction	69	82	18,8%	803	719	-10,5%	252	4,2%	263
Wood and Upholstery	112	103	-8,0%	748	822	9,9%	291	0,9%	294
Hides and Leather	138	127	-8,0%	704	746	6,0%	638	-1,0%	632
Tobacco	28	37	32,1%	262	245	-6,5%	262	12,8%	296
Paper	87	57	-34,5%	461	321	-30,4%	214	-32,4%	145
Books	99	104	5,1%	601	655	9,0%	234	7,0%	250
Art and Precision Work	200	91	-54,5%	1.136	1.071	-5,7%	344	-30,1%	240
Transport	176	38	-78,4%	1.681	462	-72,5%	799	-75,5%	196
INDUSTRY TOTAL	3.857	2.715	-29,6%	22.236	19.542	-12,1%	8.828		7.025
Purchasing and Sales	14.378	11.515	-19,9%	29.862	24.573	-17,7%	13.340	-18,8%	10.830
Banking	115	109	-5,2%	5.574	3.818	-31,5%	3.471	-18,4%	2.834
Insurances	153	57	-62,7%	2.105	1.434	-31,9%	1.065	-47,3%	561
Commercial Intermediaries	391	282	-27,9%	2.241	1.795	-19,9%	995	-23,9%	757
Hotels	844	532	-37,0%	1.609	1.521	-5,5%	1.452	-21,2%	1.144
Entertainment	89	43	-51,7%	400	327	-18,3%	239	-35,0%	155
COMMERCE TOTAL	15.970	12.538	-21,5%	41.791	33.468	-19,9%	20.562		16.282
INDUSTRY/COMMERCE TOTAL	19.827	15.253	-23,1%	64.027	53.010	-17,2%	29.390		23.307

Sources: see Table 16

Remark:
(c) Estimate 1920 = (1 + CORR. 20) x PC20
with CORR. 20 = (a+b) ÷ 2.

TABLE 18

Estimated employment level for white-collar workers and manual workers in positions of authority in industry on 31 October 1926

	In companies with more than 10 manual workers			In companies with fewer than 10 manual workers			Total white-collar workers and manual workers in authority		
	Males	Females	Total	Males	Females	Total	Males	Females	Total
Fishing	57	15	72	82	23	105	139	38	177
Mines	7.826	134	7.960	484	54	538	8.310	188	8.498
Quarries	1.963	114	2.077	199	43	242	2.162	157	2.319
Metal	20.937	2.884	23.821	1.650	513	2.163	22.587	3.397	25.984
Ceramics	1.346	164	1.510	143	23	165	1.489	187	1.675
Glass	1.519	151	1.670	177	35	212	1.696	186	1.882
Chemicals	6.789	1.036	7.825	1.143	283	1.427	7.932	1.319	9.252
Food	5.445	1.255	6.700	1.059	348	1.407	6.504	1.603	8.107
Textiles	6.242	1.507	7.749	372	112	484	6.614	1.619	8.233
Clothing	1.318	1.889	3.207	653	559	1.212	1.971	2.448	4.419
Construction	1.697	302	1.999	273	124	398	1.970	426	2.397
Wood and Upholstery	1.722	512	2.234	399	151	550	2.121	663	2.784
Hides and Leather	1.355	540	1.895	162	77	239	1.517	617	2.134
Tobacco	707	274	981	99	25	124	806	299	1.105
Paper	865	212	1.077	64	20	84	929	232	1.161
Books	1.771	567	2.338	236	92	329	2.007	659	2.667
Art and Precision Work	1.863	695	2.558	432	236	668	2.295	931	3.226
Transport	4.726	220	4.946	1.028	105	1.133	5.754	325	6.079
INDUSTRY TOTAL	68.148	12.471	80.619	8.656	2.823	11.479	76.804	15.294	92.098

Sources:
- Number of white-collar workers and manual workers in authority in companies with more than 10 manual workers: Enquête sur la situation des industries 1926, vol. II, p. 16.
- Number of white-collar workers in companies with fewer than 10 manual workers: own estimate based on proportions in ESC 1937, vol II. pp. 8-25 (see text).
- Transport = own estimate: see text.

TABLE 19

Percentage of manual workers in authority in combined total of white-collar workers and manual workers in authority on 27 february 1937

	Men	Women
Fishing	98,2%	0,0%
Mines	70,2%	6,8%
Quarries	44,2%	0,0%
Metal	30,5%	2,2%
Cermaics	41,7%	4,0%
Glass	36,5%	3,8%
Chemicals	23,3%	9,6%
Food	18,3%	20,1%
Textiles	42,5%	29,9%
Clothing	18,2%	38,0%
Construction	51,5%	1,2%
Wood and Upholstery	29,6%	5,3%
Hides and Leather	24,8%	16,8%
Tobacco	23,1%	35,7%
Paper	29,6%	12,1%
Books	14,6%	2,5%
Art and Precision Work	20,7%	10,9%
Transport	14,5%	0,0%
Purchasing and Sale	15,9%	52,7%
Banking	0,1%	0,0%
Insurance	0,4%	0,2%
Commercial Intermediaries	2,1%	1,0%
Hotels	31,8%	14,5%
Entertainment	5,5%	2,5%

Source: own calculation on basis of ESC 1937, vol. I, p. 87; vol. II, pp. 8-27, vol. III, pp. 54-55.

TABLE 20

Estimated level of unemployment of white-collar workers in industry and commerce

year	(1)	(2)	(3)	(4)	(5)	(6)	(7)	(8)	(9)	year
1920	4,7%	12,6%	2,69	2,69	12,6%	4,7%			4,7%	1920
1921				2,76	12,1%	4,4%			4,4%	1921
1922				2,83	3,9%	1,4%			1,4%	1922
1923				2,90	1,6%	0,5%			0,5%	1923
1924				2,97	1,3%	0,4%			0,4%	1924
1925				3,04	1,9%	0,6%			0,6%	1925
1926				3,11	1,8%	0,6%			0,6%	1926
1927				3,18	2,3%	0,7%			0,7%	1927
1928				3,24	1,2%	0,4%			0,4%	1928
1929				3,31	1,7%	0,5%			0,5%	1929
1930	3,4%	11,5%	3,38	3,38	4,3%	1,3%			1,3%	1930
1931				3,24	12,4%	3,8%			3,8%	1931
1932				3,09	20,2%	6,5%			6,5%	1932
1933				2,95	18,8%	6,4%			6,4%	1933
1934				2,80	20,5%	7,3%			7,3%	1934
1935				2,66	18,8%	7,1%			7,1%	1935
1936	5,4%	12,8%	2,37	2,51	12,9%	5,1%	5,1%	6,5%	6,5%	1936
1937				2,37	10,6%	4,5%	3,5%	4,5%	4,5%	1937
1938				2,37	12,8%	5,4%	3,6%	4,6%	4,6%	1938
1939				2,37	15,6%	6,6%	4,0%	5,1%	5,1%	1939

(1) Level of unemployment of white-collar workers in industry and commerce (including transport) in reference years.
    1920 = 15 April 1920 (own calculation based on Enquête sur la situation des employés privés (15 avril 1920), p. 5).
    1930 = 31 December 1930 (own calculation: see Table 14).
    1937 = 27 February 1937 (own calculation: see Table 15).
(2) Level of unemployment of manual workers in industry (excluding transport) in sample years.
    1920 = yearly average.
    1930 = 31 December 1930.
    1937 = 27 February 1937.
    Source: GOOSSENS M. et al., Interwar Unemployment in Belgium, pp. 303-304.
(3) Ratio of unemployed manual workers to unemployed white-collar workers in sample years = (2) ÷ (1).
(4) Estimated ratio of unemployed manual workers to unemployed white-collar workers in all years. 1920-1937 = linear interpolation of (3); 1938-1939 = 1937 figure.
(5) Level of unemployment of manual workers in industry: yearly averages. Source: see (2).
(6) Estimate of level of unemployment of white-collar workers in industry and commerce = (5) ÷ (4).
(7) Level of unemployment of insured white-collar workers (Belgische economische statistieken 1929-1940, p. 385).
(8) Estimated level of unemployment of white-collar workers in industry and commerce (1936-1939) = (7) x 4.5 ÷ 3.5.
(9) Level of unemployment included for white-collar workers in industry and commerce. 1930-1935: (6); 1936-1939: (8).

Remark: the level of unemployment refers only to the number of fully unemployed persons.

TABLE 21

Employment, level of unemployment and total workforce of white-collar workers (excluding manual workers in positions of authority) in census years

	Men			Women		
	(1)	(2)	(3)	(1)	(2)	(3)
	INDUSTRY			**INDUSTRY**		
1920	35.000	4,1%	36.496	5.884	3,3%	6.085
1926	51.460	0,5%	51.719	12.933	0,4%	12.985
1930	57.401	3,0%	59.176	16.645	2,4%	17.054
1937	65.158	4,8%	68.443	15.589	3,6%	16.171
	PURCHASING AND SALES			**PURCHASING AND SALES**		
1920	15.521	5,0%	16.338	5.124	3,7%	5.321
1926						
1930	22.952	3,6%	23.809	11.626	2,7%	11.949
1937	26.624	4,3%	27.820	13.608	3,8%	14.146
	BANKING			**BANKING**		
1920	15.112	4,8%	15.874	2.833	4,1%	2.954
1926						
1930	23.266	3,5%	24.110	3.817	3,0%	3.935
1937	16.313	10,5%	18.227	2.533	5,4%	2.678
	INSURANCES			**INSURANCES**		
1920	4.407	4,8%	4.629	560	4,1%	584
1926						
1930	4.442	3,5%	4.603	1.431	3,0%	1.475
1937	5.446	10,5%	6.085	1.876	5,4%	1.983
	COMMERCIAL INTERMEDIARIES			**COMMERCIAL INTERMEDIARIES**		
1920	3.847	4,8%	4.041	750	4,1%	782
1926						
1930	6.005	3,5%	6.223	1.778	3,0%	1.833
1937	6.998	10,5%	7.819	2.012	5,4%	2.127
	HOTELS			**HOTELS**		
1920	529	4,8%	556	978	4,1%	1.020
1926						
1930	678	3,5%	703	1.301	3,0%	1.341
1937	799	10,5%	893	773	5,4%	817
	ENTERTAINMENT			**ENTERTAINMENT**		
1920	239	4,8%	251	151	4,1%	157
1926						
1930	482	3,5%	499	319	3,0%	329
1937	1.275	10,5%	1.425	608	5,4%	643

Sources and Remarks :
(1) Employment: 1920 = 31 December; 1926 = 31 October; 1930 = 31 December; 1937 = 27 February.

The employment figures were obtained as follows :

	Ewc	=	(1 X) x Ewc+mwa
where	Ewc	=	employment of white-collar workers
	Ewc+mwa	=	employment of white-collar workers + manual workers in authority (see Tables 14-18)
	X	=	proportion of manual workers in authority in total number of white-collar workers + manual workers in authority (see Table 19).

(2) Level of unemployment: 1920 = 15 April 1920; 1926 = yearly average; 1930 = 31 December; 1937 = 27 February.

Sources:

1920 and 1926 = own calculation based on Table 20 (level of unemployment of all white-collar workers in industry and commerce in 1920 and 1926 respectively) and Table 14 (differentiation of unemployment figures by sector and sex based on unemployment figures on 31 December 1930).

1930 = Table 14

1937 = Table 15.

(3) Workforce = (1) x [1 + (2)].

Remarks:

for the banking, insurance, commercial intermediaries, hotels and entertainment sectors, the average unemployment figure was included because only an aggregate unemployment figure was published for these sectors in the 1937 census.

TABLE 22

Employment of white-collar workers (excluding manual workers in positions of authority) in industry and commerce: 1920-1939

year	(1)	(2)	(3)	(4)	(5)	(6)	(7)	(8)	(9)	(10)	(11)	(12)	(13)	(14)	(15)	(16)	(17)	year
1920	34.984	15.526	15.107	4.405	3.846	529	239	74.635	5.883	5.123	2.832	560	750	978	150	16.275	90.910	1920
1921	37.523	16.292	15.944	4.418	4.067	545	263	79.052	7.011	5.775	2.934	647	853	1.011	167	18.399	97.452	1921
1922	41.067	17.573	17.274	4.559	4.414	577	296	85.760	8.304	6.574	3.112	753	980	1.071	189	20.983	106.744	1922
1923	43.896	18.472	18.242	4.595	4.669	597	324	90.796	9.498	7.278	3.233	847	1.092	1.111	208	23.267	114.063	1923
1924	46.465	19.237	19.082	4.598	4.892	612	349	95.235	10.652	7.945	3.334	937	1.198	1.144	225	25.434	120.669	1924
1925	48.917	19.944	19.866	4.587	5.100	626	373	99.413	11.784	8.593	3.426	1.024	1.300	1.174	242	27.543	126.956	1925
1926	51.450	20.691	20.689	4.585	5.318	640	397	103.770	12.931	9.254	3.524	1.113	1.405	1.206	259	29.692	133.462	1926
1927	53.245	21.404	21.480	4.577	5.527	654	421	107.309	13.932	9.904	3.618	1.200	1.508	1.237	276	31.674	138.983	1927
1928	55.272	22.230	22.380	4.591	5.765	671	448	111.358	14.982	10.593	3.727	1.293	1.618	1.273	294	33.779	145.137	1928
1929	57.058	22.940	23.166	4.582	5.974	685	472	114.877	15.980	11.241	3.820	1.380	1.720	1.303	310	35.755	150.631	1929
1930	58.515	23.490	23.796	4.543	6.142	694	492	117.673	16.902	11.829	3.891	1.459	1.813	1.326	325	37.544	155.217	1930
1931	58.447	23.425	22.232	4.600	6.163	698	603	116.169	16.472	11.895	3.626	1.494	1.810	1.222	361	36.881	153.050	1931
1932	58.259	23.354	20.541	4.603	6.117	694	699	114.268	16.041	11.947	3.362	1.523	1.803	1.120	394	36.189	150.457	1932
1933	59.589	23.990	19.635	4.764	6.282	713	815	115.789	15.944	12.271	3.195	1.592	1.843	1.050	436	36.331	152.119	1933
1934	60.295	24.367	18.394	4.831	6.325	719	911	115.843	15.722	12.488	2.993	1.643	1.862	969	473	36.151	151.993	1934
1935	61.661	25.028	17.534	4.987	6.485	739	1.022	117.456	15.635	12.820	2.829	1.712	1.903	901	515	36.315	153.770	1935
1936	63.221	25.761	16.805	5.177	6.690	763	1.139	119.557	15.581	13.184	2.674	1.788	1.951	835	560	36.571	156.128	1936
1937	65.712	26.826	16.636	5.554	7.137	815	1.301	123.980	15.687	13.699	2.558	1.894	2.032	780	614	37.264	161.244	1937
1938	66.904	27.349	15.826	5.731	7.325	838	1.417	125.390	15.551	13.990	2.383	1.961	2.069	708	656	37.318	162.708	1938
1939	67.849	27.783	14.896	5.859	7.450	853	1.521	126.210	15.374	14.240	2.200	2.019	2.098	633	695	37.259	163.470	1939

(1) Male white-collar workers in industry
(2) purchasing and sales
(3) banking
(4) insurance
(5) commercial intermediaries
(6) hotels
(7) entertainment
(8) Total male white-collar workers = (1)+(2)+(3)+(4)+(5)+(7).
(9) Female white-collar workers in industry
(10) purchasing and sales
(11) banking
(12) insurance
(13) commercial intermediaries
(14) hotels
(15) entertainment
(16) Total female white-collar workers = (9)+(10)+(11)+(12)+(14)+(15).
(17) Total male and female white-collar workers = (8)+(16).

Method of calculation: see text.

TABLE 23

Estimate of average pay of white-collar workers in 1937

		(1)	(2)	(3)	(4)	(5)	(6)	(7)	(8)	(9)	(10)	(11)
INDUSTRY	Men	65.712	4.689	65.000	8.128	30.000	52.895	1.666	19.992	24.442	2,5%	26.055
	Women	15.687					15.687	871	10.452	10.452	2,1%	11.098
PURCHASING AND SALES	Men	26.826			8.973		17.853	1.457	17.484	21.670	2,4%	23.078
	Women	13.699					13.699	723	8.676	8.676	1,6%	9.167
BANKING	Man	16.636	1.079	65.000			15.557	1.542	18.504	21.520	7,7%	24.104
	Women	2.558					2.558	1.037	12.444	12.444	8,2%	14.003
INSURANCE	Man	5.554	105	65.000			5.449	1.637	19.644	20.501	2,3%	21.812
	Women	1.894					1.894	1.027	12.324	12.324	2,5%	13.137
COMMERCIAL INTERMEDIARIES	Man	7.137	702	65.000			6.435	1.591	19.092	23.608	6,3%	26.099
	Women	2.032					2.032	977	11.724	11.724	6,3%	12.961
HOTEL	Man	815					815	1.486	17.832	17.832	2,0%	18.916
	Women	780					780	733	8.796	8.796	2,0%	9.331
ENTERTAINMENT	Man	1.301					1.301	1.306	15.672	15.672	2,0%	16.625
	Women	614					614	800	9.600	9.600	2,0%	10.184
TOTAL	Man	123.981	6.575	65.000	17.101	30.000	100.305	1.597	19.165	23.090		
	Women	37.264					37.264	838	10.052	10.052		

(1) Total number of white-collar workers (excluding manual workers in authority) for the whole of 1937 (see Table 23).
(2) Estimated number of white-collar workers with annual earnings of over BF 50,000: see text.
(3) Average annual pay of white-collar workers with annual earnings of over BF 50,000 in February 1937 (excluding any 13th month and bonus payments) = own calculation.
(4) Estimate of number of commercial travellers: see text.
(5) Average annual pay of commercial travellers in February 1937 + own estimate.
(6) Number of white-collar workers with annual earnings below BF 50,000 excluding commercial travellers = (1)-(2)-(4).
(7) Average monthly pay of white-collar workers with annual earnings of less than BF 50,000 excluding commercial travellers in February 1937. Source: industry: ESC 1937, vol. IV, p. 50; purchasing and sales: own calculation based on ESC 1937, vol. V, p. 40; other sectors: ESC 1937, vol. V, p. 40.
(8) Average annual pay of white-collar workers with annual earnings of less than BF 50,000 excluding commercial travellers, based on monthly earnings in February 1937 = (7) x 12.
Remark: this figure takes no account of any 13th month or bonus payments.
(9) Average annual pay of all white-collar workers (excluding any 13th month and bonus payments) based on monthly earnings for February 1937 = [(2) x (3) + (4) x (5) + (6) x (8)] ÷ (1).
(10) Incremental factor for any 13th month or bonus payments: see text.
(11) Average annual pay of all white-collar workers including any 13th month and bonus payments, and including an incremental factor for rise in pay in the course of 1937 (estimate: 4%) = (9) x 1.04 x [1+(10)].

TABLE 24

Combined index of average pay of railway staff and average hourly wage of skilled manual workers in industry

year	(1)	(2)	(3)	(4)	year
1920	5.262	32,1	41,3	36,7	1920
1921	5.873	35,8	44,3	40,1	1921
1922	5.799	35,3	44,1	39,7	1922
1923	6.451	39,3	50,3	44,8	1923
1924	8.799	53,6	57,1	55,4	1924
1925	9.369	57,1	57,1	57,1	1925
1926	10.676	65,1	63,6	64,3	1926
1927	13.533	82,5	76,5	79,5	1927
1928	14.472	88,2	85,6	86,9	1928
1929	16.620	101,3	101,4	101,4	1929
1930	17.544	106,9	107,2	107,1	1930
1931	17.356	105,8	100,2	103,0	1931
1932	16.482	100,5	90,9	95,7	1932
1933	15.551	94,8	88,5	91,7	1933
1934	15.050	91,7	85,1	88,4	1934
1935	14.639	89,2	82,3	85,7	1935
1936	15.724	95,8	89,4	92,6	1936
1937	16.407	100,0	100,0	100,0	1937
1938	17.981	109,6	105,0	107,3	1938
1939	18.059	110,1	106,2	108,1	1939

(1) Average pay of railway staff (own calculation based on Annual Reports of State Railways and NMBS).
(2) Index of average pay of railway staff (1937 = 100).
(3) Index of average hourly wage for skilled manual workers in industry (1937 = 100). CASSIERS I., Une statistique des salaires horaires, p. 73.
(4) Combined index = mathematical average of (2) and (3).

TABLE 25

Total pay of white-collar workers (excluding manual workers in positions of authority) in industry and commerce: 1920-1939 (in BF millions)

year	(1)	(2)	(3)	(4)	(5)	(6)	(7)	(8)	(9)	(10)	(11)	(12)	(13)	(14)	(15)	(16)	(17)	(18)	(19)	year
1920	334	131	134	35	37	4	1	7	683	24	17	15	3	4	3	1	1	66	750	1920
1921	392	151	154	39	43	4	2	8	791	31	21	16	3	4	4	1	1	82	873	1921
1922	425	161	165	40	46	4	2	9	852	37	24	17	4	5	4	1	1	92	944	1922
1923	513	191	197	45	55	5	2	10	1.018	47	30	20	5	6	5	1	1	115	1.133	1923
1924	670	246	255	56	71	6	3	14	1.320	65	40	26	7	9	6	1	1	156	1.476	1924
1925	728	263	273	57	76	7	4	15	1.422	75	45	27	8	10	6	1	2	174	1.596	1925
1926	862	307	321	64	89	8	4	18	1.674	92	55	32	9	12	7	2	2	211	1.884	1926
1927	1.103	393	411	79	115	10	6	22	2.138	123	72	40	13	16	9	2	3	277	2.416	1927
1928	1.252	446	469	87	131	11	6	25	2.427	144	84	45	15	18	10	3	3	323	2.750	1928
1929	1.507	537	566	101	158	13	8	31	2.920	180	104	54	18	23	12	3	3	399	3.319	1929
1930	1.632	580	614	106	172	14	9	33	3.161	201	116	58	21	25	13	3	4	442	3.603	1930
1931	1.568	557	552	103	166	14	10	31	3.001	188	112	52	20	24	12	4	4	417	3.418	1931
1932	1.452	516	474	96	153	13	11	29	2.742	170	105	45	19	22	10	4	4	379	3.122	1932
1933	1.423	507	434	95	150	12	12	27	2.662	162	103	41	19	22	9	4	3	364	3.025	1933
1934	1.389	497	392	93	146	12	13	25	2.568	154	101	37	19	21	8	4	3	348	2.916	1934
1935	1.377	495	362	93	145	12	15	24	2.524	149	101	34	19	21	7	5	3	339	2.863	1935
1936	1.525	550	375	105	162	13	18	26	2.774	160	112	35	22	23	7	5	3	368	3.141	1936
1937	1.712	619	401	121	186	15	22	27	3.104	174	126	36	25	26	7	6	3	404	3.507	1937
1938	1.870	677	409	134	205	17	25	28	3.366	185	138	36	28	29	7	7	4	433	3.799	1938
1939	1.911	693	388	138	210	17	27	28	3.414	184	141	33	29	29	6	8	3	435	3.849	1939

(1) Male white-collar workers in industry
(2) purchasing and sales
(3) banking
(4) insurance
(5) commercial intermediaries
(6) hotels
(7) entertainment
(8) offices of colonial companies
(9) Total pay of male white-collar workers = sum of (1) to (8)
(10) Female white-collar workers in industry
(11) purchasing and sales
(12) banking
(13) insurance
(14) commercial intermediaries
(15) hotels
(16) entertainment
(17) offices of colonial companies
(18) Total pay of female white-collar workers = sum of (10) to (17).
(19) Total pay of male and female white-collar workers in industry and commerce = (9) + (18).

TABLE 26

Estimate of pay of white-collar workers not listed in the industrial and commercial censuses

year	(1)	(2)	(3)	(4)	(5)	(6)	(7)	(8)	(9)	(10)	(11)	year
1920	14.818					8.393		8.393	3.460	29	135	1920
1921			14.818	7.167	106			8.694	3.779	33	149	1921
1922			14.879	7.828	116			8.994	3.748	34	150	1922
1923			14.940	7.764	116			9.295	4.227	39	171	1923
1924			15.001	8.757	131			9.596	5.223	50	213	1924
1925			15.062	10.819	163			9.897	5.387	53	222	1925
1926			15.123	11.158	169			10.197	6.068	62	253	1926
1927			15.183	12.571	191			10.498	7.497	79	315	1927
1928			15.244	15.531	237			10.799	8.198	89	348	1928
1929			15.305	16.982	260			11.099	9.562	106	410	1929
1930	15.427	100,0	15.366	19.807	304	11.400	100,0	11.400	10.100	115	438	1930
1931		98,6	15.427	20.922	323		98,6	11.245	9.716	109	416	1931
1932		96,9	15.218	20.126	306		97,2	11.080	9.024	100	380	1932
1933		98,1	14.953	18.694	280		98,0	11.169	8.647	97	368	1933
1934		98,0	15.133	17.912	271		97,9	11.160	8.340	93	354	1934
1935		99,2	15.120	17.276	261		98,7	11.255	8.088	91	348	1935
1936		100,9	15.311	16.754	257		99,8	11.379	8.735	99	381	1936
1937		104,6	15.566	18.094	282		102,1	11.637	9.433	110	425	1937
1938		105,7	16.130	19.541	315		102,6	11.699	10.120	118	460	1938
1939		106,2	16.300	20.964	342		102,9	11.725	10.200	120	466	1939
			16.391	21.130	346							

(1) Number of male white-collar workers not listed in the industrial and commercial censuses = estimate based on the PC 1920 and 1930.
(2) Index of number of male white-collar workers in industry and commerce = based on Table 22, column 8.
(3) Number of male white-collar workers in the industrial and commercial censuses:
   - 1920-1930 : linear interpolation of (1)
   - 1930-1939 : 1930 figure x (2).
(4) Estimate of average annual pay of male white-collar workers not listed in the industrial and commercial censuses = 75% of the average annual pay of white-collar workers in industry (see text).
(5) Total pay in BF millions of male white-collar workers not listed in the industrial and commercial censuses = (3) x (4) ÷ 1,000,000.
(6) Number of female white-collar workers not listed in the industrial and commercial censuses = estimate based on the population censuses of 1920 and 1930.
(7) Index of number of female white-collar workers in industry and commerce = based on Table 22, column 16.
(8) Number of female white-collar workers not listed in the industrial and commercial censuses:
   - 1920-1930 : linear interpolation of (6)
   - 1930-1939 : figure of 1930 x (7).
(9) Estimate of average annual pay of female white-collar workers not listed in the industrial and commercial censuses = 85% of the average annual pay of female white-collar workers in industry (see text).
(10) Total pay in BF millions of female white-collar workers not listed in industrial and commercial censuses = (8) x (9) ÷ 1,000,000.
(11) Total pay in BF millions of male and female white-collar workers not listed in the industrial and commercial censuses = (5) + (10).

TABLE 27

Total wagebill of domestic staff, border-workers and seasonal workers employed abroad. Summary table (in BF millions)

year	(1)	(2)	(3)	(4)	year
1920	369	85	55	140	1920
1921	375	76	82	158	1921
1922	376	98	58	156	1922
1923	474	155	58	213	1923
1924	526	204	99	303	1924
1925	619	219	116	335	1925
1926	674	301	146	447	1926
1927	848	608	216	823	1927
1928	936	831	254	1.085	1928
1929	1.142	923	263	1.185	1929
1930	1.320	986	278	1.264	1930
1931	1.318	729	249	979	1931
1932	1.255	626	187	813	1932
1933	1.237	625	85	710	1933
1934	1.202	597	145	742	1934
1935	1.190	615	164	779	1935
1936	1.184	747	217	963	1936
1937	1.179	724	202	926	1937
1938	1.203	630	151	780	1938
1939	1.215	388	93	481	1939

(1) Total wagebill of domestic staff at current prices: see Table 31 column 4.
(2) Total wagebill of border-workers at current prices: see Table 35 column 5.
(3) Total wagebill of seasonal workers employed abroad at current prices: see Table 37 column 3.
(4) Total wagebill of border-workers and seasonal workers employed abroad at current prices = (4) + (7).

TABLE 28

Domestic staff in the censuses of 1920 and 1930

	1920			1930		
	Males	Females	Total	Males	Females	Total
GROUP I: GUARDING AND MANAGEMENT OF PROPERTY						
Stewards, administrators, managers, receivers	721	196	917	421	369	790
Special guards and watchmen of goods, yachts, fisheries, woods, etc.	3.864	124	3.988	3.889	31	3.920
Nightwatchmen not employed by a public agency	3.030	370	3.400	3.318	26	3.344
Total group I	7.615	690	8.305	7.628	426	8.054
GROUP II: DOMESTIC STAFF (1)						
Servants responsible for tending and leading animals	5.661	86.118	91.779	3.367	76.150	79.517
Personal servants	8.423	10.075	18.498	10.745	16.274	27.019
Servants responsible for tending and leading animals	8.654	1.180	9.834	4.095	528	4.623
Housekeepers, charwomen, cleaners	1.745	18.523	20.268	781	41.951	42.732
Lady companions, readers, private stenos, private secretaries	847	3.752	4.599	336	3.752	4.088
Total group II	25.330	119.648	144.978	19.324	138.655	157.979
OVERALL TOTAL	32.945	120.338	153.283	26.952	139.081	166.033

(1) Excluding hotel, restaurant and café staff.

Sources: OC 1920, vol. III, pp. 255 and 582.
PC 1930, vol. V, pp. 95 and 193.

TABLE 29

Domestic staff in the population censuses of 1910, 1920, 1930 and 1947

year	Males	Females	Total
1910	37.069	160.869	197.938
1920	32.945	120.338	153.283
1930	26.952	139.081	166.033
1947	13.154	102.085	115.239

Sources: - 1910 : PC 1920, vol. IV, pp. 237-237
        - 1920 : see Table 28
        - 1930 : see Table 28
        - 1947 : Private servants (8,854 M and 94,477 F) + firms engaged in the cleaning and maintenance of goods and premises: cleaners (194 M and 1,239 F) and ironers, linen glossers (106 M and 6,369 F) + general occupations: nightwatchmen, overseers (4,000 M = estimate)
(General Population, Industrial and Commercial Census 1947, vol. VIII, pp. 283 and 285).

TABLE 30

Wages of domestic staff in Bussels (in BF)

year	(1)	(2)	(3)	(4)	(5)	(6)	(7)	(8)	(9)	(10)	(11)	(12)	(13)	(14)	(15)	(16)	(17)	(18)	(19)	(20)	(21)	(22)	(23)	(24)	(25)	year
1920	158	53	204	51	113	38	117	47	85	38	133	41	171	35	2.640	50	1.613	48	3.960	35			100	30	36	1920
1921	188	63	338	84	163	54	138	55	103	46	175	54	250	51	2.640	50	1.613	48	3.960	35			100	30	40	1921
1922	213	71	332	83	175	58	175	70	138	61	200	62	288	59	2.640	50	1.613	48	3.960	35	2	41	100	38	39	1922
1923	225	75	300	75	200	67	175	70	138	61	200	62	350	72	2.640	50	1.653	50	4.140	37	2	55	126	38	42	1923
1924	227	76	300	75	225	75	225	90	138	61	275	85	350	72	3.887	74	1.653	50	4.140	37	2	58	139	42	49	1924
1925	271	90	394	99	292	97	233	93	197	88	325	100	414	85	3.976	75	2.533	76	6.530	58	2	58	163	50	50	1925
1926	300	100	400	100	300	100	250	100	225	100	325	100	486	100	4.830	91	2.533	76	6.577	59	3	66	177	54	56	1926
1927	383	128	442	111	341	114	329	132	254	113	366	113	656	135	5.280	100	3.333	100	9.669	86	3	76	222	68	67	1927
1928	464	155	541	135	429	143	387	155	275	122	438	135	698	144	5.760	109	3.333	100	11.195	100	4	100	245	74	78	1928
1929	475	158	600	150	450	150	400	160	275	122	450	138	750	154	5.800	110	5.340	160			5	125	298	90	94	1929
1930	475	158	600	150	400	133	350	140	275	122	450	138	688	141	5.760	109	6.200	186			6	144	343	104	100	1930
1931	454	151	600	150	379	126	350	140	275	122	450	138	688	141	5.760	109	5.340	160			5	123	344	105	94	1931
1932	450	150	600	150	350	117	350	140	275	122	450	138	651	134	5.760	109	5.340	160			4	109	329	100	85	1932
1933	450	150	600	150	350	117	350	140	275	122	450	138	625	129	5.472	104	5.073	152					326	99	83	1933
1934	450	150	600	150	350	117	350	140	275	122	450	138	625	129									318	97	79	1934
1935	450	150	600	150	350	117	350	140	275	122	450	138	625	129									317	96	76	1935
1936	450	150	600	150	350	117	350	140	275	122	450	138	625	129									317	96	85	1936
1937	450	150	600	150	350	117	400	160	275	122	450	138	625	129									317	96	96	1937
1938	456	152	600	150	356	119	400	160	275	122	450	138	625	129									325	99	100	1938
1939	475	158	600	150	375	125	400	160	275	122	450	138	625	129									329	100	100	1939

(1) Monthly wage of cook/servant-girl. Source: Scholliers, pp. 56-58 (Cf. below)
(2) Index of (1) with 1928 = 100.
(3) Monthly wage of cook. Source: Scholliers, pp. 56-58.
(4) Index of (3) with 1928 = 100.
(5) Monthly wage of a maid. Source: Scholliers, pp. 56-58.
(6) Index of (5) with 1928 = 100.
(7) Monthly wage of chambermaid. Source: Scholliers, pp. 56-58
(8) Index of (7) with 1928 = 100.
(9) Monthly wage of nanny. Source: Scholliers, pp. 59-60.
(10) Index of (9) with 1928 = 100.
(11) Monthly wage of servant. Source: Scholliers, pp. 59-60.
(12) Index of (11) with 1920 = 100.
(13) Monthly wage of charwoman - food provided. Source : Scholliers, 59-60.
(14) Index of (13) with 1928 = 100.
(15) Annual wage of charwoman in slaughterhouse. Source: Van den Eeckhout, p. 48.
(16) Index of (15) with 1928 = 100 .
(17) Annual wage of charwoman in the Stock Exchange. Source: Van den Eeckhout, p. 43.
(18) Index of (17) with 1928 = 100.
(19) Annual wage of nightwatchman. Source: Van den Eeckhout, pp. 47-48.
(20) Index of (19) with 1928 = 100
(21) Hourly wage of gardener. Source: Scholliers, p. 70.
(22) Index of (21) with 1928 = 100.
(23) Differential index for Brussels domestic staff (1920 = 100): See text.
(24) Differential index for wages of Brussels domestic staff (1939 = 100) on basis of (23).
(25) Index of unskilled workers in industry in Belgium (1939 = 100), Source: Cassiers, p. 73.

Sources: SCHOLLIERS P., Loonlijsten van de Brusselse Arbeidsbeurs 1922-1939, passim.
VAN DEN EECKHOUT P., Lonen van Brusselse arbeiders in openbare instellingen, passim.
CASSIERS I., Une statistique des salaires horaires dans l'industrie belge, 1919-1939, passim.

TABLE 31

Total wagebill of domestic staff (in BF millions)

year	(1)	(2)	(3)	(4)	year
1920	102	209	58	369	1920
1921	101	215	59	375	1921
1922	99	218	59	376	1922
1923	122	277	74	474	1923
1924	133	311	82	526	1924
1925	153	369	96	619	1925
1926	163	406	105	674	1926
1927	200	516	131	848	1927
1928	216	575	145	936	1928
1929	257	709	176	1.142	1929
1930	291	827	203	1.320	1930
1931	285	829	203	1.318	1931
1932	267	794	195	1.255	1932
1933	258	786	193	1.237	1933
1934	246	767	188	1.202	1934
1935	239	763	187	1.190	1935
1936	234	763	187	1.184	1936
1937	228	763	187	1.179	1937
1938	229	782	192	1.203	1938
1939	228	793	194	1.215	1939

(1) Men.
(2) Women (excluding part-time charwomen).
(3) Part-time charwomen.
(4) Total.

TABLE 32

Number of Belgian or West Flanders border-workers employed in the Departement du Nord or in France according to various sources

Year	Number	Description	Source + Date of Statistic	Reference
1910	40.300	Belgian border-workers in industry and commerce in France	Belgian occupational census (31 December)	THEYS, p. 36
1921	16.660	Belgian border-workers in France	French census	LENTACKER, p. 274
	12.660	Belgian border-workers in Département du Nord	French census	LENTACKER, p. 274; THEYS, p. 37
1926	36.850	Belgian border-workers in Département du Nord	French census (7 March)	LENTACKER, p. 276; THEYS, p. 37
	42.000	Belgian border-workers in France	French census (7 March)	LENTACKER, p. 276
1926-1928	100.000 (1)	Belgian border-workers in France	?	La main d'oevre, p. 38
1929	71.769 (2)	Belgians in possession of a border-workers' card for France	Centrale Dienst voor de Statistiek (= NIS), Driemaandblad, september 1930, p. 6-12	THEYS, p. 38
	61.322	Belgian border-workers in Département du Nord	Statistiek van het "Office Regional de la Main-d'Oevre Etrangere" te Rijsel (30 april)	THEYS, p. 37
	43.573 (2)	West Flemings possessing a border-workers' card for France	Centrale Dienst voor de Statistiek (= NIS), Driemaandblad, september 1930, p. 6-12	THEYS, p. 38
	46.000	West Flanders border-workers in France	Estimate of the Belgian Commissariat for border-workers' area	THEYS, p. 38
1930	79.626	Belgian border-workers in industry and commerce in France	Belgian occupational census (31 December)	Le recensement, p. 748-749
	70.000	Belgian border-workers in France	?	La main d'oevre, p. 38
	93.000	Belgian border-workers' in France	Estimate by Belgian trade union	LENTACKER, p. 276
	46.771	West Flanders border-workers in industry and commerce in France	Belgian occupational census (31 December)	Le recensement, p. 748-749
1931	55.787	Belgian and Luxembourg border-workers in France	French census	La main d'oevre, p. 38
1934	45.000	Belgian border-workers in Département du Nord (October)	Census of "L'Office Departemental du Nord" (October)	LENTACKER, p. 279
1935	28.000	Belgian border-workers in Département du Nord (October)	Census of "L'Office Departemental du Nord" (October)	LENTACKER, p. 279
	31.227	West Flanders border-workers in France	Estimate of the Belgian "Office de Redressement Economique (November)	THEYS, p. 41 en 172
	51.500	West Flanders border-workers in France	?	LENTACKER, p. 279
1936	45.284	Belgian and Luxembourg border-workers in France	French census	La main d'oevre, p. 38
	41.000	Belgian border-workers in Département du Nord	French census	LENTACKER, p. 279
	33.720	West Flemings in possession of a border-workers' card for France	? (early 1936)	THEYS, p. 41
	29.000	West Flanders border-workers in France	Estimate of the Belgian Commissariat for the border-workers' area (mid-1936)	THEYS, p. 41
1946	42.105	Belgian border-workers in France	Belgische telling uitgevoerd door het NIS en de Nationale Dienst van Arbeid en Werkloosheid (30 april)	Algemeene telling, p. 725-726
	39.739	Belgian border-workers in Département du Nord		
	28.760	West Flanders border-workers in France		
1948	54.915	Belgian border-workers in France	Belgische telling uitgevoerd door het Steunfonds voor Werklozen (eind maart)	Telling van de grensbeiders, p. 1120-1121
	51.603	Belgian border-workers in Département du Nord		
	38.170	West Flanders border-workers in France		

Sources:
- Algemeene telling van 30 April 1946 van de grensarbeiders die in Frankrijk gaan werken, pp. 724-733.
- La main d'oeuvre frontalière dans le nord de la France, pp. 36-51.
- IT 1930, pp. 719-771.
- LENTACKER F., La frontière franco-belge, passim.
- Telling van de grensarbeiders die naar Frankrijk gaan werken, pp. 1120-1125.
- THEYS J., Een analyse van de Westvlaamse grensarbeid in Noord-Frankrijk, passim.

Comments:
(1) According to Theys (p.38) probably overestimated.
(2) According to Theys (p.38) too low because various municipalities not included.

TABLE 33

Possible indicators for the evolution of the number of border-workers employed in France

year	(1)	(2)	(3)	year
1920	61		0,955	1920
1921	54		1,001	1921
1922	77		1,068	1922
1923	87		1,167	1923
1924	108		1,130	1924
1925	107		1,000	1925
1926	125		1,019	1926
1927	109		1,410	1927
1928	126		1,408	1928
1929	123		1,410	1929
1930	123	15.715	1,410	1930
1931	105	7.821	1,410	1931
1932	91	1.115	1,410	1932
1933	99	2.014	1,410	1933
1934	92	800	1,410	1934
1935	88		1,820	1935
1936	95		1,833	1936
1937	100		1,385	1937
1938	92		1,203	1938
1939			0,820	1939

(1) Industrial production in France (1937 = 100).
Source: MITCHELL B.R., European Historical Statistics 1750-1970, London, 1978, p. 180.
(2) Number of new border-workers' passes declared valid by the "Office regional de la main-d'oeuvre étrangère" in Lille. THEYS J., op. cit.
(3) Annual average exchange rate (number of BF for one FF) = own calculation on basis of JANSSEN V., De Belgische Frank, p. 429.
After the First World War there was a statutory parity of FF 1 = BF 1, but in practice there was a floating exchange rate ranging between the extremes of FF 1 = BF 1.242 in August 1923 and FF 1 = BF 0.809 in February 1926. After the stabilization of the BF on 25 October 1926, the parity hovered around FF 1 = BF 1.41. This parity became fixed on 25 June 1928 (stabilization of the FF), from which date there was a system of fixed exchange rates in both France and Belgium. On 31 March 1935 the BF devalued (FF 1 = BF 1.957). From 1 October 1936 the FF was subject to a series of devaluations (from 1 October 1936: FF 1 = BF 1.46; from 21 July 1937: FF 1 = BF 1.28; from 12 November 1938: FF 1 = BF 0.82).

Source: JANSSEN V., op. cit., p. 429, Belgische Economische Statistieken 1919-1928, p. 6.

TABLE 34

Average annual pay of border-workers employed in France
(including employers' social security contributions)

year	(1)	(2)	(3)	(4)	(5)	(6)	year
1920	15,1	4.447	0,0%	4.447	0,955	4.245	1920
1921	15,5	4.565	0,0%	4.565	1,001	4.567	1921
1922	13,6	4.010	4,0%	4.171	1,068	4.454	1922
1923	16,1	4.723	4,0%	4.912	1,167	5.732	1923
1924	18,4	5.416	4,0%	5.633	1,130	6.366	1924
1925	19,4	5.689	4,0%	5.917	1,000	5.919	1925
1926	23,0	6.763	4,0%	7.034	1,019	7.170	1926
1927	23,1	6.794	4,0%	7.066	1,410	9.962	1927
1928	24,1	7.097	4,0%	7.381	1,408	10.388	1928
1929	26,8	7.866	4,0%	8.181	1,410	11.535	1929
1930	28,7	8.434	10,5%	9.320	1,410	13.141	1930
1931	28,5	8.393	10,5%	9.274	1,410	13.076	1931
1932	27,3	8.034	10,5%	8.877	1,410	12.517	1932
1933	26,2	7.714	10,5%	8.524	1,410	12.019	1933
1934	26,1	7.666	10,5%	8.471	1,410	11.944	1934
1935	25,7	7.545	10,5%	8.337	1,820	13.657	1935
1936	30,6	9.006	11,0%	9.997	1,833	16.488	1936
1937	38,4	9.413	11,0%	10.448	1,385	14.471	1937
1938	42,8	10.477	11,0%	11.630	1,203	13.994	1938
1939	43,5	10.665	11,0%	11.838	0,820	9.707	1939

(1) Average daily wage of a border-worker in FF excluding employers' social security contributions
 - 1921 and 1924-1939:
 - wages in the French towns, with the exception of Paris, "d'après les évaluations des Conseils de prud'hommes ou des Maires"
 - weighted arithmetic average of the daily wage of a weaver (35%), turner (25%), bricklayer (10%), carpenter (5%), and female workers in the clothing industry (25%)
 - up to and including 1936: daily wages; from 1937: hourly wages x 8. Source: Statistique Générale de la France. Annuaire Statistique
 - 1920 and 1922-1923:
 - extrapolation and interpolation of above series on basis of miners' wages. Source: COMBE P., Niveau de vie et progrès technique en France, pp. 101 and 617 (wage series 3a).
(2) Average annual pay of border-worker in FF excluding employers' social security contributions:
 - 1920-1936 : daily wage (= column 1) x number of weekly working days (6) x number of working weeks (49);
 - 1937-1939 : daily wage (= column 1) x number of weekly working days (5) x number of working weeks (49);
(3) Employers' social security contributions. Source : COMBE P., op. cit., pp. 120-121 (see text).
(4) Average annual pay of border-worker in FF including employers' social security contributions = (2) x (1+(3)).
(5) Annual average exchange rate (number of BF for 1 FF) = own calculation on basis of JANSSEN V., De Belgische frank, p. 429.
(6) Average annual pay of border-worker in BF = (4) x (5).
 With the exception of 1935-1936 : (4) x (5) x 0.9 (see text).

TABLE 35

Total wagebill of Belgian border-workers employed in France
(including employers' social security contributions)

year	(1)	(2)	(3)	(4)	(5)	year
1920		20.000	20.000	4.245	85	1920
1921	16.660		16.660	4.567	76	1921
1922		22.000	22.000	4.454	98	1922
1923		27.000	27.000	5.732	155	1923
1924		32.000	32.000	6.366	204	1924
1925		37.000	37.000	5.919	219	1925
1926	42.000		42.000	7.170	301	1926
1927		61.000	61.000	9.962	608	1927
1928		80.000	80.000	10.388	831	1928
1929		80.000	80.000	11.535	923	1929
1930	79.626	75.000	75.000	13.141	986	1930
1931	55.787		55.787	13.076	729	1931
1932		50.000	50.000	12.517	626	1932
1933		52.000	52.000	12.019	625	1933
1934		50.000	50.000	11.944	597	1934
1935		45.000	45.000	13.657	615	1935
1936	45.284		45.284	16.488	747	1936
1937		50.000	50.000	14.471	724	1937
1938		45.000	45.000	13.994	630	1938
1939		40.000	40.000	9.707	388	1939

(1) Number of Belgian border-workers employed in France according to French (1921, 1926, 1931, 1936) and Belgian (1930) censuses: see Table 32.
(2) Interpolations and extrapolations for missing years and 1930 correction : see text.
(3) Average number of Belgian border-workers employed in France = (1) and (2).
(4) Average annual pay of Belgian border-workers employed in France: see Table 34 column 6.
(5) Total wagebill of Belgian border-workers employed in France in BF 1 million = (3) x (4) ÷ 1 million.

TABLE 36

Average annual pay of seasonal workers employed in France (including employers' social security contributions)

year	(1)	(2)	(3)	(4)	(5)	(6)	(7)	(8)	year
1920	11,6	15,1		11,6	11,6	2.603	0,955	2.485	1920
1921	12,1	15,5		12,1	12,1	2.723	1,001	2.724	1921
1922	12,1	13,6		12,1	12,1	2.727	1,068	2.912	1922
1923		16,1	14,2	14,2	14,8	3.334	1,167	3.891	1923
1924	16,3	18,4		16,3	17,0	3.817	1,130	4.314	1924
1925		19,4	17,1	17,1	17,8	4.008	1,000	4.010	1925
1926	20,4	23,0		20,4	21,2	4.764	1,019	4.856	1926
1927		23,1	21,1	21,1	21,9	4.933	1,410	6.956	1927
1928	22,7	24,1		22,7	23,6	5.312	1,408	7.476	1928
1929		26,8	24,1	24,1	25,1	5.645	1,410	7.959	1929
1930	24,8	28,7		24,8	25,8	5.803	1,410	8.183	1930
1931		28,5	25,2	25,2	26,2	5.898	1,410	8.316	1931
1932	24,6	27,3		24,6	25,6	5.766	1,410	8.130	1932
1933		26,2	23,5	23,5	24,4	5.495	1,410	7.747	1933
1934	23,2	26,1		23,2	24,1	5.419	1,410	7.641	1934
1935		25,7	21,4	21,4	22,3	5.016	1,820	9.129	1935
1936		30,6	24,1	24,1	25,0	5.630	1,833	10.317	1936
1937		38,4	28,4	28,4	29,5	6.640	1,385	9.196	1937
1938	29,7	42,8		29,7	30,9	6.950	1,203	8.363	1938
1939		43,5	30,2	30,2	31,4	7.074	0,820	5.801	1939

(1) Daily wages (in FF) of male day labourers in France excluding employers' social security contributions. Source: COMBE P., op. cit., p. 617.
(2) Average daily wages (in FF) of male and female border-workers excluding employers' social security contributions (Table 34 column 1).
(3) Interpolations and extrapolations of (1): trend-corrected interpolation and extrapolation of (1) on basis of evolution (2).
(4) Daily wages (in FF) of male day labourers excluding social security contributions = (1) and (3).
(5) Daily wages (in FF) of male day labourers excluding social security contributions: 1920-1922 = (4); 1923-1939 = (4) + 4%.
(6) Annual pay (in FF) of seasonal workers = (5) , 8 x 1,800.
(7) Annual average exchange rate (number of BF for FF 1) = own calculation on basis of JANSSEN V., De Belgische frank, p. 429.
(8) Annual pay (in BF) of seasonal workers = (6) x (7).

TABLE 37

Total wagebill of seasonal workers employed in France (including benefits in kind and employer social security contributions) (in BF millions)

year	(1)	(2)	(3)	year
1920	22.000	2.485	55	1920
1921	30.000	2.724	82	1921
1922	20.000	2.912	58	1922
1923	15.000	3.891	58	1923
1924	23.000	4.314	99	1924
1925	29.000	4.010	116	1925
1926	30.000	4.856	146	1926
1927	31.000	6.956	216	1927
1928	34.000	7.476	254	1928
1929	33.000	7.959	263	1929
1930	34.000	8.183	278	1930
1931	30.000	8.316	249	1931
1932	23.000	8.130	187	1932
1933	11.000	7.747	85	1933
1934	19.000	7.641	145	1934
1935	18.000	9.129	164	1935
1936	21.000	10.317	217	1936
1937	22.000	9.196	202	1937
1938	18.000	8.363	151	1938
1939	16.000	5.801	93	1939

(1) Number of seasonal workers (LENTACKER F., op. cit., p. 394).
(2) Average annual pay in BF (see Table 10 column 9).
(3) Total wagebill (in BF million) = (1) x (2) ÷ 1 million.

TABLE 38

Statutory employer's social security contribution (in BF millions)

year	(1)	(2)	(3)	(4)	(5)	(6)	(7)	(8)	year
1920	32					32	83	114	1920
1921	28					28	91	119	1921
1922	24					24	99	123	1922
1923	32					32	122	154	1923
1924	39					39	141	181	1924
1925	40					40	142	182	1925
1926	48	18	30			96	164	260	1926
1927	69	30	74			173	210	383	1927
1928	64	32	86			183	242	426	1928
1929	71	34	103		1	208	302	509	1929
1930	78	35	116		1	230	355	584	1930
1931	84	46	184	213	1	528	295	823	1931
1932	56	97	150	243	1	548	242	790	1932
1933	58	101	148	271	1	579	233	812	1933
1934	55	98	150	257	1	560	216	777	1934
1935	56	98	149	197	1	500	219	720	1935
1936	64	111	160	274	1	610	250	860	1936
1937	94	127	173	389	1	784	300	1084	1937
1938	135	138	182	435	1	891	300	1190	1938
1939	128	130	178	401	1	838	281	1119	1939

(1) Employers' contributions to mineworkers' pensions (Annual Reports of National Pension Fund for Mineworkers).
(2) Employers' contributions to manual workers' pensions (1926: own estimate; 1927-1939: Annual Reports of ASLK: 50% of compulsory payments, excluding those of manual workers not employed by companies).
(3) Employers' contributions to white-collar workers' pensions (see Table 39, column 5).
(4) Employers' contributions to family allowances (see Table 40, column 6).
(5) Employers' contributions to job-related sickness benefit (1932: JULIN A., op. cit., p. 122; other years: own estimate).
(6) Total employers' contribution (excluding industrial accident insurance) = (1)+(2)+(3)+(4)+(5).
(7) Employers' contribution to industrial accident insurance (see Table 41, column 3).
(8) Total employers' contribution (including industrial accident insurance) at current prices = (6)+(7).

TABLE 39

Employers' contribution to white-collar workers' pensions (in BF millions)

year	(1)	(2)	(3)	(4)	(5)	year
1926	30				30	1926
1927	74				74	1927
1928	86				86	1928
1929	103				103	1929
1930	116				116	1930
1931	184				184 (*)	1931
1932	24	40	64	22	150	1932
1933	23	40	63	23	148	1933
1934	22	40	63	24	150	1934
1935	22	40	62	25	149	1935
1936	23	44	67	26	160	1936
1937	25	47	73	27	173	1937
1938	28	50	78	26	182	1938
1939	27	50	76	25	178	1939

(1) Employers' contributions to ASLK. 1926-1931: total deposits x 5/8; 1932-1939: total deposits x 4/7 (Annual Reports ASLK).
(2) Employers' contributions to National Fund for White-Collar Workers' Pensions (NKB). Total payments x 4/7 (Annual Reports of National Fund for White-Collar Workers' Pensions).
(3) Estimate of employers' contributions to private insurance companies and funds (1932-1939) = (1)+(2).
(4) Estimate of employers' contributions to Benefit Fund for White-Collar Workers (TB). 1932: total payments x 120/157; 1933: total payments x 120/155; 1938: total payments x 120/142; 1939: total payments x 120/143. (Annual Reports of Benefit Fund for White-Collar Workers).
(5) Total employers' contributions = (1)+(2)+(3)+(4).

(*): The high contribution for 1931 is due to a change introduced during that year in the period for which payments were made. Before 1931 payments were for the period from one birthday to the next of the fund-member, thereafter for a calendar year. In 1931 payments included contributions both for the calendar year 1931 and the period between the fund-member's 1930 and 1931 birthdays, and for the period between the employee's 1931 birthday and the end of the calendar year (Annual Report ASLK 1932, p. 30). For example, if the member's birthday fell on 1 July, then the 1930 payment covered the period 1 July 1929-30 June 1930, the 1931 payment the period 1 July 1930-31 December 1931, and the 1932 payment the period 1 January 1932-31 December 1932.

TABLE 40

Employers' contributions to family allowances (in BF millions)

year	(1)	(2)	(3)	(4)	(5)	(6)	year
1920					0		1920
1921	1	1	15.000	4.745	1		1921
1922	5	6	95.000	4.611	9		1922
1923	4	10	160.000	5.325	17		1923
1924	1	11	175.000	6.174	22		1924
1925	2	13	205.000	6.163	25		1925
1926	2	15	235.000	7.011	33		1926
1927		19	300.000	8.574	51		1927
1928		?	350.000	9.590	67		1928
1929		44	581.605	11.164	130		1929
1930		?	600.000	12.013	144		1930
1931						213	1931
1932						243	1932
1933						271	1933
1934						257	1934
1935						197	1935
1936						274	1936
1937						389	1937
1938						435	1938
1939						401	1939

(1) Number of new funds, 1921-1926: DE LEENER G., Les Caisses, pp. 15-16.
(2) Number of funds, 1921-1926: own calculation based on (1); 1927 and 1929: DE LEENER G., Vingt-cinq années, p. 47.
(3) Estimate of number of affiliated employees, 1927 and 1929: DE LEENER G., Vingt-cinq années, p. 48; other years: own estimate based on (2) and development of legislation.
(4) Estimate of average annual wage = weighted average hourly wage for manual workers in industry and commerce in February 1937 (BF 4.42) x incremental factor for whole of 1937 (1.043) x time worked (2,400 hours) x index of hourly wages for industry.
Sources. Hourly wage: own calculation based on ESC 1937, vol. IV, pp. 49 and 77; vol. V, pp. 38 and 54-61. Incremental factor for the whole of 1937: own calculation based on Belgian economic statistics 1929-1940, p. 199. Index of hourly wages in industry: CASSIERS I., Une statistique des salaires horaires dans l'industrie, p. 73.
(5) Estimate of employers' contributions in 1920-1930 (in BF millions) = (3) x (4) x 0.02 ÷ 1,000,000. These figures are included in Chapter 6, Table 2.
(6) Employers' contributions in 1931-1939 (in BF millions): Annual Reports of the National Settlement Fund for Family Allowances.

TABLE 41

Employers' contributions to industrial accident insurance (in BF millions)

year	(1)	(2)	(3)	year
1920	79	4	83	1920
1921	87	4	91	1921
1922	95	4	99	1922
1923	117	5	122	1923
1924	135	6	141	1924
1925	136	6	142	1925
1926	157	7	164	1926
1927	203	7	210	1927
1928	235	7	242	1928
1929	295	7	302	1929
1930	348	7	355	1930
1931	289	6	295	1931
1932	238	4	242	1932
1933	229	4	233	1933
1934	212	4	216	1934
1935	215	4	219	1935
1936	245	5	250	1936
1937	295	5	300	1937
1938	295	5	300	1938
1939	276	5	281	1939

(1) Premiums for industrial accident insurance (Industrial Accidents Report, 1948-1949-1950, pp. 16-18).
(2) Estimate of benefits paid directly by uninsured employers (= 1% of total wages of manual workers whose employers made payments into the Guarantee Fund and of workers whose employers were exempted from contributions to the Guarantee Fund) = 1% of Chapter 1, Table 1, columns 5 and 6.
(3) Total employers' contributions = (1)+(2).

TABLE 42

Pay and pensions of government staff (in BF millions).

year	(1)	(2)	(3)	(4)	(5)	(6)	(7)	(8)	(9)	(10)	year
1920	311	30	498	201	91	56	519	136	31	1.873	1920
1921	368	38	418	210	136	107	629	172	32	2.110	1921
1922	381	37	536	242	147	109	623	171	38	2.284	1922
1923	398	38	551	236	161	119	699	176	41	2.419	1923
1924	469	53	441	319	172	118	976	216	51	2.815	1924
1925	532	64	487	364	184	125	1.055	256	56	3.123	1925
1926	584	69	507	385	197	134	1.308	297	61	3.542	1926
1927	767	131	657	475	217	133	1.619	395	79	4.473	1927
1928	1.010	151	848	545	362	274	1.806	500	87	5.583	1928
1929	1.049	159	888	636	455	350	2.129	533	104	6.303	1929
1930	1.178	181	1.027	778	507	404	2.198	639	122	7.034	1930
1931	1.172	184	1.081	806	533	433	2.058	658	126	7.051	1931
1932	1.078	174	988	767	514	419	1.839	627	120	6.526	1932
1933	1.018	168	909	776	499	400	1.690	574	123	6.157	1933
1934	1.013	167	926	692	500	384	1.640	545	141	6.008	1934
1935	999	165	876	657	422	342	1.519	629	136	5.645	1935
1936	1.082	186	1.011	644	471	378	1.686	562	114	6.134	1936
1937	1.279	198	1.149	697	483	376	1.851	591	112	6.736	1937
1938	1.376	224	1.287	751	532	419	1.908	672	123	7.292	1938
1939	1.351	221	1.892	737	542	425	1.823	674	125	7.790	1939

(1) Central government: pay and pensions of civil service.
(2) Central government: pay and pensions of state education.
(3) Central government: pay and pensions of the military establishment.
(All figures: CLEMENT, P. and NEFORS, P., The Growth of a Welfare State in Belgium, passim).
(4) Local government (provinces, municipalities and COOs): pay and pensions of civil service.
(5) Local government (provinces, municipalities and COOs): pay and pensions of education service.
(6) Free education: central government pay subsidies.
(7) Belgian State Railways/NMBS: pay and pensions (Annual reports).
(8) RTT, Postal Service, Aviation Authority: pay and pensions (Accounts of the Audit Office and Documents of Chamber and Senate).
(9) Public companies controlled by the provinces and the municipalities: pay and pensions.
(10) Total.

TABLE 43

Income from employment: additions and adjustments (in BF millions)

year	(1)	(2)	(3)	(4)	(5)	year
1920	45	8	105	37	121	1920
1921	46	15	117	41	137	1921
1922	40	24	243	43	263	1922
1923	53	34	286	51	322	1923
1924	61	42	338	61	380	1924
1925	51	48	253	62	290	1925
1926	65	52	392	72	437	1926
1927	93	77	478	88	560	1927
1928	81	95	534	99	611	1928
1929	87	164	479	118	612	1929
1930	87	179	330	123	473	1930
1931	73	34	272	105	274	1931
1932	53	30	217	86	214	1932
1933	52	31	215	85	213	1933
1934	46	28	198	79	193	1934
1935	44	29	298	79	292	1935
1936	44	32	344	90	330	1936
1937	56	40	415	107	404	1937
1938	63	44	274	108	273	1938
1939	55	43	259	104	254	1939

(1) Value of coal and coke supplied free of charge to mineworkers and to workers in coke-fired blast furnace (Annales des Mines 1920-1939).
(2) Estimate of voluntary employers' contributions outside the framework of the compulsory social security system (see Table 44, column 6).
(3) Estimate of undeclared income of manual workers (see Table 45, columns 4 and 6).
(4) Estimate of expenditure on professional clothing by employees (0.6% of the aggregate wages and salaries of manual and white-collar workers employed in the private sector in Belgium)
(5) Total additions and adjustments = (1)+(2)+(3)-(4).

TABLE 44

Estimate of voluntary employers' contributions (in BF millions)

year	(1)	(2)	(3)	(4)	(5)	(6)	year
1920	2	0	30,0	6	0	8	1920
1921	6	1	33,5	7	1	15	1921
1922	6	9	34,9	7	1	24	1922
1923	6	17	41,2	8	2	34	1923
1924	7	22	49,3	10	3	42	1924
1925	8	25	50,0	10	4	48	1925
1926		33	58,1	12	8	52	1926
1927		51	71,4	14	12	77	1927
1928		67	80,1	16	12	95	1928
1929		130	95,9	19	15	164	1929
1930		144	100,0	20	15	179	1930
1931			84,9	17	17	34	1931
1932			69,9	14	16	30	1932
1933			69,0	14	17	31	1933
1934			64,2	13	15	28	1934
1935			64,0	13	16	29	1935
1936			73,0	15	18	32	1936
1937			86,5	17	23	40	1937
1938			87,3	17	27	44	1938
1939			84,1	17	26	43	1939

(1) Estimate of voluntary employers' contributions for manual and white-collar workers' pensions = 1/2 of personal payments (excluding those for mineworkers) to the annuity fund of the ASLK (ASLK Annual Reports 1920-1925).
(2) Estimate of voluntary employers' contributions for family allowances (see Chapter 4, Table 40, column 5).
(3) Index of the aggregate wages and salaries of manual and white-collar workers employed in the private sector in Belgium: 1930 = 100 (own calculation based on Chapter 1, Table 12, column 6 and Chapter 2, Table 13, column 3).
(4) Estimate of voluntary employers' contributions for medical insurance (1930 = VELGE H., o.c., p. 126; other years = estimate for 1930 linked to index (3)).
(5) Estimate of value of coal supplied free of charge to retired mineworkers or to their widows and orphans (SCHROEVEN C., o.c., Chapter 6).
(6) Total voluntary employers' contributions outside the framework of the compulsory social security system = (1)+(2)+(4)+(5).

TABLE 45

Estimate of undeclared income of workers (in BF millions)

year	(1)	(2)	(3)	(4)	(5)	year
1920	62,0	12,6%	2%	5.271	105	1920
1921	62,0	12,1%	2%	5.849	117	1921
1922	70,9	3,9%	4%	6.063	243	1922
1923	79,7	1,2%	4%	7.152	286	1923
1924	83,5	1,3%	4%	8.443	338	1924
1925	84,8	1,9%	3%	8.442	253	1925
1926	89,9	1,8%	4%	9.798	392	1926
1927	96,2	2,3%	4%	11.942	478	1927
1928	105,1	1,2%	4%	13.354	534	1928
1929	102,5	1,7%	3%	15.954	479	1929
1930	100,0	4,3%	2%	16.496	330	1930
1931	94,9	12,4%	2%	13.611	272	1931
1932	87,3	20,2%	2%	10.844	217	1932
1933	92,4	18,8%	2%	10.775	215	1933
1934	88,6	20,5%	2%	9.915	198	1934
1935	101,3	18,8%	3%	9.932	298	1935
1936	103,8	12,9%	3%	11.462	344	1936
1937	103,8	10,6%	3%	13.824	415	1937
1938	98,7	12,8%	2%	13.675	274	1938
1939	.	15,6%	2%	12.952	259	1939

(1) Index of industrial production (1929 = 100), CARBONELLE C., p. 358.
(2) Number of complete unemployed manual workers in industry (GOOSSENS M., Reconstructie van werkgelegenheidscijfers voor het Interbellum. Methodologie en resultaten, p. B5.)
(3) Expansion factor.
(4) Aggregate wages of manual workers employed in the private sector in Belgium (in 1 000 000 BF), (Chapter 1, Table 12, column 6).
(5) Estimate of undeclared income of workers (in 1 000 000 BF) = (3) x (4).

TABLE 46

Self-employed income from agriculture, horticulture and forestry (in BF millions)

year	(1)	(2)	(3)	(4)	(5)	(6)	(7)	(8)	year
1920	3.597	2.045	953	6.594	2.353	4.241	16	4.257	1920
1921	3.427	1.359	1.081	5.868	2.553	3.315	14	3.329	1921
1922	2.920	1.070	755	4.746	2.582	2.163	18	2.181	1922
1923	3.812	1.882	1.047	6.740	2.950	3.791	22	3.812	1923
1924	4.548	2.154	1.137	7.839	3.649	4.190	25	4.216	1924
1925	4.905	2.105	1.136	8.145	4.313	3.833	29	3.862	1925
1926	6.416	3.431	1.362	11.210	6.283	4.927	37	4.963	1926
1927	7.399	3.123	1.496	12.018	7.197	4.821	44	4.865	1927
1928	8.259	3.024	1.951	13.234	7.708	5.526	52	5.578	1928
1929	9.583	2.174	1.896	13.653	7.753	5.900	60	5.960	1929
1930	8.381	1.658	1.774	11.813	6.882	4.932	68	4.999	1930
1931	6.673	1.447	1.812	9.933	6.326	3.606	61	3.667	1931
1932	5.826	1.018	1.465	8.309	5.178	3.130	55	3.185	1932
1933	5.819	874	1.510	8.203	4.514	3.689	48	3.737	1933
1934	5.090	1.217	1.311	7.618	4.783	2.835	41	2.876	1934
1935	5.588	1.450	1.361	8.399	4.744	3.655	34	3.689	1935
1936	5.703	1.394	1.405	8.502	5.429	3.073	38	3.111	1936
1937	6.686	1.687	1.378	9.751	6.121	3.630	44	3.674	1937
1938	7.057	1.488	1.488	10.033	5.937	4.096	41	4.137	1938
1939	6.270	1.819	1.718	9.808	5.847	3.961	43	4.004	1939

(1) Livestock production (BLOMME J., Belgian Agriculture, p. B35).
(2) Arable production (idem).
(3) Horticultural production (idem).
(4) Gross value of agricultural and horticultural production = (1)+(2)+(3).
(5) Operational inputs (see Table 47, column 11).
(6) Income from entrepreneurship in agriculture and horticulture = (4)-(5).
(7) Income from entrepreneurship from woods not under the management of the Forestry Commission (see Table 48, column 12).
(8) Income from entrepreneurship in agriculture, horticulture and forestry in current prices = (6)+(7).

TABLE 47

Operational inputs in agriculture and horticulture (in BF millions)

year	(1)	(2)	(3)	(4)	(5)	(6)	(7)	(8)	(9)	(10)	(11)	year
1920	379	461	329	685	57	8	43	293	98	0	2.353	1920
1921	459	539	281	727	48	12	47	330	110	0	2.553	1921
1922	562	530	265	674	45	11	48	335	112	0	2.582	1922
1923	589	546	329	856	56	16	56	377	126	0	2.950	1923
1924	728	537	443	1.200	67	25	68	435	145	0	3.649	1924
1925	960	564	617	1.315	77	40	73	500	167	0	4.313	1925
1926	1.168	592	883	2.512	96	48	94	668	223	0	6.283	1926
1927	1.727	656	829	2.658	115	64	122	770	257	0	7.197	1927
1928	1.838	758	974	2.642	135	84	141	853	284	0	7.708	1928
1929	1.875	723	1.171	2.450	129	110	150	859	286	0	7.753	1929
1930	1.779	713	949	2.010	89	114	161	799	266	0	6.882	1930
1931	1.782	665	644	1.924	71	84	164	743	248	0	6.326	1931
1932	1.749	617	262	1.408	61	71	157	641	214	0	5.178	1932
1933	1.553	574	318	1.218	52	72	150	597	199	219	4.514	1933
1934	1.408	560	460	1.418	54	64	150	610	203	145	4.783	1934
1935	1.335	514	459	1.446	54	60	157	590	197	67	4.744	1935
1936	1.473	519	434	1.850	63	62	167	646	215	0	5.429	1936
1937	1.660	562	379	2.228	77	65	186	723	241	0	6.121	1937
1938	1.623	556	501	2.096	77	61	194	723	241	135	5.937	1938
1939	1.685	536	342	1.996	72	67	206	706	235	0	5.847	1939

(1) Rents
(2) Agricultural workers' wages
(3) Fertilizers
(4) Feedstuffs
(5) Planting stock and seeds
(6) Interest on borrowed operating capital
(7) Depreciation
(8) General overheads
(9) Indirect taxation
(10) Subsidies
(11) Total operational inputs: sum of columns (1)-(9) - (10)

Source : BLOMME J., Belgian Agriculture, *passim.*

TABLE 48

Self-employed income from woods managed by the forestry commission (in BF millions)

year	(1)	(2)	(3)	(4)	(5)	(6)	(7)	(8)	(9)	(10)	(11)	(12)	year
1910	559.786												1910
1920		577.599			63,90	369.151			66	24	8	16	1920
1921		579.380	216.044	37,30	62,70	363.336	12.426	58	58	21	7	14	1921
1922		581.162			61,50	357.262			75	27	9	18	1922
1923		582.943			60,20	351.144			93	33	11	22	1923
1924		584.724			59,00	344.982			110	38	13	25	1924
1925		586.506	247.730	42,20	57,80	330.776	31.696	128	128	43	14	29	1925
1926		588.287			57,50	338.403			162	55	18	37	1926
1927		590.068			57,30	338.022			197	67	22	44	1927
1928		591.850			57,00	337.632			231	78	26	52	1928
1929	593.631	593.631			56,80	337.234			266	90	30	60	1929
1930		596.282	258.963	43,40	56,60	337.319	77.809	300	300	101	34	68	1930
1931		598.934			56,70	339.485			270	92	31	61	1931
1932		601.585			56,80	341.656			239	82	27	55	1932
1933		604.236			56,90	343.833			209	72	24	48	1933
1934		606.887			57,00	346.017			178	62	21	41	1934
1935		609.539	261.333	42,90	57,10	348.206	38.631	148	148	51	17	34	1935
1936		612.190			57,20	350.401			162	57	19	38	1936
1937		614.841			57,30	352.602			188	66	22	44	1937
1938		617.493			57,50	354.808			173	62	21	41	1938
1939		620.144			57,60	357.021			179	64	21	43	1939
1950	649.308												1950

(1) Total acreage of woodland (government and privately owned) in agricultural census years = total acreage in the agricultural censuses raised by an incremental factor as explained in BLOMME J., Belgian Agriculture, passim.
(2) Total acreage of woodland in 1920-1939 = linear interpolation of (1).
(3) Acreage of woodland managed by Forestry Commission (= belonging to the state, municipalities or public institutions); Statistical Jearbook, vol. 57, 1935, p. 166; vol. 63, 1941, p. 182.
(4) Portion of woods in state ownership in total acreage of woodland = (3) ÷ (2).
(5) Portion of woods in private ownership in total acreage of woodland = 1921, 1925, 1930, 1935 : (1) - (4); intervening years: linear interpolation; after 1935: linear interpolation.
(6) Acreage of woodlands in private ownership = (2) x (5).
(7) Total net income from woods managed by the Forestry Commission (source: see (3)).
(8) Net income per hectare from woods managed by the Forestry Commission = (7) ÷ (3).
(9) Net income per hectare from woods managed by the Forestry Commission. 1921-1935: linear interpolation of (9); 1920-1921: 1921 figure linked to retail price index; 1935-1939: 1935 figure link to wholesale price index.
(10) Total net income from woods in private ownership = (6) x (9) ÷ 1,000,000.
(11) Capital income from woods in private ownership = (10) x 1/3.
(12) Self-employed income from woods in private ownership = (10) x 2/3.

TABLE 49

Entrepreneurial income of the professions, independent traders, craftsmen and partnerships: summary table (in BF millions)

year	(1)	(2)	(3)	(4)	(5)	(6)	year
1920	5.867	495	6.362	327	445	7.134	1920
1921	5.794	489	6.283	334	440	7.057	1921
1922	5.786	488	6.274	414	439	7.128	1922
1923	6.868	580	7.448	484	521	8.453	1923
1924	8.258	697	8.955	562	627	10.143	1924
1925	8.480	716	9.196	578	644	10.417	1925
1926	10.153	857	11.009	671	771	12.451	1926
1927	12.435	1.049	13.484	743	944	15.172	1927
1928	13.929	1.175	15.104	859	1.057	17.021	1928
1929	15.306	1.291	16.597	959	1.162	18.719	1929
1930	15.139	1.277	16.416	1.005	1.149	18.571	1930
1931	14.043	1.141	15.183	977	1.063	17.223	1931
1932	12.103	946	13.049	951	913	14.914	1932
1933	11.872	889	12.761	929	893	14.583	1933
1934	11.386	818	12.203	906	854	13.964	1934
1935	12.164	839	13.003	885	910	14.799	1935
1936	13.159	914	14.072	933	985	15.991	1936
1937	14.759	1.032	15.791	1.016	1.105	17.912	1937
1938	15.309	1.070	16.379	1.027	1.147	18.553	1938
1939	14.576	1.019	15.595	1.044	1.092	17.731	1939

(1) Entrepreneurial income of independent traders and craftsmen: main occupation = Table 58 column 4.
(2) Entrepreneurial income of independent traders and craftsmen: secondary occupation = Table 60 column 7.
(3) Entrepreneurial income of independent traders and craftsmen = (1) + (2).
(4) Entrepreneurial income of the professions.
(5) Entrepreneurial income of independent traders = 7% of (3).
(6) Total = (3) + (4) + (5).

TABLE 50

Direct taxes received by the central government (annual figures - in BF millions)

year	(1)	(2)	(3)	(4)	(5)	(6)	(7)	(8)	year
1919							210	210	1919
1920	54	79	54	81			29	297	1920
1921	56	114	86	126			60	442	1921
1922	76	146	145	199			88	653	1922
1923	213	322	414	333			132	1413	1923
1924	164	405	382	302			144	1396	1924
1925	194	451	453	440			360	1898	1925
1926	493	578	458	404			490	2423	1926
1927	366	777	618	397			540	2699	1927
1928	409	884	738	591			551	3172	1928
1929	458	956	946	623			618	3602	1929
1930	332	948	798	34	64		689	2866	1930
1931	436	753	727		111		650	2676	1931
1932	422	595	630		113		579	2339	1932
1933	422	529	475		191	510	754	2881	1933
1934	417	522	416		167	524	753	2799	1934
1935	305	455	379		184	501	785	2610	1935
1936	347	598	488		231	587	756	3007	1936
1937	352	716	608		248	263	641	2828	1937
1938	354	795	640		283	360	700	3132	1938
1939	346	707	588		345	593	861	3440	1939

(1) Split tax on income : land tax
(2) Split tax on income : property tax
(3) Split tax on income : trade tax
(4) Supertax
(5) Supplementary personel tax
(6) National crisistax
(7) Other direct taxes
(8) Total

Source: S. VANDENDRIESSCHE, o.c., p. 85; p. 159, 192, 224.

Number of taxpayers, tax receipts and taxable income of industrial proprietors, independent traders, craftsmen and the professions (tax receipts and taxable income in the year in which income was earned in BF millions)

year	income category	INDUSTRIAL PROPRIETORS, TRADERS, CRAFTSMAN			PROFESSIONS			OTHER		
		tax payers	tax receipts	taxable income	tax payers	tax receipts	taxable income	tax payers	tax receipts	taxable income
1920	total	311.864		2.399.000	14.432		198.000	30.544		362.000
1922	total	339.580		3.089.000	15.098		251.000	21.520		233.000
1924	- 5 000	139.566								
	5 000 - 10 000	129.462								
	10 000 - 25 000	92.223								
	25 000 - 50 000	?								
	50 000 - 100 000	?								
	+ 100 000	?								
	total	386.744		4.470.000	19.307		340.000			
1925	- 5 000	112.648								
	5 000 - 10 000	132.449								
	10 000 - 25 000	103.998								
	25 000 - 50 000	?								
	50 000 - 100 000	?								
	+ 100 000	?								
	total	?								
1926	- 5 000	91.961								
	5 000 - 10 000	133.102								
	10 000 - 25 000	127.397								
	25 000 - 50 000	?								
	50 000 - 100 000	?								
	+ 100 000	?								
	total	?								
1927	- 5 000	83.122								
	5 000 - 10 000	124.869								
	10 000 - 25 000	141.773								
	25 000 - 50 000	?								
	50 000 - 100 000	?								
	+ 100 000	?								
	total	?		6.800.000			450.000			

1920 Legislative Chambers, House of Representatives, Bulletin van Vragen en Antwoorden, ordinary session 1924-1925, 16 December 1924, p. 53; MAHAIM E., La fortune et le bien-être, p. 526.

1922 MAHAIM E., o.c., pp. 526 and 533; BAUDHUIN F., Quel est le revenu actuel de la Belgique? pp. 53-56.

1924 BAUDHUIN F., Finances belges. La stabilisation et ses conséquences, p. 16; De Middenstandspost. Weekblad van den Landsbond van den Christe-lijken Middenstand van België", vol. 13, 1938, p. 41.

1925 COLLIN F., o.c., p. 16.

1926 COLLIN F., o.c., p. 16.

1927 BAUDHUIN F., Le revenu national en 1930, p. 374; COLLIN F., o.c., p. 16.

1928 Legislative Chambers, Senate, Bulletin van Vragen en Antwoorden, ordinary session 1930-31, 26 February 1931, pp. 241-242; Banque Nationale de Belgique. Bulletin d'Information et de Documentation, vol. 6, 1931, p. 209.

1929 Legislative Chambers, Senate, Bulletin van Vragen en Antwoorden, ordinary session 1931-32, 7 July 1932, pp. 569-571.

1930 NIS, Driemaandblad, vol. 20, 1934, p.8; Legislative Chambers, Senate, Bulletin van Vragen en Antwoorden, 1933-1934 session, 10 July 1934, pp. 447-448; BAUDHUIN F., La Belgique en 1936. Les revenus, p. 124.

1932 Legislative Chambers, Senate, Bulletin van Vragen en Antwoorden, 1935-36 session, 5 March 1936, pp. 194-195.

1935 VAN DER AA E.A., Studie over het opzetten eener statistiek der in de mobiliënbelasting, de bedrijfsbelasting, de nationale crisisbelasting en de aanvullende personele belasting aangeslagen inkomsten en het rendement dezer belastingen (1945 financial year - earnings acquired in 1944), pp. 836-837.; Legislative Chambers, House of Representatives, Parliamentary Documents, 1937-38 session, no. 1296, 5 July 1938, p. 8.

Note: Year in which income was earned = financial year (i.e. year in which tax was assessed) - 1.

TABLE 52

Comparison of the numbers of independent traders and industrial entrepreneurs according to the censuses and the fiscal statistics

ICS 1930 (INDUSTRIAL AND COMMERCIAL CENSUS OF 1930)

Industry
a) workshop proprietors	207,381
b) home industry proprietors	+3,084
c) proprietors with main occupation outside industry and commerce	-2,244
d) idle establishments	+14,338
Total : self-employed with main occupation in industry	222,559

Sources:
a) ICS 1930, p. 1342;
b) ICS 1930, p. 1420;
c) OC 1930, p. 768;
d) own calculation on basis of ICS 1930, p. 1342.

Commerce
a) proprietors without other occupation in commerce or industry	234,033
b) proprietors with main occupation outside industry and commerce	-16,344
Total : main occupation self-employed in commerce	217,689

Sources:
a) ICS 1930, pp. 1446-1447;
b) OC 1930, p. 768

ESC 1937 (ECONOMIC AND SOCIAL CENSUS OF 1937)

Industry
a) establishments (workshops) in operation	235,421
b) idle establishments (workshops)	+12,808
c) estimate of difference between proprietors and establishments	+2,000
Total : estimated number of proprietors	250,229

Sources:
a) and b) ESC 1937, vol. 1, p. 87.
c) rounded-off difference between number of proprietors with main occupation in industry in 1930 (222,535, see above) and number of establishments in industry in 1930 (220,871, see ICS 1930, p. 1342).

Commerce
a) independent traders without salaried personnel (main occupation)	248,360
b) establishments with salaried personnel	+35,027
Total : estimated number of proprietors with main occupation	283,387

Sources:
a) ESC 1937, vol, III, p. 132 (excluding personal care).
b) ESC 1937, vol, III, pp. 25-26 (excluding personal care)

OCCUPATIONAL CENSUS 1930

proprietors with main occupation in industry	222.535
proprietors with main occupation in commerce	217.317

Source:
OC 1930, p. 753.

GENERAL CENSUSES OF 1920 AND 1930	1920	1930
proprietors with main occupation in industry	181.241	217.041
proprietors with main occupation in commerce	207.891	269.147

Sources:
PC 1920, vol. III, pp. 232-252, 566-580;
PC 1930, vol. V, pp. 72-79, 188-193.

FISCAL STATISTICS 1920, 1930, 1935	1920	1930	1935
	342.408	446.378	547.098

See Table 49. In 1920 the category "other" was added (see text).

TABLE 53

Number of industrial entrepreneurs and independent traders according to the adapted fiscal statistics

year	(1)	(2)	(3)	(4)	year
1920	357.048		357.048		1920
1921		363.074	363.074	1,7%	1921
1922	369.100		369.100	1,7%	1922
1923		379.922	379.922	2,9%	1923
1924	390.744		390.744	2,8%	1924
1925		396.045	396.045	1,4%	1925
1926		401.347	401.347	1,3%	1926
1927		406.648	406.648	1,3%	1927
1928	411.949		411.949	1,3%	1928
1929	432.401		432.401	5,0%	1929
1930	446.378		446.378	3,2%	1930
1931		464.670	464.670	4,1%	1931
1932	482.961		482.961	3,9%	1932
1933		504.340	504.340	4,4%	1933
1934		525.719	525.719	4,2%	1934
1935	547.098		547.098	4,1%	1935
1936		543.549	543.549	-0,6%	1936
1937	540.000		540.000	-0,7%	1937
1938		540.000	540.000	0,0%	1938
1939		540.000	540.000	0,0%	1939

(1) Fiscal statistics figures (see Table 51).
   1920: 311,864 industrial proprietors and independent traders in FS + 30,544 other in FS + 15,000 FS underestimation
   1922: 339,580 industrial proprietors and independent traders in FS + 21,520 other in FS + 8,000 FS underestimation
   1924: including 4,000 persons in the "professions" category (see text)
   1937: own estimate on basis of ESC 1937 (see text).
(2) Linear interpolations for missing years.
   1938-39: the same figure as 1937.
(3) = (1) and (2).
(4) Annual percentage increase.

TABLE 54

Taxable income of industrial proprietors, independent traders and craftsmen: homogenization of the fiscal statistics (in BF millions)

year	Original fisc.stat.	Estimate 1928 1929, 1932	Adjustments			Adjusted fisc.stat.
	(1)	(2)	(3)	(4)	(5)	(6)
1920	2.399		362		327	3.088
1922	3.089		233		294	3.616
1924	4.470			46	645	5.161
1927	6.800				972	7.772
1928		7.389			1.053	8.442
1929		8.746				8.746
1930	8.651					8.651
1932		7.335				7.335
1935	7.372					7.372

(1) See Table 51.
(2) Estimated taxable income on basis of number of taxpayers per income band (see Table 51) and average taxable income per income band (respectively BF 4,500, BF 7,500, BF 17,500, BF 37,500, BF 70,000 and BF 250,000).
(3) Taxable income of the "other" group: see Table 51.
(4) 4,000 taxpayers in the "professions" category x average income of the "industrial proprietors, independent traders and craftsmen" category: (own calculation on basis of Table 51).
(5) Income upon invested capital subject to financial securities tax: see Table 55 column 10.
(6) = (1)+(2)+(3)+(4)+(5).

TABLE 55

Estimated taxable income from invested capital of industrial proprietors, independent traders and craftsmen: 1920-1928 (in BF millions)

year	(1)	(2)	(3)	(4)	(5)	(6)	(7)	(8)	(9)	(10)	year
1920	1.293	2.761	4.054	68,1%	480	327	11,8%			327	1920
1922	1.260	3.322	4.582	72,5%	405	294	8,8%			294	1922
1924	1.630	4.516	6.146	73,5%	878	645	14,3%			645	1924
1927		6.800						14,3%	972	972	1927
1928	2.080	7.389	9.469	78,0%	1.350	1.053	14,3%			1.053	1928

(1) Income from employment of farmers = subjected to trade tax (sources: see sources to Table 51).
(2) Income from employment of industrial proprietors, independent traders and craftsmen = subject to trade tax (= Table 51 columns 1+2+3+4).
(3) Income from employment of farmers, industrial proprietors, independent traders and craftsmen = (1) + (2).
(4) Share of (2) and (3).
(5) Income from invested capital of farmers, industrial proprietors, independent traders and craftsmen (= subject to financial securities tax).

Sources:
1920: MAHAIM E., La fortune et le bien-être, p. 523; 1922: Idem, pp. 522-523.
1924: BAUDHUIN, Quel est le revenu actuel de la Belgique, p. 54;
1928: BAUDHUIN, Le revenu national en 1930, p. 373.

(6) Estimated income from invested capital of industrial proprietors, independent traders and craftsmen = (4) x (5).
(7) Ratio of income from invested capital to income from employment of industrial proprietors, independent traders and craftsmen = (6) , (2).
(8) Estimated ratio of income from invested capital to income from employment of industrial proprietors, independent traders and craftsmen in 1927 and 1929 = interpolation and extrapolation of the ratio in 1924 and 1928.
(9) Estimated income from invested capital of industrial proprietors, independent traders and craftsmen = (2) x (8).
(10) Income from invested capital of industrial proprietors, independent traders and craftsmen = (6) and (9).

TABLE 56

Entrepreneurial income of independent traders and craftsmen: incremental coefficients of the NIS

year	%	year	%	year	%	year	%
1948	80%	1959	50%	1970	40%	1980	40%
1949	70%	1960	50%	1971	40%	1981	40%
1950	60%	1961	50%	1972	40%	1982	40%
1951	50%	1962	50%	1973	40%	1983	40%
1952	50%	1963	50%	1974	40%	1984	40%
1953	50%	1964	50%	1975	40%	1985	40%
1954	50%	1965	45%	1976	40%	1986	40%
1955	50%	1966	45%	1977	40%	1987	40%
1956	50%	1967	45%	1978	40%	1988	40%
1957	50%	1968	45%	1979	40%		
1958	50%	1969	45%	1980	40%		

Sources: Statistisch Bulletin, 1956, p. 606; Statistisch Tijdschrift, 1963, p. 1152; Statistisch Tijdschrift, 1965, p. 1388; Statistische Studien, no. 33, 1973, p. 3; since 1970 consistently 40% (communication by Mr. Hermans, NIS official).

TABLE 57

Conversion of taxable into actually earned entrepreneurial income of independent traders and craftsmen (in BF millions)

year	(1)	(2)	(3)	(4)	(5)	(6)	(7)	(8)	(9)	(10)	(11)	(12)	year
1920	3.088	+60 %	+30 %			+90 %	5.867	38		17.300	36		1920
1921													1921
1922	3.616	+60 %				+60 %	5.786	38	-1%	16.975	36	-2%	1922
1923													1923
1924	5.161	+60 %				+60 %	8.258	54	43%	25.067	53	48%	1924
1925													1925
1926													1926
1927	7.772	+60 %		+5 %		+60 %	12.435	81	51%	39.775	83	59%	1927
1928	8.442	+60 %		+5 %	+10 %	+65 %	13.929	91	12%	43.758	92	10%	1928
1929	8.746	+60 %		+5 %	+10 %	+75 %	15.306	100	10%	47.702	100	9%	1929
1930	8.651	+60 %			+10 %	+75 %	15.139	99	-1%	49.132	103	3%	1930
1931													1931
1932	7.335	+60 %		-5 %	+10 %	+65 %	12.103	79	-20%	38.335	80	-22%	1932
1933													1933
1934													1934
1935	7.372	+60 %		-5 %	+10 %	+65 %	12.164	79	1%	35.089	74	-8%	1935
1936													1936
1937													1937
1938													1938
1939													1939

(1) Taxable income according to adjusted fiscal statistics (see Table 54 column 6).
(2) Overall incremental coefficient.
(3) Incremental coefficient for inadequate fiscal machinery.
(4) Reduction coefficient for weak economy and incremental coefficient for boom years.
(5) Incremental coefficient for lump-sum assessment.
(6) Annual incremental coefficient = (2)+(3)+(4)+(5).
(7) Estimated actually earned entrepreneurial income = (1) x [1+(6)].
(8) Index of actually earned entrepreneurial income = index of (7) with 1929 = 100.
(9) Growth rate of actually earned entrepreneurial income in relation to previous observation year.
(10) Private consumption of food, beverages, tobacco, clothing and other personal items, transport (with the exception of trams, busses and rail), leisure activities (= entertainment, hotels, restaurants, cafes, books, newspapers and magazines),
Source: SCHROEVEN C., Consumption, passim.
(11) Index of (10) with 1929 = 100.
(12) Growth rate of (10) in relation to previous observation year.

TABLE 58

Estimated entrepreneurial income of independent traders and craftsmen in years without fiscal statistics (in BF millions)

year	(1)	(2)	(3)	(4)	year
1920	5.867	17.300		5.867	1920
1921		17.043	5.794	5.794	1921
1922	5.786	16.975		5.786	1922
1923		20.499	6.868	6.868	1923
1924	8.258	25.067		8.258	1924
1925		26.288	8.480	8.480	1925
1926		31.981	10.153	10.153	1926
1927	12.435	39.775		12.435	1927
1928	13.929	43.758		13.929	1928
1929	15.306	47.702		15.306	1929
1930	15.139	49.132		15.139	1930
1931		45.026	14.043	14.043	1931
1932	12.103	38.335		12.103	1932
1933		36.485	11.872	11.872	1933
1934		33.917	11.386	11.386	1934
1935	12.164	35.089		12.164	1935
1936		37.958	13.159	13.159	1936
1937		42.575	14.759	14.759	1937
1938		44.162	15.309	15.309	1938
1939		42.047	14.576	14.576	1939

(1) Entrepreneurial income in years with fiscal statistics (Table 57 column 7).
(2) Private consumption of food, beverages, tobacco, clothing and other personal items, transport (with the exception of trams, buses and rail), leisure activities (= entertainment, hotels, restaurants, cafes, books, newspapers and magazines):
Source: SCHROEVEN C., Consumption, passim.
(3) Estimated entrepreneurial income in years without fiscal statistics: 1921-1934: trend-corrected interpolation on the basis of (2). 1936-1939: extrapolation on basis of growth rates of (2).
(4) Entrepreneurial income of independent traders and craftsmen (main occupation): (1) and (3).

TABLE 59

Number of independent traders and craftsmen as secondary occupation on 31 December 1930

Main occupation	Secondary occupation		
	industrial proprietors	commercial proprietors	total
Manual worker or white-collar worker in commerce or industry	992	42.906	43.898
Unemployed in commerce or industry	187	12.656	12.843
Professions, farmer, agricultural labourer	2.244	16.344	18.588
Total	3.423	71.906	75.329

Source: OC 1930, passim.

TABLE 60

Entrepreneurial income of independent traders and craftsmen (secondary occupation)
(in BF millions)

year	(1)	(2)	(3)	(4)	(5)	(6)	(7)	year
1920	5.867	342.048	17.153		57.723	8.576	495	1920
1921	5.794	351.574	16.482		59.330	8.241	489	1921
1922	5.786	361.100	16.023		60.938	8.012	488	1922
1923	6.868	375.922	18.270		63.439	9.135	580	1923
1924	8.258	390.744	21.134		65.940	10.567	697	1924
1925	8.480	396.045	21.412		66.835	10.706	716	1925
1926	10.153	401.347	25.297		67.730	12.648	857	1926
1927	12.435	406.648	30.579		68.624	15.290	1.049	1927
1928	13.929	411.949	33.812		69.519	16.906	1.175	1928
1929	15.306	432.401	35.398		72.970	17.699	1.291	1929
1930	15.139	446.378	33.915	75.329	75.329	16.958	1.277	1930
1931	14.043	464.670	30.221		75.500	15.110	1.141	1931
1932	12.103	482.961	25.060		75.500	12.530	946	1932
1933	11.872	504.340	23.540		75.500	11.770	889	1933
1934	11.386	525.719	21.657		75.500	10.829	818	1934
1935	12.164	547.098	22.234		75.500	11.117	839	1935
1936	13.159	543.549	24.209		75.500	12.104	914	1936
1937	14.759	540.000	27.332		75.500	13.666	1.032	1937
1938	15.309	540.000	28.350		75.500	14.175	1.070	1938
1939	14.576	540.000	26.993		75.500	13.496	1.019	1939

(1) Total entrepreneurial income of independent traders and craftsmen (main occupation) = Table 58 column 4.
(2) Number of independent traders and craftsmen (main occupation) = Table 53 column 3.
(3) Average entrepreneurial income of independent traders and craftsmen (main occupation) = (1) ÷ (2).
(4) Number of independent traders and craftsmen (secondary occupation) on 31 December 1930 = Table 11.
(5) Number of independent traders and craftsmen (secondary occupation): 1920-1930: (4) linked to evolution (2); 1931-1939: see text.
(6) Average entrepreneurial income of independent traders and craftsmen (secondary occupation) = 50% of (3).
(7) Total entrepreneurial income of independent traders and craftsmen (secondary occupation) = (5) x (6).

TABLE 61

Capitalized interest on savings deposits held by private individuals with the ASLK (in BF millions)

year	(1)	(2)	(3)	(4)	(5)	(6)	(7)	year
1920	1.444	13	1.494	37	1.365	2,7%	3,0%	1920
1921	1.640	15	1.700	45	1.583	2,8%	3,0%	1921
1922	1.776	9	1.834	49	1.743	2,8%	3,0%	1922
1923	1.888	15	1.960	57	1.846	3,1%	3,3%	1923
1924	2.133	14	2.217	70	2.068	3,4%	3,6%	1924
1925	2.464	-2	2.552	90	2.385	3,8%	4,0%	1925
1926	2.562	33	2.693	98	2.566	3,8%	4,0%	1926
1927	3.264	43	3.424	117	3.038	3,9%	4,0%	1927
1928	3.954	60	4.171	157	3.732	4,2%	4,4%	1928
1929	5.129	107	5.433	197	4.729	4,2%	4,4%	1929
1930	7.254	165	7.653	234	6.540	3,6%	4,0%	1930
1931	8.845	29	9.115	241	8.464	2,8%	3,0%	1931
1932	9.461	32	9.813	320	9.446	3,4%	3,6%	1932
1933	9.698	-13	9.964	279	9.800	2,8%	3,0%	1933
1934	10.208	-44	10.452	288	10.132	2,8%	3,0%	1934
1935	10.251	44	10.584	289	10.223	2,8%	3,0%	1935
1936	11.091	58	11.456	307	10.876	2,8%	3,0%	1936
1937	12.113	43	12.489	333	11.908	2,8%	3,0%	1937
1938	12.318	6	12.671	347	12.489	2,8%	3,0%	1938
1939	11.638	-19	11.961	342	12.190	2,8%	3,0%	1939

(1) Total savings deposits of private persons on 30 November (*Belgische economische statistieken*, 1919-1928, p. 26; 1929-1940, p. 191).
(2) Net deposits (= deposits minus withdrawals) in December. Source: see (1), pp. 25-26, pp. 190-191.
(3) Total savings deposits on 31 December, including capitalized interest. Source: see (1).
(4) Capitalized interest = (3) - (1) - (2).
(5) Average annual total savings deposits (own calculation : average of the monthly totals. Source for the monthly totals: see (1). The sum for December = excluding capitalized interest).
(6) Implicit ASLK rate of interest = (4) / (5).
(7) Explicit ASLK rate of interest (1920-1930 : ASLK Annual Report 1930, p. 18; 1929-1939 : Belgische economische statistieken, p. 14. In 1923 the rate of interest to the end of June was 3.0%, and from July 3.6%.

TABLE 62

Interest on ex-servicemen's endowment passbooks with the ASLK (in BF millions)

year	(1)	(2)	(3)	(4)	(5)	(6)	year
1920							1920
1921		13		844	844	42	1921
1922		116		767	806	40	1922
1923		123		680	724	36	1923
1924		117		594	637	32	1924
1925		114		507	550	28	1925
1926	2	189		340	424	21	1926
1927	8	63	301		321	16	1927
1928	7	49	278		290	14	1928
1929	8	33	270		274	14	1929
1930	10	23	273		272	14	1930
1931	10	20	278		276	14	1931
1932	7	22	278		278	14	1932
1933	5	23	290		284	14	1933
1934	6	20	293		292	15	1934
1935	6	23	279		286	14	1935
1936	6	18	297		288	14	1936
1937	7	16	304		301	15	1937
1938	6	20	306		305	15	1938
1939	3	21	305		306	15	1939

(1) Deposits (source : ASLK annual reports).
(2) Withdrawals (source : ASLK annual reports).
(3) Balance at 31 December in 1927-1939 (source : ASLK annual reports).
(4) Balance at 31 December in 1921-1926 (own calculation on the basis of (1), (2), (3) : see text).
(5) Average annual balance (own calculation on the basis of (3) and (4) : see text).
(6) Interest = 5% of (5).

TABLE 63

Interest on savings deposits with private savings banks (in BF millions)

year	(1)	(2)	(3)	(4)	(5)	(6)	(7)	(8)	(9)	(10)	(11)	(12)	year
1920	133	10	12	290	30	376	851	43	894	894	3,5%	31	1920
1921	149	11	20	400	35	450	1.065	53	1.118	1.006	3,5%	35	1921
1922	158	13	27	491	37	518	1.244	62	1.306	1.212	3,5%	42	1922
1923	180	15	30	604	38	573	1.440	72	1.512	1.409	3,8%	54	1923
1924	191	18	30	722	41	635	1.637	82	1.718	1.615	4,1%	66	1924
1925	222	20	30	822	45	682	1.821	91	1.912	1.815	4,5%	82	1925
1926	248	27	30	938	48	619	1.910	96	2.006	1.959	4,5%	88	1926
1927	223	50	54	1.196	59	706	2.288	114	2.403	2.204	4,5%	99	1927
1928	276	80	56	1.409	66	809	2.697	135	2.831	2.617	4,9%	128	1928
1929	364	118	77	1.710	76	944	3.289	164	3.454	3.143	4,9%	154	1929
1930	504	160	100	1.999	100	1.133	3.996	200	4.196	3.825	4,5%	172	1930
1931	588	210	108	2.183	122	1.275	4.486	224	4.710	4.453	3,5%	156	1931
1932	589	220	105	2.080	131	1.208	4.333	217	4.550	4.630	4,1%	190	1932
1933	548	193	94	2.051	133	1.198	4.217	211	4.428	4.489	3,5%	157	1933
1934	307	166	91	1.906	133	1.143	3.745	187	3.932	4.180	3,5%	146	1934
1935	197	140	82	270	100	971	1.760	88	1.848	2.890	3,5%	101	1935
1936	80	142	80	265	95	924	1.586	79	1.665	1.757	3,5%	61	1936
1937	115	161	80	286	92	913	1.648	82	1.731	1.698	3,5%	59	1937
1938	108	175	81	285	87	890	1.625	81	1.707	1.719	3,5%	60	1938
1939	74	147	81	278	78	829	1.488	74	1.562	1.634	3,5%	57	1939

(1) Savings deposits with savings banks of socialist cooperatives affiliated with Office Coopérative Belge.
(2) Savings deposits with Christian workers' savings banks.
(3) Savings deposits with savings banks of neutral cooperatives.
(4) Savings deposits with Catholic agricultural savings banks.
(5) Savings deposits with various company savings banks (Cockerill; Ougrée-Marihaye; Vieille Montagne).
(6) Savings deposits with various savings banks of mortgage companies (Antwerpse Hypotheekkas; Belgische Hypotheekmaatschappij en Spaarkas; Banque Hypothécaire et Immobilière d'Anvers, from 1935 : Antwerpse Maatschappij van Deposito's en Hypotheken; Hypotheek- en Beleggingsmaatschappij van Antwerpen).
(7) Total savings deposits (excluding the savings deposits with banks) with savings banks cited in VANTHEMSCHE G., De Belgische spaarbanken tijdens het interbellum = (1)+(2)+(3)+(4)+(5)+(6).
(8) Estimate of savings deposits with savings banks not cited in VANTHEMSCHE, op.cit., = 5 % of (7).
(9) Total savings deposits at end of the year = (7)+(8).
(10) Total average annual savings deposits = own calculation on basis of (9).
(11) Rate of interest = ASLK rate of interest (Table 61 column 7) increased by 0.5 %.
(12) Interest on savings deposits with private savings banks = (10)x(11).

Source for column (1) - (6) : VANTHEMSCHE G., De Belgische spaarbanken tijdens het Interbellum, p. 197-199. Figures are missing in Vanthemsche for certain savings banks in certain years. The missing figures were estimated on the basis of the known years and the evolution of the deposits at the other savings banks.

TABLE 64

Interest on savings deposits : summary overview (in BF millions)

year	(1)	(2)	(3)	(4)	(5)	year
1920	38	31	0,3	1,9	72	1920
1921	88	35	0,4	1,9	126	1921
1922	91	42	0,4	2,3	136	1922
1923	95	54	0,4	1,9	151	1923
1924	104	66	0,5	2,9	174	1924
1925	120	82	0,6	4,9	207	1925
1926	122	88	0,6	3,1	214	1926
1927	137	99	0,7	3,2	240	1927
1928	176	128	0,7	2,8	308	1928
1929	217	154	0,9	3,9	376	1929
1930	255	172	1,1	5,0	433	1930
1931	262	156	1,4	3,8	423	1931
1932	344	190	1,5	3,6	539	1932
1933	302	157	1,6	2,9	463	1933
1934	312	146	1,7	2,5	462	1934
1935	312	101	1,7	2,3	417	1935
1936	331	61	1,8	1,9	396	1936
1937	358	59	1,9	2,9	423	1937
1938	373	60	1,9	3,5	439	1938
1939	368	57	1,8	3,7	431	1939

(1) ASLK. Sum of Table 61, column 4, increased by 1.6% for interest on savings deposits of private persons paid in the course of the financial year + Table 62, column 6, increased by 1.5% for interest on deposit passbooks or non-profit making organisations.
(2) Private savings banks (Table 63 column 12).
(3) Municipal savings banks.
(4) Parastatal financial institutions (excl. ASLK).
(5) Total = (1)+(2)+(3)+(4).

TABLE 65

Interest on bank deposits (in BF millions)

year	(1)	(2)	(3)	(4)	(5)	(6)	(7)	(8)	(9)	(10)	(11)	(12)	(13)	(14)	(15)	(16)	year
1920	8.184	8.271	0	827	7.444	0	827	7.444	4,25%	3,50%	1,50%	0	29	112	141	105	1920
1921	9.613	8.518	1.095	852	7.666	547	839	7.555	4,33%	3,50%	1,50%	24	29	113	166	125	1921
1922	10.510	9.506	1.004	951	8.555	1.050	901	8.111	4,40%	3,50%	1,50%	46	32	122	199	150	1922
1923	11.562	10.156	1.406	1.016	9.140	1.205	983	8.848	4,44%	3,80%	1,67%	54	37	148	239	179	1923
1924	12.055	9.815	2.240	982	8.834	1.823	999	8.987	5,06%	4,10%	2,50%	92	41	225	358	268	1924
1925	15.797	11.264	4.533	1.126	10.138	3.386	1.054	9.486	5,44%	4,50%	3,00%	184	47	285	516	387	1925
1926	17.975	14.294	3.681	1.429	12.865	4.107	1.278	11.501	6,64%	4,50%	3,09%	273	58	355	686	514	1926
1927	23.507	18.692	4.815	1.869	16.823	4.248	1.649	14.844	5,01%	4,50%	1,78%	213	74	264	551	413	1927
1928	26.347	21.481	4.866	2.148	19.333	4.840	2.009	18.078	4,61%	4,90%	1,59%	223	98	287	609	457	1928
1929	30.438	22.199	8.239	2.220	19.979	6.553	2.184	19.656	4,70%	4,90%	1,50%	308	107	295	710	532	1929
1930	33.152	24.181	8.971	2.418	21.763	8.605	2.319	20.871	3,51%	4,50%	1,15%	302	104	240	646	485	1930
1931	29.863	21.782	8.081	2.178	19.604	8.526	2.298	20.683	2,30%	3,50%	1,00%	196	80	207	483	363	1931
1932	25.367	18.501	6.866	1.850	16.651	7.474	2.014	18.127	2,65%	4,10%	1,00%	198	83	181	462	346	1932
1933	25.254	18.418	6.836	1.842	16.576	6.851	1.846	16.614	2,75%	3,50%	1,00%	188	65	166	419	314	1933
1934	22.179	17.243	4.936	1.724	15.518	5.886	1.783	16.047	2,54%	3,50%	0,92%	150	62	148	360	270	1934
1935	19.103	16.067	3.036	1.607	14.460	3.986	1.665	14.989	2,10%	3,50%	0,60%	84	58	90	232	174	1935
1936	20.612	17.312	3.300	1.731	15.581	3.168	1.669	15.021	1,92%	3,50%	0,50%	61	58	75	194	146	1936
1937	19.631	16.343	3.288	1.634	14.709	3.294	1.683	15.145	1,75%	3,50%	0,50%	58	59	76	192	144	1937
1938	16.313	14.592	1.721	1.459	13.133	2.505	1.547	13.921	2,12%	3,50%	0,50%	53	54	70	177	133	1938
1939	13.154	11.934	1.220	1.193	10.741	1.471	1.326	11.937	2,50%	3,50%	0,50%	37	46	60	143	107	1939

(1) Total deposit amount at 31 December.
  1920-1929 : DURVIAUX R., o.c., p. 121 (amount in gold francs divided by depreciation coefficient).
  1930-1933 : VAN DER WEE H., TAVERNIER K., De Nationale Bank van België, p. 433.
  1934 :   linear interpolation between 1933 and 1935.
  1935-1939 : (2)+(3).
(2) Demand deposits and time deposits of no more than one month, deposit passbooks at 31 December.
  1920-1927 : VAN DER WEE H., TAVERNIER K., o.c., p.432.
  1928-1929 : EYSKENS G., o.c., p. 160.
  1930-1933 : VAN DER WEE H., TAVERNIER K., o.c., p. 432.
  1934 :   linear interpolation between 1933 and 1935.
  1935-1939 : Annual Reports Banking Commission.
(3) Time deposits of more than a month on 31 December.
  1920-1927 : (1)-(2).
  1928-1929 : EYSKENS G., o.c., p. 160.
  1930-1934 : (1)-(2).
  1935-1939 : Annual Reports Banking Commission.
(4) Deposit passbooks amount on 31 December = 10 % of (2).
(5) Amount of demand deposits and time deposits of at least one month, deposit passbooks on 31 December = 90 % of (2).
(6) Average annual amount of time deposits of more than one month = own calculation on basis of (3).
(7) Average annual amount of deposit passbooks = own calculation on basis of (4).
(8) Average annual amount of demand deposits and time deposits of no more than one month = own calculation on basis of (5).
(9) Rate of interest on time deposits of more than one month.
  1920-1925 : rate of interest on time deposits of 6 months with a large Brussels bank (DURVIAUX R., o.c., p. 122).
  1926-1928 : interpolation on basis of the yield on the perpetual state loan of 3 %.
  1929-1939 : Rate of interest on time deposits of 6 months with Belgian banks (*Belgische Economische Statistieken* 1929-1940, p. 14).
(10) Rate of interest on deposit passbooks.
  1920-1939 : ASLK rate of interest (Table 61 column 7) increa-sed by 0.5 %.
(11) Rate of interest on demand and time deposits of no more than one month.
  1920-1925 : rate of interest on demand deposits with a large Brussels bank (DURVIAUX R., o.c., p. 122).
  1926-1928 : interpolation on basis of the private discount rate for commercial paper.
  1929-1939 : rate of interest on demand deposits with Belgian banks (Belgische economische statistieken 1929-19-40, p. 14).
(12) Total interest (accruing to private individuals, companies and abroad) on time deposits of more than a month = (6)x(9).
(13) Total interest (accruing to private individuals, companies and abroad) on time deposits = (7)*(10).
(14) Total interest (accruing to private individuals, companies and abroad) on demand and time deposits of no more than a month = (8)x(11).
(15) Total interest (accruing to private individuals, companies and abroad) on bank deposits = (12)+(13)+(14).
(16) Interest on bank deposits accruing to private individuals = 75 % of (15).

TABLE 66

Imputed interest on the actuarial reserves or life insurance companies (in BF millions)

year	(1)	(2)	(3)	(4)	(5)	(6)	(7)	(8)	(9)	(10)	year
1919	11			96			5				1919
1920	13	12	0	113	105	4	6	5	0	4	1920
1921	15	14	0	131	122	4	7	6	0	5	1921
1922	18	17	1	157	144	5	8	7	0	6	1922
1923	22	20	1	192	175	6	10	9	0	7	1923
1924	28	25	1	244	218	8	12	11	0	9	1924
1925	38	33	1	332	288	10	17	14	1	12	1925
1926	46	42	2	402	367	13	20	18	1	15	1926
1927	54	50	2	471	436	15	24	22	1	18	1927
1928	72	63	3	628	550	19	31	27	1	23	1928
1929	100	86	3	873	751	26	44	38	1	31	1929
1930	130	115	5	1.135	1.004	35	57	50	2	41	1930
1931	154	142	6	1.344	1.239	43	67	62	2	51	1931
1932	177	166	7	1.545	1.445	51	77	72	3	60	1932
1933	192	185	7	1.725	1.635	57	86	82	3	67	1933
1934	200	196	8	1.919	1.822	64	96	91	3	75	1934
1935	200	200	8	2.221	2.070	72	111	104	4	84	1935
1936	206	203	8	2.498	2.360	83	125	118	4	95	1936
1937	212	209	8	2.824	2.661	93	141	133	5	106	1937
1938	219	216	9	3.100	2.962	104	155	148	5	117	1938
1939	222	221	9	3.329	3.215	113	166	161	6	127	1939

(1) ASLK : actuarial reserves op 31 December (Annual Reports ASLK : balance of the insurance fund).
(2) ASLK : average annual actuarial reserves = own calculation on basis of (1).
(3) ASLK : imputed interest : 1920-1921 : 3 % of (2); 1922-1939 = 4 % of (2).
(4) Private life insurance companies : actuarial reserves on 31 December.
1919-1931 : (1) * 8.7.
1932-1939 : Rapports sur l'execution de la loi du 25 juin 1930 relative au contrôle des entreprises d'assurances sur la vie.
(5) Private life insurance companies : average annual actuarial reserves = own calculation on basis of (4).
(6) Private life insurance companies : imputed interest = 3.5 % of (5).
(7) Employers' provident funds : actuarial reserves on 31 December = 5 % of (4).
(8) Employers' provident funds : average annual actuarial reserves = own calculation on basis of (7).
(9) Employers' provident funds : imputed interest = 1920-1921 : 3 % of (8); 1922-1939 : 4 % of (8).
(10) Total imputed interest on actuarial reserves = (3)+(6)+(9).

TABLE 67

Interest from mortgage loans accruing to private individuals (in BF millions)

year	(1)	(2)	(3)	(4)	(5)	year
1916	127	51				1916
1917	105	42				1917
1918	160	64				1918
1919	530	212				1919
1920	930	372	740	4,94%	37	1920
1921	1.058	423	1.113	5,34%	59	1921
1922	1.233	493	1.564	5,61%	88	1922
1923	1.619	648	2.148	5,58%	120	1923
1924	1.694	678	2.614	6,14%	160	1924
1925	2.064	826	3.067	6,55%	201	1925
1926	1.819	728	3.372	7,69%	259	1926
1927	2.463	985	3.864	8,32%	321	1927
1928	3.649	1.460	4.676	7,91%	370	1928
1929	4.671	1.868	5.866	7,77%	456	1929
1930	5.178	2.071	7.112	7,84%	558	1930
1931	5.323	2.129	8.514	6,42%	547	1931
1932	4.031	1.612	9.141	6,07%	555	1932
1933	3.223	1.289	8.970	6,17%	553	1933
1934	2.454	982	8.084	6,07%	491	1934
1935	2.505	1.002	7.014	5,74%	403	1935
1936	2.566	1.026	5.912	5,63%	333	1936
1937	2.614	1.046	5.345	5,25%	281	1937
1938	2.985	1.194	5.250	5,08%	267	1938
1939	2.253	901	5.169	5,04%	261	1939

(1) Mortgage registrations (1913 and 1919-1939 : TECHEUR P., Le crédit immobilier en Belgique de 1802 à 1954, p. 136-138; 1916-1918 : interpolation based on BUYST E., Residential Building, Table III-8).
(2) Mortgage registrations by private persons : 40 % of (1).
(3) Outstanding mortgage debt with private individuals.
(4) Rate of interest, see TECHEUR P., o.c., pp. 137-138).
(5) Interest amount on mortgage loans accruing to private individuals = (3) x (4).

TABLE 68

Interest for private individuals. Various categories (in BF millions)

year	(1)	(2)	(3)	year
1920	640	77	360	1920
1921	800	103	460	1921
1922	930	123	560	1922
1923	1.000	143	615	1923
1924	1.050	155	995	1924
1925	1.070	181	1.375	1925
1926	1.080	192	1.765	1926
1927	1.080	147	1.695	1927
1928	1.110	182	1.740	1928
1929	1.010	211	1.780	1929
1930	1.060	265	1.765	1930
1931	1.090	330	1.600	1931
1932	1.200	408	1.570	1932
1933	1.290	405	1.460	1933
1934	1.340	358	1.225	1934
1935	1.140	362	845	1935
1936	1.230	365	830	1936
1937	1.340	329	665	1937
1938	1.340	262	610	1938
1939	1.410	236	560	1939

(1) Interest on government stocks accruing to private individuals
(2) Interest from a bond loan transacted bij a company
(3) Imputed interest in connection with the free services of banks

Source: PEETERS S., Reconstruction, Annex B.

TABLE 69

Rent (received or imputed) credited to private individuals (in BF millions)

year	(1)	(2)	(3)	(4)	year
1920	1.079	357	686	750	1920
1921	1.269	427	691	1.005	1921
1922	1.425	524	772	1.177	1922
1923	1.832	552	890	1.494	1923
1924	2.117	680	1.013	1.784	1924
1925	2.529	893	1.091	2.331	1925
1926	2.835	1.088	1.298	2.625	1926
1927	3.382	1.598	1.571	3.409	1927
1928	4.220	1.706	1.912	4.014	1928
1929	5.117	1.748	2.460	4.405	1929
1930	7.761	1.669	2.830	6.600	1930
1931	8.903	1.665	2.635	7.933	1931
1932	9.549	1.629	2.502	8.676	1932
1933	9.551	1.446	2.368	8.629	1933
1934	9.470	1.308	2.180	8.599	1934
1935	9.058	1.236	2.102	8.192	1935
1936	9.108	1.364	2.144	8.327	1936
1937	9.227	1.538	2.300	8.465	1937
1938	9.370	1.502	2.400	8.473	1938
1939	9.580	1.559	2.377	8.762	1939

(1) Gross rent from improved properties (Table 71, column 7).
(2) Gross leasehold rent from unimproved properties (Table 72, column 3).
(3) Charges = depreciation, maintenance, mortgage interest (Table 73, column 3).
(4) Net rent in current prices = (1) + (2) - (3).

TABLE 70

Housing rent index for Belgium (1936-1938 = 100)

year	(1)
1920	16,3
1921	18,8
1922	20,6
1923	26,1
1924	29,3
1925	34,0
1926	37,0
1927	42,8
1928	52,7
1929	62,9
1930	94,7
1931	106,7
1932	112,3
1933	110,5
1934	107,9
1935	101,6
1936	100,4
1937	99,8
1938	99,8
1939	100,5

(1) Belgian rent index (BUYST E., Het inkomen uit onroerend patrimonium toevloeiend aan particulieren: België, 1920-1939, in "Workshop on Quantitative Economic History", tabel 5).

TABLE 71

Gross income from improved properties credited to private individuals

year	(1)	(2)	(3)	(4)	(5)	(6)	(7)	(8)	(9)	(10)	year
1920	1.972.803				3.235	6.381	16,3	1.041	38	1.079	1920
1921	2.002.757				3.251	6.510	18,8	1.223	46	1.269	1921
1922	2.038.139				3.267	6.659	20,6	1.369	56	1.425	1922
1923	2.072.911				3.283	6.806	26,1	1.773	59	1.832	1923
1924	2.111.115				3.300	6.966	29,3	2.044	73	2.117	1924
1925	2.157.853				3.316	7.156	34,0	2.433	96	2.529	1925
1926	2.203.279				3.333	7.343	37,0	2.718	117	2.835	1926
1927	2.239.636				3.349	7.502	42,8	3.209	173	3.382	1927
1928	2.277.245				3.366	7.666	52,7	4.036	184	4.220	1928
1929	2.315.449				3.383	7.833	62,9	4.930	187	5.117	1929
1930	2.354.153				3.400	8.004	94,7	7.583	178	7.761	1930
1931	2.393.651				3.417	8.179	106,7	8.725	178	8.903	1931
1932	2.430.804				3.434	8.348	112,3	9.374	175	9.549	1932
1933	2.463.643				3.451	8.503	110,5	9.396	155	9.551	1933
1934	2.492.605				3.468	8.646	107,9	9.329	141	9.470	1934
1935	2.520.088	3.577	100,0	3.577	3.486	8.785	101,6	8.925	133	9.058	1935
1936	2.548.517		98,8	3.534	3.503	8.928	100,4	8.961	147	9.108	1936
1937	2.578.269		98,2	3.514	3.521	9.078	99,8	9.061	166	9.227	1937
1938	2.607.188		98,2	3.514	3.538	9.225	99,8	9.208	162	9.370	1938
1939	2.633.323				3.556	9.364	100,5	9.411	169	9.580	1939

(1) Number of families on 30 June.
(2) Average gross rent in 1935 for residential dwellings and commercial properties (in BF).
(3) Rent index (1935 = 100) : calculated from Table 70, column 6.
(4) Average annual gross rent for residential and commercial properties = (2) x (3) / 100.
(5) Total annual gross rent (actually received or imputed) from improved properties (excluding agricultural buildings) credited to private individuals (in BF mlns) = (1) x (4)/ 1,000,000.
(6) Total annual gross rent (actually received or imputed) from agricultural buildings (in 1 000 000 BF) = 9.7% of Chapter 7 (Commercial Income from Agriculture, Horticulture and Forestry) Table 47, column 1.
(7) Housing rent index (1936-1938 = 100), see Table 70.
(8) Gross rent for residential duellings and commercial properties in current prices (in 1 000 000 BF) = $\dfrac{(6) \times (7)}{100}$
(9) Gross rent (actually received or imputed) from agricultural buildings (in 1 000 000 BF).
(10) Total annual gross rent (actually received or imputed) credited to private individuals (in 1 000 000 BF) = (5) + (6).

TABLE 72

Gross income from unimproved properties credited to private individuals (in BF millions)

year	(1)	(2)	(3)	year
1920	341	16	357	1920
1921	413	14	427	1921
1922	506	18	524	1922
1923	530	22	552	1923
1924	655	25	680	1924
1925	864	29	893	1925
1926	1.051	37	1.088	1926
1927	1.554	44	1.598	1927
1928	1.654	52	1.706	1928
1929	1.688	60	1.748	1929
1930	1.601	68	1.669	1930
1931	1.604	61	1.665	1931
1932	1.574	55	1.629	1932
1933	1.398	48	1.446	1933
1934	1.267	41	1.308	1934
1935	1.202	34	1.236	1935
1936	1.326	38	1.364	1936
1937	1.494	44	1.538	1937
1938	1.461	41	1.502	1938
1939	1.516	43	1.559	1939

(1) Gross income from agricultural land credited to private individuals (leases: actually received or imputed) = 90% of Chapter 7, "Commercial Income from Agriculture, Horticulture and Forestry)" Table 47, column 1.
(2) Gross income from ownership of woodland credited to private individuals, Table 48, column 12.
(3) Gross income from unimproved properties credited to private individuals = (1) + (2).

TABLE 73

Total charges (in BF millions)

year	(1)	(2)	(3)	(4)	year
1920	455	175	56	686	1920
1921	434	172	85	691	1921
1922	463	192	117	772	1922
1923	515	215	160	890	1923
1924	557	241	215	1.013	1924
1925	575	251	266	1.091	1925
1926	684	288	326	1.298	1926
1927	832	338	400	1.571	1927
1928	969	485	459	1.912	1928
1929	1.202	682	576	2.460	1929
1930	1.332	851	647	2.830	1930
1931	1.206	789	640	2.635	1931
1932	1.140	733	629	2.502	1932
1933	1.059	690	619	2.368	1933
1934	974	654	551	2.180	1934
1935	988	655	459	2.102	1935
1936	1.060	699	386	2.144	1936
1937	1.176	779	345	2.300	1937
1938	1.235	830	334	2.400	1938
1939	1.220	838	319	2.377	1939

(1) Depreciation, see BUYST E., Inkomen..., Table 5.
(2) Maintenance costs, see ibidem.
(3) Mortgage interest charges, see ibidem.
(4) Total charges = (1) + (2) + (3).

TABLE 74

Dividends, proceeds from investments abroad, directors' bonuses, donations to private individuals resident in Belgium: summary table (in BF millions)

year	(1)	(2)	(3)	(4)	(5)	(6)	year
1920	850	24	255	152	28	1.309	1920
1921	510	9	173	86	17	794	1921
1922	725	18	215	127	24	1.109	1922
1923	1.264	39	207	229	42	1.782	1923
1924	1.360	64	284	268	45	2.021	1924
1925	1.300	75	325	270	43	2.013	1925
1926	1.740	98	466	359	58	2.721	1926
1927	2.027	112	580	416	91	3.226	1927
1928	2.519	122	683	500	101	3.925	1928
1929	3.142	112	675	584	121	4.634	1929
1930	2.931	110	714	550	136	4.442	1930
1931	2.222	75	523	408	99	3.327	1931
1932	1.876	50	379	332	42	2.679	1932
1933	1.844	49	396	326	29	2.644	1933
1934	1.827	52	449	326	39	2.692	1934
1935	2.201	74	459	404	45	3.182	1935
1936	2.844	107	451	533	70	4.004	1936
1937	3.293	131	480	625	86	4.615	1937
1938	3.248	122	357	609	79	4.415	1938
1939	2.741	82	238	493	65	3.618	1939

(1) Dividends paid to Belgian companies principally trading in Belgium to private individuals resident in Belgium = Table 75 column 15.
(2) Dividends paid out by Belgian companies principally trading in the colonies or abroad to private individuals resident in Belgium = Table 76 column 7.
(3) Income from investment abroad (excluding dividends paid to Belgian companies) accruing to private individuals resident in Belgium = Table 77 column 7.
(4) Directors' bonuses = Table 78 column 4.
(5) Corporate grants to households or non-profit making institutions serving households = Table 78 column 6.
(6) Total and current prices = (1) + (2) + (3) + (4) + (5).

TABLE 75

Dividends paid by Belgian companies principally trading in Belgium (in BF millions)

year	(1)	(2)	(3)	(4)	(5)	(6)	(7)	(8)	(9)	(10)	(11)	(12)	(13)	(14)	year
1920	850	160	1.010	84,2%										850	1920
1921	510	60	570	89,5%										510	1921
1922	725	120	845	85,8%										725	1922
1923	1.264	263	1.527	82,8%										1.264	1923
1924	1.360	427	1.787	76,1%										1.360	1924
1925	1.300	500	1.800	72,2%										1.300	1925
1926	2.203													1.740	1926
1927	2.494	810	3.013	73,1%					2.395	2.395		72,7%	1.740	2.027	1927
1928	2.788								2.898	2.772		73,1%	2.027	2.519	1928
1929	2.201								3.479	3.334		75,5%	2.519	3.142	1929
1930	1.416								4.028	3.891		80,8%	3.142	2.931	1930
1931	1.351								3.547	3.667		79,9%	2.931	2.222	1931
1932	1.479								2.447	2.722		81,6%	2.222	1.876	1932
1933	1.291								2.135	2.213		84,8%	1.876	1.844	1933
1934	1.924	216	1.507	85,7%	1.851	2.201	316	492	2.183	2.171		84,9%	1.844	1.827	1934
1935	2.362	346	2.270	84,8%	2.317	2.844	551	713	2.167	2.171	81,7%	84,1%	1.827	2.201	1935
1936	2.871	623	2.985	79,1%	3.019	3.293	767	877	2.868	2.693	80,0%			2.844	1936
1937	2.552	580	3.451	83,2%	3.384	3.248	913	815	3.786	3.557	79,0%			3.293	1937
1938		404	2.956	86,3%	3.202	2.741	782	544	4.297	4.169	79,9%			3.248	1938
1939					2.587		465		3.984	4.062	83,4%			2.741	1939
1940									3.052	3.285					1940

(1) Fiscal statistics: dividends paid by Belgian companies principally trading in Belgium.
(2) Fiscal statistics: dividends paid by Belgian companies principally trading abroad or in the colonies.
(3) Fiscal statistics: dividends paid by all Belgian companies = (1) + (2).
(4) Fiscal statistics: (1) ÷ (3).
(5) Return-on-capital statistics (according to the year in which dividends were paid): dividends paid by Belgian companies principally trading in Belgium.
(6) Return-on-capital statistics (according to activity year): dividends paid by Belgian companies principally trading in Belgium = own calculation on basis of (5) : see text.
(7) Return-on-capital statistics (according to year in which dividends were paid) : dividends paid by Belgian companies principally trading abroad or in the colonies.
(8) Return-on-capital statistics (according to activity year): dividends paid by Belgian companies trading abroad or in the colonies = own calculation on basis of (7): see text.
(9) Return-on-capital statistics (according to year in which dividends were paid): dividends paid by all Belgian companies: 1927-1934 = total figure from the return-on-capital statistics; 1935-1940 = (5) + (7).
(10) Return-on-capital statistics (according to activity year): dividends paid by all Belgian companies = own calculation on basis of (9): see text.
(11) Return-on-capital statistics: (6) ÷ (10).
(12) Estimated share of dividends paid by Belgian companies principally trading in Belgium in relation to dividends paid by all Belgian companies: see text.
(13) Estimate of dividends paid by Belgian companies principally trading in Belgium (1926-1934) = (10) x (12).
(14) Dividends paid by Belgian Companies principally trading in Belgium. 1921-1925 = (1); 1926-1934 = (13); 1935-1939 = (6).

Sources:

- fiscal statistics 1920-1922 (= 1921-1923 financial years): House of Representatives, Bulletin van Vragen en Antwoorden, ordinary session 1924-1925, 14 December 1924, p. 53: question no. 6 by R. De Bruyne; MAHAIM E., La fortune et le bien-être, p. 528.
- fiscal statistics 1923 (= 1924 financial year): BAUDHUIN F., Quel est le revenu actuel de la Belgique, p. 54; MAHAIM, E., o.c., p. 528.
- fiscal statistics 1924-1925 (= 1925-1926 financial years): BAU-DHUIN F., Finances belges. La stabilisation et ses conséquences, p. 238.
- fiscal statistics 1927 (=1928 financial year): BAUDHUIN F., Le revenu national en 1930, p. 375 ; Idem, Le système fiscal belge et la crise (1928-1935), p. 182.
- fiscal statistics 1928-1933 (= 1929-1934 financial years): BAUDHUIN F., Le système fiscal, p. 182.
- fiscal statistics 1934-1938 (= 1935-1939 financial years), L'évolution de la structure des revenus d'après les statistiques fiscales, p. 20.
- return-on-capital statistics 1927-1928: Belgische economische statistieken 1919-1928, pp. 19-22.
- return-on-capital statistics 1929-1940: Idem 1929-1940, pp. 160-187.

TABLE 76

Dividends paid by Belgian companies principally trading in the colonies or abroad
(in BF millions)

year	(1)	(2)	(3)	(4)	(5)	(6)	(7)	year
1920	160					160	24	1920
1921	60					60	9	1921
1922	120					120	18	1922
1923	263					263	39	1923
1924	427					427	64	1924
1925	500					500	75	1925
1926			2.395	27,3%	655	655	98	1926
1927	810		2.772	26,9%	745	745	112	1927
1928			3.334	24,5%	815	815	122	1928
1929			3.891	19,2%	749	749	112	1929
1930			3.667	20,1%	736	736	110	1930
1931			2.722	18,4%	500	500	75	1931
1932			2.213	15,2%	337	337	50	1932
1933			2.171	15,1%	327	327	49	1933
1934	216		2.171	15,9%	344	344	52	1934
1935	346	492				492	74	1935
1936	623	713				713	107	1936
1937	580	877				877	131	1937
1938	404	815				815	122	1938
1939		544				544	82	1939

(1) Fiscal statistics: dividends paid by Belgian companies principally trading in the colonies or abroad = Table 75 column 2.
(2) Return-on-capital statistics (according to activity year): dividends paid by Belgian companies principally trading in the colonies or abroad = Table 75 column 8.
(3) Return-on-capital statistics (according to activity year): dividends paid by all Belgian companies = Table 75 column 10.
(4) Estimated share of dividends paid by Belgian companies principally trading in the colonies or abroad in relation to dividends paid by all Belgian companies = 100% - Table 75 column 12.
(5) Estimate of dividends paid by Belgian companies principally trading in the colonies or abroad (1926-1934) = (3) x (4).
(6) Dividends paid by Belgian companies principally trading in the colonies or abroad: 1920-1925 = (1); 1926-1934 = (5); 1935-1939 = (2).
(7) Dividends paid by Belgian companies principally trading in the colonies or abroad accruing to private individuals resident in Belgium = 15% of (6).

TABLE 77

Income from investments abroad (including dividends from Belgian companies) (in BF millions)

year	(1)	(2)	(3)	(4)	(5)	(6)	(7)	year
1920	510	160		510	255	765	255	1920
1921	345	60		345	173	518	173	1921
1922	430	120		430	215	645	215	1922
1923	414	263		414	207	621	207	1923
1924	568	427		568	284	852	284	1924
1925	650	500		650	325	975	325	1925
1926		655	931	931	466	1.397	466	1926
1927	1.160	745		1.160	580	1.740	580	1927
1928		815	1.366	1.366	683	2.048	683	1928
1929		749	1.350	1.350	675	2.025	675	1929
1930		736	1.429	1.429	714	2.143	714	1930
1931		500	1.045	1.045	523	1.568	523	1931
1932		337	757	757	379	1.136	379	1932
1933		327	793	793	396	1.189	396	1933
1934	897	344		897	449	1.346	449	1934
1935	917	492		917	459	1.376	459	1935
1936	901	713		901	451	1.352	451	1936
1937	960	877		960	480	1.440	480	1937
1938	714	815		714	357	1.071	357	1938
1939		544	477	477	238	715	238	1939

(1) Fiscal statistics: income from investments abroad (excluding dividends from Belgian companies), Sources: see Table 75.
(2) Dividends paid by Belgian companies principally trading in the colonies or abroad (Table 76 column 6).
(3) Income from investments abroad (excluding dividends from Belgian companies): trend-corrected interpolation of (1) on the basis of (2).
(4) Income from investments abroad (excluding dividends from Belgian companies and excluding tax fraud) = (1) and (3).
(5) Estimate of tax fraud = 50% of (4).
(6) Income from investments abroad (excluding dividends from Belgian companies and including tax fraud) = (4) + (5).
(7) Income from investments abroad accruing to private individuals resident in Belgium = 1/3 of (6).

TABLE 78

Directors' bonuses and corporate grants to households or non-profit making organizations serving households (in BF millions)

year	(1)	(2)	(3)	(4)	(5)	(6)	year
1920	850	160	1.010	152	97	28	1920
1921	510	60	570	86		17	1921
1922	725	120	845	127	110	24	1922
1923	1.264	263	1.527	229		42	1923
1924	1.360	427	1.787	268	260	45	1924
1925	1.300	500	1.800	270		43	1925
1926	1.740	655	2.395	359		58	1926
1927	2.027	745	2.772	416	450	91	1927
1928	2.519	815	3.334	500	500	101	1928
1929	3.142	749	3.891	584	689	121	1929
1930	2.931	736	3.667	550	751	136	1930
1931	2.222	500	2.722	408		99	1931
1932	1.876	337	2.213	332	611	42	1932
1933	1.844	327	2.171	326		29	1933
1934	1.827	344	2.171	326		39	1934
1935	2.201	492	2.693	404	502	45	1935
1936	2.844	713	3.557	533		70	1936
1937	3.293	877	4.169	625		86	1937
1938	3.248	815	4.062	609		79	1938
1939	2.741	544	3.285	493		65	1939

(1) Dividends paid by Belgian companies principally trading in Belgium (Table 75 column 14).
(2) Dividends paid by Belgian companies principally trading in the colonies or abroad (Table 76 column 6).
(3) Total dividends paid by Belgian companies = (1) + (2).
(4) Estimate of directors' bonuses = 15% of (3).
(5) Fiscal statistics: directors' income subject to trade tax (the figures relate to the year in which the income was earned, not to the tax year (year of earning = tax year -1).
   Source: see Chapter 8, "Entrepreneurial income of the professions, independent traders, craftsmen and partnerships".
(6) Corporate grants to households and non-profit making institutions serving households = Chapter 12 Table 81 column 5.

TABLE 79

Saving of corporations: summary table (in BF millions)

year	(1)	(2)	(3)	year
1920	383	-1	382	1920
1921	230	-4	226	1921
1922	326	-1	325	1922
1923	569	-2	566	1923
1924	612	3	615	1924
1925	585	7	592	1925
1926	783	5	788	1926
1927	2.059	14	2.073	1927
1928	1.988	58	2.046	1928
1929	2.396	100	2.496	1929
1930	3.257	120	3.378	1930
1931	2.290	57	2.347	1931
1932	-24	11	-13	1932
1933	-623	49	-574	1933
1934	-171	50	-121	1934
1935	-361	44	-317	1935
1936	88	48	136	1936
1937	329	44	373	1937
1938	41	47	88	1938
1939	-50	46	-4	1939

(1) Undistributed profits of companies limited by shares = Table 81 column 6.
(2) Undistributed profits of autonomous public institutions = Table 83 column 6.
(3) Total at current prices = (1) + (2).

TABLE 80

Net profit of Belgian joint-stock companies principally trading in Belgium (in BF millions)

year	(1)	(2)	(3)	(4)	(5)	(6)	(7)	(8)	(9)	(10)	(11)	(12)	(13)	(14)	(15)	year
1920											850		60%	1.417	1.417	1920
1921											510		60%	850	850	1921
1922											725		60%	1.208	1.208	1922
1923											1.264		60%	2.107	2.107	1923
1924											1.360		60%	2.267	2.267	1924
1925											1.300		60%	2.167	2.167	1925
1926											1.740		60%	2.901	2.901	1926
1927					6.492	238	6.254		73,1%	4.573	2.027	44%			4.573	1927
1928					7.106	332	6.774		74,5%	5.045	2.519	50%			5.045	1928
1929					8.315	363	7.952		75,8%	6.030	3.142	52%			6.030	1929
1930					9.508	719	8.789		77,2%	6.784	2.931	43%			6.784	1930
1931					7.483	1.185	6.298		78,5%	4.946	2.222	45%			4.946	1931
1932					4.667	2.048	2.620		79,9%	2.093	1.876	90%			2.093	1932
1933					3.906	2.104	1.802		81,2%	1.464	1.844	126%			1.464	1933
1934					4.054	1.669	2.385		82,6%	1.970	1.827	93%			1.970	1934
1935	2.454	1.010	1.444	2.260	3.882	1.220	2.662	84,9%			2.201	97%			2.260	1935
1936	3.476	944	2.532	3.498	5.693	1.170	4.523	77,3%			2.844	81%			3.498	1936
1937	4.224	404	3.820	4.287	7.141	469	6.672	64,3%			3.293	77%			4.287	1937
1938	4.788	345	4.443	3.933	8.342	435	7.907	49,7%			3.248	83%			3.933	1938
1939	4.216	453	3.763	3.231	6.979	804	6.175				2.741	85%			3.231	1939
1940	3.835	781	3.054		5.974	806	5.168	52,3%								1940

(1) Return-on-capital statistics (according to year in which dividends were distributed): net profit of Belgian companies principally trading in Belgium with a positive net result.
(2) Return-on-capital statistics (according to year in which dividends were distributed): net loss of Belgian companies principally trading in Belgium with a negative net result.
(3) Return-on-capital statistics (according to year in which dividends were distributed): net result of Belgian companies principally trading in Belgium = (1) - (2).
(4) Return-on-capital statistics (according to activity year): net result of Belgian compa-nies principally trading in Belgium = own calculation on basis of (3): see text.
(5) Return-on-capital statistics (according to year in which dividends were distributed): net profit of all Belgian companies with a positive net result, including an incremental factor of 35 % for underestimation.
(6) Return-on-capital statistics (according to year in which dividends were distributed): net loss of all Belgian companies principally trading in Belgium with a negative net result.
(7) Return-on-capital statistics (according to year in which dividends were distributed): net result of all Belgian companies = (5) - (6).
(8) Share of net result of Belgian companies principally trading in Belgium in relation to net result of all Belgian companies in 1935-1939 = 4 ÷ 7.
(9) Estimated share of net result of Belgian companies principally trading in Belgium in relation to net result of all Belgian companies in 1927-1934 = Chapter 11 Table 75 column 12: see also text.
(10) Estimate of net result of Belgian companies principally trading in Belgium 1927-1934 = (7) x (9).
(11) Dividends distributed by Belgian companies principally trading in Belgium = Chapter 11 Table 75 column 14.
(12) Ratio of dividends distributed/net result of Belgian companies principally trading in Belgium: 1927-1934 = (11) ÷ (10); 1935-1939 = (11) ÷ (4).
(13) Estimate of ratio of dividends distributed/net result of Belgian companies principally trading in Belgium (1920-1926) = own estimate: see text.
(14) Estimate of net result of Belgian companies principally trading in Belgium (1920-1926) = (11) ÷ (13).
(15) Net result of Belgian companies principally trading in Belgium: 1920-1926 = (14); 1927-1934 = (10); 1935-1939 = (4).

TABLE 81

Profits reserved by Belgian joint-stock companies principally trading in Belgium (in BF millions)

year	(1)	(2)	(3)	(4)	(5)	(6)	year
1920	1.417	850	128	28	28	383	1920
1921	850	510	77	17	17	230	1921
1922	1.208	725	109	24	24	326	1922
1923	2.107	1.264	190	42	42	569	1923
1924	2.267	1.360	204	45	45	612	1924
1925	2.167	1.300	195	43	43	585	1925
1926	2.901	1.740	261	58	58	783	1926
1927	4.573	2.027	304	91	91	2.059	1927
1928	5.045	2.519	378	101	101	1.988	1928
1929	6.030	3.142	471	121	121	2.396	1929
1930	6.784	2.931	440	136	136	3.257	1930
1931	4.946	2.222	333	99	99	2.290	1931
1932	2.093	1.876	281	42	42	-24	1932
1933	1.464	1.844	277	29	29	-623	1933
1934	1.970	1.827	274	39	39	-171	1934
1935	2.260	2.201	330	45	45	-361	1935
1936	3.498	2.844	427	70	70	88	1936
1937	4.287	3.293	494	86	86	329	1937
1938	3.933	3.248	487	79	79	41	1938
1939	3.231	2.741	411	65	65	-50	1939

(1) Net profit = Table 80 column 15.
(2) Distributed dividends = Table 75 column 14.
(3) Estimate of directors' bonuses = 15% of (2).
(4) Estimate of staff bonuses = 2% of (1).
(5) Estimate of grants to households and to non-profit making institutions serving households = 2% of (1).
(6) Reserved profits = (1)-(2)-(3)-(4)-(5).

TABLE 82

Reserved profits: comparison with results from other sources (in BF millions)

year	(1)	(2)	(3)	(4)	(5)	year
1920	383	800				1920
1921	230					1921
1922	326					1922
1923	569					1923
1924	612					1924
1925	585					1925
1926	783	2.600	1.500			1926
1927	2.059					1927
1928	1.988	3.091				1928
1929	2.396	3.648				1929
1930	3.257	3.028	3.250			1930
1931	2.290	1.955				1931
1932	-24	1.171				1932
1933	-623	873				1933
1934	-171	558				1934
1935	-361	678	(900)			1935
1936	88	1.090	1.500	15.460		1936
1937	329		1.500	15.656	196	1937
1938	41		1.250	15.203	-453	1938
1939	-50			14.630	-573	1939
1940				14.575		1940

(1) Reserved profits of Belgian companies principally trading in Belgium = Table 81 column 6.
(2) Reserved profits subject to corporation tax:
   1920: MAHAIM E., La fortune et le bien-être, 523.
   1926: BAUDHUIN F., Le revenu national en 1930, p. 374.
   1928-1935: Le rendement de la taxe professionnelle de 1928 and 1935, p. 16 (in 1935: 678 million).
   1935-1936: Legislative Chambers, Bulletin van Vragen en Antwoorden, ordinary session 1950-1951, no. 5, 9 January 1951, p. 173 (in 1935: BF 900 million).
(3) Baudhuin's Estimates:
   1926 and 1930: BAUDHUIN F., o.c., pp. 374 and 376.
   1936 and 1937: BAUDHUIN F., La Belgique en 1937. Les finances belges en 1937, p. 126.
   1938: BAUDHUIN F., Placements. Principes permanents d'économie privée. (Cours à l'université de Louvain), 3rd edition, 1944, p. 49.
(4) Return-on-capital statistics (according to year in which dividends were distributed): reserves of Belgian companies principally trading in Belgium. Belgische economische statistieken 1929-1940, pp. 174-186.
(5) Return-on-capital statistics (according to activity year): reserves of Belgian companies principally trading in Belgium = own calculation on basis of (4): see text.
(6) Return-on-capital statistics (according to activity year): growth in reserves of Belgian companies principally trading in Belgium = own calculation on basis of (5).

TABLE 83

Undistributed profits of autonomous public companies (in BF millions)

year	(1)	(2)	(3)	(4)	(5)	(6)
1920	0,3	-1,4	0,2	0,0	0,0	-1,0
1921	0,2	-4,0	0,1	0,0	0,0	-3,6
1922	0,4	-2,1	0,2	0,0	0,0	-1,5
1923	0,4	-3,3	0,4	0,0	0,0	-2,5
1924	0,4	1,2	0,8	0,0	0,0	2,5
1925	0,3	5,4	0,9	0,0	0,0	6,6
1926	0,4	3,3	1,4	0,0	0,0	5,1
1927	6,6	5,3	1,6	0,3	0,4	14,3
1928	43,3	7,8	2,0	2,2	2,6	57,8
1929	80,6	8,9	1,5	4,0	4,8	99,9
1930	106,9	0,1	1,5	5,3	6,4	120,3
1931	58,2	-9,1	1,6	2,9	3,5	57,2
1932	15,7	-8,2	2,0	0,8	0,9	11,2
1933	46,9	-4,8	1,9	2,3	2,8	49,2
1934	48,1	-5,1	1,8	2,4	2,9	50,1
1935	45,0	-8,7	2,9	2,2	2,7	44,2
1936	41,2	-2,8	4,6	2,1	2,5	47,6
1937	39,8	-4,7	4,0	2,0	2,4	43,6
1938	47,6	-9,9	4,5	2,4	2,9	47,4
1939	45,6	-7,9	3,2	2,3	2,7	45,8

(1) ASLK. *Source* : annual reports.
(2) Nationale Maatschappij van Buurtspoorwegen. *Source:* annual reports.
(3) Gemeentekrediet, Centraal Bureau voor Hypothecair Krediet (from 1936 onwards), Tijdelijk Kredietfonds ten behoeve van de Middenstand (1935-37) / Nationale Kredietkas ten behoeve van de Middenstand (1938-39), Herdiscontering- en Waarborginstituut (from 1936 onwards), Nationaal Instituut voor Landbouwkrediet (from 1938 onwards). *Source:* annual reports.
(4) Other government institutions with special statutes (5% of (1)).
(5) Intercommunale enterprises (6% of (1)).
(6) Total = (1)+(2)+(3)+(4).

TABLE 84

Direct taxation of companies: (in BF millions)

year	(1)	(2)	(3)	(4)	(5)	year
1920	38	27	16		82	1920
1921	64	39	22		125	1921
1922	77	35	23		134	1922
1923	113	54	26		193	1923
1924	102	86	28		216	1924
1925	83	96	32		211	1925
1926	93	110	74		277	1926
1927	207	147	53		408	1927
1928	202	164	59		426	1928
1929	247	182	66		495	1929
1930	291	220	53		564	1930
1931	242	176	70		487	1931
1932	156	131	67		354	1932
1933	93	114	69	112	388	1933
1934	70	111	69	84	334	1934
1935	45	95	53	53	245	1935
1936	54	129	57	65	305	1936
1937	87	155	58	52	352	1937
1938	11	182	59	7	258	1938
1939	0	160	61	0	221	1939

(1) Trade tax (see Table 85 column 7).
(2) Financial securities tax (see Table 86 column 2).
(3) Land tax (see Table 86 column 4).
(4) National crisis tax (1933-1936 - (1) x 1.2; 1937-1938 = (1) x 0.6; 1939 = (1) x (1.2).
(5) Total at current prices = (1)+(2)+(3)+(4).

TABLE 85

Estimate of trade tax paid by companies (per financial year in BF millions)

year	(1)	(2)	(3)	(4)	(5)	(6)	(7)	year
1920					383	38	38	1920
1921		800		64	230		64	1921
1922					326	77	77	1922
1923					569	113	113	1923
1924					612	102	102	1924
1925					585	83	83	1925
1926					783	93	93	1926
1927		2.600		207	2.059		207	1927
1928					1.988	202	202	1928
1929		3.091		247	2.396		247	1929
1930	291	3.648	8,0%	291	3.257		291	1930
1931		3.028		242	2.290		242	1931
1932		1.955		156	-24		156	1932
1933		1.171		93	-623		93	1933
1934		873		70	-171		70	1934
1935		558		45	-361		45	1935
1936		678		54	88		54	1936
1937		1.090		87	329		87	1937
1938					41	11	11	1938
1939					-50	0	0	1939

Note: The trade tax payable in tax year t relates to the profits stated in the balance sheets for the year ending 31 December 1929 or some time in the course of 1930, depending on whether or not the companies' accounting year corresponded with the calendar year. For the sake of simplicity it has been assumed that all companies concluded their balance sheets at 31 December, so that the trade tax in year t was levied in its entirety on the reserved profits of year t-1.

(1) Estimate of trade tax paid by companies in 1930 financial year (= on reserved profit of 1929): see text.
(2) Reserved profits of companies subject to trade tax in financial year t (= reserved profit of t-1). *Sources:* see Table 82 column 2.
(3) Average tax rate in 1930 = (1) ÷ (2).
(4) Estimate of trade tax paid by companies in the years for which the fiscally reserved profit is known = (2) x (3).
(5) Reserved profit of companies limited by shares: Table 82 column 1.
(6) Estimate of trade tax paid by companies in the years for which the fiscally reserved profit is not known:
1920: 64 (= figure for 1921, see column 4) x 118 (= total trade tax revenues in 1920, see Chapter 8 Table 2 column 3) ÷ 218 (= total trade tax revenues in 1921, see Chapter 8 Table 2 column 3).
1922 -1926 and 1928: trend-corrected interpolation on basis of (5).
1938-1939: extrapolation on basis of evolution (5).
(7) Trade tax paid by companies = (4) and (6).

TABLE 86

Estimate of financial securities tax and land tax paid by companies
(annual figures - in BF millions)

year	(1)	(2)	(3)	(4)	year
1920	137	27	108	16	1920
1921	195	39	150	22	1921
1922	174	35	151	23	1922
1923	270	54	175	26	1923
1924	432	86	185	28	1924
1925	482	96	211	32	1925
1926	549	110	490	74	1926
1927	737	147	353	53	1927
1928	822	164	394	59	1928
1929	910	182	441	66	1929
1930	1.101	220	353	53	1930
1931	879	176	464	70	1931
1932	653	131	450	67	1932
1933	569	114	458	69	1933
1934	554	111	463	69	1934
1935	473	95	352	53	1935
1936	644	129	379	57	1936
1937	775	155	385	58	1937
1938	910	182	390	59	1938
1939	800	160	408	61	1939

(1) Total receipts from financial securities tax (Bulletin van de directe belastingen, no. 181, February 1943, p. 68).
(2) Estimate of financial securities tax paid by companies = 20% of (1).
(3) Total receipts from land tax (Source: see (1)).
(4) Estimate of land tax paid by companies = 15% of (3).

TABLE 87

Imputed net rent accruing to the government (in BF millions)

year	(1)	(2)	(3)	year
1920	54,5	5.923	113	1920
1921	54,2	6.357	121	1921
1922	52,7	6.818	126	1922
1923	58,3	7.177	146	1923
1924	65,5	7.427	170	1924
1925	63,8	7.653	171	1925
1926	75,5	7.699	203	1926
1927	88,9	7.542	235	1927
1928	98,0	7.417	254	1928
1929	117,3	7.364	302	1929
1930	124,4	7.446	324	1930
1931	110,3	7.613	294	1931
1932	99,8	7.689	269	1932
1933	91,7	7.701	247	1933
1934	85,8	7.810	235	1934
1935	86,2	7.967	240	1935
1936	91,4	8.483	271	1936
1937	102,6	9.321	335	1937
1938	106,4	10.004	373	1938
1939	102,7	10.093	363	1939

(1) Price index Other Buildings (1936-38 = 100).
(2) Gross capital stock buildings public and other government on mid-year basis at 1936-38 prices.
(3) Total imputed net rent at current prices = (2) x 0.035 x (1) / 100.

TABLE 88

Income from property and entrepreneurial income accruing to the central government: total excluding income derived from the railways, post office, telegraph and telephone
(in BF millions)

year	(1)	(2)	(3)	(4)	(5)	(6)	(7)	(8)	year
1920								75	1920
1921								97	1921
1922								95	1922
1923	8	62	70	57	7	64	3	137	1923
1924	11	25	36	70	14	84	3	123	1924
1925	164	44	208	64	14	78	3	289	1925
1926	33	37	70	109	23	132	4	206	1926
1927	31	60	91	127	38	165	3	259	1927
1928	107	23	130	141	52	193	4	327	1928
1929	191	40	231	195	56	251	7	489	1929
1930	136	75	211	100	36	136	15	362	1930
1931	18	32	50	55	28	83	9	142	1931
1932	2	30	32	22	16	38	7	77	1932
1933	0	43	43	21	28	49	7	99	1933
1934	8	41	49	14	33	47	7	103	1934
1935	5	31	36	12	22	34	7	77	1935
1936	1	63	64	12	36	48	8	120	1936
1937	2	100	102	12	87	99	8	209	1937
1938	1	65	66	17	80	97	9	172	1938
1939	1	62	63	23	79	102	6	171	1939

(1) Proceeds from the investment of the available Exchequer monies.
(2) Other interest on government receivables.
(3) Interest on government receivables = (1) + (2).
(4) Share in the operating profit of the National Bank of Belgium.
(5) Entrepreneurial income and share in the operating profit of other public enterprises (excluding railways, post offices, telegraph and telephone).
(6) Share in the operating profit of public enterprises (excluding railways, post offices, telegraphs and telephones) = (4) + (5).
(7) Dividends accruing to the central government.
(8) Total: 1923-1939 = (3)+(6)+(7); 1920-1922: estimate on basis of the Accounts of the Audit Office (Final accounts of the budget of the Belgian State).

Source:
- 1923-1939: Accounts of the Audit Office (Final accounts of the budget of the Belgian State).
- 1920-1922: Estimate on the basis of the Books of the Audit Office: Final accounts of the budget of the Belgian State.

TABLE 89

Income from property and entrepreneurial income accruing to the central government: income derived from the railways (in BF millions)

year	(1)	(2)	(3)	(4)	(5)	(6)	(7)	(8)	(9)	year
1920	864									1920
1921	998									1921
1922	1.126									1922
1923	1.271	1.203	68						68	1923
1924	1.691	1.747	-56						-56	1924
1925	1.730	1.784	-54						-54	1925
1926	1.381	1.554	-173						-173	1926
1927				270	135		405		405	1927
1928				200	100		300		300	1928
1929				200	100		300		300	1929
1930				100	50		150		150	1930
1931							0		0	1931
1932							0		0	1932
1933							0	-20	-20	1933
1934						2	2	-20	-18	1934
1935						6	6	-20	-14	1935
1936					21	7	28	-22	6	1936
1937						9	9	-27	-18	1937
1938						10	10	-32	-22	1938
1939						10	10	-32	-22	1939

(1) Current State Railways receipts.
(2) Current State Railways expenditure.
(3) Net State Railways = (1) - (2).
(4) Share of the State in the profits of the NMBS.
(5) Dividend on the NMBS preference shares assigned to the State but not issued ("super-dividend").
(6) Interest on the profit-sharing bonds of the NMBS issued to the State.
(7) Total income accruing to the State = (4)+(5)+(6).
(8) Price-reducing subsidies.
(9) Income from property and entrepreneurial income from the Railways accruing to the government = (3)+(7)+(8).

Source: Accounts of the Audit Office (Final accounts of the budget of the Belgian State).

TABLE 90

Income from property and entrepreneurial income accruing to the central government: income deriving from the post office and the telegraph and telephone company

year	(1)	(2)	(3)	(4)	(5)	(6)	year
1920	40			52			1920
1921	57			63			1921
1922	105			73			1922
1923	111	123	-12	74	70	4	1923
1924	149	169	-20	101	100	1	1924
1925	184	196	-12	170	150	20	1925
1926	228	223	5	222	183	39	1926
1927	285	294	-9	237	188	49	1927
1928	334	358	-24	274	250	24	1928
1929	368	405	-37	313	297	16	1929
1930	402	486	-84				1930
1931	426	478	-52				1931
1932	417	419	-2				1932
1933	400	385	15				1933
1934	406	331	75				1934
1935	412	320	92				1935
1936	429	348	81				1936
1937	453	366	87				1937
1938	460	398	62				1938
1939	443	383	60				1939

(1) Post Office: current receipts.
(2) Post Office: current expenditure.
(3) Post Office: balance = (1)-(2).
(4) Telegraph and Telephone: current receipts.
(5) Telegraph and Telephone: current expenditure.
(6) Telegraph and Telephone: balance = (4)-(5).

Source: Boeken van het Rekenhof: Final accounts of the budget of the Belgian State.

TABLE 91

Income from property and entrepreneurial income accruing to the central government: total (in BF millions)

year	(1)	(2)	(3)	(4)	(5)	(6)	(7)	(8)	year
1920	75				956	1.077	-121	-46	1920
1921	97				1.118	1.195	-77	20	1921
1922	95				1.304	1.213	91	186	1922
1923	137	68	-12	4				197	1923
1924	123	-56	-20	1				48	1924
1925	289	-54	-12	20				243	1925
1926	206	-173	5	39				77	1926
1927	259	405	-9	49				704	1927
1928	327	300	-24	24				627	1928
1929	489	300	-37	16				768	1929
1930	362	150	-84					428	1930
1931	142	0	-52					90	1931
1932	77	0	-2					75	1932
1933	99	-20	15					94	1933
1934	103	-18	75					160	1934
1935	77	-14	92					155	1935
1936	120	6	81					207	1936
1937	209	-18	87					278	1937
1938	172	-22	62					212	1938
1939	171	-22	60					209	1939

(1) Total excluding income deriving from the railways, Post Office, Telegraph and Telephone (Table 88 column 8).
(2) Income deriving from the railways (Table 89 column 9).
(3) Income deriving from the Post Office (Table 90 column 3).
(4) Income deriving from the Telegraph and Telephone (Table 90 column 6).
(5) Total current receipts of the State Railways, Post Office, Telegraphs and Telephone (Accounts of the Audit Office : Final accounts of the budget of the Belgian State) = Table 89 column 1 + Table 90 column 1 + Table 90 column 4.
(6) Total current expenditure of the State Railways, Post Office, Telegraph and Telephone Company (estimate on the basis of the Accounts of the Audit Office (Final accounts of the budget of the Belgian State).
(7) Total net balances of the railways, Post Office, Telegraph and Telephone Company = (5)-(6).
(8) Income from property and entrepreneurial income accruing to the central government = (1)+(2)+(3)+(4)+(7).

TABLE 92

Statutory pension funds: interest on actuarial reserves (in BF millions)

year	(1)	(2)	(3)	year
1920	14	5	19	1920
1921	15	6	21	1921
1922	16	8	24	1922
1923	17	11	28	1923
1924	19	13	32	1924
1925	20	15	35	1925
1926	24	18	41	1926
1927	32	20	52	1927
1928	43	24	66	1928
1929	56	28	84	1929
1930	71	34	106	1930
1931	90	43	133	1931
1932	115	49	164	1932
1933	139	52	191	1933
1934	157	53	210	1934
1935	176	53	228	1935
1936	195	53	248	1936
1937	215	54	270	1937
1938	238	58	296	1938
1939	261	62	323	1939

(1) Interest on actuarial reserves of statutory pension funds (Table 93 column 8).
(2) Interest on actuarial reserves of funds for industrial accident insurance (Table 94 column 7).
(3) Total = (1) + (2).

TABLE 93

Interest on actuarial reserves of statutory pension funds (in BF millions)

year	(1)	(2)	(3)	(4)	(5)	(6)	(7)	(8)	year
1919				336	1,10	370			1919
1920				354	1,10	390	380	14	1920
1921				381	1,10	419	404	15	1921
1922				407	1,10	448	433	16	1922
1923				434	1,10	477	463	17	1923
1924				466	1,10	512	495	19	1924
1925				501	1,10	551	532	20	1925
1926				641	1,10	705	628	24	1926
1927				892	1,10	981	843	32	1927
1928				1.185	1,10	1.303	1.142	43	1928
1929				1.541	1,10	1.695	1.499	56	1929
1930				1.919	1,10	2.111	1.903	71	1930
1931				2.440	1,10	2.684	2.398	90	1931
1932				2.831	1,22	3.454	3.069	115	1932
1933				3.229	1,22	3.940	3.697	139	1933
1934				3.625	1,22	4.423	4.181	157	1934
1935				4.054	1,22	4.946	4.684	176	1935
1936				4.469	1,22	5.453	5.200	195	1936
1937				4.944	1,22	6.032	5.742	215	1937
1938	6.659	5.458	1,22	5.458	1,22	6.659	6.345	238	1938
1939				5.960	1,22	7.272	6.966	261	1939

(1) Total actuarial reserves as at 31 December 1938 (ASLK Annual Report 1948, p. 43).
(2) ASLK Pension Fund as at 31 December 1938 (ASLK Annual Report 1939, p. 28).
(3) = (1) ÷ (2).
(4) ASLK Pension Fund as at 31 December (ASLK Annual Report 1939, p. 28).
(5) Incremental factor (see text).
(6) Total actuarial reserves at 31 December = (4) x (5).
(7) Average annual total actuarial reserves = own calculation on basis of (6) (see text).
(8) Interest on annual average total actuarial reserves = (7) x 3.75%.

TABLE 94

Interest on actuarial reserves of industrial accident insurance funds (in BF millions)

year	(1)	(2)	(3)	(4)	(5)	(6)	(7)	year
1913		23	8	31	125			1913
1920		28	10	38	153	139	5	1920
1921		31	12	43	174	163	6	1921
1922		49	14	63	254	214	8	1922
1923		62	15	77	311	283	11	1923
1924		86	18	104	420	365	14	1924
1925		89	22	111	448	434	16	1925
1926		100	25	125	505	476	18	1926
1927		114	30	144	581	543	20	1927
1928		133	34	167	674	628	24	1928
1929		159	39	198	799	737	28	1929
1930		203	48	251	1.013	906	34	1930
1931		246	59	305	1.231	1.122	42	1931
1932		268	68	336	1.356	1.294	49	1932
1933		270	78	348	1.404	1.380	52	1933
1934		260	89	349	1.410	1.407	53	1934
1935		251	96	347	1.401	1.406	53	1935
1936		254	101	355	1.434	1.418	53	1936
1937		256	107	363	1.465	1.450	54	1937
1938	1.606	287	111	398	1.606	1.535	58	1938
1939		307	116	424	1.710	1.658	62	1939

(1) Total definitive actuarial reserves as at 31 December 1938 (definitive actuarial reserves of private companies and employer's funds and definitive actuarial reserves of the ASLK Industrial Accidents Fund) (ASLK Annual Report 1948, p. 45).
(2) Provisional actuarial reserves as at 31 December of the private companies and employers' funds (Three-yearly industrial accidents reports: e.g. 1933-1935 report, pp. 35-48).
(3) Definitive actuarial reserves as at 31 December of the ASLK Industrial Accidents Fund (ASLK Annual Reports).
(4) = (2) + (3).
(5) Total definitive actuarial reserves as at 31 December = (4) x 1.606 ÷ 398.
(6) Average annual total definitive actuarial reserves = own calculation on basis of (5): see text.
(7) Interest on average annual total definitive actuarial reserves = (6) x 3.75%.

TABLE 95

Income from property and entrepreneurial income (excluding imputed rent) accruing to other government (in BF millions)

year	(1)	(2)	(3)	(4)	year
1920	41	10	0	52	1920
1921	63	10	1	74	1921
1922	78	12	1	91	1922
1923	87	16	1	105	1923
1924	101	20	1	122	1924
1925	127	23	2	152	1925
1926	133	26	2	160	1926
1927	196	23	4	223	1927
1928	271	32	6	309	1928
1929	264	32	7	303	1929
1930	246	37	6	289	1930
1931	277	42	7	326	1931
1932	230	37	4	271	1932
1933	283	40	8	330	1933
1934	438	84	10	532	1934
1935	439	78	14	531	1935
1936	428	77	10	515	1936
1937	453	80	10	544	1937
1938	434	81	9	525	1938
1939	402	72	8	481	1939

(1) Municipalities (Table 96 column 13).
(2) Public Welfare Committees (Table 96 column 18).
(3) Provinces (Table 97 column 8).
(4) Total = (1) + (2) + (3).

TABLE 96

Income from property and entrepreneurial income (excluding imputed rent) accruing to the municipalities and public welfare committees
(in BF millions)

year	(1)	(2)	(3)	(4)	(5)	(6)	(7)	(8)	(9)	(10)	(11)	(12)	(13)	(14)	(15)	(16)	(17)	(18)	year
1920				18	33				71	64	7	8	41					10	1920
1921				17	31				98	72	27	32	63					10	1921
1922				20	37				119	84	34	41	78					12	1922
1923				27	51				133	102	30	36	87					16	1923
1924				34	64				165	134	30	37	101					20	1924
1925				39	74				149	105	44	53	127					23	1925
1926				44	82				171	128	43	51	133					26	1926
1927				39	73				373	270	103	123	196					23	1927
1928				54	101				392	251	141	170	271					32	1928
1929				55	103				439	305	134	161	264					32	1929
1930				62	117				530	423	107	129	246					37	1930
1931				71	134				520	400	120	144	277					42	1931
1932				64	119				451	359	92	111	230					37	1932
1933				68	127				494	364	129	155	283					40	1933
1934				143	269				555	414	141	169	438					84	1934
1935				134	251				585	428	157	188	439					78	1935
1936				131	246				181	30	152	182	428					77	1936
1937				137	257				185	23	163	196	453					80	1937
1938				139	260				171	26	145	174	434					81	1938
1939	285	55	230	122	230	220	48	172	170	27	143	172	402	89	22	67		72	1939
1941	286	70	216														0		1941

384

(1) Municipal property and charges: municipal revenues in 1939 and 1941 (Statistical Yearbook, vol. 66, 1944, p. 150).
(2) Municipal property and charges: total municipal expenditure in 1939 and 1941 (Idem, p. 151).
(3) Municipal property and charges: balance of municipalities in 1939 and 1941 = (2) - (1).
(4) Municipal property and charges: income of 14 municipalities with over 40,000 inhabitants (VAN AUDENHOVE M., o.c., vol. 35, 1981, pp. 214-215).
(5) Municipal property and charges: balance of ordinary municipalities in 1920-1939 = (4) x 230 ÷ 122.
(6) Municipal enterprises or equivalent agencies: income of all the municipalities in 1939 (Statistical Yearbook, vol. 66, 1944, p. 150).
(7) Municipal enterprises or equivalent agencies: expenditure of all the municipalities in 1939 (Idem, p. 151).
(8) Municipal enterprises or equivalent agencies: balance of all the municipalities in 1939 = (6) - (7).
(9) Municipal enterprises or equivalent agencies: income of 14 municipalities with over 40,000 inhabitants (VAN AUDENHOVE M., o.c., vol. 35, 1981, pp. 214-215).
(10) Municipal enterprises or equivalent agencies: expenditure of 14 municipalities with over 40,000 inhabitants (Idem).
(11) Municipal enterprises or equivalent agencies: balance of 14 municipalities with over 40,000 inhabitants = (9) - (10).
(12) Municipal enterprises or equivalent agencies: balance of all municipalities in 1920-1939 = (11) x 172 ÷ 143.
(13) Income from property and entrepreneurial income accruing to municipalities = (5) + (12).
(14) Public Welfare Committees: income from property of all municipalities in 1941 (Statistical Yearbook, vol.66, 1944, p. 155).
(15) Public Welfare Committees: expenditure on property by all municipalities in 1941 (Idem).
(16) Public Welfare Committees: balance from property of all municipalities in 1941 = (14) - (15).
(17) Ratio (16 ÷ (3) in 1941.
(18) Public Welfare Committees: balance from property of all the municipalities in 1920-1939 = (5) x (17).

Note. Relates only to current income and expenditure.

TABLE 97

Income from property and entrepreneurship (excluding imputed rent) accruing to the provinces (in BF millions)

year	(1)	(2)	(3)	(4)	(5)	(6)	(7)	(8)	year
1920	0	0	0				0	0	1920
1921	1	0	0				1	1	1921
1922	1	1	0				1	1	1922
1923	2	1	0				1	1	1923
1924	2	1	1				1	1	1924
1925	2	1	1				1	2	1925
1926	3	2	1				1	2	1926
1927	4	3	1				3	4	1927
1928	7	5	2				4	6	1928
1929	9	6	3				4	7	1929
1930	10	7	3				3	6	1930
1931	11	7	4				3	7	1931
1932	5	3	2				3	4	1932
1933	14	9	5				4	8	1933
1934	19	13	6				4	10	1934
1935	29	19	9				4	14	1935
1936	17	11	6				4	10	1936
1937	18	12	6				5	10	1937
1938	15	10	5				4	9	1938
1939	11	7	4	11	7	4	4	8	1939

(1) Property and charges: income (Statistical Yearbook).
(2) Property: expenditure = 67% of (1): see text.
(3) Balance from property and charges = (1) - (2).
(4) Provincial enterprises or equivalent agencies: income in 1939 (Statistical Yearbook, vol. 66, 1944, p. 142).
(5) Provincial enterprises or equivalent agencies: expenditure in 1939 (Idem).
(6) Provincial enterprises or equivalent agencies: balance in 1939 = (4) - (5).
(7) Provincial enterprises or equivalent agencies: balance in 1920-1939 = own calculations on basis of balance in 1939 (column 6) and balance of municipal enterprises (see Table 96 column 12).
(8) Total = (3) + (7).

Note: relates only to current income and expenditure.

TABLE 98

Interest on the government debt (in BF millions)

year	(1)	(2)	(3)	year
1920	864	133	997	1920
1921	1.234	135	1.368	1921
1922	1.309	174	1.482	1922
1923	1.548	201	1.749	1923
1924	1.673	242	1.915	1924
1925	1.807	250	2.057	1925
1926	1.985	262	2.247	1926
1927	2.284	271	2.555	1927
1928	2.227	300	2.527	1928
1929	2.144	330	2.474	1929
1930	2.068	396	2.464	1930
1931	1.932	428	2.361	1931
1932	1.845	484	2.329	1932
1933	1.888	519	2.407	1933
1934	1.879	532	2.410	1934
1935	1.853	549	2.402	1935
1936	1.796	491	2.288	1936
1937	1.786	510	2.296	1937
1938	1.725	519	2.244	1938
1939	1.782	545	2.327	1939

(1) Interest on the State debt (see Table 99 column 12).
(2) Interest on local government debt (see Table 102 column 15).
(3) Interest on the public debt at current prices = (1) + (2).

TABLE 99

Interest on the public debt (in BF millions)

year	(1)	(2)	(3)	(4)	(5)	(6)	(7)	(8)	(9)	(10)	(11)	(12)	year
1920					738				126	1,000	126	864	1920
1921					1.063				171	1,000	171	1.234	1921
1922					1.131				178	1,000	178	1.309	1922
1923					1.231				317	1,000	317	1.548	1923
1924					1.349				325	1,000	325	1.673	1924
1925					1.385				421	1,000	421	1.807	1925
1926					1.282				703	1,000	703	1.985	1926
1927					1.338				946	1,000	946	2.284	1927
1928					1.280				947	1,000	947	2.227	1928
1929	1.060	93	28	20	1.201	734	0	209	943	1,000	943	2.144	1929
1930	1.063	53	29	20	1.165	673	0	230	903	1,000	903	2.068	1930
1931	1.069	48	31	5	1.152	619	0	185	804	0,970	780	1.932	1931
1932	1.142	70	49	1	1.261	575	15	14	603	0,968	584	1.845	1932
1933	1.189	95	80	0	1.364	558	69	13	640	0,819	524	1.888	1933
1934	1.262	80	74	0	1.415	558	14	10	582	0,797	464	1.879	1934
1935	1.007	90	131	18	1.247	536	60	10	606	1,000	606	1.853	1935
1936	1.108	74	114	28	1.323	430	38	5	473	1,000	473	1.796	1936
1937	1.248	72	93	25	1.437	335	14	0	349	1,000	349	1.786	1937
1938	1.305	37	63	0	1.405	294	25	0	320	1,000	320	1.725	1938
1939	1.331	83	65	0	1.479	272	31	0	303	1,000	303	1.782	1939

(1) Interest on consolidated domestic debt (Belgische economische statistieken 1929-1940, p. 151).
(2) Interest on short and medium-term domestic debt (Idem, p. 152).
(3) Charges without associated consolidated capital (Idem, p. 151).
(4) Charges without associated short and medium-term capital (Idem, p. 152).
(5) Interest on total domestic debt:
   - 1920-1928: MICHIELS J., Kritische periodes in de evolutie van de rijksschuld: 1926, p. 32.
   - 1929-1940: (1)+(2)+(3)+(4).
(6) Interest on consolidated domestic debt, excluding intergovernmental debt (Belgische economische statistieken, p. 151).
(7) Interest on short and medium-term foreign debt, excluding intergovernmental debt (Idem, p. 152).
(8) Interest on intergovernmental debt (Table 101 column 11).
(9) Interest on total foreign debt (without exchange rate adjustment 1931-1934):
   - 1920-1928: MICHIELS J., o.c., p. 32.
   - 1929-1940: (6)+(7)+(8).
(10) Exchange rate adjustment 1931-1934: see text.
(11) Interest on total foreign debt (with exchange rate adjustment 1931-1934) = (9) x (10).
(12) Interest on total government debt = (5) + (11).

TABLE 100

interest on government funds (1933-1939) according to the return on capital statistics
(in BF millions)

year	(1)	(2)	(3)	(4)	(5)	(6)	(7)	year
1933	854	57	201	746	617	18	2.493	1933
1934	929	49	221	764	569	11	2.543	1934
1935	948	51	226	697	482	15	2.419	1935
1936	1.202	69	217	545	477	15	2.525	1936
1937	1.032	92	206	551	332	15	2.228	1937
1938	1.130	136	191	587	313	15	2.372	1938
1939	1.143	156	202	600	267	?	2.368	1939

(1) Coupons of domestic State loans (figures based on the budgets).
(2) Coupons of Congo loans.
(3) Coupons of provincial and municipal loans (confined to those quoted on the Brussels stock exchange).
(4) Coupons of loans issued by various bodies (= loans of public utilities; figures derived from the balance sheets and reports drawn up by these bodies).
(5) Coupons of foreign State loans.
(6) Coupons of the foreign loan of the City of Antwerp.
(7) Total.

Other comments:
- Relates to coupons that became payable in year X.
- The figures included relate not just to the loans placed with the public but also those placed with financial institutions.

Source: Belgische economische statistieken 1929-1940, pp. 160-182.

TABLE 101

Interest on the intergovernmental debt: 1929-1940 (in BF millions)

year	(1)	(2)	(3)	(4)	(5)	(6)	(7)	(8)	(9)	(10)	(11)	year
1929	412	89	323					734	1.138	64,5%	209	1929
1930	458	87	371					673	1.089	61,8%	230	1930
1931	380	85	295					619	987	62,7%	185	1931
1932	138	83	55	20	14,45	5%	14				14	1932
1933	137	81	56	18	14,45	5%	13				13	1933
1934	126	79	47	14	14,45	5%	10				10	1934
1935	157	77	80	10	20,07	5%	10				10	1935
1936	147	75	72	6	16,02	5%	5				5	1936
1937	170	73	97	0			0				0	1937
1938	71	71	0	0			0				0	1938
1939	67	67	0	0			0				0	1939
1940	66	66	0	0			0				0	1940

(1) Consolidated debt: other charges (= interest + redemption of capital) (Belgische economische statistieken 1929-1940, p. 1). This item comprises the charges relating to the following debts:
    a) 3% Army and Air Force debt
    b) loan from the US entered into during the war
    c) loan from the US entered into after the ceasefire
    d) costs of internment in the Netherlands
    e) UK reconstruction loans
    f) Gemeentekrediet annuities (capitalization) and annuities to buy off railway licences.

(2) Charges of a) and f):
    - 1938-1940: see (1)
    - 1929-1937: own estimate on basis of 1938-1940.

(3) Charges of b) c) d) e): (1) - (2).
(4) Outstanding debt of d) in guilders (Belgische economische statistieken 1929-1940, pp. 148-149).
(5) Exchange rate: number of BF to the guilder at the end of the year (JANSSEN V., De Belgische frank, p. 435).
(6) Interest rate on d) = 5% (VANDENDRIESSCHE S., Evolutie van de Belgische centrale overheidsuitgaven sinds 1919, p. 1091).
(7) Interest on the debt of d) in BF = $(4) \times (5) \times (6)$.
(8) Interest on the foreign consolidated debts (excluding intergovernmental debt): Belgische economische statistieken, p. 151.
(9) Interest + redemption of foreign consolidated debt (excluding intergovernmental debt): Idem, p. 151.
(10) = $(8) \div (9)$.
(11) Interest on the intergovernmental debt:
    - 1929-1931: $(3) \times (10)$.
    - 1932-1939: (7).

TABLE 102

Interest on local government debt (provinces and muni-cipalities) (in BF milli-ons)

year	(1)	(2)	(3)	(4)	(5)	(6)	(7)	(8)	(9)	(10)	(11)	(12)	(13)	(14)	(15)	year
1920												86	65%	133	133	1920
1921												87	65%	135	135	1921
1922												112	65%	174	174	1922
1923												130	65%	201	201	1923
1924												156	65%	242	242	1924
1925												162	65%	250	250	1925
1926												169	65%	262	262	1926
1927												175	65%	271	271	1927
1928												194	65%	300	300	1928
1929	3.133	2.898	360	0	6.391	119	90	209	6.600	5,00%	330	213	65%	330	330	1929
1930	3.633	3.634	360	0	7.627	211	90	301	7.928	5,00%	396	236	60%		396	1930
1931	4.114	3.692	360	0	8.166	312	90	402	8.568	5,00%	428	269	63%		428	1931
1932	4.613	4.247	360	0	9.220	369	89	458	9.678	5,00%	484	280	58%		484	1932
1933	4.885	4.447	360	0	9.692	600	86	686	10.378	5,00%	519	302	58%		519	1933
1934	5.074	4.600	212	0	9.886	663	83	746	10.632	5,00%	532	344	65%		532	1934
1935	5.312	4.561	295	0	10.168	731	82	813	10.981	5,00%	549	353	64%		549	1935
1936	5.725	5.346	295	0	11.366	808	113	921	12.287	4,00%	491	310	63%		491	1936
1937	5.949	5.579	300	0	11.828	816	104	920	12.748	4,00%	510	313	61%		510	1937
1938	6.306	5.295	300	141	12.042	825	102	927	12.969	4,00%	519	315	61%		519	1938
1939	6.675	5.566	291	165	12.697	820	101	921	13.618	4,00%	545	346	64%		545	1939

(1) Outstanding municipal debt at the Gemeentekrediet van België (Belgische economische statistieken 1929-1940, p. 159).
(2) Outstanding municipal debt on public domestic issues (Idem).
(3) Outstanding municipal debt on public issues abroad (Idem).
(4) Outstanding municipal debt with private individuals = debt placed with private citizens of the municipality or with financial institutions excluding the Gemeentekrediet (Idem).
(5) Total outstanding municipal debt = (1)+(2)+(3)+(4).
(6) Outstanding provincial debt with the Gemeentekrediet van België (NBB, Idem).
(7) Outstanding provincial debt on public issued in Belgium (Idem).
(8) Total outstanding provincial debt = (6)+(7).
(9) Total outstanding local government debt = (5)+(8).
(10) Average rate of interest on the total outstanding local government debt (own calculation: see text).
(11) Interest charges on the total outstanding local government debt (1920-1940) = (9)x(10).
(12) Interest charges and annuities of 14 municipalities with over 40,000 inhabitants (Statistical Yearbook).
(13) Share of interest charges and annuities of 14 municipalities with over 40,000 inhabitants in interest charges on the total outstanding local government debt: 1929-1939 = (12) ÷ (11) ; 1920-1928 = share in 1929.
(14) Interest charges on the total outstanding local government debt (1920-1929) = (12) ÷ (13).
(15) Interest charges on the total outstanding local government debt (1920-199) - (11) and (14).

TABLE 103a

Depreciation of dwellings

year	(1)	(2)	(3)	(4)	(5)	(6)	year
1919		1526	79,2	120,80			1919
1920	52,50	1530	79,6	121,73	0,81	0,42	1920
1921	49,80	1542	80,0	123,29	0,81	0,40	1921
1922	52,50	1564	80,4	125,68	0,82	0,43	1922
1923	57,50	1593	80,8	128,65	0,84	0,48	1923
1924	60,70	1619	81,2	131,40	0,86	0,52	1924
1925	61,60	1656	81,6	135,08	0,88	0,54	1925
1926	72,70	1684	82,0	138,05	0,90	0,65	1926
1927	87,00	1706	82,4	140,55	0,92	0,80	1927
1928	98,90	1734	82,8	143,57	0,94	0,93	1928
1929	120,60	1774	83,2	147,62	0,96	1,15	1929
1930	130,30	1807	83,6	151,12	0,98	1,28	1930
1931	115,30	1835	84,0	154,23	1,01	1,16	1931
1932	107,70	1871	84,5	158,04	1,03	1,11	1932
1933	97,90	1907	84,9	161,88	1,05	1,03	1933
1934	87,90	1936	85,3	165,17	1,08	0,95	1934
1935	87,90	1967	85,7	168,65	1,10	0,97	1935
1936	93,00	1996	86,2	171,99	1,12	1,05	1936
1937	101,70	2021	86,6	175,02	1,15	1,17	1937
1938	105,30	2043	87,0	177,81	1,17	1,23	1938
1939	102,50	2060	87,5	180,18	1,19	1,22	1939

(1) Weighted price index of building costs of dwellings 1936-1938 = 100. Calculated from: BUYST E., Residential Building, Table II-14.
(2) Annual evolution of the stock of dwellings in thousands; according to Idem, Annex 10, Table 1.
(3) Average cost price of new buildings in 1936-1938 in BF thousands; calculated according to Idem, Table II-9.
(4) Stock of dwellings in BF billions in 1936-1938 prices: (3) x (2) : 1,000.
(5) Depreciation of dwellings in BF billions in 1936-1938 prices: column (4) year "t-1" divided by 150.
(6) Depreciation of dwellings in BF billions at current prices; column (5) multiplied by column (2) and divided by 100.

TABLE 103b

Depreciation of other buildings and plant and equipment, public sector

year	(1)	(2)	(3)	(4)	(5)	(6)	(7)	(8)	(9)	(10)	year
1919	34,94	44,20		5,74			0,47				1919
1920	54,50	82,57	0,09	6,11	0,78	0,03	0,57	0,17	0,12	0,07	1920
1921	54,20	54,87	0,09	6,61	0,92	0,04	0,74	0,23	0,13	0,07	1921
1922	52,70	47,68	0,10	7,03	0,83	0,05	0,91	0,23	0,15	0,08	1922
1923	58,30	70,78	0,11	7,33	0,72	0,06	0,98	0,13	0,17	0,10	1923
1924	65,50	73,80	0,11	7,53	0,61	0,07	1,03	0,11	0,17	0,12	1924
1925	63,80	72,07	0,11	7,78	0,67	0,07	1,08	0,12	0,18	0,12	1925
1926	75,50	95,27	0,12	7,62	0,25	0,07	1,09	0,07	0,19	0,16	1926
1927	88,90	109,46	0,11	7,46	0,26	0,07	1,10	0,08	0,19	0,18	1927
1928	98,00	112,03	0,11	7,37	0,32	0,07	1,09	0,06	0,19	0,19	1928
1929	117,30	122,56	0,11	7,36	0,40	0,07	1,09	0,06	0,18	0,22	1929
1930	124,40	106,74	0,11	7,53	0,59	0,07	1,12	0,10	0,18	0,22	1930
1931	110,30	80,34	0,11	7,69	0,58	0,07	1,13	0,07	0,19	0,18	1931
1932	99,80	72,01	0,12	7,68	0,40	0,08	1,12	0,06	0,19	0,17	1932
1933	91,70	64,33	0,12	7,72	0,45	0,07	1,13	0,07	0,19	0,15	1933
1934	85,80	61,42	0,12	7,90	0,60	0,08	1,12	0,05	0,19	0,15	1934
1935	86,20	69,74	0,12	8,03	0,55	0,07	1,10	0,05	0,19	0,15	1935
1936	91,40	80,45	0,12	8,93	1,10	0,07	0,96	0,09	0,19	0,17	1936
1937	102,60	110,26	0,13	9,71	1,32	0,06	0,79	0,06	0,20	0,21	1937
1938	106,40	108,36	0,15	10,30	1,19	0,05	0,73	0,07	0,20	0,21	1938
1939	102,70	109,76	0,15	9,89	1,01	0,05	0,67	0,06	0,20	0,21	1939
1948	393,02	435,23									1948

(1) Price index of building costs of other buildings, 1936-1938=100 according to VAN MEERTEN M., Capital Formation in Belgium, Chapter 2.
(2) Price index for costs of plant and equipment, 1936-1938=100. Idem.
(3) Depreciation of other buildings in BF billions at 1936-1938 prices; column (4) year "t-1" divided by 40.
(4) Stock of other buildings in BF billions at 1936-1938 prices; 1938 value obtained by dividing 1948 value in column (10) by 1948 value in column (1) and multiplying by 100 and subsequently by 40; 1939 value obtained by adding 1938 value to 1939 value in column (5) and deducting the average value in the years 1925-1935 in column (6); 1919-1937 values obtained by deducting the value for year "t" in column (5) from the value in year "t+1" and adding the average value for the years 1925-1935 in column (5).
(5) Gross investment in other buildings in BF billions at 1936-1938 prices. CLEMENT, P., The Growth, Chapter 5.
(6) Depreciation of plant and equipment in BF billions at 1936-1938 prices; column (7) year "t-1" divided by 15.
(7) Stock of plant and equipment in BF billions at 1936-1938 prices; 1938 value obtained by dividing 1948 value in column (12) by 1948 value in column (2) and multiplying by 100 and subsequently by 15; 1939 value obtained by adding 1939 value in column (9) to 1938 value and deducting the 1924 value in column (8); 1934-1937 values obtained by deducting the value in year "t" in column (8) from the value in year "t+1" and adding the value for year "t-15" in column (8); 1929-1933 values obtained by deducting the value in year "t" in column (8) from the value in "t+1" and adding a quarter of the value in 1919 in column (8); 1919-1928 values obtained by deducting the value in year "t" in column (8) from the value in year "t+1" and adding the average value in the years 1925-1935 in column (8).
(8) Gross investment in plant and equipment in BF billions at 1936-1938 prices. CLEMENT, P., The Growth, Chapter 5.
(9) Depreciation of government capital stock in BF billions at 1936-1938 prices; sum of columns (3) and (6)
(10) Depreciation of government capital stock in BF billions at current prices; 1920-1939 values column (9) multiplied by 0.93 * column (1) and 0.07 * column (2), and consequently divided by 100; 1948 value calculated from the National Income Commission, pp. 78 and 161.

TABLE 104

Depreciation of other buildings and plant and equipment, private sector and totals

year	(1)	(2)	(3)	(4)	(5)	(6)	(7)	(8)	(9)	(10)	(11)	(12)	(13)	(14)	(15)	(16)	year
1919	34,9	44,2			1,84									0,09			1919
1920	54,5	82,6	1,20	47,86	3,38	1,39	20,91	3,87		0,31	0,65	1,15	0,07	0,13	3,83	2,43	1920
1921	54,2	54,9	1,24	49,54	1,78	1,54	23,04	4,93	0,12	0,32	0,67	0,84	0,07	0,15	4,05	2,13	1921
1922	52,7	47,7	1,24	49,63	1,68	1,65	24,69	4,46	0,13	0,33	0,65	0,78	0,08	0,15	4,21	2,10	1922
1923	58,3	70,8	1,24	49,62	1,68	1,72	25,82	3,94	0,15	0,35	0,72	1,22	0,10	0,17	4,33	2,69	1923
1924	65,5	73,8	1,24	49,60	2,18	1,72	25,85	2,84	0,17	0,37	0,81	1,27	0,12	0,18	4,37	2,91	1924
1925	63,8	72,1	1,25	50,09	2,00	1,78	26,72	3,67	0,17	0,38	0,80	1,28	0,12	0,21	4,48	2,95	1925
1926	75,5	95,3	1,26	50,39	1,66	1,82	27,27	3,37	0,18	0,39	0,95	1,73	0,16	0,24	4,57	3,74	1926
1927	88,9	109,5	1,26	50,36	1,81	1,78	26,64	2,17	0,19	0,40	1,12	1,94	0,18	0,30	4,55	4,34	1927
1928	98,0	112,0	1,26	50,47	2,03	1,76	26,47	2,64	0,19	0,41	1,24	1,98	0,19	0,33	4,56	4,66	1928
1929	117,3	122,6	1,27	50,81	2,64	1,80	27,02	3,36	0,19	0,41	1,49	2,21	0,22	0,37	4,62	5,44	1929
1930	124,4	106,7	1,29	51,76	2,99	1,91	28,62	4,41	0,18	0,41	1,61	2,04	0,22	0,40	4,78	5,54	1930
1931	110,3	80,3	1,33	53,05	2,15	2,03	30,42	5,45	0,19	0,41	1,46	1,63	0,18	0,38	4,96	4,81	1931
1932	99,8	72,0	1,34	53,51	1,44	2,33	34,89	5,48	0,19	0,42	1,34	1,67	0,17	0,34	5,30	4,62	1932
1933	91,7	64,3	1,33	53,26	1,63	2,47	37,03	3,29	0,19	0,43	1,22	1,59	0,15	0,31	5,47	4,30	1933
1934	85,8	61,4	1,33	53,19	1,33	2,61	39,16	3,16	0,19	0,43	1,14	1,60	0,15	0,32	5,64	4,15	1934
1935	86,2	69,7	1,32	52,82	1,03	2,78	41,63	2,85	0,19	0,44	1,14	1,94	0,15	0,33	5,83	4,52	1935
1936	91,4	80,4	1,30	52,16	1,22	2,68	40,20	2,43	0,19	0,44	1,19	2,16	0,17	0,36	5,74	4,92	1936
1937	102,6	110,3	1,29	51,68	1,50	2,50	37,57	2,31	0,20	0,44	1,33	2,76	0,21	0,40	5,59	5,86	1937
1938	106,4	108,4	1,29	51,49	1,55	2,36	35,39	2,28	0,20	0,45	1,37	2,56	0,21	0,43	5,46	5,79	1938
1939	102,7	109,8	1,28	51,35	1,48	2,28	34,17	2,72	0,20	0,45	1,32	2,50	0,21	0,46	5,40	5,71	1939
1948	393,0	435,2		51,13			32,89	2,39			6,73	14,87	3,50				1948

(1) Price index of building costs of other buildings, 1936-1938=100 according to VAN MEERTEN M., Capital Formation in Belgium, Chapter 2.
(2) Price index for costs of plant and equipment, 1936-1938=100. Idem.
(3) Depreciation of other buildings in BF billions at 1936-1938 prices; column (4) year "t-1" divided by 40.
(4) Stock of other buildings in BF billions at 1936-1938 prices; 1938 value obtained by dividing 1948 value in column (11) by 1948 value in column (1) and multiplying by 100 and subsequently by 40; 1939 value obtained by adding 1938 value to 1939 value in column (5) and deducting the average value in the years 1925-1935 in column (6); 1919-1937 values obtained by deducting the value for year "t" in column (5) from the value in year "t+1" and adding the average value for the years 1925-1935 in column (5).
(5) Gross investment in other buildings in BF billions at 1936-1938 prices. Idem, Chapter 5.
(6) Depreciation of plant and equipment in BF billions at 1936-1938 prices; column (7) year "t-1" divided by 15.
(7) Stock of plant and equipment in BF billions at 1936-1938 prices; 1938 value obtained by dividing 1948 value in column (12) by 1948 value in column (2) and multiplying by 100 and subsequently by 15; 1939 value obtained by adding 1939 value in column (9) to 1938 value and deducting the 1924 value in column (8); 1934-1937 values obtained by deducting the value in year "t" in column (8) from the value in year "t+1" and adding the value for year "t-15" in column (8); 1929-1933 values obtained by deducting the value in year "t" in column (8) from the value in "t+1" and adding a quarter of the value in 1919 in column (8); 1919-1928 values obtained by deducting the value in year "t" in column (8) from the value in year "t+1" and adding the average value in the years 1925-1935 in column (8).
(8) Gross investment in plant and equipment in BF billions at 1936-1938 prices. Idem, Chapter 5.
(9) Depreciation of government capital stock in BF billions at 1936-1938 prices; sum of column (9) in table 103b.
(10) Depreciation in agriculture, forestry and fishing in BF billions at 1936-38 prices. VAN MEERTEN M., o.c., Chapter 4.
(11) Depreciation of other buildings in BF billions at current prices; 1920-1939 values column (3) multiplied by column (1) and divided by 100; 1948 value calculated from the National Income Commission, pp. 78 and 161.
(12) Depreciation of plant and equipment in BF billions at current prices; 1920-1939 values column (6) multiplied by column (2) and divided by 100; 1948 value calculated from National Income Commission, pp. 78 and 161.
(13) Depreciation of government capital stock in BF billions at current prices; column (10) from table 103b.
(14) Depreciation in agriculture, forestry and fishing in BF billions at current prices according to VAN MEERTEN M., o.c., Chapter 4.
(15) Total depreciation in BF billions at 1936-1938 prices; sum of columns (3), (6), (9) and (10) and column (6) Table 103a.
(16) Total depreciation in BF billions at current prices; sum of columns (11), (12), (13) and (14) and column (7) Table 103a.

TABLE 105

Indirect taxes (in BF millions)

year	(1)	(2)	(3)	(4)	(5)	(6)	(7)	(8)	(9)	(10)	(11)	(12)	year
1920	211	132	204	48	2	15	0		42		-6	648	1920
1921	251	200	183	94	3	20	9		35	0	-8	778	1921
1922	396	280	226	351	4	22	16	8	36	-2	-13	1.311	1922
1923	364	365	280	496	29	40	15	9	31	-8	-15	1.614	1923
1924	433	420	321	642	39	48	18	0	35	-2	-15	1.945	1924
1925	551	430	323	698	48	52	36	24	45	0	-18	2.139	1925
1926	709	630	422	1.541	110	68	52	20	56	0	-22	3.572	1926
1927	901	796	557	2.545	83	73	62	23	70	0	-15	5.082	1927
1928	1.097	901	840	2.746	87	76	73	25	82	0	-15	5.899	1928
1929	1.319	991	971	2.642	95	79	56	30	83	0	-33	6.245	1929
1930	1.336	975	645	1.699	89	73	44	33	93	0	-39	4.957	1930
1931	1.303	1.029	556	1.653	85	59	42	33	71	0	-30	4.803	1931
1932	1.556	1.062	526	1.847	96	57	39	32	66	22	-53	5.254	1932
1933	1.496	1.245	526	2.042	136	59	39	32	148	-38	-20	5.665	1933
1934	1.497	1.232	409	1.992	152	50	49	32	70	-40	-19	5.414	1934
1935	1.456	1.302	521	2.177	150	47	64	32	125	-9	-20	5.830	1935
1936	1.554	1.286	494	2.412	160	45	72	34	141	-48	-18	6.124	1936
1937	1.587	1.414	546	2.816	176	48	72	34	91	-46	-24	6.714	1937
1938	1.544	1.505	486	2.565	199	48	72	35	81	-30	-20	6.485	1938
1939	1.438	1.534	389	2.501	220	44	66	33	157	0	-19	6.363	1939

(1) Customs duties and statistical duties.
(2) Excise and special consumption taxes.
(3) Registration and transfer.
(4) Stamp duty and equivalent taxes (transfer tax).
(5) Motor vehicle tax.
(6) Entertainment tax.
(7) Betting and gaming taxes.
(8) Corkage taxes on the sale of fermented beverages.
(9) Other indirect taxes.
(10) Balance of the joint receipts with the Grand Duchy of Luxembourg.
(11) Stray items and repayments of incorrectly levied indirect taxes (approximate estimate).
(12) Total = sum of (1) up to and including (11).

Sources:

- 1923-1939: Accounts of the Audit Office: Final accounts of the budget of the Belgian State. For (1), (2), (3), (4) and (5) nearly the same figures may be found in VANDENDRIESSCHE S., o.c.
- 1920-1922: (1) (2) (5) (6) (7) (8): Accounts of the Audit Office: Final accounts of the budget of the Belgian State ; (3) (4) VANDENDRIESSCHE S., o.c., p. 89 ; (9): Estimate on the basis of the Accounts of the Audit Office: Final accounts of the budget of the Belgian State; VANDENDRIESSCHE S., o.c., p. 89.

TABLE 106

Subsidies (in BF millions)

year	(1)	(2)	(3)	(4)	(5)	(6)	year
1920						4	1920
1921						4	1921
1922						4	1922
1923	3	0	0	0	1	4	1923
1924	4	0	0	0	0	4	1924
1925	4	0	0	0	0	4	1925
1926	2	0	0	0	0	2	1926
1927	2	0	0	0	0	2	1927
1928	3	0	0	6	5	14	1928
1929	3	0	0	0	10	13	1929
1930	7	0	0	0	8	15	1930
1931	7	0	0	0	1	8	1931
1932	7	0	0	0	2	9	1932
1933	2	0	0	11	6	19	1933
1934	5	12	0	14	11	42	1934
1935	5	11	25	16	6	63	1935
1936	7	13	34	12	1	67	1936
1937	8	13	0	17	11	49	1937
1938	15	14	9	22	9	69	1938
1939	16	10	78	26	1	131	1939

(1) Agriculture and horticulture.
(2) Commerce and shipping.
(3) Energy.
(4) Aviation.
(5) Other sectors.
(6) Total

Sources:
- 1920-1922 : own estimate.
- 1923-1939 : Accounts of the Audit Office: Final accounts of the budget of the Belgian State.

TABLE 107

Belgian national income, 1920-1939 (nominal terms, in 1 000 000 BF)

Category (source)	1920	1921	1922	1923	1924	1925
Wages and salaries of manual workers in the private sector (1)	5.808	6.429	6.507	7.628	9.003	9.006
Wages and salaries of white-collar workers in the private sector (2)	952	1.098	1.167	1.387	1.796	1.934
Wages and salaries of domestic staff (3)	369	375	376	474	526	619
Wages and salaries of border and seasonal workers (3)	140	158	156	213	303	335
Employers social security contributions (4)	122	134	147	188	223	230
Wages and salaries of government personnel (5)	1.944	2.125	2.281	2.396	2.883	3.221
Entrepreneurial income in agriculture, horticulture and foresty (7)	4.257	3.329	2.181	3.812	4.216	3.862
Entrepreneurial income of the professions (8)	327	334	414	484	562	578
Entrepreneurial income of independant traders (8)	6.362	6.283	6.274	7.448	8.955	9.196
Entrepreneurial income of partnerships (8)	445	440	439	521	627	644
Interest accruing to the personal sector (9)	1.295	1.678	1.993	2.215	2.811	3.433
Rent accruing to the personal sector (10)	750	1.005	1.177	1.494	1.784	2.331
Dividends, bonuses and donations accruing to the personal sector (11)	1.309	794	1.109	1.782	2.021	2.013
Savings by corporations (12)	382	226	325	567	615	592
Direct taxes paid by companies (13)	82	125	134	193	216	211
Income from capital and entrepreneurial income accruing to the government (14)	138	236	427	476	372	601
Interest on public debt (15)	-997	-1.368	-1.482	-1.749	-1.915	-2.057
NET NATIONAL INCOME (NNI) or NET NATIONAL PRODUCT AT FACTOR COST (NNPf)	23.684	23.401	23.625	29.529	34.999	36.749
Depreciation (16)	2.430	2.130	2.100	2.690	2.910	2.950
GROSS NATIONAL INCOME (GNI) or GROSS NATIONAL PRODUCT AT FACTOR COST (GNPf)	26.114	25.531	25.725	32.219	37.909	39.699
Indirect taxation (17)	648	778	1.311	1.614	1.945	2.139
Subsidies (17)	-4	-4	-4	-4	-4	-4
GROSS NATIONAL PRODUCT AT MARKET PRICE (GNPm)	26.758	26.305	27.032	33.829	39.850	41.834

	1926	1927	1928	1929	1930	1931	1932	1933	1934	1935	1936	1937	1938	1939
	9.457	12.781	14.224	17.003	17.697	14.983	12.311	12.177	11.291	11.189	12.643	15.083	15.064	14.413
	2.274	2.907	3.295	3.968	4.307	4.112	3.779	3.662	3.538	3.469	3.802	4.224	4.577	4.642
	674	848	936	1.142	1.320	1.318	1.255	1.237	1.202	1.190	1.184	1.179	1.203	1.215
	447	824	1.085	1.186	1.264	978	813	710	742	779	964	926	781	481
	312	460	521	673	763	857	820	843	805	749	892	1.124	1.234	1.162
	3.663	4.737	5.824	6.378	7.119	7.080	6.526	6.177	6.030	5.735	6.242	6.880	7.444	7.930
	4.963	4.865	5.578	5.960	4.999	3.667	3.185	3.737	2.876	3.689	3.111	3.674	4.137	4.004
	671	743	859	959	1.005	977	951	929	906	885	933	1.016	1.027	1.044
	11.010	13.484	15.104	16.597	16.416	15.184	13.049	12.761	12.204	13.003	14.073	15.791	16.379	15.595
	771	944	1.057	1.162	1.149	1.063	913	893	854	910	985	1.105	1.147	1.092
	4.039	3.914	4.190	4.396	4.607	4.404	4.678	4.552	4.221	3.425	3.395	3.288	3.168	3.132
	2.625	3.409	4.014	4.405	6.600	7.933	8.676	8.629	8.598	8.192	8.328	8.465	8.472	8.762
	2.721	3.226	3.925	4.634	4.442	3.327	2.679	2.644	2.692	3.182	4.004	4.615	4.415	3.618
	788	2.073	2.046	2.496	3.377	2.347	-13	-574	-121	-317	136	373	88	-4
	277	408	426	495	564	487	354	388	334	245	305	352	258	221
	481	1.214	1.256	1.457	1.147	843	779	862	1.137	1.154	1.241	1.427	1.406	1.376
	-2.247	-2.555	-2.527	-2.474	-2.464	-2.361	-2.329	-2.407	-2.410	-2.402	-2.288	-2.296	-2.244	-2.327
	42.926	54.282	61.813	70.436	74.312	67.199	58.426	57.220	54.898	55.077	59.950	67.226	68.556	66.356
	3.740	4.340	4.660	5.440	5.540	4.810	4.620	4.300	4.150	4.520	4.920	5.860	5.790	5.710
	46.666	58.622	66.473	75.876	79.852	72.009	63.046	61.520	59.048	59.597	64.870	73.086	74.346	72.066
	3.572	5.082	5.899	6.245	4.957	4.803	5.254	5.665	5.414	5.830	6.124	6.714	6.485	6.363
	-2	-2	-14	-13	-15	-8	-9	-19	-42	-63	-67	-49	-69	-131
	50.236	63.702	72.358	82.108	84.794	76.804	68.291	67.166	64.420	65.364	70.927	79.751	80.762	78.298

TABLE 108

Share of the various income categories, 1920-1939 (nominal terms, in BF millions)

Category (source)	1920	1921	1922	1923	1924	1925
Wages and salaries of manual workers in the private sector (1)	21,71	24,44	24,07	22,55	22,59	21,53
Wages and salaries of white-collar workers in the private sector (2)	3,56	4,17	4,32	4,1	4,51	4,62
Wages and salaries of domestic staff (3)	1,38	1,43	1,39	1,4	1,32	1,48
Wages and salaries of border and seasonal workers (3)	0,52	0,6	0,58	0,63	0,76	0,8
Employers social security contributions (4)	0,46	0,51	0,54	0,56	0,56	0,55
Wages and salaries of government personnel (5)	7,26	8,08	8,44	7,08	7,23	7,7
Entrepreneurial income in agriculture, horticulture and foresty (7)	15,91	12,66	8,07	11,27	10,58	9,23
Entrepreneurial income of the professions (8)	1,22	1,27	1,53	1,43	1,41	1,38
Entrepreneurial income of independant traders (8)	23,78	23,88	23,21	22,02	22,47	21,98
Entrepreneurial income of partnerships (8)	1,66	1,67	1,62	1,54	1,57	1,54
Interest accruing to the personal sector (9)	4,84	6,38	7,37	6,55	7,05	8,21
Rent accruing to the personal sector (10)	2,8	3,82	4,35	4,42	4,48	5,57
Dividends, bonuses and donations accruing to the personal sector (11)	4,89	3,02	4,1	5,27	5,07	4,81
Savings by corporations (12)	1,43	0,86	1,2	1,68	1,54	1,42
Direct taxes paid by companies (13)	0,31	0,48	0,5	0,57	0,54	0,5
Income from capital and entrepreneurial income accruing to the government (14)	0,52	0,9	1,58	1,41	0,93	1,44
Interest on public debt (15)	-3,73	-5,2	-5,48	-5,17	-4,81	-4,92
Depreciation (16)	9,08	8,1	7,77	7,95	7,3	7,05
Indirect taxation (17)	2,42	2,96	4,85	4,77	4,88	5,11
Subsidies (17)	-0,01	-0,02	-0,01	-0,01	-0,01	-0,01
GROSS NATIONAL PRODUCT AT MARKET PRICE (GNPm)	100,0	100,0	100,0	100,0	100,0	100,0

1926	1927	1928	1929	1930	1931	1932	1933	1934	1935	1936	1937	1938	1939
18,83	20,06	19,66	20,71	20,87	19,51	18,03	18,13	17,53	17,12	17,83	18,91	18,65	18,41
4,53	4,56	4,55	4,83	5,08	5,35	5,53	5,45	5,49	5,31	5,36	5,3	5,67	5,93
1,34	1,33	1,29	1,39	1,56	1,72	1,84	1,84	1,87	1,82	1,67	1,48	1,49	1,55
0,89	1,29	1,5	1,44	1,49	1,27	1,19	1,06	1,15	1,19	1,36	1,16	0,97	0,61
0,62	0,72	0,72	0,82	0,9	1,12	1,2	1,26	1,25	1,15	1,26	1,41	1,53	1,48
7,29	7,44	8,05	7,77	8,4	9,22	9,56	9,2	9,36	8,77	8,8	8,63	9,22	10,13
9,88	7,64	7,71	7,26	5,9	4,77	4,66	5,56	4,46	5,64	4,39	4,61	5,12	5,11
1,34	1,17	1,19	1,17	1,19	1,27	1,39	1,38	1,41	1,35	1,32	1,27	1,27	1,33
21,92	21,17	20,87	20,21	19,36	19,77	19,11	19	18,94	19,89	19,84	19,8	20,28	19,92
1,53	1,48	1,46	1,42	1,36	1,38	1,34	1,33	1,33	1,39	1,39	1,39	1,42	1,39
8,04	6,14	5,79	5,35	5,43	5,73	6,85	6,78	6,55	5,24	4,79	4,12	3,92	4
5,23	5,35	5,55	5,36	7,78	10,33	12,7	12,85	13,35	12,53	11,74	10,61	10,49	11,19
5,42	5,06	5,42	5,64	5,24	4,33	3,92	3,94	4,18	4,87	5,65	5,79	5,47	4,62
1,57	3,25	2,83	3,04	3,98	3,06	-0,02	-0,85	-0,19	-0,48	0,19	0,47	0,11	-0,01
0,55	0,64	0,59	0,6	0,67	0,63	0,52	0,58	0,52	0,38	0,43	0,44	0,32	0,28
0,96	1,91	1,74	1,77	1,35	1,1	1,14	1,28	1,76	1,77	1,75	1,79	1,74	1,76
-4,47	-4,01	-3,49	-3,01	-2,91	-3,07	-3,41	-3,58	-3,74	-3,67	-3,23	-2,88	-2,78	-2,97
7,44	6,81	6,44	6,63	6,53	6,26	6,77	6,4	6,44	6,92	6,94	7,35	7,17	7,29
7,11	7,98	8,15	7,61	5,85	6,25	7,69	8,43	8,4	8,92	8,63	8,42	8,03	8,13
0	0	-0,02	-0,02	-0,02	-0,01	-0,01	-0,03	-0,07	-0,1	-0,09	-0,06	-0,09	-0,17
100,0	100,0	100,0	100,0	100,0	100,0	100,0	100,0	100,0	100,0	100,0	100,0	100,0	100,0

Source:

The figures in brackets next to the various categories refer to the chapters in which the figures were calculated; within these chapters the statistical material in question was included in the following tables:

Chapter 1: Table 12, supplemented by the adjustments in Chapter 6, Table 43, columns 4 and 5
Chapter 2: Table 13, supplemented by the adjustments in
Chapter 6: Table 45, columns 9 and 10
Chapter 3: Table 27, column 1 for the domestic staff, column 4 for the border and seasonal workers
Chapter 4: Table 38, supplemented by the adjustments in Chapter 6, Table 4, column 2
Chapter 5: Table 42
Chapter 7: Table 46, column 8
Chapter 8: Table 49, column 4 for the professions, column 3 for the independent traders and craftsmen and column 5 for the partnerships
Chapter 9: Table 64-68
Chapter 10: Table 69, column 4
Chapter 11: Table 74, column 6
Chapter 12: Table 79, column 3
Chapter 13: Table 84, column 5
Chapter 14: Table 87, column 3 + Table 91 column 8 + Table 92 column 3 + Table 95 column 4
Chapter 15: Table 98, column 3
Chapter 16: Table 104, column 17
Chapter 17: Table 105, column 12 for the indirect taxes, Table 106, column 6 for the subsidies

SELECTIVE BIBLIOGRAPHY[1]

SECTION 1. SOURCES

I. Unpublished sources[2]

A. National Institute for Statistics, Brussels.

Commissie van het nationaal inkomen. Het Belgisch nationaal inkomen van 1948 tot 1954 (dossier of December 1955).

B. Private archives

Payroll records of the Van der Wee shoe factory (Lier), 1924-1943.

II. Published sources[3]

A./ Quantative reports, articles and studies ; official sources
Algemene Volks-, Nijverheids- en Handelstelling op 31 december 1947. Brussels, Nationaal Instituut voor de Statistiek, 1949-1954, 14 vol.
Algemeene telling van 30 april 1946 van de grensarbeiders die in Frankrijk gaan werken. In : "Statistisch Bulletin", vol. 32, 1946, pp.724-733.
Annales des mines de Belgique. Brussels, 1920-1940.
Belgisch Staatsblad (Le moniteur belge). Brussels, 1920-1940.
Belgische economische statistieken, 1919-1928. In : "Tijdschrift voor documentatie en voorlichting van de Nationale Bank van België", special number, 1929.
Belgische economische statistieken, 1929-1940. In : "Tijdschrift voor documentatie en voorlichting van de Nationale Bank van België", special number, 1940.
Belgische economische statistieken, 1941-1950. In : "Tijdschrift voor documentatie en voorlichting van de Nationale Bank van België", 2 vol., s.d.

---

[1] This bibliography is not exhaustive : only sources, books and articles that were really used are mentioned.
[2] Certain chapters and parts of chapters are based on the studies of Blomme, Clement, Schroeven and Van Meerten (cfr. infra, Sec.2, Literature). Unpublished sources used in these studies are not mentioned in this bibliography.
[3] See footnote 2.

Belgische economische statistieken, 1950-1960. In : "Tijdschrift voor documentatie en voorlichting van de Nationale Bank van België", 2 vol., s.d.

Belgische Senaat. Parlementaire bescheiden. Brussels, Senaat, 1920-1940.

Bestuurlijk jaarverslag over de zeevisscherij. Brussels, Ministerie van Verkeerswezen, 1920-1940.

Boeken van het Rekenhof. Opmerkingen en documenten aan de wetgevende lichamen voorgelegd. Brussels, Kamer der Volksvertegenwoordigers, 1920-1940.

Bulletin de l'Institut de Recherches Economiques. Louvain, 1920-1940.

Bulletin mensuel du commerce extérieur de l'Union Economique Belgo-Luxemburgeoise. Brussels, 1932-1940.

Caisse nationale de compensation pour allocations familiales. Rapports du conseil d'administration et de la direction. Brussels, 1920-1940.

Comité National de l'Alimentation. Deuxième rapport : le régime alimentaire actuel de la population belge, ses caractéristiques et l'influence qu'auraient sur lui les mesures envisagées pour lutter contre les restrictions des importations en temps de guerre. Dans : "Bulletin de la Santé Publique", vol. 4, 1939, pp. 783-819.

De ontwikkeling van de inkomstenstructuur volgens de belastingstatistieken. In : "Nationale Bank van België. Tijdschrift voor Documentatie en Voorlichting", vol.28, 1953, pp. 16-23.

DE BRUYNE J.-P., *L'évolution des prix des immeubles urbains de l'agglomération bruxelloise de 1878 à 1952.* In : "Bulletin de l'Institut de Recherches Economiques", vol. 22, 1956, pp. 57-93.

DE LEENER G., *L'approvisionnement en produits alimentaires de la Belgique.* In : "Banque Nationale de Belgique. Bulletin d'information et de Documentation", vol. 14, 1939.

Economische en Sociale Telling van 27 februari 1937. Brussels, Centrale Dienst voor de Statistiek, 8 vol., s.d.

Enquête sur la production. Rapport général. Paris ; Nancy ; Strasbourg, Bureau International du Travail, 1923-1925, 5 vol.

Enquête sur la situation des employés privés (15 avril 1920). Brussels, Ministère de l'Industrie et du Travail, 1923.

Enquête sur la situation des industries (établissements de 10 ouvriers et plus), 31 octobre 1926. Brussels, Ministère du Travail et de la Prèvoyance Sociale, 1927-1928, 2 vol.

Evolution des taux de l'intérêt en Belgique depuis la première guerre mondiale (1919-1958). In : "Bulletin de l'Institut de Recherches Economiques", vol. 25, 1959, pp. 75-122.

Gemeentekrediet van België. Verslagen van den Beheerraad en van het Toezichtskomiteit. Brussels, 1920-1940.

Herdisconteering- en Waarborginstituut. Verslag van het Bestuurscomité en verslag der reviseuren. Brussels, 1935-1940.

Hoofdkas voor het Klein Beroepskrediet. Verslag over de werkzaamheden van de hoofdkas. Balans. Brussels, 1930-1940.
Inkomens der natuurlijke personen onderworpen aan de bedrijfsbelasting en de aanvullende personele belasting of de supertaks. Statistiek opgemaakt door de administratie der belastingen. In : "Bulletin der Belastingen", vol. 37, 1961, pp. 1911-1940.
Jaarverslagen Nationaal Pensioenfonds voor Mijnwerkers. Brussels, 1920-1940.
Jaarverslagen Nationale Kas voor Bediendenpensioenen. Brussels, 1930-1940.
JULIN A., *Résultats principaux d'une enquête sur les budgets d'ouvriers et d'employés en Belgique.* In : "Bulletin de l'Institut International de Statistique", 1934, passim.
Kamer der Volksvertegenwoordigers. Parlementaire documenten van België. Brussels, Kamer der Volksvertegenwoordigers, 1890-1961.
L'evolution de la structure des revenus d'après les statistiques fiscales. In: "Banque Nationale de Belgique. Bulletin d'Information et de Documentation", vol. 28, 1953, pp. 16-23.
La main-d'oeuvre frontalière dans le nord de la France. In : "Etudes et conjuncture", 1949, pp. 36-51.
La main-d'oeuvre belge en France. In : "Banque Nationale de Belgique. Bulletin d'Information et de Documentation", vol.7, 1932, pp. 38-46.
La situation des industries belges en décembre 1919. Brussels, Ministère de l'Industrie, du Travail et du Ravitaillement, 1919.
La situation des industries belges en juin 1920. Brussels, Ministère de l'Industrie, du Travail et du Ravitaillement, 1920.
La situation des industries belges en décembre 1920. Brussels, Ministère de l'Industrie, du Travail et du Ravitaillement, 1921.
Le moniteur des intérêts matériels. Brussels, 1920-.
Le mouvement des salaires en Belgique de 1922 à 1932. In : "Banque Nationale de Belgique. Bulletin d'Information et de Documentation", vol. 7, 1932, pp. 97-202.
Le recensement de l'industrie et de commerce au 31 décembre 1930. Analyse sommaire des résultats. Première partie : recensement professionel. In : "Revue du Travail", vol. 43, 1934, pp. 719-771.
Le recensement de l'industrie et de commerce au 31 décembre 1930. Analyse sommaire des résultats. Deuxième partie : recensement industriel. In : "Revue du Travail", vol. 44, 1935, pp. 171.
Le rendement de la taxe professionnelle de 1928 à 1935. In : "Banque Nationale de Belgique. Bulletin d'Information et de Documentation", vol. 13, 1938, pp. 11-16.
Nationale Maatschappij van Buurtspoorwegen. Verslagen voorgelegd door den Raad van Beheer en door den Raad van Toezicht. Brussels, 1920-1940.
Nationale Verrekenkas voor Gezinsvergoedingen. Verslagen, rekeningen en statistieken voorgelegd aan de algemene vergadering van 21 december 1952. Brussels, 1930-.

Population. Recensement général du 31 décembre 1910. Brussels, Ministère de l'Intérieur, 1912-1916, 5 vol.

Population. Recensement général du 31 décembre 1920. Brussels, Ministère de l'Intérieur, 1926, 5 vol.

Population. Recensement général de 1930. Brussels, Ministère de l'Intérieur, 1934-1937, 8 vol.

Prijzen-, arbeids- en sociale statistieken, 1900-1964. Brussels, Nationaal Instituut voor de Statistiek, 1965.

Raming van het globaal bedrag der jaarloonen van de werklieden en bedienden uit de nijverheid, den handel en den landbouw. In : "Statistisch Bulletin", vol. 29, 1943, pp. 333-335.

Rapports relatifs à l'exécution des lois coördonnées sur la réparation des dommages resultant des accidents du travail. Brussels, Ministère de l'Industrie et du Travail - Ministère du Prèvoyance Sociale, 1905-1940.

Rapport sur l'exécution de la loi du 25 juin 1930 relative au contrôle des entreprises d'assurances sur la vie pendant l'année X, présenté aux chambres législatives par Monsieur le Ministre du Travail et de la Prévoyance sociale. Brussels, 1930-1940.

Rapports sur l'exécution de la loi du 25 juin 1930 relative au contrôle des entreprises d'assurances sur la vie pendant l'année 1930 -. Brussels, Ministère du Travail et de la Prévoyance Sociale, 1931-1940.

Rapports sur les opérations de la Caisse d'Amortissement et de la Caisse des Consignations pendant les années 1923-. Brussels, 1924-1940.

Recensement de l'industrie et du commerce (31 décembre 1910). Brussels, Ministère de l'Industrie et du Travail, 1913-1921.

Revue du Travail. Brussels, Ministère de l'Emploi et du Travail, 1920-1940.

Statistiek der belastbare kadastrale inkomsten en van het rendement der grondbelasting en der nationale crisisbelasting op de inkomsten uit onroerende goederen (fiscaal dienstjaar 1943). In : "Statistisch Bulletin", vol. 32, 1946, pp. 734-742.

Statistiek van de belastbare inkomens onderworpen aan de bedrijfsbelasting en de nationale crisisbelasting en aan de aanvullende personele belasting (dienstjaar 1949 - inkomsten verworven in 1948). In : "Statistisch Bulletin", vol. 40, 1954, pp. 1096-1125.

Statistiek van de belastbare inkomens onderworpen aan de bedrijfsbelasting en de nationale crisisbelasting en aan de aanvullende personele belsting (dienstjaar 1950 - inkomsten verworven in 1949). In : "Statistisch Bulletin", vol. 41, 1955, pp. 506-592.

Statistiek van de belastbare inkomens aangeslagen in de bedrijfsbelasting en in de aanvullende personele belasting (dienstjaar 1946 - inkomsten verworven in 1945). In : "Statistisch Bulletin", vol. 36, 1950, pp. 584-598.

Statistiek van de belastbare inkomens aangeslagen in de bedrijfsbelasting en in de aanvullende personele belasting (dienstjaren 1947 en 1948 - inkomsten ver-

worven in 1946 en 1947). In : "Statistisch Bulletin", vol. 39, 1953, pp. 351-372.
Statistiques des accidents du travail élaborées d'après les documents fournis en exécution de la loi du 24 décembre 1903 sur la réparation des dommages résultant des accidents du travail. Brussels, Ministère de l'Industrie et du Travail - Ministère des Affaires Economiques, 1906-1913, 1921, 1922, 1931, 1937-1940.
Statistique générale de la France. Annuaire statistique. Paris, 1920-1940.
Statistiek van de levensverzekeringen. In : "Statistisch Bulletin", vol. 34, 1948, pp. 106-112.
Statistisch jaarboek voor België en Belgisch Kongo. Brussels, Nationaal Instituut voor de Statistiek, 1920-1940.
Telling van de grensarbeiders die naar Frankrijk gaan werken. Toestand einde maart 1948. In : "Statistisch Bulletin", vol. 34, 1948, pp. 1120-1126.
Telling van de personen welke een bezoldigde betrekking of functie uitoefenen ten laste van de Rijksbegroting. In : "Statistisch Bulletin", vol. 34, 1948, pp. 2042-2079.
Tijdelijk kredietfonds ten behoeve van den middenstand. Verslag van het bestuurscomité aan den heer Minister van Financiën en aan den heer Minister van Economische Zaken. Brussels, 1935-1946.
Tijdschrift voor documentatie en voorlichting van de Nationale Bank van België (Banque Nationale de Belgique. Bulletin d'Information et de Documentation), Brussels, 1920-1940.
Une enquête sur la nature et le coût de l'alimentation des classes laborieuses portant sur 1.500 ménages. In : "Revue du Travail", vol. 23, 1922, pp. 690-696.
Verslag over de verrichtingen en de toestand van de Algemene Spaar- en Lijfrentekas. Brussels, 1920-1940.
Wetgevende Kamers. Kamer der Volksvertegenwoordigers. Bulletin van Vragen en Antwoorden. Brussels, 1920-1940.
Wetgevende Kamers. Senaat. Bulletin van Vragen en Antwoorden. Brussels, 1920-1940.

B/ Contemporary literature
ARENDT J., *Les conditions d'existence des travailleurs et des entreprises en Belgique en 1935 et 1936.* Brussels, 1936.
BAUDHUIN F., *Economie agraire.* Louvain, 1945.
BAUDHUIN F., *Essai sur les classes moyennes.* In : "Banque Nationale de Belgique. Bulletin d'Information et de Documentation", vol. 8, 1933, pp. 317-322.
BAUDHUIN F., *Finances belges. La stabilisation et ses conséquences.* In : "Editions de la Société d'Etudes morales, sociales et juridiques", Brussels ; Paris, 1928.

BAUDHUIN F., *Finances belges. La stabilisation et ses conséquences.* Brussels ; Paris, 1928.
BAUDHUIN F., *Histoire économique de la Belgique, 1914-1939.* Brussels ; Louvain, 1944, 2 vol.
BAUDHUIN F., *La Belgique en 1936. Les revenus.* In : "Bulletin de l'Institut des Sciences Economiques", vol. 8, 1936-1937, pp. 121-133.
BAUDHUIN F., *La Belgique en 1937. Les finances belges en 1937.* In : "Bulletin de l'Institut de Sciences Economiques", vol. 9, 1937-1938, pp. 101-118.
BAUDHUIN F., *Le revenu national en 1930.* In : ""Banque Nationale de Belgique. Bulletin d'Information et de Documentation", vol. 5, 1930.
BAUDHUIN F., *Le système fiscal belge et la crise (1928-1935).* In : "Banque Nationale de Belgique. Bulletin d'Information et de Documentation", vol. 13, 1938, pp. 178-189.
BAUDHUIN F., *Les finances belges en 1938.* In : "Bulletin de l'Institut de Recherches Economiques", vol. 10, 1938-1939, pp. 111-137.
BAUDHUIN F., *Prix, consommation et revenu national.* In : "Bulletin de l'Institut de Recherches Economiques", vol. 13, 1947, pp. 409-429.
BAUDHUIN F., *Quel est le revenu actuel de la Belgique ?* In : "Banque Nationale de Belgique. Bulletin d'Information et de Documentation", vol. 2, 1927.
BONVOISIN P., *L'épargne et l'activité des banques en 1929.* In : "Bulletin de l'Institut de Sciences Economiques", vol. 1, 1929-1930, pp. 137-158.
CHLEPNER B.S., *Les finances publiques, la monnaie et le marché financier.* In : "La Belgique restaurée", MAHAIM, E. (ed.), Brussels, 1926, pp. 393-504.
CLAVIER C., *La fortune belge à la veille de la guerre.* Brussels, 1919.
COLLIN F., *Verslag nopens den ambachts- en handeldrijvenden middenstand.* Brussels, 1937.
DECHESNE L., *La crise financière, conséquence de la réforme fiscale.* In : "Revue économique internationale", vol. 24, 1932, pp. 398-402.
DE LEENER G., *Les caisses de compensation des allocations familiales en Belgique. Leur rôle - leur législation - leur avenir.* Brussels, 1929.
DE LEENER G., *Vingt années de régime des allocations familiales en Belgique.* Brussels, 1947.
DE LOCHT L., *Un aperçu sur la situation des employées.* In : "Revue du Travail", vol. 20, 1919, pp. 974-994.
De Middenstandspost. Weekblad van den Landsbond van den Christelijken Middenstand van België, vol. 13, 1938.
DE VISSCHERE F.E., *Het Belgische belastingwezen en zijn grondbeginselen. Een studie over zijn wording en ontwikkeling sedert 1830.* In : "Economisch-sociale bibliotheek. Monografieën", VAN GOETHEM ; F., SAP, G. (eds.), vol. 9, Brussels ; Antwerp ; Leuven ; Ghent, 1935.
EYSKENS G., *La bourse et les banques en 1931.* In : "Bulletin de l'Institut de Sciences Economiques", vol. 3, 1931-1932, pp. 153-163.
GENIN E., *Les prêts hypothécaires en Belgique et leur destination.* In : "Bulletin de l'Institut des Sciences Economiques" vol. 4, 1932-1933, pp. 257-261.

GILIS H., *Le bilan dans la société anonyme. Etude juridique, economique, financière et comptable*. Brussels ; Renaix, 1927.
HAIDANT P., *Précis de législation industrielle et sociale*. Brussels ; Liège ; Paris, 1932.
HANON DE LOUVET C., *Analyse et discussion de bilans*. Brussels, 1944.
JULIN A., *Enquête sur les charges sociales de l'industrie*. Brussels, Editions du Comité Central Industriel de Belgique, 1933.
KIEHEL C.A., *Unemployment insurance. A development of the Ghent and Liège systems*. New York, 1932.
LOECKX F., *L'évolution de l'impôt sur les revenus en Belgique*. In : "Revue Economique Internationale", vol. 29, 1937, pp. 289-322.
MAHAIM E., *La fortune et le bien-être*. In : "La Belgique restaurée", MAHAIM E. (ed.), Brussels, 1926, pp. 507-611.
MAHAIM E. (ed.), *La Belgique restaurée*. Brussels, 1926.
MAUCO G., *Les étrangers en France. Leur rôle dans l'activité économique*. Paris, 1932.
NEELS G., *De tijdelijke uitwijking naar Frankrijk beschouwd uit het arrondissement Brugge*. In : "De Gids op Maatschappelijk Gebied", vol. 19, 1924, pp. 469-481 and pp. 568-589.
NEUMANN H., *De l'intérêt d'une présentation claire des bilans et comptes de pertes et profits des S.A. et la nécessité d'une réforme du régime actuel*. In : "Revue de la Banque", vol. 14, 1950, pp. 217-228.
NICOLAI E., *Salaires et budgets ouvriers en 1853 et 1891*. Brussels, 1895.
Onze Belgen die een deel des jaars in Frankrijk verblijven. Verslag op het Congres van Luik in 1898 voorgebracht door G. Eylenbosch, schrijver van den Belgischen Volkbond. Gent, 1898.
ROGER C., *La politique d'alimentation en Belgique. Deuxième partie. La consommation des denrées alimentaires en Belgique avant la guerre actuelle*. Brussels, 1942.
RONSE E., *L'émigration saisonnière belge*. Ghent, 1913.
RONSE E., *Les formes nouvelles de l'émigration belge*. In : "Revue Catholique Sociale et Juridique", vol. 26, (1921), pp. 133-150.
VAES U., *La société anonyme et le sort des actionnaires*. In : "Bulletin de l'Institut de Sciences Economiques", vol. 2, 1930-1931, pp. 27-38.
VAN DER AA E.R., *Studie over het opzetten eener statistiek der in de mobiliënbelasting, de bedrijfsbelasting, de nationale crisisbelasting en in de aanvullende personeele belasting aangeslagen inkomsten en van het rendement dezer belastingen (fiscaal dienstjaar 1945 - inkomsten verworven in 1944)*. In : "Statistisch Bulletin", vol. 32, 1946, pp. 835-857.
VANDERVELDE E., *L'exode rural et le retour aux champs*. Paris, 1903.
VELGE H., *Le mouvement social en 1930 -*. In : "Bulletin de l'Institut des Sciences Economiques", vol. 2 - , 1930-1931 -.

VELGE H., *Les lois belges d'assurance et de prévoyance sociales. Accidents du travail, maladies professionnelles, vieillesse et décès prématuré, chômage involontaire, allocations familiales.* Brussels, 1933.

WAUWERMANS P., *Manuel pratique des sociétés anonymes.* Brussels, 1924.

Section 2. Literature

A Standardized System of National Accounts. Paris, OECD, 1952 and 1958.

AVONDTS,G. SCHOLLIERS P., *Gentse prijzen, huishuren en budgetonderzoeken in de negentiende en twintigste eeuw.* In : "Centrum voor Hedendaagse Sociale Geschiedenis. De Gentse textielarbeiders in de negentiende en twintigste eeuw.", dossier 5, Brussels, 1977.

BLOMME J., *The Economic Development of Belgian Agriculture, 1880-1980. A Quantitative and Qualitative Analysis.* In : "Studies in Belgian Economic History", vol. 3, Brussels, 1992.

BUBLOT G., *La production agricole belge. Etude economique séculaire, 1846-1955.* Louvain, 1957.

BUYST E., *An Economic History of Residential Building in Belgium between 1890 and 1961.* In : "Studies in Belgian Economic History", vol. 1, Brussels, 1992.

BUYST E., *Het inkomen uit onroerend vermogen toevloeiend aan particulieren: België, 1920-1939.* In : "Workshop in Quantitative Economic History. Research Paper 94.01", Leuven, 1994.

BUYST, E., *New GNP Estimates for the Belgian Economy During the Interwar Period.* In "Review of Income and Wealth", vol. 43, 1997, pp. 357-375.

BUYST, E., *Rent Control and Virtual Prices. A Case Study for Interwar Belgium.* In "Journal of Economic History", vol. 57, 1997, pp. 654-673.

BUYST, E., NACKAERTS, P., and PEPERMANS, G., *Some Aspects of Gross Domestic Fixed Capital Formation in Manufacturing and in Dwellings: Belgium, 1920-1939.* In: "Workshop on Quantitative Economic History", vol. 87.03. Leuven, 1987.

BUYST, E., SMITS, J.P. and VAN ZANDEN, J.L., *National Accounts for the Low Countries, 1800-1990.* In: "Scandinavian Economic History Review", vol. 43, 1995, pp. 53-76.

CARBONELLE C., *Recherches sur l'évolution de la production en Belgique de 1900 à 1957.* In : "Cahiers économiques de Bruxelles", vol. 3, 1959, pp. 353-377.

CASSIERS I., *Une statistique des salaires horaires dans l'industrie belge, 1919-1939.* In : "Recherches economiques de Louvain", vol. 46, 1980, pp. 57-85.

CHADEAU E., *L'économie nationale aux XIXe en XXe siècles.* In : "Annuaire statistique de l'économie française aux XIXe en XXe siècles", vol. 1, Paris, 1988.

CLEMENT P., *The Growth of a Welfare State in Belgium. A History of the Belgian Public Finances*. In : "Studies in Belgian Economic History", Brussels, 2000.

COMBE P., *Niveau de vie et progrès technique en France (1860-1939). Contribution à l'étude de l'économie française contemporaine. Postface (1939-1949)*. Paris, 1956.

COPPIETERS B., *De statistieken over de arbeidsongevallenverzekering als bron voor de berekening van de totale loonsom der arbeidersklasse in België*. In : "Tijdschrift voor Sociale Geschiedenis", vol. 13, 1987, pp. 94-111.

COPPIETERS B., HENDRIX, G., *De koopkrachtevolutie van loontrekkenden in periodes van economische depressie : een vergelijking voor de jaren 1929-1939 en 1974-1984*. In : "Belgisch Tijdschrift voor Nieuwste Geschiedenis", vol. 17, 1986, pp. 275-307.

COPPIETERS B., *Schatting van de koopkracht en de loonevolutie van arbeiders en bedienden in de privé-sector tijdens de periode 1906-145 op basis van de statistieken betreffende de arbeidsongevallenverzekering*. In : "Centrum voor Politocologie", werkdocument nr. 4, Brussels, VUB, 1985.

CRETEN L., *De gezinsbestedingen in België, 1853-1974. Een studie van de Belgische budgetenquêtes* (Unpublished Dissertation Economics Department KUL, 1982).

CRISPIELS J., *Les droits de douane et d'accise de 1914 à 1940*. In : "Histoire des finances publiques en Belgique", Brussels ; Paris, Institut Belge de Finances Publiques, vol. 1, 1950, pp. 603-641.

DAVIN L.E., *La dette publique de 1919 à 1939*. In : "Histoire des finances publiques en Belgique", Brussels ; Paris, Institut Belge de Finances Publiques, vol. 2, 1954, pp. 291-375.

De nationale rekeningen van België, 1953-1962. In : "Statistisch Tijdschrift", vol. 49, 1963, pp. 1119-1261.

De nationale rekeningen van België, 1963-1971. In : "Statistisch Tijdschrift", vol. 58, 1972, pp. 371-433.

DE BIOLLEY T., GILOT A., *The capital stock of the Belgian economy : evaluation and analysis*. Brussels, 1987.

DEHEM R., *Emploi et revenus en économie ouverte. Theorie et application à l'évolution belge et britannique de 1919 à 1939*. In : "Bulletin de l'Institut de Recherches Economiques", vol. 12, 1946, pp. 41-115.

DELORY F., *Les finances des chemins de fer belges*. In : "Histoire des finances publiques en Belgique", Brussels ; Paris, Institut belge de finances publiques, 1955, vol. 3, pp. 101-143.

DEPRIMOZ J., *Le salaire et le niveau de vie en Belgique de 1936 à 1951*. Paris, 1954.

DEREYMAEKER R., *De methode der nationale boekhouding en haar toepassing in België*. In : "Statistisch Tijdschrift", vol. 4, 1957, pp. 818-844.

DUPRIEZ L., *Les rémunérations en Belgique de 1936 à 1952*. In : "Bulletin de l'Institut de Recherches Economiques", vol. 12, 1952, pp. 433-475.

DURVIAUX R., *La banque mixte. Origine et soutien de l'expansion économique de la Belgique.* Brussels, 1947.
FEINSTEIN C.H., *National Income, expenditure and output of the United Kingdom, 1855-1965.* In : "Studies in the national income and expenditure of the United Kingdom", vol. 6, Cambridge, 1972.
FRANK M., *Analyse macroéconomique de la fiscalité belge, 1913-1958.* Brussels, 1960.
GADISSEUR J., *Le produit physique de l'économie belge, 1831-1913. Présentation critique des données statistiques* (Ph.D. Dissertation, Economics Department, State University of Liège, 1979-1980, 9 vol.)
GENIN E., *Les impôts sur la circulation juridique des biens en Belgique après 1914.* In : "Histoire des finances publiques en Belgique", Brussels ; Paris, Institut Belge de Finances Publiques, vol. 1, 1950, pp. 543-602.
GOBYN R., *De woningnood en het probleem van de voorlopige huisvesting in België na de Eerste Wereldoorlog.* In : "Resurgam : de Belgische wederopbouw na 1914", SMETS M. (ed.), Brussels, 1985, pp. 169-187.
GOOSSENS M., *De Belgische arbeidsmarkt tijdens het Interbellum.* In : "Tijdschrift voor Economie en Management", vol. 33, 1988, pp. 109-125.
GOOSSENS M., *Het looninkomen van arbeiders in privé-dienst tijdens het Interbellum (1920-1939) : berekeningsmethode en resultaten.* In : "Workshop on Quantitative Economic History", Discussion Paper 87.06, Leuven, 1987.
GOOSSENS M. et al., *Interwar Unemployment in Belgium.* In : "Interwar Unemployment in International Perspective", EICHENGREEN, B., HATTON, T.J. (eds.) (NATO ASI Series. Series D. Behavioural and Social Sciences), vol. 23, Dordrecht, Boston, London, 1988, pp. 289-324.
GOOSSENS M., *Reconstructie van werkgelegenheidscijfers voor het Interbellum. Methodologie en resultaten.* In : "Workshop on Quantitative Economic History", Discussion Paper 87.01, Leuven, 1987.
Groupe d'études de la comptabilité nationale. Premiers éléments d'une comptabilité nationale de la Belgique, 1948-1951. Brussels, 1954.
Groupe d'études de la comptabilité nationale. Economie belge et comptabilité nationale, 1948-1954. Brussels, 1955.
HENAU A., *De Belgische huishuren gedurende het Interbellum.* In: "Workshop on Quantitative Economic History", vol. 91.01, Leuven, 1991.
Het Belgisch nationaal inkomen van 1948 tot 1954. In : "Statistisch Bulletin", vol. 42, 1956, pp. 581-618.
JANSSENS V., *De Belgische frank. Anderhalve eeuw geldgeschiedenis.* Antwerp; Amsterdam, 1976.
KAHN B., *Depreciatie.* Brussels, Nationaal Instituut voor de Statistiek, 1961.
KUZNETS S., *Economic Growth of Nations. Total Output and Production Structure*, Cambridge 1971.
LE BRUN J., *Het juridisch statuut van de spaarbanken.* In : "De Belgische Spaarbanken. Geschiedenis, recht, economische functie en instellingen", Tielt, Belgische Spaarbankenvereniging ed., 1986, pp. 299-377.

LECAT E. *Le financement des télégraphes et des téléphones.* In : "Histoire des Finances Publiques en Belgique", Brussels ; Paris , Institut belge de Finances Publiques, 1955, vol. 3, pp. 145-191.
LEEMAN A., *De woningmarkt in België (1890-1950).* Kortrijk, 1955.
LENTACKER F., *La frontière franco-belge. Etude géographique des effets d'une frontière sur la vie des relations.* Lille, 1974.
MADDISON A., *Dynamic Forces in Capitalist Development. A Long-Run comparative View.* Oxford, 1991.
MATTHEWS R.C.O. et al., *British Economic Growth, 1856-1973*, Oxford 1973.
MICHIELS J., *Kritische periodes in de evolutie van de rijksschuld : 1926* (Unpublished Dissertation, Economics Department KUL, 1983).
MITCHELL B.R., *European Historical Statistics, 1750-1970.* London, abridged edition, 1978.
MOESEN W., VAN ROMPUY V., *Inleiding tot de openbare financiën.* Leuven ; Amersfoort, 1986.
MOREAU L., *Le bilan des sociétés par actions, le compte des résultats, interprétation et unification.* Brussels, 1919.
NEIRYNCK M., *De lonen in België sedert 1846.* Leuven, 1943.
NEUILLE J., *Les investissements publiques en Belgique (1830-1950).* Paris, 1951.
OLAERTS S., *Kritische periodes in de evolutie van de rijksschuld : 1935* (Unpublished Dissertation, Economics Department KUL, 1983).
OLISLAEGERS O., *Naar een uitbreiding van de nationale rekeningen. Tweede deel. Het Europese stelsel van geïntegreerde economische rekeningen.* In : "Statistisch Tijdschrift", vol. 55, 1969, pp. 988-999.
PEETERS S. et al., *Reconstruction of the Belgian National Income, 1920-1939. Methodology and Results.* In : "Workshop on Quantitative Economic History", Discussion Paper 86.01, Leuven, 1986.
PHELPS BROWN E.H., BROWNE M.H., *A Century of Pay. The Course of Pay and Production in France, Germany, Sweden, the United Kingdom and the United States of America, 1860-1960.* London ; Melbourne ; Toronto ; New York, 1968.
PIRARD J., *Le pouvoir central belge et ses comptes économiques, 1830-1913.* In : "Histoire quantitative et développement de la Belgique", LEBRUN P. (ed.), vol. 6 (1-3), Brussels, 1980-1985.
PUTMAN R., *Les impôts directs en Belgique de 1914 à 1940.* In : "Histoire des finances publiques en Belgique", Institut Belge de Finances Publiques, Brussels ; Paris, vol. 1, 1950, pp. 357-541.
RAPORT A., *Vijfentwintig jaar Vereniging Privé-Spaarkassen.* In : "De Belgische Spaarbanken. Geschiedenis, recht, economische functie en instellingen", Tielt, Belgische Spaarbankenvereniging ed., 1986, pp. 251-296.
SCHEPENS L., *Van vlaskutser tot franschman. Bijdrage tot de geschiedenis van de Westvlaamse plattelandsbevolking in de negentiende eeuw.* Bruges, 1976.

SCHOLLIERS E., *Prijzen en lonen te Antwerpen en in het Antwerpse (zestiende-negentiende eeuw)*. In : "Documenten voor de geschiedenis van prijzen en lonen", VERLINDEN, C. (ed.), vol. II B, Bruges, 1965, pp. 641-1056.

SCHOLLIERS E., *Un indice du loyer : les loyers anversois de 1500 à 1873*. In : "Studi in onore di A. Fanfani", vol. 5, Milan, 1962, pp. 593-617.

SCHOLLIERS P., *Lonen in de Belgische nijverheid, 1913-1940 : de enquête Davin*. In : "Centrum voor Hedendaagse Sociale Geschiedenis. Lonen en prijzen in België in de negentiende en twintigste eeuw", Loonreeks 2, Brussels, VUB, 1979.

SCHOLLIERS P., *Loonindexering en sociale vrede. Koopkracht en klassenstrijd in België tijdens het Interbellum*. In : "Centrum voor Hedendaagse Sociale Geschiedenis", Brussels, VUB, 1985.

SCHOLLIERS P., *Loonlijsten van de Brusselse Arbeidsbeurs, 1922-1939*. In : "Centrum voor Hedendaagse Sociale Geschiedenis. Lonen en prijzen in België in de negentiende en twintigste eeuw", Loonreeks 3, Brussels, VUB, 1979.

SCHOLLIERS P., VAN DEN EECKHOUT P., *De Brusselse huishuren : 1880-1940*. In : "Centrum voor Hedendaagse Sociale Geschiedenis. Lonen en Prijzen in België in de negentiende en twintigste eeuw", Prijzenreeks 1, Brussels, 1979.

SCHROEVEN C., *Consumer Expenditure in Interwar Belgium (1920-1939)*. In : "Studies in Belgian Economic History", Brussels, 1994.

TECHEUR P., *Le crédit immobilier en Belgique de 1802 à 1954*. In : "Bulletin de l'Institut de Recherches Economiques et Sociales", vol. 23, 1957, pp. 95-138.

THEYS J., *Een analyse van de Westvlaamse grensarbeid in Noord-Frankrijk*. Bruges, 1969.

TIMMERMANS A.P., *La dette publique*. In : "Université de Louvain. Institut des sciences economiques appliquées. Collection du Centre de Recherches en Economie et Gestion des Entreprises", vol. 15, Courtrai, 1958.

VAN AUDENHOVE M., *Geschiedenis van de gemeentefinanciën*. In : "Gemeentekrediet van België. Driemaandelijks tijdschrift", vol. 35, 1981, pp. 203-236 ; vol. 36, 1982, pp. 83-114, 243-274.

VANDENDRIESSCHE S., *Evolutie van de Belgische centrale-overheidsuitgaven sinds 1919. Onderzoek naar de determinerende factoren*. In : "Ministerie van Financiën. Documentatieblad", 1977, nr. 11, pp. 37-112, nr. 12, pp. 145-23 ; 1978, nr. 2, pp. 131-232, nr. 4, pp. 129-178, nr. 6, pp. 49-130 and nr. 7, pp. 101-168.

VAN DEN EECKHOUT P., *Lonen van Brusselse arbeiders in openbare instellingen (1809-1934) : bouwvakkers, ziekenhuis- en stadspersoneel*. In : "Centrum voor Hedendaagse Sociale Geschiedenis. Lonen en prijzen in België in de negentiende en twintigste eeuw", Loonreeks 1 , Brussels, VUB, 1979.

VAN DEN EYNDE F., *De statistiek inzake inkomstenbelastingen*. In : "Bulletin der Belastingen", vol. 37, 1961, pp. 1911-1940.

VANDEPUTTE R., *Fernand Collin en zijn tijd.* Tielt, 1985.
VANDEPUTTE R., *Handboek voor verzekeringen en verzekeringsrecht.* Antwerp, 1969.
VAN DER WEE, H. DANCET G., *De Belgische Nationale Boekhouding, 1920-1982: Geschiedenis van haar reconstructiemethodologie,* in: "Actuele economische problemen. Theorie en politiek", VAN ROMPUY, V. (ed.), Leuven 1986, pp. 146-150 and pp. 155-158.
VAN DER WEE H., TAVERNIER K., *De Nationale Bank van België en het monetaire gebeuren tussen de twee wereldoorlogen.* Brussels, 1975.
VAN DER WEE H., VERBREYT M., *Mensen maken geschiedenis. De Kredietbank en de economische opgang van Vlaanderen.* Tielt, 1985.
VAN MEERTEN M., *Capital Formation in Belgium (1900-1995).* In : "Studies in Belgian Economic History", Leuven, 2003.
VANTHEMSCHE G., *De Belgische spaarbanken tijdens het Interbellum.* In : "De Belgische Spaarbanken. Geschiedenis, recht, economische functie en instellingen", Tielt, Belgische Spaarbankenvereniging ed., 1986, pp. 161-209.
VANTHEMSCHE G., *De werkloosheid in België tijdens de crisis van de jaren 1930* (Ph.D. Dissertation, History Department Free University Brussels, 1987, 3 vol.)
VANTHEMSCHE G., *De werkloosheid in België : 1929-1940.* Berchem, 1989.
VERAGHTERT K., *Het economisch leven in België, 1918-1940.* In : "Nieuwe Algemene Geschiedenis der Nederlanden", vol.14, Haarlem, 1979, pp. 53-101.
VERAGHTERT K., *Van spaarkas tot spaarbank (1940-1975).* In : "De Belgische Spaarbanken. Geschiedenis, recht, economische functie en instellingen", Tielt, Belgische Spaarbankenvereniging ed., 1986, pp. 211-251.
VRANCKEN F. ; SEULEN E., *Financement et liquidation de la première guerre mondiale.* In : "Histoire des finances publiques en Belgique", Institut Belge de Finances Publiques (ed.), Brussels ; Paris, vol. 2, 1954, pp. 1-34.
WARD M., *The Measurement of Capital.* Paris, OECD, 1976.

www.ingramcontent.com/pod-product-compliance
Ingram Content Group UK Ltd.
Pitfield, Milton Keynes, MK11 3LW, UK
UKHW021837140426
5217IPUK00021B/1493